# Growing Up

by
## Alexandra J. McClanahan

Foreword by
## Carl H. Marrs

Publication of this volume is made possible
in part by a grant from the
Alaska Federation of Natives.

The CIRI Foundation is the recipient of any
proceeds from the sale of this book.

### THE CIRI FOUNDATION
Anchorage, Alaska

10 9 8 7 6 5 4 3

All photographs, including front cover, by Chris Arend Photography,
except as noted:
Austin Ahmasuk photo by Peggy Fagerstrom;
Brad Angasan photo by Fritz Johnson;
Sharon Anderson photo, courtesy Sharon Anderson;
Andrew Guy photo by Sue Gamache, courtesy Calista Corporation;
Jaeleen Kookesh-Araujo photo, courtesy John Whitman Photography;
Matt McDaniel photo, courtesy Jostens/Campus Images;
Jaylene Wheeler photo, courtesy Jaylene Wheeler; and
Ricardo Worl photo, courtesy Byrnes Photography.

———————■———————

Printed by Thomson-Shore, Dexter, Michigan
Maps by Thomas Glazier, Land & GIS Technician, CIRI
Design by Tina Wallace, 𝕿𝖔𝖉𝖉 𝕮𝖔𝖒𝖒𝖚𝖓𝖎𝖈𝖆𝖙𝖎𝖔𝖓𝖘

*For Natasha and all the others*
*born after. . .*

# *Table of Contents*

3. **Arctic Slope Region** ................ *Page 77*
*Bobbi Quintavell* .................. *Page 79*
*Rex Allen Rock, Sr.* ............... *Page 91*

4. **Bering Straits Region** ............. *Page 101*
*Austin Ahmasuk* ..................... *Page 103*
*Jaylene Z. Wheeler* ............... *Page 115*

5. **Bristol Bay Region** .................. *Page 129*
Trefon's son → *Brad Angasan* ........................ *Page 131*
BBNC CEO *Jason Metrokin* ...................... *Page 143*

6. **Calista Region** .......................... *Page 155*
*Andrew Guy* ........................... *Page 157*
*George Owletuck* .................. *Page 167*
*Deborah Vo* ........................... *Page 181*

7. **Chugach Region** ....................... *Page 195*
*James W. LaBelle, Jr.* ............ *Page 197*
Pebble Finance Director → *Matt McDaniel* .................... Page 208

8. **Cook Inlet Region** .................... *Page 219*
*Doris Hunter-Whitley* ........... *Page 221*
*Gloria O'Neill* ....................... *Page 238*

9. **Doyon Region** .......................... *Page 251*
*Dawn Dinwoodie* .................. *Page 253*
*Carrie Irwin* .......................... *Page 272*

10. **Koniag Region** ........................ *Page 287*
*Sharon Anderson* .................. *Page 289*
*Kim Eaton-Olson* .................. *page 300*

# Foreword
## by Carl H. Marrs

You might say this book has been 20 years in the making. Although its actual development has taken about two years, it really goes back to what I've been hoping for years now – that someone would start documenting the effects of the Alaska Native Claims Settlement Act of 1971 to preserve its history for future generations. A couple years ago it occurred to me that there is no better time to start than now, and so we at CIRI made the commitment to begin that documentation.

I view this book as a first step in a long process whereby we will document and catalog as much as we can about ANCSA and the Native experience in Alaska, running the gamut from these young people to our elders. We begin by talking to some of the people who are the closest to being our next leaders. *Growing Up Native in Alaska* is a way to bring the voices of younger Alaska Natives and all their perspectives to the forefront. We need to ensure these voices are heard, as well as learn from them.

We begin with our younger adults precisely because many of these people were left out of ANCSA, and it's time we took a good, hard look at where that leads us as Native people.

Our youth are our future. Culturally and economically, we have to start relying on them. Although they don't have the historical perspective on ANCSA that their elders do, it is they who will live with it in the next generation. Where does their sense of belonging come from? What are their hopes for their children? Who are their heroes?

ANCSA was very specific about what Congress was trying to accomplish. It was to be undertaken "in conformity with the real economic and social needs of Natives." In other words, it is our duty as Native corporations to advance not just economically, but socially. ANCSA goes beyond people running successful corporations. It is about our cultural and traditional values.

When George Miller, Kenaitze Indian Tribe President and later CIRI's first President, testified before the House Subcommittee on Indian Affairs about settling Alaska Native claims in October 1969, he said he was concerned about using any revenues derived from the settlement of Alaska Native land claims for education, health and welfare and housing. He told the committee education was the number one priority.

In 1966, the average age of death for Alaska Natives was 34 and a half years, about half that for other Americans. That dismal statistic was caused by a host of factors, not the least of which was that when ANCSA was signed, Alaska Natives played virtually no role in the Alaska economy. Many of our problems are still with us. The need for jobs and economic development in our small rural communities is more pressing than ever. But today Alaska Natives have a place at the table where statewide issues are discussed, and the reason we do is largely because ANCSA has created dynamic business entities that have themselves created institutions where the real economic and social needs of Alaska Natives are addressed as their first priority.

Many Alaska Natives will be given the opportunity to assume leadership positions as a result of Native corporations and corporation-funded scholarships. CIRI's own educational foundation has awarded grants and scholarships to more than 1,500 students. The CIRI Foundation has been instrumental in the development of this book, and the Foundation is the recipient of any proceeds from the sale of this book.

For decades now people have been talking about the "loss" of Native culture. Entire careers have been built around the desire to capture some aspects of our cultures before they are gone forever. These efforts are important. The death of each speaker of a Native language is truly the toll of the bell for each of us. What I think we sometimes overlook, however, is the fact that cultures can evolve and change, too. If the ANCSA experience has been a journey, we can't simply follow the roadmap of the past to continue it into the future. Our elders knew this, and they urged emphasis on education in every forum where their voices could be heard. In fact, we save our cultures by educating ourselves.

The creation of Native corporations has given us the opportunity to integrate successful business operations into the fabric of our cultures. We can take pride in our heritage as Alaska Natives and as shareholders.

You don't have to lose your culture by getting an education. The young people who speak frankly on the following pages are all struggling with their identities and where they fit into their respective cultures. One of the issues they raise is where those who get an education fit in. In his interview, Rex Rock, Sr., points out that people in rural Alaska villages need to welcome those who left to get an education with open arms: "Instead of being afraid that this kid's coming back to take my job, we have to open our arms and say, 'Here, come on in. You went out there. You sacrificed, and if you feel strongly you want to come back and work for your people, get in here.'"

We can live in both worlds, and the people in this book are living proof that it's not a question of survival, it's a question of where we want to go. As we look to the future, we start our look at ANCSA at the beginning – of the next generation.

Like many of the current Native leaders, I didn't have a formal education. We learned corporate systems in what amounted to on-the-job training as our corporations grew from some of the state's smaller business entities to some of its largest and most successful businesses. Back in those early days, disagreements were occasionally settled in fistfights rather than at the negotiating table. When corporate revenues were counted in hundreds of thousands of dollars, as opposed to hundreds of millions, that was okay. Today, our corporations have grown substantially. Tomorrow's leaders will be selected from among those who have the requisite training.

Years from now when we look back to determine how well Native corporations have done, we can perhaps judge best by the hopes of the next generation and their vision for the future. If that vision is of a society where our differences are celebrated and where our cultures are vibrant – alive and evolving and not just preserved in museums – then we will have succeeded. The journey to that vision will not be realized unless our people are educated.

# *Introduction*

"So that's why I
remember ANCSA
passing – because it had
to deal with my identity."

*– George Owletuck*

A generation of Alaska Natives is finding its place in Alaska Native history by defining what it means to be Alaska Native at the beginning of a new century.

Cultures clashed 30 years ago when Congress passed the Alaska Native Claims Settlement Act of 1971, and the reverberations of that clash are still being heard and felt today. This book concerns itself with the human results of the act, the social implications stemming from an unprecedented decision by Congress that has been called an extraordinary national experiment.

Twenty-seven Alaska Natives born between 1957 and 1976 were selected for interviews based on their potential as leaders and because they have struggled in one way or another with what it means to be an Alaska Native today. Some have grown up in an urban environment and are now trying to learn about their cultural heritage, some have chosen to remain in the community where their families have their roots, and still others seek to maintain ties in both the city where they work and the village where they grew up.

Participants were selected based on a representative sample of Alaska's geographic regions, as well as their leadership qualities, such as serving on a village or regional corporation board of directors, completing higher education, teaching or participating in activities to foster appreciation of Native culture. In addition, a representative of the Native corporation created to represent Alaska Natives living outside Alaska was included. Although Brenda Takes Horse is a shareholder of the Thirteenth Regional Corporation, she grew up in Alaska. The goal was to include people born both before and after the act, as well as men and women. In other words, diversity was important.

All of the interviews for *Growing Up Native in Alaska* were tape recorded, and a transcript was made of each interview. Participants edited their transcripts and had the final say on what was included.

The impacts of the act, known as ANCSA, are profound. Families of Alaska Natives were directly affected. Leaders who spent countless hours lobbying and fund-raising often sacrificed critical time with their children. Brad Angasan, the son of one of the leaders of the Bristol Bay Native Corporation, talked in his interview about how the act actually split his family:

"It stripped our family of its structure. With structure you have frame, walls, windows. When my dad became involved with

14

ANCSA, our family structure crumbled. And 20 years later we're finally getting the windows up. Our family structure is once again healthy, but with a lot of consequences. No longer are my father and mother married."

Whatever the act's flaws, it has created new entities which offer a sense of belonging – but only to those who are shareholders. Jaeleen Kookesh Araujo, a young attorney from the Sealaska Region, is concerned about those left out.

"There are going to be a lot of young Native people left out of this corporate structure, and it's really sad. Eventually, there may be a problem because you're going to have a lot of young, talented Alaska Native people going out to get educated. They're going to have a lot of expertise and education in ways that might benefit the corporation, and yet you have to wonder if they're really going to want to be involved in these Native corporations that they don't even belong to."

Jaeleen looks to the future.

"I just get so frustrated with the whole argument that people have about further slicing the pie and cutting the pie into smaller and smaller pieces, which means they get smaller and smaller dividends. In talking to other young Alaska Natives when I worked as an intern at Sealaska Corporation, we were saying, 'Who says the pie was baked only for you?'"

Sharon Anderson, who is originally from Ouzinkie, points to the divisions that ANCSA has created:

"As more time goes on, more people are not part of the corporation and don't really share in the benefits, such as dividends. To me, it's just a way of dividing people. And there really shouldn't be division, especially within families."

Blood quantums and where people place their allegiance are other difficult issues facing these people. Jason Metrokin, a business development officer for the National Bank of Alaska who grew up in Anchorage, has ties to more than one region.

"I was born in 1972. My mother is from Revere, Massachusetts. My father is a Koniag shareholder. In fact, he's the current Koniag President. I'm not a shareholder of Koniag. I'm a Bristol Bay shareholder through inherited shares from my grandfather, Walter Metrokin."

Many of the people on these pages have overcome tremendous obstacles against very difficult odds. Some have overcome poverty and others have dealt with discrimination both from their own people and from the larger society.

But if these young people are only a small sample of the Alaska Native community's best and brightest, they are living examples of people with high hopes for the future. And one is struck by their lack of bitterness and anger. Ricardo Worl, from Juneau, recalled a humiliating experience when as a third grader his teacher called him to the front of the room to demonstrate Tlingit dancing.

"She opened a page in one of her piano music books, and the name of the song was 'Ten Little Indians.' And so she tried to coax me to get up in front of the class and perform this Tlingit dance while she played 'Ten Little Indians' on the piano.

"I told her, 'I can't. I don't have my regalia. I usually dance with a blanket.'

"She said, 'Well, you don't need a blanket.' She gave me somebody's coat and wrapped it around me and said, 'Here's your blanket.' And she led me up to the front of the class. . .

"I couldn't move. I was just so embarrassed."

Ricardo went on to get a degree in anthropology from Dartmouth and has focused his career on Alaska and maintaining his tie to the Alaska Native community. He continues to take great pride in his Native heritage and expends much of his energy finding ways to work with young people.

George Owletuck is from the Calista Region and is the son of a non-Native father and Yup'ik mother. He was adopted by a Yup'ik family, and when he was enrolled after passage of ANCSA he was struck by how to describe himself:

"The reason I remember is because on the line, it said: 'What percentage Native are you?' Blood quantum level. I knew that I could put in 100 percent Native, and I'd get away with it. But since I was taught to be truthful, I put in 50 percent Alaska Native. It stands on that record to this date. So that's why I remember ANCSA passing, because it had to deal with my identity. Who am I? Am I Alaska Native? Or, am I some mixture thereof?"

The original intent of this effort was to discover how this generation of Alaska Natives views ANCSA. The people who speak to us on the following pages answer that question, but they go further and give us an unexpected look at the process of forming an identity.

Former CIRI President Roy Huhndorf has described ANCSA as an extraordinary national experiment in federal relations with

16

Native Americans. He points to the fact that corporations, not reservations, were organized to administer the proceeds from the historical land claims settlement for Alaska Natives. Some of these people and their peers are those who will run the corporations in the future. They will carry the "experiment" to the next stage, and in so doing they will stamp this generation's imprimatur into the act.

At passage, the act provided benefits only to the people who were alive on December 18, 1971, the date the law was signed by President Nixon. All people of at least one-quarter Native blood quantum who enrolled to participate in ANCSA were issued shares of stock in Native corporations that managed the land and money provided by the act. As enacted, the act prevented shareholders from selling their stock for 20 years. That meant that shareholders could not even give any of their shares to those born after 1971. The only means by which those born after December 18, 1971, could obtain shares in corporations before 1991 was through inheritance.

Many people feared the effect this "cut-off" date would have on those born after ANCSA was passed. Unlike a traditional tribe, where one was born into membership, ANCSA corporation stock was a Western concept. Shares went only to people alive in 1971. Concerns about what would happen to those born after, as well as other issues, led to a successful effort in the 1980's to amend the act.

Amendments passed in 1988 radically altered ANCSA by continuing restrictions on stock sales in perpetuity unless a majority of shareholders voted to lift them. In addition to a number of other changes, shareholders are now allowed to "gift" stock to others and corporations that so desire are authorized to issue new stock to those born after 1971. Since passage of these amendments, shareholders of three of the 13 regional corporations have voted to create new stock. They are Arctic Slope Regional Corporation, Doyon Ltd., and NANA Regional Corporation. A few of the village corporations also have created new stock.

What was radical about the amendments was that they allowed Native corporations to emphasize their Nativeness. Issuing new stock to those born after 1971 could only lead to dilution of the monetary value of stock. But if stock were valued because it gave the shareholders a way to "belong" rather than being an instrument for increasing equity, the amendments made perfect sense.

The people who led the fight for ANCSA in the late 1960's were mostly young Natives. In fact, many leaders at the time the act was passed were the same age as those interviewed for *Growing Up Native in Alaska*. The earlier generation of leaders could see that there was a unique window of opportunity for Alaska Natives who had made claim to most of Alaska and were desperately trying to preserve their hold on the only thing that was truly precious to them, the land. Part of the opportunity resulted from the discovery of oil at Prudhoe Bay in the late 1960's and the fact that the Trans-Alaska Pipeline was under consideration. The Alaska Native land claims put a dark cloud over oil and other developments within Alaska.

ANCSA has had a profound impact on the aboriginal people of Alaska. It has been hailed by some as a social experiment on a grand scale, while its critics have said that it forced a foreign Western system on tribal peoples and threatened their ties to the land. Aboriginal peoples who had become increasingly marginalized within Alaska desperately fought to gain title to their lands, as the State of Alaska doggedly insisted on its land entitlement from the Statehood Act and oil companies pushed for a pipeline to transport Prudhoe Bay's riches to market.

ANCSA marked a critical change in the approach of the U.S. government toward the nation's aboriginal peoples. Alaska Natives retained 44 million acres – about 10 percent of the entire land area of Alaska – and were paid nearly $1 billion in cash for lands lost. The settlement was the government's most generous in terms of land and money to Native people ever in American history.

The land claims told only part of the story, however. Thirty years ago, Alaska Natives struggled with the most basic of human needs. Most villagers obtained their water by chopping ice from rivers. Sewage facilities were rudimentary "honey" bucket systems or outhouses; electricity was years away and communication was virtually non-existent. Television was unheard of in most areas of Alaska, and even telephones were rare except for the state's larger cities.

For Alaska Natives, discrimination was a fact of life. Jobs were scarce. And even the most basic of human needs, a way to maintain health, was elusive. Successive waves of diseases, ranging from smallpox to tuberculosis, had ravaged Native people for decades. Entire villages were decimated by disease following the earliest Western contact in the late 1700's and early 1800's.

In 1966, a major step in the fight for lands was taken when a statewide Native organization was created. That organization became the Alaska Federation of Natives. Before the decade of the 1960's had ended, Alaska Natives had filed claims to nearly the entire 375 million acres of land within Alaska, and the Alaska Federation of Natives had mounted a full-scale effort to gain fee simple title to Native lands. At the same time, because the state had been granted 104 million acres under the Alaska Statehood Act of 1958, state officials were filing claims to some of the Alaska Natives' most important lands. Late in 1966, Interior Secretary Stewart L. Udall initiated a "land freeze" that was a moratorium on the process of patenting state land selections in order to preserve the status of Alaskan lands until the Native claims were settled. When vast oil reserves were discovered at Prudhoe Bay in 1968, lifting the freeze became the absolute top priority of developers and state officials.

ANCSA, therefore, was the product of intense pressures. Working in Alaska Natives' favor was a growing social realization within the United States that Indian treaties of the past had mostly been a license to steal lands from the nation's aboriginal peoples. It was time to try something new. Rather than creating reservations, with their attendant ties to the Bureau of Indian Affairs and the Department of the Interior, Congress adopted ANCSA in 1971, creating more than 200 village corporations and 12 regional corporations in Alaska. A thirteenth regional corporation was authorized later for Natives living outside of Alaska, but was only granted money and no land.

In a break from the past, ANCSA granted land in fee simple title and cash. The land and money went to corporations that would be created for villages and traditional Native regions within Alaska and managed by boards of directors comprised of Alaska Natives themselves.

While the idea of creating corporations was innovative, it was what some considered an insurmountable challenge for the nearly 80,000 Alaska Natives alive at the time of passage. One business leader in Anchorage has said that throwing millions of dollars on people who had never had a checking account and authority to spend that kind of money was very dangerous. That was the view of many non-Natives at the time.

Few Native people had college degrees, and even fewer knew anything about corporate enterprises. Despite their inexperience, however, many have succeeded in Western terms.

How Alaska Native corporations overcame such odds is

another story that eventually will be told. Many of the corporations have not only managed to survive, but they have become leading business entities within Alaska. Arctic Slope Regional Corporation is at the top of *Alaska Business Monthly's* "Top 49'ers" list, which ranks Alaskan-owned businesses by gross revenues. The corporation's goal is to achieve gross revenues of $1 billion by the year 2001. And while the act has led to the creation of some of the most successful corporations that exist in the state – Native or non-Native – it also has spawned some corporations that have struggled mightily for nearly 30 years just to survive.

One of the early leaders was Byron Mallott, former CEO of Sealaska Corporation and the Executive Director of the Alaska Permanent Fund. Mallott was in his 20's during the fight for ANCSA. He said that as a young Native fighting for ANCSA in the 1960's he listened to the elders of the time. Even then, Native identity was the key issue.

"They didn't say go out and make dividends for us. They didn't say go out and become corporate CEO's. They didn't say go out and be a big part of the state's economic future and let us stalk the corridors of power. They didn't say go out and invest in oil wells.

"They said go out and save who we are."

While many of the corporate leaders of the 1970's had to focus their full attention on creating a corporation where none existed before, the leaders of tomorrow must find a way to mix business with culture, a task some thought impossible. It is the next wave of Alaska Natives who will determine what the performance standards of Native corporations will be.

Their first task has been to determine who they are and what it means to be Native today. They struggle for answers to many questions on the following pages: What does culture mean to an Alaska Native raised in Anchorage whose parents are from some tiny remote village? What does culture mean to someone who has grown up in a one-room home without telephones, without television or even electricity and without sewage facilities and who is now a practicing attorney?

How does being a shareholder compare to being a tribal member? Is being a shareholder an important part of one's identity?

What would happen if shareholders decided to lift restrictions on the sale of stock and control of corporations went to non-Natives?

Is blood quantum important? Where do people of less than

one-quarter blood quantum fit into the Alaska Native community?

Why would a corporation issue new stock to Alaska Natives born after 1971? Should the stock be issued to all those born after or only the first generation? What happens in families when some of the children are shareholders and some are not?

Is it important to marry within the group?

These are not questions that were overlooked 30 years ago. But the leaders of that era were hamstrung by the limitations placed upon them. People without the most basic community services and facing the loss of everything that is most precious to them can hardly be expected to debate at length precisely how the corporate structure should be altered to best serve their grandchildren. The goal was to grab hold of what could be saved and hold on as tightly as humanly possible.

But it is the children and the grandchildren who will grapple with ANCSA future issues. The oldest among this group was 14 years old at the time ANCSA was passed, and the youngest were born five years after it passed. All of these people and their families have been profoundly affected by the act. Even nearly 30 years after the act was passed, some critics feel it was a mistake. Others see great benefits, but they hope the act will remain a living document that can be changed as needed.

For these young leaders who share their stories, the act is a fact of life. For them, it's not a question of whether the act should have been passed, but how it can be shaped and changed in the future to better meet the needs of the Alaska Native people.

On these pages you will find stories of courage and inspiration. Many of the comments concern the future. And some speak to the spiritual. As Ricardo Worl gave his interview, it was a beautiful clear winter day with delicate blue skies. The snow-covered Chugach Mountains were pink, then white as the sun rose higher. As he spoke, he stopped abruptly and said:

"An eagle just flew by the window. That must be a good sign."

*– Alexandra J. McClanahan*

**Carl H. Marrs** is President and CEO of Cook Inlet Region, Inc., known as CIRI. CIRI is one of 13 regional corporations established under the terms of the Alaska Native Claims Settlement Act of 1971. A respected business leader in the Alaskan community, Marrs has been named often as one of the "Top 25 Most Powerful Alaskans" by the *Alaska Journal of Commerce*.

With 6,900 shareholders, CIRI is one of the most financially successful of the regional corporations. Its principal lines of business include real estate, construction services and heavy equipment sales and leasing, communications, tourism and natural resource development. The corporation also supports a number of nonprofit organizations designed to promote the social and cultural well-being of CIRI shareholders and other Alaska Natives.

Marrs began his career with CIRI in 1973. Since then, he has held a variety of senior-level positions. A CIRI shareholder of Aleut descent, Marrs was born and reared in Seldovia. He attended Stanford University's Graduate School of Business for Executives in 1983 and the Amos Tuck School of Business for Executives at Dartmouth College in 1986.

---

**Alexandra J. McClanahan** is the CIRI Historian. A journalist originally from Nebraska who came to Alaska in 1982 to work for *The Anchorage Times*, a former Anchorage daily newspaper, McClanahan is the author of a previous oral history, *Our Stories, Our Lives*, featuring 23 Alaska Native elders from each of the state's major geographical regions who enrolled to Cook Inlet Region as provided in the Alaska Native Claims Settlement Act of 1971. She also served as publisher and president of *The Tundra Times* from 1986 until 1991. Under her direction, the newspaper focused much of its attention on promoting sobriety within Alaska. McClanahan left that newspaper, Alaska's only statewide Native weekly newspaper, when she and her husband John Shively adopted a six-day-old baby girl. Natasha Hensley Shively is a shareholder of NANA Regional Corporation, and her birth mother is an Inupiaq Eskimo from Kotzebue.

*Our Stories, Our Lives* was published in 1986 by The CIRI Foundation under the direction of Dr. Lydia Hays, the Foundation's Executive Director.

# *Acknowledgements*

The people who are featured in this book are due very special recognition for their courage and honesty in talking about themselves, their families and their cultures. They have taught me a great deal, and I am in their debt. I feel a spiritual connection to them because they allowed me into their lives and because this work is as much the result of prayer as work.

Carl H. Marrs, Barbara Donatelli and Mark Kroloff deserve most of the credit for *Growing Up Native in Alaska* because the three of them decided that rather than waiting for someone to capture the "ANCSA story," they would create an environment at CIRI where it could be explored in all its depth.

Also deserving of recognition for making this book a reality is the Alaska Federation of Natives, which assisted with funding. I am especially indebted to AFN President Julie Kitka, whose support was critical to this book. I also thank Frank Hill of AFN.

I am grateful to my beautiful daughter Natasha Hensley Shively for her patience with me and because she personified for me the audience for this work. As an adopted Inupiaq, she, too, will struggle with her identity. I hope that this book will give her and all the others "born after" some tools for forging their identities. I am also grateful to my husband, John Shively, who has never wavered in his loyal support for me, as well as my parents.

Sincere thanks are due to William J. Van Ness, Jr., who as a staff member for Senator Henry M. Jackson, contributed significantly to the development of the Alaska Native Claims Settlement Act. The idea for interviews with young leaders came directly from conversations with Van Ness, as well as discussions with Carl Marrs, Roy Huhndorf, Byron Mallott and Janie Leask.

I owe a special debt of gratitude to Professors Stephen Haycox and Ronald Spatz of the University of Alaska Anchorage, both of whom gave me a great deal of much needed guidance and support.

Dr. Lydia Hays offered advice and suggestions, and her assistance was invaluable, as was The CIRI Foundation, which has published this work.

Many other people at CIRI have helped in a variety of ways – Sophie Minich, Allison Knox, Hallie Bissett, Beth Van Couwenberghe, Sharon Boling, Keith Sanders, Dustin Lorah, Hazel Felton and others. Thomas Glazier deserves recognition for his work on the maps. In fact, I owe a debt to everyone at the corporation, all of whom contribute to making CIRI a place that honors culture, family, integrity and honesty.

I thank Dale R. Lindsey for teaching me more about rewriting than any writing coach I have ever had.

Finally, I am so grateful to elders I have interviewed for other projects. They have given me the gift of their stories, and through them I have learned that listening can be a magical, spiritual act.

# *Glossary of Terms*

**AFN** – The Alaska Federation of Natives, a statewide organization formed in 1966 to fight for Alaska Native rights and champion Native claims to land within Alaska.

**Afterborns** – A term used to describe Alaska Natives born after the passage of the Alaska Native Claims Settlement Act of December 18, 1971. Unless a majority of the shareholders votes to create stock for those born after passage, the only way they can become shareholders is through inheritance or if someone "gifts" stock to them. Of the 12 regional corporations within Alaska, three have created stock for those born after: Arctic Slope Regional Corporation, Doyon Ltd., and NANA Regional Corporation.

**Aleuts** – The indigenous Native people of the Aleutian Islands, some of whom were moved by the Russians to the Pribilof Islands to undertake the fur seal harvest. The Pribilovians were forced to leave their homes during World War II and put into camps in Southeastern Alaska for the duration of the war. Many died due to the camps' unsanitary conditions.

**ANCSA** – The acronym for the Alaska Native Claims Settlement Act.

**Athabascans** – The indigenous Indians living throughout Interior Alaska and Cook Inlet.

**BIA** – The Bureau of Indian Affairs.

**Enrolled** – Alaska Natives who participated in the Alaska Native Claims Settlement Act were required to enroll in order to become shareholders of a Native regional corporation and a Native village corporation. Those who enrolled only to a Native regional corporation and not also to a village are known as "at-large" shareholders. The term also is used for Alaska Natives who are not shareholders in a Native corporation, but who are enrolled members to a particular Native group or tribe.

**Eskimo** – The name given to several groups of indigenous peoples generally from the northern and western portions of Alaska.

**ICC** – The Inuit Circumpolar Conference, an organization that was the dream of Alaska Inupiaq leader Eben Hopson of Barrow. The organization was formed when Hopson called upon the Inuit (Eskimo) leaders of Greenland, Canada, the United States and the then-USSR to form an international organization. The first meeting was hosted by Hopson in Barrow in 1977. Meetings are held every three years.

**IRA Councils** – Native tribal councils organized under the Indian Reorganization Act. The Indian Reorganization Act (also known as the Wheeler-Howard Act) was enacted by Congress in 1934. The act authorizes constitutions and bylaws for tribal governments, but due to an unintentional error in drafting, it was not immediately applicable in Alaska. It was amended in 1936 to include Alaska.

**Inupiat** – The indigenous people of northern Alaska who are generally the arctic tundra people. The language is known as Inupiaq.

**New Native** – One of the terms used to describe Alaska Natives born after the passage of the Alaska Native Claims Settlement Act of December 18, 1971.

**"1991" Amendments** – Amendments to the Alaska Native Claims Settlement Act that prevented the lifting of the restrictions on the sale of Native corporation stock. As passed in 1971, ANCSA authorized the sale of Native corporation stock in 1991, 20 years after passage. The amendments allow for such sales to take place only if a majority of a corporation's shareholders vote to authorize the sales. In addition, the amendments authorize the creation of stock for "New Natives," as well as the gifting of stock.

**Nonprofit Corporations** – Each Native regional corporation has one or more nonprofit organizations concerned with social needs of the people.

**North Slope Borough** – A unit of local government for northern Alaska created in 1972 and encompassing 88,000 square miles. The borough reaches from the Canadian border to Point Hope on the Chukchi Sea.

**Regional Corporation** – Instead of creating reservations for Alaska Natives, the Alaska Native Claims Settlement Act called for the creation of 12 regional corporations and 205 village corporations. Generally speaking, the regional corporations encompassed traditional Native boundaries of the indigenous people within Alaska. In addition to the 12 regional corporations within Alaska, ANCSA authorized the creation of a thirteenth regional corporation to represent Alaska Natives living outside Alaska.

**Section 7(i)** – The section of ANCSA that requires regional corporations to share 70 percent of their resource revenues on their ANCSA lands with each other. Section 7(j) calls for half of the shared revenues that a regional corporation receives to be shared with its village corporations and at-large shareholders.

**Subsistence** – The livelihood of people who survive by living off the land. For Alaska Natives, the term includes requirements for survival as well as the cultural and spiritual aspects of carrying on the traditions of the past.

**Tlingit** – Indians of Southeast Alaska whose northern territory extended to Yakutat and whose southern boundary was near Ketchikan.

**Tribal Council** – A traditional Native government.

**UAA, UAF, UAS** – The University of Alaska Anchorage, University of Alaska Fairbanks and University of Alaska Southeast in Juneau.

**Venetie decision** – In a 1998 decision the U.S. Supreme Court ruled in the State of Alaska's favor that the Village of Venetie is not "Indian Country." The case was argued on December 10, 1997. The Ninth Circuit Court of Appeals had upheld Venetie's "Indian Country" status, and the State of Alaska appealed the Ninth Circuit Court decision. The case was considered to be a major setback for tribal advocates in Alaska.

**Yup'ik** – Eskimo people whose territory generally included western Alaska south of the Inupiaq people. The people of St. Lawrence Island are Siberian Yupik.

# Thirteen Regional Corporations created under ANCSA

ALEU

**Thirteenth Region**

Seattle

HAWAII

ALASKA

N

*Not to scale*

*Twelve Regions in the State of Alaska*

# *Ahtna Region*

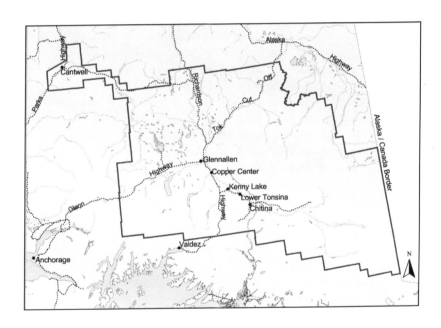

***PAUL MAYO*** *was born November 15, 1964, in Fairbanks. Except for several years in Cantwell where his father and mother, Leonard and Louise Mayo, Grandfather Jake Tansy and other family members taught him many of his subsistence and cultural skills, he grew up in Fairbanks. After graduating from high school, he went to the University of Alaska Fairbanks and received his Bachelor's of Business Administration Finance Degree in 1989.*

*His aunt, Ruby John, was a vocal advocate for the Alaska Native Claims Settlement Act in the late 1960's and a leader in the Ahtna Region. She died August 9, 1999.*

*Mayo's father is from Rampart in the Doyon Region, and his mother Louise Tansy Mayo is from Cantwell in the Ahtna Region. In 1971, the entire family enrolled as shareholders in Cantwell.*

*Mayo is currently employed as the Realty Director for Tanana Chiefs Conference, Inc., of Fairbanks.*

*A shareholder of Cantwell Yedetena Na Corporation and Ahtna, Inc., Mayo is a member of the Ahtna, Inc., Board of Directors. He is the youngest member of the Ahtna Board.*

*Mayo and his wife Tammy have three children, Ryan, Kristina and Katie. He was interviewed January 22, 1999.*

I don't think the Native corporate structure is always negative. A lot of people are always saying it's not a good thing, but there are good things about it. You've got to take the best from what you've got. It's already happened. I can see benefits of a tribal perspective, but you need economic vitality. You need cash to survive. You can write grants and get the basic village funding from the government every year, but that's not the only way to go. You need to get some type of independence. You need to bring in money to survive. That's the way the world is.

I was born and raised here in Fairbanks. I moved to Cantwell in 1973 and went to school there for a year, and then came back to Fairbanks. From 1976 through 1980, I went back to Cantwell during my junior high years. And I went two years of high school in Cantwell. During that part of my life, I was able to learn how to hunt and everything else from my grandpa Jake Tansy, and my father, Leonard Mayo.

I went to the regular school system – public schools here – to Denali School in Fairbanks, and then at West Valley High School. I then went to the University of Alaska Fairbanks from 1983 to 1989. I spent a couple of semesters off on construction, and during the summers I did construction. I got a Bachelor's of Business Administration Finance degree from the University.

My dad is from Rampart. And my mom, Louise Tansy Mayo, is from Cantwell. That's how I'm connected to Ahtna – through Cantwell as an Ahtna shareholder enrolled to Ahtna. Half my family comes from this region, Doyon, and half from the Ahtna Region. I have numerous aunts, uncles and cousins. I have two brothers, Scott and Adam. They are both younger, but they are both shareholders.

My mom got us enrolled. That's why we're enrolled to Ahtna. When they were doing the initial enrollment, we enrolled to Cantwell, not Rampart. We don't go to Rampart that often, even though my dad's from there. He also enrolled to Cantwell.

*What did you think of your elementary education?* I was very shy, especially in kindergarten. In elementary school, they used to split up the classes in reading groups – a group that needed remedial help and another group that was more advanced. Nearly every time we were split up, I was put into the remedial group. It was only after being in there a couple weeks – until the test scores came back – I was moved into the advanced courses. So that's something I noticed about elementary school. There were a lot of bright Native kids who went to school with me. We competed with each other, went to spelling bees and everything else.

*Was that discrimination?* In retrospect, yes. It was based on what we looked like and probably because we didn't talk very much. It was only after our test scores came back that we were moved into where we were supposed to be.

I only had one incident of a teacher that could have been prejudiced. That was sixth grade. She was so bad that we reported her to our parents. The parents contacted the school principal, and she was reprimanded for the things she said about Native kids. She would say things about how Native kids often get into trouble, have a higher incidence of crime, suicide, and they couldn't see very well because of vitamin deficiencies.

*How did you feel when the teacher made these statements?* We kept quiet – my friends, Harold, Glenn, Dudley and Bobby. That's all I remember. I think the other kids (non-Native) knew better, that she shouldn't have been saying those things.

*Otherwise discrimination wasn't a problem?* No. I was able to adapt to elementary school well because I grew up here in town, and I grew up with television. We seemed to gather a lot from television

– Sesame Street, all of the old shows of the '60's, early '70's.

*Did you learn your Native language?* When we went to Cantwell, between '76 and '80, my mom taught bilingual to the whole school. The non-Native children went to the class, too, and learned. *Did your mother speak it at home?* Not always. She spoke it to her sisters and brothers, her mom and dad, but we didn't learn it on our own. We listened, and we only know a few words. My father didn't speak any Native language. Rampart was influenced very early on by miners and became very Westernized quickly.

*Was there a point where you felt you were an Alaska Native?* Our mom let us know very early on that we were Alaska Native, and we took a lot of pride in that. As you remember during the early '70's, there was a lot about Black Power, Red Power, and so on. And there was a lot of pride in ethnicity, with Wounded Knee and so on. Even as kids you still knew things like that. We saw the protests. I started reading the newspaper when I was in fifth grade. I've read it every day since. Our mom instilled us with a lot of pride in those days. And then later, she explained that you're not supposed to be "proud," exactly, but it's called *ingee*. It's just a saying that you shouldn't be proud. In the Western world, it's like "knock on wood," or, "what goes around, comes around," that kind of saying. Or, "never make fun of people." *Ingee* kind of covers all of that. Even the Bible says, "Don't be proud. Don't have a lot of pride." I know the Bible, but I'm not religious. *Ingee* is just a knowing feeling.

I grew up in a place called Chena Courts. There were two-bedroom apartments, and there must have been 36 units. All of my friends from that apartment complex were Native. Nearly the whole complex was Native. We went to Denali School. We all walked together to school. That was from first grade all the way through sixth. We all knew we were Natives. We were all very happy with that. There were older kids that were high schoolers, and they were very proud, too.

*Is the feeling of being an Alaska Native positive?* Positive. As I get older, I realize if someone says something against me as an Alaska Native, often it's that person who has a problem or needs to resolve conflict within himself. When I went to college, they called it "projection" of their own bad qualities.

It's only after I've traveled to many different cities that I see some Fairbanks residents could be considered prejudiced. People see the downtown drunks and so on, and so they formulate an immediate stereotype. And then, for instance, you may go to a store here and not be helped right away. I found out if you went to other cities, they call you "sir," and they help you right away. I've gotten a couple of cold shoulders by businesses downtown in Fairbanks, but not always. It's only been 10 percent of the time. Otherwise, people are really nice here. I've read all of these books about customer service, and I'm a licensed appraiser. So I think maybe it's a Fairbanks thing. Most people are nice. It's just you remember most incidents where you are discriminated against. Now, we don't make a big deal out of it. The way I see it is the person's having a bad day or he or she is thinking about something else. They're at work, but maybe their kid is sick. I don't label everything as prejudice. Not unless it's blatant, and then you take action.

*How did you decide to go to college?* Like I said, I grew up in this place called Chena Courts, and I remember my mom and dad looking at a three-bedroom ranch in a new subdivision. We went with a realtor, and my mom and dad were probably just looking. Maybe they didn't even try. I was only eight or nine. And the down payment was 300 dollars, and it was 1973. I didn't like living in Chena Courts because when we went to school, the kids made fun of where we lived. So I was thinking, "I don't want to just cruise through life, barely getting by and being embarrassed." So when I was 16 years old, there used to be all of these get-rich seminars. I went, and I met these wealthy people, and they said they all had gotten business degrees. And so, I thought I might as well get at least a Bachelor's. So I got a degree in Finance to learn about money. And I wanted to learn how to buy houses.

I got my own house after only two years of employment – it's a zero lot line, and we live in a good place – because I knew the system.

*Your parents didn't have the 300 dollars?* My parents sort of sabotaged themselves. They grew up in a time period where they weren't served in restaurants and so on. My mom has a degree in education. My dad went through the eighth grade. They think they are deserving of less. Still, we try to help them along. They still cling to these old ideas of, "I can't do this." "I can't do that." Or, "We shouldn't do that." Back then, I guess we didn't have the 300.

Growing up, my mom and dad used to drink quite a bit. But we always had lots to eat and were to school on time. It was just that you remember when they did drink. They quit about 1980 or 1981. A lot of people in Cantwell quit at the same time. It seems that a lot of these people are the same age. I'm glad they all quit in Cantwell because there's no more drinking like there used to be. There used to be big gatherings up at the bar, with fights. Although some people still drink, it doesn't seem as destructive as before.

*Did you tell yourself that wouldn't happen to you?* Not really. I think I just do it responsibly. Because I went to college, I realized I could drink and have fun. But if I drink, I'm going to get up early the next day. I'm not going to sleep in or pick up another bottle the next day. I go to a lot of the villages, and people will go on binges for days, weeks, until the money runs out. I could never understand that. I always thought I could go have a good time, but I'll be up early the next day, back to work.

*When the kids made fun of you, was it because you were Native or low-income?* Three of my friends were from the same apartment complex. The rest were from an apartment complex called Birch Park that was a HUD project. We were easy to identify. And the kids knew that these were places that were poor. Oftentimes, there were a few bad apples that would cause problems, a few young Native kids who would routinely beat up other kids, no matter who they were.

*College?* I liked it. I worked construction in the summer, and I literally was in ditches with a shovel. And that was hard, twelve hours a day. And then other times, I was holding a sign for traffic. That was the hardest thing to do because it's a very boring job. I'd rather be shoveling. But I didn't want to do that type of work, so college became easy. The good thing about construction is that it disciplines you. You learn to sleep for just several hours only. So when you get to college, it's just easy. There's nothing bad about going to class and reading books.

And then there was a fear of poverty, a fear that if I didn't get a degree, I was going to be mediocre, embarrassed because I'm poor.

I have been married 11 years. I have a six-year-old boy, a four-year-old girl and a two-year-old girl. They are Ryan, Kristina and Katie. My wife is non-Native. My children are three-eighths exactly because I'm three-quarter Indian. My dad is a quarter white, and my mom is a quarter white.

*How did you become a member of the Ahtna board?* It's because of my Auntie Ruby John and others in Cantwell. My aunts and my mom are very forceful. My Aunt Ruby is politically active, and my mom's very sharp also. Also my uncles. They said, "Why don't you run for the Cantwell seat?" And so I did. I got on in 1992, and then three years later I got in at-large. Part of it is, just like any town, any community, there's conflict. And it seemed as if I caused less trouble than others did. Maybe I didn't offend as many as the others did. So I guess I was the choice.

*Are you the youngest member of the board?* I think I am at 34. Most of them are in their 40's or 50's or older. I think way differently from them, but we're still able to be businesslike, still disciplined.

*How do you feel about being on your board? Did you always want to be on?* No. It's something I didn't even think of. Even before 1992 and still now, I don't like conflict that much, but I've learned to deal with it. And the best training I got was from my aunts and my mom. For some reason, when they want to get their point across, they'll say it loudly. They'll say things forcefully to you and even almost insult you to get a point across. I've seen them in action against me and other people who were on the opposite side of the table. That's where I've learned to deal with conflict constructively. I don't take things personally. If somebody's going to yell and get excited, I'm able to see more or less that's just their way of communicating. So I can take these types of situations a lot better.

One time we were supposed to have a meeting with an electric company, and it was felt that they didn't treat us right. Four company representatives came to Cantwell for a powerline discussion. Even before the meeting got started, the council members – my aunts and my mom – said, "Nope. Kick them out." So we kicked them out. (Laughs.) We didn't even have a meeting with them. They came all the way to Cantwell, thinking they were going to get something done, but we literally threw them out of the hall.

I said, tactfully to the electric company representatives, "Oh, they said we don't have to hear from you today."

It's a good experience. I've learned. The best thing to do is learn people's behavior. It's helped me. I have 15 people on my staff here. It has helped me learn how to deal with them, learn their behavior, so I don't have to have a knee-jerk reaction when somebody does something. You kind of learn: let's wait a little bit, see if they're having problems or something.

We've gotten five new staff members in the past five months. It's basically because a lot of talented people that we have in Realty that we've grown so much. We manage Native allotments and restricted townsites. That's the trust responsibility program through the Bureau of Indian Affairs. We manage about 2,200 parcels and about 500 townsites.

*Are you involved in the village?* Yes, I'm on the shareholder committee that was formed after the merger with Ahtna as an advisory committee to the corporation. There is a village council, and I'm a member of the village, but council members are people who live there year-round.

*Native hero?* My first one growing up was Geronimo. Like I said, during those days there was a lot of pride. There were big black-and-white posters, and we had one in our house. It was Geronimo himself, holding a rifle, kneeling down. All of our friends in Chena Courts had things like that, too. I admire his tenacity, his ability to fight against tremendous odds. And then next was Billy Mills, and everybody knows of Billy Mills. Seeing him in person in Glennallen a few years ago was tremendous. There are always people you admire, people you work with.

*Your feelings on ANCSA?* It avoided the reservation system. I don't have many bad feelings about ANCSA because I have a degree in business. I think the best way to enhance people's lives is to get them out of poverty. And using ANCSA as a vehicle was not such a bad thing. Part of the problem is that not everybody's benefiting equally from Native corporations. There's a lot of animosity from shareholders who think that the corporations aren't doing enough for them. But, to me, generally speaking, I think people should help themselves first. It seems like the people who complain the most are not doing something for themselves first to maximize their own opportunities.

The other thing is that Native corporations own land and are state-chartered. The only thing about fee simple title is that it's not as protected as land under federal jurisdiction. It just would seem better if the land was under federal jurisdiction. It seems like there are more federal protections.

*Would you like to see a change?* Just for land purposes, yes. ANCSA didn't work at the village level for Cantwell for 14(c)3 lands. If the population keeps increasing, it doesn't benefit Cantwell as well.

*Do you remember when ANCSA was passed?* I remember around 1972, there were meetings of all of my relatives around Cantwell. We'd go to my grandpa's house and get around all these maps. That's when I first started seeing things, but I didn't know what they were about. It was just a time for me to play with my cousins. *Did it seem like a good thing?* When we got the dividend checks, yes.

Once I got on the board and got more active, I could see things better and the potential for growth. To me, it was best to help make a more powerful corporation for helping the Native people – to make them economically and financially strong. It seems, in general, Ahtna is trying to do that. We have a very talented CEO, Darryl Jordan. He's doing everything he can. He has the personal commitment – because he's a shareholder – to make sure that the corporation grows responsibly. And we've grown quite a bit this past year.

*Is there a clash between the culture and corporations?* Yes, there is a clash. On one level, you want to maintain the lifestyle. For instance, the way my mom and dad grew up, when you're hungry or the kids are hungry, you go out and you get your moose or caribou or whatever or your fish. But you have all of these political forces from everywhere taking all of these rights they used to have. And so, there's a situation where you cannot maintain your own culture. Cantwell is a cash economy. Oftentimes, Native corporations are criticized for being limited or having a limited scope and not helping. They're viewed as just trying to make a profit, and Native corporations are just benefiting management and a few select individuals. Profit-wise, you're in a competitive environment where you're trying to increase revenue. There's a lot of clash there between the haves and the have-nots. For me, because of the way I grew up, I can think both ways in the dichotomy. I know my culture. But I know profit. Profit is not an evil thing. Money is not an evil thing. It's what people do with that money or their attitudes toward that and how they treat other people – that's where it could be not a good thing.

Profitwise, the complaints out of Cantwell are that they want to get their homesites. That's number one on their list. Under the merger agreement, each shareholder is entitled to five acres, perpetual lease. And that's been very slow coming about. And the second would be: "Where's my dividend?" But they say that jokingly. "What's our dividend this year, Paul?" Number one is land. They want their five acres.

*Your goals?* Right now, I have a heady feeling. This past year, I've traveled. I've always wanted to travel. I've always wanted to drive across a desert. And these things have happened through Ahtna and through Tanana Chiefs. I've taken training with Tanana Chiefs, and I've gone to appraisal courses in Albuquerque, Phoenix, San Diego, Denver. And then with Ahtna, I've been to Sacramento, Reno,

Miami. We're going to other places, maybe even New York. I like to see different perspectives when I travel. I like to see what America is like.

For goals, I want to raise my family really well. I want to be married forever. That's the way my mom and dad and their moms and dads seem to have been raised. Once you're married, you take care of your children. So number one is treating my family really well, and always having a stable environment. Also, I want to become a better person by treating people better. If I say something mean, I can apologize for doing that. I don't want to be prideful or fight with anyone for years on end.

Then there are financial goals. I want to get a bigger house. The goal I always had when I was younger was that I was going to be a millionaire by the time I was 30. I'm doing fine. I'm not rich, but I'm happy, so that's fine.

*What are you seeing on your travels?* When I go to different cities, I see different traffic patterns. You see people in different neighborhoods, different ethnic groups. I see the potential for growth, money, maybe things that Native corporations can capitalize on. I observe other types of businesses, everything from cellular phone companies, computers to sports franchises like basketball, football.

After you come back from these larger places, Fairbanks seems like a village. It's very cold, but there is hardly any traffic, and it's really nice to come back to, actually, after being down in all that traffic and being with all those people. I don't mind visiting Outside. You get a different perspective. But I also know from learning about other people that people are the same everywhere in a lot of ways.

*Goals for your children?* My children like to read. We have lots of children's books. They see us reading all the time, so by example, they read a lot. A goal is to get them very educated and to later experience their culture, to hunt, fish and take part in the other activities. And a big deal lately – focusing on their emotional intelligence, making sure that they're going to be OK in that respect also. We want to make sure that they're going to be well-balanced people. For instance, if my kids lose their temper, we help them try to do it in a tactful way. Let them know it's OK to get mad every once in awhile, but that you can't do certain things. And another goal, of course, is having enough money for them to go to college.

*Goals for Ahtna?* Ahtna has grown way beyond expectation.

Right now, we've grown beyond Glennallen. We've had to move some operations to Anchorage because that's the central business area for Alaska. Our goal is to make Ahtna a powerful corporation that's viable. Generally, that means not to compete against other Native corporations. We're not going to have a dog-eat-dog world against each other. But we've grown beyond the Ahtna Region, and that was a goal – to lessen our dependence on the Alyeska Pipeline. I think people were hanging on to that too tight. We've diversified ourselves from that and grown into other areas.

They've accepted me, but it's almost like I'm an outsider because I'm from Cantwell. Glennallen is on the Richardson Highway, and we're way across the Denali Highway on the Parks Highway. We're the farthest away from Copper Center. Oftentimes when people talk, they'll say, "Oh, you guys are 'out of the way.'"

"Out of the way," we've heard that from our former CEO. "You guys are kind of out of the way, you know. It takes a long time to get there." And then if the village of Cantwell is listening to this, that's not always that tactful. (Laughs.)

*Your goal for ANCSA in the future?* That the corporations remain strong. I don't think it's a structure you can change that much. I know there are some village corporations transferring land to the tribal entities. I hope not to see corporations in general start selling off land. I know of only one small corporation selling land in this region. The goal is for Native corporations in general to remain strong companies that represent the people and take care of the people. For instance, for many years Ahtna has offered jobs. Many people have benefited.

I don't think the Native corporate structure is always negative. A lot of people are always saying it's not a good thing, but there are good things about it. You've got to take the best from what you've got. It's already happened. I can see benefits of a tribal perspective, but you need economic vitality. You need cash to survive. You can write grants and get the basic village funding from the government every year, but that's not the only way to go. You need to get some type of independence. You need to bring in money to survive. That's the way the world is. If tribal entities could find some way to bring in revenue, then that would be OK. It's going to be hard to maintain the culture if you have these threats – even subsistence rights are being attacked. If tribal entities can't fight that, then it's going to be difficult. You've got to have financial strength. You've got to have political clout to deal with all these forces.

**SUE SHERMAN** *was born on January 9, 1962, and grew up in Lower Tonsina, about 12 miles north of the village of Chitina in Southcentral Alaska. Her father Al Taylor, a non-Native originally from California, worked for the Bureau of Land Management in Fire Management, and he also owned a sawmill. Her mother Agnes Taylor is Athabascan originally from the village of Chitina.*

*Sherman is from the Caribou Clan of the Ahtna people. She is a shareholder of Chitina Native Corporation and Ahtna, Inc. Sherman graduated from Kenny Lake School with a class of nine. She began working for Ahtna in 1985. While working and raising her two young children, Sherman attended classes at Prince William Sound Community College, where she obtained an Associate of Arts Degree. Sherman began moving up in the corporation through work in Land and Resources and recently worked as Chief Operating Officer for the Ahtna in Glennallen.*

*Sherman lives in Glennallen with her daughter Dana and son Randy. She has gifted stock to both of her children. She was interviewed January 8 and 19, 1999.*

**I** hope that in the future the regional corporations are better able to balance culture with business and that we don't turn into just big business. I hope we always remain unique. Our uniqueness comes from our traditional values. I hope that that never goes away. There is too much focus on big business. It's great to aim for bottom-line success, but I hope we are all keeping our ties to the culture. We don't need to be another IBM and GM. We need to be what we are, Native corporations.

I grew up outside of a little town called Chitina. Chitina is in Southcentral Alaska. Right now it is a major dipnet fishery. Actually, the area I grew up in was a little place called Lower Tonsina, about 12 miles north of Chitina. I lived there until I was 18. We didn't have running water, electricity or even a phone – none of those types of amenities. My dad worked for the Bureau of Land Management in Fire Management. He also owned a sawmill, so he was also self-employed. My mother was a homemaker. My mom is Athabascan; my father is a non-Native from California. He was introduced to Alaska through his father, who came up to work on the railroad in the Kennecott Mine days.

My dad left Alaska and joined the Navy but loved Alaska and the Chitina area so much that he returned and met and married my mother. I am the youngest of six children. My parents are Al Taylor and Agnes Taylor. There were three boys and three girls in our family.

*Was it a subsistence lifestyle?* We lived somewhat a subsistence lifestyle, but since my father was from California, I was introduced to the Western ways of life also. But we sure ate a lot of fish, and a lot of moose meat, too.

My mother can understand Athabascan. She probably doesn't speak it as well as she would like to, but she understands and can speak it to an extent. I think the reason my mother doesn't speak it as well is because she grew up in Chitina during the Kennecott days and there was a strong non-Native influence on the village people at that time.

*Did you learn it?* Just words here and there. I couldn't hold a conversation with anyone. I might be able to pick out a few words, but that's about it.

I graduated from a small school called Kenny Lake School. My high school years were during the Pipeline days, which caused a little bit more of an influx in that school, made it a little larger. But it still was a very small school, nine people in my graduating class. Five of us were Native students.

*Discrimination?* Very little. There was some joking about "salmon crunching," but our school was small – and there was a small percentage of Native students there, but I don't ever remember knowing the difference in school. I don't know how to explain it. I knew there was a difference. I knew we were Alaska Native, but we didn't recognize a difference in the school that I went to. The non-Native kids were our friends, and we were their friends, and we dated each other, caught rides after school with each other. We were in the same sports programs. So, it actually was a very nice school to go to in that respect.

I went to the local community college after I tried going to a school of cosmetology in Anchorage, which wasn't for me, so I decided not to do that and went back to Glennallen. I was married then and had a child. This was when I was in my early 20's. And then I began school at Prince William Sound Community College, where I finally got a two-year degree, an Associate of Arts Degree.

In the meantime, I began working for Ahtna in 1985. Over 14 years I went from being their receptionist to being the Chief Operating Officer.

*When did you first feel "I'm an Alaska Native"?* When I went to work for Ahtna. That probably was the point that I really recognized what it meant to be an Alaska Native. I grew up around Alaska Natives. Our neighbors were Natives. We ate dried fish over at their house. Smoked fish, we had all of that. But I guess it never occurred to me that that was a different lifestyle than other people lived. And then I came to Ahtna, and I started to become more involved with the region and where people lived and how they lived and how people would fight for a subsistence lifestyle. I learned about clans and the differences among our people. I am from the Caribou Clan. Being exposed to more of the Ahtna people I then became aware that I was a part of something very special.

I wasn't aware of it before because it was just there. My mother took me to potlatches when I was younger. I've been to many potlatch ceremonies, but to me it was just our way of life. It didn't occur to me that other people didn't live like this. And I guess maybe if it did, it didn't bother me that I lived differently. So it always was a positive thing.

*Social problems in the village?* Yes. I saw alcohol abuse. And the town of Chitina centered around a bar. So there was a lot of alcohol abuse. *Did that have an effect on you?* Yes, probably. But alcohol didn't just affect the Native people. The non-Natives that lived there had alcohol problems. So I never looked at it as solely a Native issue. We had some serious alcohol problems in my family, too. And that was from both sides, my non-Native side and my Native side. I learned that there are no boundaries with alcoholism.

*Did you see these things and say, "That's not going to happen to me"?* Yes, definitely, I also said living without electricity, telephone, running water and sewer wasn't the life for me, either. That was probably part of my drive to climb the corporate ladder and to make a little more money.

*Do you feel you have a tie to your Native culture?* Yes, very much so. I think it's just being among the people, living out in the region, knowing the issues that they face and understanding them. Just being a part of that life, I think. I continue to go to potlatch ceremonies, continue to spend time with my friends and family at the fishwheel, even though I don't have my own. The only way I can practice a subsistence way of life is through them. I work and don't have the time to go out and cut fish or hunt. Well, maybe I just don't take the time to do that, so I depend on my friends and family to help me out. *The spiritual side?* I would say just the ceremony of the potlatch, the way that our people deal with the passing on of our people and how everyone rallies around each other and how through the generations we have continued to keep that alive. It's something that I hope we never stop doing.

*Native hero or heroine?* I've thought about that question. I can't think of just one. There are so many people that I admire. I admire the early leaders. I admire the people that went out there and fought for the land claims in the early days when there wasn't per diem. There wasn't this "lavish" lifestyle that many of us are able to live in now, the nice hotels. Today, we go to lobby in Juneau or fly off to Washington, D.C., and the corporation pays for it. I admire the people who didn't have that, but still had it in them to go and fight for the people and fight for the land. I think those guys are the real heroes.

In our region it would be Roy S. Ewan, Markle Ewan, Sr., Oscar Craig, John Billum, Sr. Those are the guys that I think are some of the real the heroes. I understand that the wives had bake sales, and that was how they raised money to be able to do these things. Can you imagine that? Who would have the energy to do that these days? I look at myself: would I do that? Would I take my own funding and go out and do something like that, fight for the people? Would any of us do it if we didn't get to go to our corporations and say, "Here's my expense report for that last trip to Juneau"?

I learned a lot from Roy Ewan. He was the President/CEO of our corporation for many years and I worked with him a lot of those years. Roy would invite me to meetings, negotiating sessions and his visits with people. I didn't realize it then, but this was his way of mentoring me. I learned a lot of negotiation skills from him. I learned a lot of things from him, like how to not always take everything so personally. Roy always said, "It's business. Don't take it personally." I've seen him upset with people, and then the next day he'd meet with them again. "This is business; this is not personal," he'd say. I always admired that. I learned from it. I don't always practice it, but I learned from it.

I also have to mention Walter Charley from Chitina when I talk of true Native heroes. He really was a very special man. He passed on about four years ago. He was a spokesman for Ahtna people statewide, and he very much tried to bring people together. I never saw Walter in the middle of conflict. I never saw him taking sides. I always admired that. And he would seek wisdom from anyone, even a young person. I always thought that was a wonderful thing – to be big enough to say he could learn from anyone. We certainly learned a lot from him.

*Your goals?* I've been with the corporation for 14 years. I guess my goal is to always stay involved at some level. But I hope this isn't all I do in my life. And I guess I want to teach my kids to be involved in the corporation, to always respect the people, whether they choose to live in the region or not. Of course, my dreams for my children are that they get an excellent education and they pursue all grand and wonderful things. Also, my goal for me is to support them in anything they do, which is what my parents did for me. Especially my mother who supported me in anything that I was involved in.

I have a daughter Dana who is 12, and my son Randy is 17. *Have they shown any interest in Ahtna?* Actually, both have. My son has worked for the nonprofit, for Copper River Native Association, for the past two summers, and he has enjoyed that. He's helped out in the housing improvement program, so he's gotten a chance to get around some of the Native people, and he's enjoyed that. And I have been happy that he's had that exposure to them. My daughter has a very big interest in languages, and a big interest in the Ahtna language. She spends time trying to learn Ahtna words. Sometimes she practices them with her grandmother. And that's great.

*What about the fact that they're not shareholders?* They're shareholders. I gifted them stock, and I believe that everyone should gift their children stock. *Do they understand what it's about?* No, I don't think they do. They were pleased to get their dividend check. (Laughs.) *Has Ahtna considered adding the young people?* Ahtna is considering that. I think the Ahtna people really want to include our descendants. I think of it as their birthright. *Is it a big issue in Ahtna?* I have heard it's a growing issue. People say, and this is very true, "Why should the kids become interested? They have no stake in this."

We need to grow new leaders. We always need to grow new leaders. And you can't grow them from children who have no stake in the company. They have no reason to become interested in something that they're not a part of. So I do think we need to make them a part of it.

*Ahtna was active in land claims from the early 1900's. Do people feel they got enough recognition?* Ahtna people are a humble people. They really are. I don't think it really bothers them if they didn't get the recognition. They were there. I know recently we did a book on Ahtna history. I have heard, and it is documented in that book, that the word "Ahtna" comes from "Chitina." It actually means "lower Copper River people." But when they were fighting for land claims, they named it "Ahtna" for the Ahtna Region. And so the whole region has adopted this word "Ahtna." And then it was transformed into "the people of the Copper River," rather than "the people of the Lower Copper River."

*How do Ahtna people feel about being the smallest regional corporation?* I guess it doesn't bother us that much to be the smallest region. We tell people when we describe who we are. I was in Albuquerque recently, and we had a lot of introductions. I was at a Native American women's conference. I explained that I work for one of the 12 regional corporations, and that we are the smallest. (Laughs.) It doesn't bother us to say that. Being small makes us unique. It makes us more of a family. We don't have a lot of dissension from shareholders. You don't see our shareholders write to the newspaper and air our dirty laundry. Because they know us. They know the leaders personally. If they're mad, they're going to call Sue Sherman up and say, "Sue, I'm mad." They're going to tell me, or I'm going to hear it. And so we're still small enough that we're more personal to our shareholders. And I think that makes us unique, and it makes us special. When I hear shareholders' names, I know they are shareholders. We have 1,200 shareholders, and I could probably name 90 percent of them.

*Your region is facing tremendous pressure from sport fishermen coming into the area. Is that a concern?* Yes, this is scary. I look at the improvements in the Glenn Highway, and I think, "Oh, how wonderful. Now I can drive to Anchorage in three and a half hours." And the road is so nice. Well, that road goes both ways. And the more that road is improved, the more we've become Anchorage's backyard. And why not? It's a beautiful region. But it is an incredible influx on our resources, our fisheries, our game, on our quiet way of life. So we look at that, and I don't think we know how to put our arms around it or what we should do about it in the future. We are right at the gateway to a large national park. Wrangell-St. Elias is right there in our backyard. It's 13.2 million acres. And they are just now this year beginning to build a visitors' center, which will start the attraction. We look forward to probably another Denali National Park in terms of popularity with the tourists. And we need to plan for that. I think the Ahtna people realize it's coming. We just don't know what to do with it yet.

*The fishing?* Chitina is the largest dipnet fishery in Alaska and it's very popular. The Klutina River is a wonderful, beautiful river, probably one of the best king salmon fisheries in Alaska. It's becoming quite popular. We have the Gulkana River. It's completely overrun by people. Ahtna owns the banks of all these rivers, and we're just now starting to be able to set in place programs to try to control access. And then we hope to funnel some of these people to other areas to try to minimize some of the damages that they do to the land by just the abundance of people.

*Do people understand it's Ahtna land?* I don't think that many of them know. And that education process from our standpoint is expensive and time-consuming, and it's unfortunate that we have to spend our time informing people. *Is there much help from the state?* No, not the state or the federal government, very little help at all.

We have land in Cantwell. The Denali National Park is near there. We've been hard hit with visitors on our land. But it's beautiful land, so who can blame them?

*Was it a good idea to set up corporations as opposed to reservations?* When I recently visited Albuquerque, New Mexico, I met a lot of women from a reservation. I don't have a really good understanding of how that all works. They seem to have the same politics that we have. They have the issues of Native hire, and also family hire. I realize that there is a great deal of difference between corporations and reservations, but I don't really understand the reservation system. I can't really say one is better than the other when I know only one.

*What do you hope the corporations will do in the future?* I hope that in the future the Native corporations are better able to balance culture with the business and that we don't just turn into big business. I hope we always remain unique. Our uniqueness comes from our traditional values, and that should never go away. I truly believe that right now there is too much focus on big business. It's great to aim for bottom-line success, but I hope that we are all keeping our ties to the culture. We don't need to be another IBM or GM. We need to be what we are, Native corporations.

One of the things that is unique about Ahtna is that we're more village oriented than other corporations. We merged with seven of our eight village corporations, and in that merger we went a step further than ANCSA. In order to protect our villages, it was set up so that they are allowed to have a say in the development of the lands in their village. They have a veto power with Ahtna. It's one we listen to. Many times, management doesn't like it. We tell the village, "It's going to make us so much money." But the people say they don't want it for subsistence reasons or they want to maintain their same lifestyle. Sometimes as management all we can see is the economics of development, and we don't see their part of it. I think that balance between us needs to stay.

I believe in the merger. It's been a good thing. It has united us. It's important. Ahtna had a lot of small villages, so joining together was the way to go. Our elders that put that together were wise.

Our villages have vetoed a few things. What was set up was a shareholder village organization that is similar to the former corporation board. They are reasonable in their vetoes. Because we're small we're able to work together and work things out.

We recently had a veto in one of our northern villages, an area of a mining development, and we were able to work through that. We met with the villagers, listened to their concerns, talked about the pros and cons of development, how we could take steps to alleviate those concerns and understand them. The process gave the staff greater appreciation for their lifestyle and what they wanted to protect. We were able to make that work with the promise that we'd keep them in the loop.

# *Aleut Region*

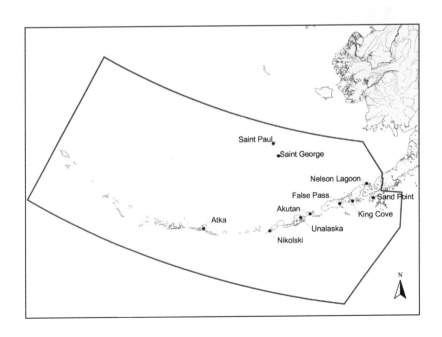

*JEFFERY KAUFFMAN was born January 1, 1970, in Anchorage. His mother is originally from St. George Island in the Pribilofs, and his father is from Michigan. His mother was actually born in Funter Bay in Southeast Alaska in 1943 when the Aleut people from the Pribilof Islands were forcibly removed from their homes during World War II. They were placed in abandoned canneries, and many people died in the difficult conditions there.*

*Kauffman moved to St. Paul with his mother and sisters in 1978 when his parents were divorced. He has lived on the island most of his life except for a year in high school when he lived in Florida and the years that he attended college.*

*Kauffman is a shareholder in The Aleut Corporation. He is enrolled as an "at-large" shareholder and therefore does not have stock in the St. Paul village corporation, Tanadgusix Corporation.*

*Kauffman received his Bachelor's Degree in Elementary Education from the University of Alaska Anchorage in 1998. He is also a commercial fisherman and maintains a 32-foot fishing vessel.*

*He and his wife Jessica are the parents of one daughter, Taylor Renee. Both Jeffery and Jessica are teachers in the St. Paul school system. Jeffery coaches basketball and Native Youth Olympics and teaches English, history and Physical Education, and Jessica is a third/fourth grade teacher. He was interviewed February 24, 1999.*

**O**ur Native corporations will put you through school basically, and it's pretty exciting for these young kids to know. It's there for the taking. If you do well, if you go and you try, they sure support you. They're very generous.

I was born in Anchorage. My mother is from St. George, and my dad is from Michigan. I have two sisters. One is older and one is younger. We lived in Anchorage until 1978 when my parents got divorced and we moved here to St. Paul with my mother. My dad moved to California. So I've been here in St. Paul since then with my family, with the exception of the time I was in high school and college. I have a degree in elementary education. And I'm currently teaching at the St. Paul school.

My mother's name is Edna Floyd. Her maiden name is Philemonof, and my dad's name is John Kauffman.

My older sister Renee and I are both shareholders – at large – so we're shareholders of just The Aleut Corporation. My younger sister Margaret is not a shareholder. I think she's going to inherit some shares from my grandfather. He passed away, and I think my mom is going to give some of those to my younger sister since she's not a shareholder.

*Do you remember Anchorage?* I do remember a little bit about it. I went to school at Chester Creek Elementary, off of Muldoon Road. I don't remember much more than that. *How about your education on St. Paul?* Back then a lot of our teachers came from Georgia. I think the education was good.

*Did you experience discrimination?* I did when I came here to St. Paul. I certainly did. I was considered the "white boy" from out of town and got in some fights over that. It was bad when I was in second and third grade, but it seems to be much more accepted now.

People eventually realized I was from home, that I am Aleut and that my roots are here. So I haven't experienced it since I was a kid. Everybody knows me here now, so there are no problems.

*Was the discrimination hard on you?* It was pretty hard to take. I remember getting in fights a lot, kids trying to beat me up. Yeah, there was some discrimination. And I remember being a kid, too, and coming from St. Paul and going to St. George with my mother – she has relatives there – and getting beat up there too, as well. I guess just being from St. Paul, there was some discrimination in St. George. I don't remember why, but there was some discrimination between Aleuts from St. Paul and St. George even though we're so close together.

*Did you discuss this with your mother?* Yes, I sure did. And she stuck up for me any way she could. I remember her calling my friends' parents when I was young. I think this went on through – it must have been fourth grade before it finally went away and people started to lay off a little bit.

I remember it was difficult. I did go to high school in Florida for a year when I was in tenth grade, and I remember being referred to as "Eskimo." That's what I was to them. They liked me, and I was on the basketball team and everything else. But that's what they called me. I was "Eskimo." (Laughs.) I don't think they meant it to be negative, but I didn't feel very good. It didn't bother me so much at the time, but when I came home, it seemed weird. I didn't like it.

*Did you have a sense of being Alaska Native?* When I was in high school I served on the Alaska Federation of Natives Youth Council. I guess the more that I learned about it through high school, the more it meant to me. Since I was eight years old, we lived with my grandfather, and our home was very rich in culture. He's passed away now, but my grandfather and my mother and other family members speak Aleut. So I was around that constantly. And then there's the religion, and just the Aleut way of life – the hunting and the fishing and everything else since I was a boy. I have been involved in all that.

*Do you speak the language?* Unfortunately, no. I just know a few selected words. And my mother is a bilingual teacher, but somehow I didn't get it. (Laughs.)

*Do you have a tie to your culture?* Definitely. There is a tie there. There's a lot. Being here and being associated with everything that goes on here.

*Your wife?* She's Athabascan from Galena. Her name is Jessica Kauffman. She was originally a Housemann. And her grandfather was Edgar Nollner, who was part of that original serum run to Nome that started the Iditarod. He just passed away. She's rich with culture. Her grandfather's pretty famous in the Interior.

We have one daughter, Taylor Renee. She's 18 months now.

*Do you know much about the history of the Pribilofs?* Yes, we've heard a lot of the stories, especially from my grandfather's days. He was raised here in St. Paul. They were evacuated out to Funter Bay in Southeastern Alaska in World War II, and my mom was actually born there. Things like that, sure. And about how St. Paul was discovered, and the fur seals and the government and how they treated us. Things like that.

I went my first year of college in Oregon, and then I went the rest of the time to the University of Alaska Anchorage. My older sister is also a teacher, and my younger sister has an associate's degree in business management. She's a hotel manager now.

I wanted to play basketball in college, so I went to Oregon and did that for a year. Then I came home and worked various jobs. I worked construction. I've always fished since I've been a kid. I just didn't want to do that type of work forever, and then I got a job as a teacher's aide at the school. I was a para-professional there at the school. And then I decided it was time that I get my degree. I decided I wanted to teach like my mom and my sister. My grandmother on my dad's side was also a teacher. I've always enjoyed being around kids, so I wanted to go and finish. I figured if I was going to be in the school, I might as well be a teacher. So I went back and I finished up and got that degree.

Many young people from rural areas do not go to college. But there are more and more every day getting degrees. We've got a lot of kids from here in college now. And some of them are actually graduating.

*What about sports?* Sports have always been important to me. Since I was a kid, I've always been involved in baseball and basketball and whatever. Throughout high school and even into college, I was involved in sports. And now I'm coaching on the high school level, so it's still important to me. I coach basketball, and I'll be coaching the Native Youth Olympics.

*Why did you go to St. Paul?* I came home just because it's a good place to be. The loan that I got through the state of Alaska – if

60

I come to rural Alaska and teach for five years, it's 100 percent forgiven. So between my wife and me, we're talking about 70,000 dollars. So that was one reason for going to the Bush. And I have a commercial fishing boat here, so that helped me to decide to come home. We actually signed to go to the Lower Yukon School District. And we just at the last minute changed our minds. There was only one position open, but we still chose to come here. My wife took that job, and I worked as a full-time substitute for awhile, and I did some other things last year as we waited for another position to come available. And it's just a good place. My mother lives here, and I've got aunts and uncles and cousin here. St. Paul's a nice place.

*Was it hard to find housing?* Housing is very difficult on St. Paul, but fortunately the school district provides teacher housing. We do have to pay for it, but it's a nice house, a pretty good deal.

*Did you participate in subsistence activities?* My grandfather didn't do a lot of hunting, but I do have uncles and cousins who have always taken me out for duck hunting. We'd go out for kitiwakes or we'd go sea lion hunting or we'd go get a seal. And I've always fished since I was young. I don't do it so much now. My wife doesn't eat it, and I've never been a heavy eater of the subsistence foods. But I do go occasionally, and I do go bird hunting. But usually, when we do that I go with a friend or a cousin and we'll distribute it to the community.

*Why do you like St. Paul?* It's just a great place to live. It's a small community. It's about 750 people. I know everybody in this community. It's just very friendly, very relaxed. It's a slow pace. There are a lot of things happening, but still it's slow-paced. I can drive five minutes to work, or I can drive right down the street to my mom's house. It's very beautiful. We have a brand new harbor down there, and there are boats coming and going all the time. It's very active that way in the fishing sense. We've always ridden motorcycles. There are a lot of beaches, and they are beautiful. We drive the beaches or walk them and look for ivory. There are no trees here. It's all tundra and dunes and beaches. The people are kind, and it's just a close-knit community.

There certainly is some drug abuse and some alcohol abuse. Fortunately, it's not as bad here as it is in some of the other communities. We just recently had a death where a guy was drinking at five o'clock in the morning. He was an Aleut and he was married and his wife was from the Interior. Still, there's a problem. The kids seem to do really well with it though. There doesn't seem to be as much alcohol or drug abuse among the kids, with our new rec center. We're doing really well. And people are really conscious now of alcohol abuse, and it's talked about now more than it ever has been. I think they're trying to make people aware. They're trying to control that.

*Was ANCSA a good idea?* I think it was great, and it was for a good purpose: To turn the lands over to the Natives. I feel good about it. I like it – having the regional corporations and the village corporations. Unfortunately, we're "at large" shareholders so we didn't get any title to lands like some people got from the village corporations as village shareholders. But I know that our village corporation and also our regional corporation do a lot of good things for us and for this community. I know that. I studied a little bit about it in high school. We had an Alaska history class in college, and I remember studying some about it then.

*Was it better to create corporations instead of reservations?* I don't know enough about it. One of my cousins is the president of the tribal council now, and they wanted to turn this place into a reservation. And they're still trying to do this with tribal law. I'm not sure about all that stuff. I know that the corporations have been outstanding. I know that our village corporation, Tanadgusix Corporation, and our regional corporation, The Aleut Corporation, are both excellent. They do a lot of things for the community, and they really protect our land. They make sure nobody's coming in here and taking over. They want to keep it under Native control, and it just seems that the corporations are doing a good job. They have many programs of all different types for people, even for drug abuse. They'll pay for the rehabilitation. They provide lots of jobs for people around here. I know the corporations are doing a good job, and I don't know about reservations, how that would affect us.

I know that in our village corporation especially there's a real balance there between profit and culture. We're trying to make profit, and I think they're doing an excellent job. I know that Tanadgusix Corporation owns the West Coast International in Anchorage. They bought half of the Paramount, another West Coast hotel in Seattle. They paid for that, and now they're a 10-percent owner of a new one going up in Oregon. And those companies on the Outside provide lots of money for the corporations. A lot of that money is spent right here in St. Paul to better this community. So I think they need to make a profit. They're making it elsewhere, but they bring a lot of it home and they provide a lot of jobs locally. And they do a lot of good things for our roads and our harbor. They provide our cable. They run the tour industry here. They really protect the land, so I know they're real conscious of protecting St. Paul from Outside control. So I think there's a real balance in our village corporation.

*What about the amendments to the Alaska Native Claims Settlement Act that allowed Native corporations to maintain Native control?* Around here they want to keep control. They don't want it being turned over to big companies such as Trident and Unisea and these other fish companies that come in here and look at us as dollars. They're trying to keep that from happening. Around here, I think the village corporation has the first rights to buy someone's land if people want to sell. And they do exercise that right if something becomes available. They will buy it up.

*What about the concept of creating new stock for those born after the act?* My wife's corporation, Doyon, did that. My wife fell under that. She was born in '74, but she is a shareholder, and I think that's a good thing. However, I don't know about diluting the shares down so much that they're just not worth anything. I don't know. We recently took a vote on that at The Aleut Corporation. I voted in favor of that, probably for my younger sister, and I guess the kids I'm teaching. If they're not shareholders of the corporation someday, I'm not sure what will happen. I think the Doyon system of having the new stock revert back to the corporation when they pass on works well. A lot of the younger people won't ever be shareholders the way we're set up now.

*How do your students feel about that?* They do mention it once in awhile. Not a lot. They basically feel like they're part of that corporation somehow. I don't know why. We've talked about it a little bit.

*Your goals for the future?* As far as my goals, I've accomplished a lot of them. I wanted to get my own boat. I wanted to get married and have kids. I'd like to buy a house someday. We'd like to build a house here within the next five years or so. I don't know how long I'll stay. I know that I want to stay here. I like being here. So as long as we're happy here, we'd like to build and settle here for awhile. And maybe someday, we'd kind of like to move to the Anchorage or Palmer area. But for now, we're very happy here. I'd like to go on and get my Master's Degree in Administration, and my wife wants to get hers in Special Education. We own the boat, and we have a family, and things are going well.

*Goals for the Native community?* I hope they really take care of this island and make sure that the future is good for the kids. I was involved politically with our community development group for the Central Bering Sea. I don't know that I like to get involved with politics. I think we have some good people in there now that are doing a good job and really care about what happens here. And they really seem to know what they're doing. I guess as far as our goals for the Native community – just to keep the heritage and the culture alive. My mom does Aleut dancing, and she teaches the language to the kids. And we need to keep our religion alive out here. We need to keep going to church. I think that's about it.

Our corporations have been outstanding in supporting students. It's amazing how much money they put out. I used the Teacher Student Loan, but I don't think I would have if it hadn't been forgivable. Our Native corporations will put you through school basically, and it's pretty exciting for these young kids to know. It's there for the taking. If you do well, if you go, and you try, they sure support you. They're very generous.

*PATIENCE P. MERCULIEF was born on August 20, 1973, on St. Paul Island. Her mother is from St. Paul, and her father is from St. George. Like her parents, Patience attended high school and graduated from Mt. Edgecumbe in Sitka in Southeast Alaska.*

*Merculief has a Bachelor's of Business Administration Degree with an emphasis in International Business, as well as a Bachelor's Degree in Japanese studies from the University of Alaska Fairbanks.*

*As an Alaska Native who was born after 1971, Merculief is not a shareholder in either the village corporation for St. Paul, Tanadgusix Corporation, nor her regional corporation, The Aleut Corporation. She is an enrolled member of the St. Paul tribal council.*

*Merculief has worked for the Aleutian Housing Authority as a housing specialist, implementing the national Native American Housing Assistance and Self-Determination Act. The Authority serves 10 Aleutian region villages, including St. Paul, St. George, Unalaska, King Cove, Sand Point, Nelson Lagoon, False Pass, Akutan, Atka and Nikolski. She has since moved home to St. Paul to work for a fisheries organization.*

*She feels she gained valuable experience within her region and the rest of Alaska by working in Anchorage. She is also considering working on an advanced degree in public policy. She was interviewed December 9, 1998.*

**A**nd then there's just the pull of the islands. I miss the ocean and the waves and the isolation of it. I miss the wind, the storms we have. (Laughs.) People will say, "What? You're crazy!" But that's what makes it unique, and we don't have that here. And just the air – it's fresh and clean, moist. Summers are my favorite time there, though. It's really green, lush green, and beautiful. . . You're on this small speck of land in the middle of the Bering Sea.

I am from St. Paul Island and was born there. In the past we had doctors, and children were born on the island. But now the mothers are brought in from St. Paul and the kids are born here in Anchorage. I had a discussion with one of my friends about that, about how Natives from rural villages are flying into Anchorage or regional centers to give birth. Now children can't really say, "I was born on St. Paul," or, "I was born in such and such" any more. When you're filling out forms, they want to know your place of birth, too, and then you can't put your hometown but have to put "Anchorage." Think about it. This has many undertones, undercurrents to it.

My parents are both from the islands, St. Paul and St. George, and were born on the islands. I am the eldest of seven children. I have two brothers and four sisters. My two youngest sisters are going to school on St. Paul, one sister is at Mt. Edgecumbe High School, and the other is going to the University of Alaska Southeast in Juneau. One brother is going to school here at the University of

Alaska Anchorage and the other one has finished his Associate Degree from UAS and is living on St. Paul.

*Did you get a good education at St. Paul?* I feel I did, but I feel it was lacking in some ways. They could have pushed me more. I remember when I was in fifth or sixth grade I moved up a grade so I was with the class one level ahead of me. We didn't have a high school there back then and after eighth grade you had to leave. My mom didn't want me leaving early so I stayed back a year. And I remember that being a pretty boring year because I already had done that work. I remember going in the library a lot, doing my own assignments or writing or other things. But basically, I think they did give a good education.

Since they didn't offer a high school education on the island, you had to go elsewhere – Mt. Edgecumbe in Sitka or Chemewa High School, which is in Oregon. Or, you could come to Anchorage. But the majority of students went to Mt. Edgecumbe where my parents went to school. I had heard good things about it. So my eighth grade year I was excited. I was doing my application and I was all ready and prepped to go.

I think they offer an excellent education there – a lot better than what I could have gotten on St. Paul, a rural place. The island now has a high school that goes up to 12th grade and graduates students, but I think many of students still choose to leave.

I knew all along that I wanted to go to college. I just remember ever since I was little, knowing that education was the way for me. Education has always been important to me. And I knew that one day I'd want to support myself, and I saw education as being the way to do that. Reading was my favorite pastime when I was a kid. My parents stressed the importance of an education. They never really said, "You're going to college. You better get A's." They just had a supportive environment for wanting to learn, getting a good education.

Even thinking back now I remember being small and saying, "Yes, I'm going to go to school. Yes, I'm going to get an education. Yes, I'm going to be able to support myself someday." I guess I was very independent.

I received a Bachelor of Business Administration degree with an emphasis in International Business and a Bachelor's in Japanese studies. I lived in Japan for a year, studied the language so I could speak it, read it and write it.

*Social problems in the community?* There were. There was a lot of drinking, alcohol abuse, drug abuse, smoking, chewing tobacco and stuff within the community. So yeah, there are a lot of social problems, just like in many small places. *What kept you from drinking or taking drugs?* I never really saw it as an option, I guess. (Laughs.) Well, it was respect for my parents, but also I didn't want to get in trouble with them. Growing up and seeing all the problems alcohol and drug abuse cause was also a factor.

*When did you have a sense of being Native?* I can't really remember when. I think the underlying sense was always there, but maybe it was in high school where I began to realize more what it meant or felt like to be an Alaska Native. Before that my world was St. Paul. We'd go through Anchorage, and my grandma had moved to Seattle, so we'd go there and visit her. So I knew Alaska was really different. But I hadn't really met people from other places in the state until I went to high school and got a sense of where they came from, where they lived, what their culture was like.

I don't really remember if we studied other Alaskan cultures when I was in grade school or junior high. But Mt. Edgecumbe was where I got the sense of what it was to be a Native from Alaska, what it was to be an Aleut, how being an Aleut was different from being Tlingit or Haida or Athabascan or Inupiaq or Yup'ik. I think there I got a sense of how all the Alaska Natives were different and how they were the same.

*Discrimination?* In grade school I remember cases of reverse discrimination, the teachers' kids being picked on a lot because they weren't Native and they weren't from the island. They were outsiders coming in. Some of the kids would be friends and have a good time, but other kids would just pick on them and harass them.

*Did you talk to your parents about discrimination?* No. I don't think it ever affected me so strongly or upset me so strongly where I needed to talk to my parents. I probably didn't even recognize it that much back then. People were different – different personalities, different attitudes. I didn't recognize it as discrimination.

*Did you experience discrimination later?* Not really that affected me. I knew there was a lot of discussion at high school because it was mostly Natives at Mt. Edgecumbe, but there were some non-Natives. And the non-Native students said, "We're being treated differently," or "You don't accept as many non-Natives into the school." I remember that coming up in high school. In college we had discussions about affirmative action and how it was looked upon and what effect it had and didn't have on different people.

*Ties to your Aleut culture?* I do. But what I saw when I was meeting people from other Native cultures and seeing their cultures was that ours was different. It wasn't as directly strong as theirs because we've been so influenced by the Russians and then the government. The Russians brought the Aleuts to St. Paul and St. George in the 1700's to harvest the fur seals and so that really affected the lives of the people. Traditional Aleut culture and what the Russians brought is sort of what the Aleut culture has become. It's now a combination of the two. Even in the language – there are a lot of Russian words mixed in when people speak Aleut. When I was growing up, I remember in kindergarten and first grade having Aleut taught, but that was the only time that language was taught. What we have is Russian Christmas, Russian New Year's. We had people going masquerading. So I guess our culture was centered around the church and the church holidays.

The church is still important. My grandfather – my mom's dad – was a priest. He became a priest in his 40's or 50's. So she grew up with him being strict and being a priest and the church being very important in her life and she passed it on to us.

They're trying to bring back the language now, teach it in school. And they're trying to bring back Aleut dance. They started an Aleut dance group on St. Paul. I'm not sure how much of the dancing is what was actually done hundreds of years ago and how much is what we think they might have been. But they're bringing the costumes back. It's really hard to get information on Aleut culture and Aleut history. It's sparse. What's out there is limited. In college, I did papers and was interested in researching Aleuts and Aleut culture, and I didn't find that much. I'd keep finding the same information. I don't know if the Russians kept records. Maybe they have more records of the Aleuts they first met and what their culture was like. By the time the U.S. got here, people were already in that mixed culture.

I know words and phrases, and I like listening when the elders talk. I pick out a word here and a word there. But the grammar and everything, I don't really understand. I'm very interested in learning it, but I don't know how to start. I was just going to have my aunt, Jeannie Gromoff, tutor me. She recently moved back here from Seattle, and I was thinking she would be a good source. She's in her

60's right now. She's been speaking English so much and not really having people around her to speak Aleut with, she'll have to stop and think, "Am I pronouncing this right? Am I saying this right?" I'm working with her a little bit. And then Paul Fratis – he's from the islands – and he has moved to Anchorage for health reasons. I question him on Aleut words and Aleut phrases.

*Are you interested in Aleut dance?* Yes. But there's no place here really to learn or to start. The Atka Dancers have a group that was started recently and they're becoming pretty well known. I'd like to question them and see where they got their dances from and just talk to them more about their dancing. There are the Atka Dancers and a dance group on St. Paul. I know there are Alutiiq Dancers from Kodiak, which are a little different from Aleut.

*Native hero?* Not really apart from my elders who I admire for who they were and what they did. Not really one person. I have a lot of respect for the elders. They were evacuated during World War II and taken to Funter Bay in Southeast Alaska. They sure had to go through a lot. And most of them have a really good sense of humor, which I admire. They kind of find the humor in the worst situation and make you laugh. So that's what I really admire about them.

*Did people talk much about the forced evacuation of the islanders during World War II?* No. It's something they preferred just not to talk about. I was probably in junior high when I learned of it. I'm not really sure. I probably even heard references, listening to my mom talk or my aunts talk. But I think it was probably in junior high or high school that I got the full picture of what had happened and why they were evacuated and what it must have been like for them.

I was shocked that that would happen. I was shocked at the behavior of the U.S. government and how the people from the Pribilofs were treated. They were taken to abandoned canneries in Southeast Alaska with no running water, no jobs, no anything. That was just shocking. It was hard to believe. I'd heard that a lot of the elders died, and a lot of the children, including some that were born there died. Because not only were the conditions real bad, they were exposed to new diseases.

*How did your family fare there?* I think my grandfather was a priest around then, and I think he was able to find a house for himself and his family to live in. I don't really know much about their conditions or what they did while they were there though.

70

I think in some ways, too, it was the way a lot of the people got more educated about how badly they were being treated. I think during that time they started working closely with the Alaska Native Brotherhood group in Sitka, trying to gain more rights for themselves as Alaska Natives. I heard stories about the government checking people's mail. They didn't want the story of what was happening, how the conditions were on the island, to get out. So my grandfather would have to smuggle letters out to try to get information or help or learn – legally – what he could do – what was wrong, what was right.

*Why do you miss St. Paul?* One big reason is my family, celebrating holidays together, birthdays and the closeness it brings. And then there's just the pull of the islands. I miss the ocean and just the waves and the isolation of it. I miss the wind, the storms we have. (Laughs.) People will say, "What? You're crazy!" But that's what makes it unique, and we have that here. And just the air – it's fresh and clean, moist. Air here and in Fairbanks is really dry.

Summers are my favorite time there, though. It's really green, lush and beautiful. And recently, I just went through a hard decision-making process about whether I wanted to move back. There was an opening on St. Paul as the manager for the 10-plex apartment building there. And I'd be able to have my own place and live there, working for Aleutian Housing Authority on a part-time basis. I was saying, "Should I go back?" There's a really strong pull to go back, and a pull to stay in Anchorage. So I'm trying to decide what to do. I was going to go back and then recently I just decided to stay here for awhile longer. And I feel – even though I wanted to go back and I was ready to go back, I wasn't 100 percent sure about the decision and comfortable with it. I was saying, "I don't want to make this big of a change now." So I decided to stay in Anchorage because of my work opportunities and social life opportunities.

It was a hard decision to make. Housing is hard to find on St. Paul. I'm used to living on my own and having my own place. It'd be hard for me to go back and live with my parents, which is one of the reasons I'd be tempted to go back for this job. I'd be able to have my own apartment, my own place, on St. Paul.

*What about the isolation there?* Growing up there, I never really felt isolated because it was the environment I grew up with and it was what I was used to. But it's different for other people in Alaska, from maybe Bethel or Nome, where they could get on their snow machines in winter and go visit the next village. On St. Paul, there's no village next to you. The only way you can get off the island is by airplane, two and a half hours. St. George is the closest community. They're about 40 miles south of St. Paul, and planes don't have regular trips back and forth so people don't go in between those two islands as much as you might imagine.

The island itself isn't too large. If you go hiking to the middle of the island you can look around and see water all around you – 360 degrees. And I know a lot of people would be shocked by that. You're on this small speck of land in the middle of the Bering Sea.

*Is there a sense of peace there?* I find it peaceful. You can look into yourself more and you're more in touch, I think, with what's really valuable, the basics in life. In the city, there are so many distractions, so many other things pulling on you that you could lose track of what's really important in life.

It is expensive to travel. I could get to Seattle cheaper than I could get to St. Paul because it's 600 or 700 dollars round trip. That would factor into the isolation feeling. A lot of people don't have the money to travel back and forth a lot, so you do get isolated. Between the islands, it's about 120 dollars roundtrip. There's not anyone locally who flies and charters between the islands.

*Your feelings on ANCSA?* I was born in 1973, and the closing date was December 18, 1971, for when you get shares in a corporation. So I'm not a shareholder in The Aleut Corporation, and I'm not a shareholder in our local village corporation. And they haven't added new shareholders to the system. I think they messed up there. When I think of the Alaska Native Claims Settlement Act, I have a lot of mixed feelings about it. I don't think they were looking into the future – forecasting where will this leave us in 20 years, 40 years, 60 years? What will this develop into?

Right now, I won't be a shareholder until my parents pass away if they leave their shares to me. I have two brothers and four sisters. You've got shares from two people divided among their children. Then you'll end up in 20 years with Aleuts who are shareholders and Aleuts who are not shareholders in the corporation. In that way the Alaska Native Claims Settlement Act could really divide a culture and a people. I mean it took what was a traditional Native culture and it brought in this whole foreign idea of corporations and businesses. I don't know. I've been doing a lot of thinking about it in recent years, especially since I went into college, about how it affects me, how it's affected everybody. I'm still thinking on it: What does this

72

do? How could we improve it in the future? What do we need to do?

Even now you have adult Aleuts who are shareholders in The Aleut Corporation and adult Aleuts who are not shareholders. And if The Aleut Corporation is supposed to be representing all Aleuts, then it's not doing that right now.

When they worked on ANCSA, I get the feeling that they were steam-rolling through it, trying to come up with something different from reservations they had in the Lower 48. Alaska was becoming a state, and they were trying to give the Natives something, some money and some land. And the Natives wanted something in return for their other land, but I don't think they were sure about how they wanted to receive it. I know what it ended up is that they got it in the form of corporations, a foreign concept brought into the Native communities. They didn't know about big business and corporations. They had to get educated and learn about it. It was a whole new process. They had this money and this land.

They tried to make the corporations into something that would benefit all Alaska Natives, but they weren't thinking 20, 40, 50 years into the future. They were thinking right now. With corporations, land could be bought and sold. So maybe in 50, 60, 70 years, they could be even non-Native owned or operated corporations.

In some ways, I think: Why should I care what they do? Why should I be involved? Because I don't have a stake in that besides being Aleut. I'm not a shareholder and I don't have a voice in that corporation unless I am a shareholder. I'm sure if I went to talk to them they'd listen to me. But legally, you really don't have ground to stand on within the corporate structure. You can't be on the board of directors. You can't get elected because you're a non-shareholder. I could beg someone to give me one or two shares to get my foot in the door. I know some corporations have passed shares on to people born after 1971.

*Is there a clash between profit, culture?* Definitely. There is a clash between the profit-making corporation and the culture and what the values of the culture are. Corporations are businesses out there to make money. In the culture, there's a lot of sharing going on, a lot of doing what's best for the people or the community, not what would bring the most money into the community. The businesses are run around money and making money. Providing benefits for rural communities is usually a money-losing operation. So the corporation says, "Well, we don't want to get involved with that. We'd lose money." That's a typical corporation attitude. So there's definite a clash of values.

*What about the success of some corporations and their clout?* I think that's good. You have the positive and the negative both where the corporations are concerned. That's one of the positives – where they can use their status as a corporation and their influence in helping their people or the Natives of Alaska. So in one way, that did give them a voice.

There's no one right answer. It's just going to take a lot of work to make it work for the cultures and the businesses and the people.

Something I definitely would like to see done is have people like myself born after 1971 made shareholders of the corporations. I'm still trying to learn what I can about the corporations and how they operate, trying to get a sense of what they should be doing that they're not doing or what's lacking in our communities that they could help with. Another thing I see is you have a little community and in many places they have two governments. They have the city government and tribal government. And some places they work together well, and some places they clash because they both want to supply the services. In St. Paul, there's definitely a clash between the city and the tribal government both wanting to be the main government. I just read an article about one village where the government and the city combined, where they were connected, cooperating and working together. That made more sense to me for providing the services and benefiting the community as a whole.

*Your work?* I work for the Aleutian Housing Authority. There's a new law that was just passed – the Native American Housing Assistance and Self-Determination Act – and it gives more control to the tribes. So there's a lot of change right now. We serve 10 communities – St. Paul, St. George, Unalaska, King Cove, Sand Point, Nelson Lagoon, False Pass, Akutan, Atka and Nikolski. Everyone has problems, something they want fixed or more houses built. It's a challenge to meet that. You have a lot of people living with maybe two families in one household, especially where people my age are getting married, having kids, and there are no apartments or houses for them to move into. So they end up staying with their parents or maybe with friends. So there's definitely a demand there. Even in some of the smaller communities where there are enough houses, they need upgrades or weatherization.

One thing I enjoy is being able to meet people from the other

Aleut communities. St. Paul and St. George are isolated from the rest of the Aleutian Chain. I've been to Unalaska before and know people there, but I haven't been to any of the other communities. I hope to be able to visit them.

*It's expensive to build there?* Yes, just the logistics of getting the equipment and people out there is a challenge itself. You either barge it up from Seattle or you fly it in by plane from Anchorage or Seattle.

If I went back to St. Paul on my own, I'd be living with my parents because there is just no place for me to find my own apartment or my own house. There are a few people who have built their own houses there, but even getting land from the village corporation is a struggle. The Alaska Housing Finance Corporation has programs to make loans, where people could build their own houses or upgrade their houses, but a big struggle is just getting that information out to the people, trying to educate them on what's here in Anchorage, what's here to help you.

*Personal goals?* Ideally I'd like to still be involved with St. Paul or be able to travel and work with St. Paul, maybe even move back there and raise my family there whenever I decide to do that. But I would like to also have a voice in working with The Aleut Corporation, saying, "Hey, we need to be included for the future of the corporation as well as our own future." In a lot of ways, I feel like I got a broader perspective going to Mt. Edgecumbe and then UAF and meeting Natives from all over Alaska. I also enjoy working with Natives from other places. I've got a lot of friends who are from all over Alaska. Working somewhere in the overall picture would be exciting to me – statewide.

I've been thinking about going to graduate school, but I'm not sure where I want to go – maybe to get my MBA or maybe I want to go into public policy. I've been tossing some ideas around. I want to get some work experience before I go on to school, so I'll wait for awhile.

# *Arctic Slope Region*

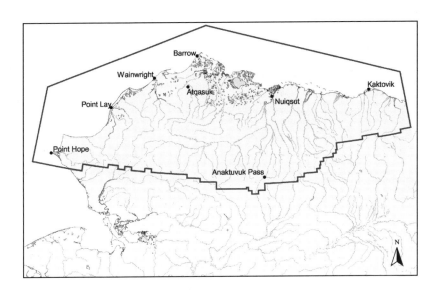

 **ROBERTA J. (BOBBI) QUINTAVELL** *was born September 28, 1961, in Barrow. She is a shareholder in Arctic Slope Regional Corporation, one of three Native regional corporations that has voted to issue stock to shareholders born after December 18, 1971. Quintavell currently serves as assistant to the Chief Executive Officer of Petro Star, Inc., a subsidiary of ASRC. She and her husband Keith R. Quintavell live in Palmer. She has two daughters, Kimmialuk A. Smith and Raelynn I. Quintavell.*

*Quintavell was raised by her grandparents and she grew up speaking Inupiaq with them. She feels that learning her Native language has had a major impact on her life.*

*She has a Bachelor's of Business Administration Degree with a minor in Political Science from the University of Alaska Anchorage. She has worked as community health aide, a fuel tank farm operator, an itinerant community health aide, a video production assistant and a fuel manager. In addition, she served as the Executive Director of Arctic Slope Native Association, Ltd., from 1991 to 1994. As part of her work as a management trainee for Arctic Slope Regional Corporation from 1994 to 1998, she developed a computer forecasting model for projecting total shareholders as a result of issuing stock to those born after 1971. She was interviewed July 16 and 22, 1998.*

When I'm in a corporate boardroom, and we're faced with a corporate decision, a real important aspect of making that decision, for me, is to look at it through what I feel is the Inupiaq point of view. How is this going to benefit the Inupiaq people as a whole? Does the economic benefit of any particular decision outweigh what it might cost us culturally? I try to keep that in my mind foremost, not only in the way I conduct myself on a day-to-day basis, but in the decisions I make.

I was born in Barrow, and raised, in part, by my grandparents Ned and Faye Nusunginya. My grandfather, Papa, was a minister so we traveled between the North Slope villages. So, while I was born in Barrow, I always say that I grew up on the North Slope because we spent a lot of time in Kaktovik, Point Hope. I certainly traveled between the other villages as well. I have two brothers, an older brother Eric Voss, and a younger brother Vernon "Poe" Brower, and two sisters, an older sister Jana Harcharek, and a younger sister Lorene "Asi" Young. My parents are Sally Brower and Robert Brower, Jr.

My grandparents lived a very traditional lifestyle, which afforded me many opportunities, one of which was to learn the Inupiaq language. While it wasn't my first language, it certainly has had huge impacts on my life. I continue to practice speaking it fluently – as fluently as I can, trying to learn as many of the old words and use those as often as I can.

Elementary school was real interesting for me. Since my grandparents practiced a very traditional lifestyle, we would leave town and go out to the various camps in the spring, and I wouldn't be back until Thanksgiving. So the school year would start, and I wouldn't be there. While making supply runs Papa would register me for school and pick up all my homework. I would have a teacher and be in a class before I even knew who my teacher would be, and even who my classmates would be. So, consequently, phonics was a real interesting task. It certainly had its pros and cons. It certainly made my academic career very challenging, later in life. Knowing what I know now, I wouldn't give up what I gained in lieu of that time in the classroom.

*College?* I recently graduated from UAA with a degree in Business Management and a minor in political science.

Speaking both languages has had a tremendous impact on how I look at the world. When I'm in a corporate boardroom, and we're faced with a corporate decision, a real important aspect of making that decision, for me, is to look at it through what I feel is the Inupiaq point of view. How is this going to benefit the Inupiaq people as a whole? Does the economic benefit of any particular decision outweigh what it might cost us culturally? I try to keep that in my mind foremost, not only in the way I conduct myself on a day-to-day basis, but in the corporate decisions that I make. So it gets kind of complicated sometimes, because there are diametrically opposing values in some cases. A lot of the principles and the values of being Inupiaq can be applied in many business decisions that you make. It's like having principles and values in the Western world. Just because ours are a little different doesn't mean that they're any less important or that the differences will create controversy.

I've always had it in my head that I was going to give back to the community. That's always been something that's very important to me. For a time I worked as a community health aide. I started the job and didn't receive any training for six months. That was probably the scariest six months of my life. I ended up being responsible for the entire community. I started this position in Anaktuvuk Pass, and then when I left, I worked as an itinerant health aide out of Barrow, so I went to some of the other outlying villages.

In this position I had the opportunity to work with a woman

whom the village considered to be their mid-wife. We delivered a baby. That was when I decided that that was not the career for me. I'm in this clinic in Anaktuvuk Pass, I had the doctor on the phone, and the mother had been in labor for a few hours. I was thinking we have everything under control, I know exactly what I'm getting into, I know exactly what I'm going to do. I've read about this. I understand what's required of me. If anything happens I've always got the doc on the phone. When things started happening – the baby was born – there I was holding this baby, and I realized, this person's whole life is ahead of him, and he's depending on me. We had held the mail plane over, and they got on.

I got back to the clinic, and I sat down in my chair. From this far, far away distance, I hear this, "Bobbi? Bobbi?" The doctor's still on the phone. He laughs at me, and he says, "You know, it sounded like things went really well." That is when I knew, most definitely, this is not the career for me. I just didn't want that responsibility. The baby was great, the mom was great, everything went well. I had really good support. I certainly cannot take the credit by myself.

Once I got back to Barrow, I did a number of jobs. A job I particularly enjoyed was working for then-Mayor George Ahmaogak as a village liaison for the Planning Department. In that position, I was able to really develop some good relationships in the outlying villages. The job entailed getting the leadership of those communities to identify capital projects that they felt necessary for the development of their village and to assist in securing the funding for the development of those capital projects. The idea was to assist the communities in building the infrastructure they now enjoy. That was a very rewarding position in many respects. It allowed me to continue in my quest for knowledge in regard to the culture. Every time we had a project going up, we looked at the cultural implications that it had, not just site-related, not just community related, but the long-term impacts that it may bring to a community. These were all fun, rewarding topics to discuss and explore with the village leaders.

*When did you have a sense of being an Alaska Native?* Always. It's always been very important. Both my parents and my grandparents felt it important to communicate to us in many different ways how important it was to understand that we were Inupiat and that it was OK to have different values or to be judged differently. Just because you're different doesn't make you good or bad. It just makes you different.

*Did you feel any ties to your non-Native background?* At times, especially I think in junior high school. I found myself in a kind of a precarious situation more than once because there weren't very many of us that were half-breeds at the time. Now you walk into the middle school and you have more half-breed than full-blooded Inupiats for the most part. But at the time I was going through middle school, we were definitely in the minority. We were sometimes made to feel that we were less than everyone else. So I really had an ax to grind in both directions. I based a lot of my early decisions on the fact that I would succeed in both environments, regardless of any negative criticism that may come my way.

*Was there discrimination?* Absolutely, I have experienced discrimination. I think that to some extent everyone experiences discrimination. Some forms are more obvious than others. I had the name calling, having your behavior or options excused because of your race, made to feel that the only reason you are where you are is because of your race, without any consideration for your talent and abilities. For me, the most hurtful form of discrimination has come from within the Inupiaq community.

*How important was the church?* I often wonder just how important. It was a real part of my daily life as I was growing up. It really instilled my sense of responsibility to the community. One of the things that I struggle with today – I'm not sure is directly tied to religion, but tied principally to our family values – is our sense of commitment to the community at large versus your sense of commitment to your immediate family. Part of what we did with the church and for the community as a representative of the church very often was to place the needs of the community above the needs of our family. So, that was just part of the way we lived our life. If something had to be done, you found the resources to get up and go do it. You just did it. You didn't ask questions why, you didn't sit there and agonize over "Why me? Why can't it be somebody else?" You just got up and made the best of the situation. There were situations that were not so good and not so much fun to be in, but you did it.

I see people struggle with some of the decisions they have to make today, between balancing the needs of their family versus the needs of the community. My sense of community is so strong that there are times when I make decisions I very often don't consider the impact on my immediate family. I make a decision. I go forward. I do it. My husband will come up and say, "But didn't you think that maybe we would want to spend that time with you and that maybe you don't have time to take on all this responsibility? Let somebody else do it." Sometimes I have to be hit in the face with it before I understand that, well, maybe I should spend more time at home. Perhaps it is because I was raised with a real community orientation, and having extended family members being so important.

Family members aren't always defined by blood relation, either. You care for the community as a whole. Sometimes I wonder if that was instilled in us because of the religion or if it was just part of the way my family is, regardless of the religious affiliation. I think that's the point I'm trying to make. There's that part of me that no longer practices the religion on an active daily basis that would like to feel that it's grounded in our family principles and values.

*Do you have a Native hero?* I have to think about that one. There are certainly a lot of people that have been very influential in my life. I suppose if I had to distinguish one from many it would be my mother Sally Brower. Certainly Eileen MacLean *(North Slope leader and legislator who is deceased)* would be very near the top of the list. She has been very influential in my life. But, I could name a half a dozen others. Certainly, in junior high and high school, listening to AFN, and having had the opportunity to participate at a couple of the AFN conventions when Janie Leask was president – I certainly value her opinions. I don't always agree with them, but I didn't always agree with my mother or Eileen. Jacob Adams is another. They all play many different roles in the community, so it's not fair to pick any one person as a hero, because they all carried many different parts of the Alaska Native struggle.

Etok *(Charlie Edwardsen, one of the early leaders in the development of ANCSA)* is a fine example. I love Etok to bits. I think that his role in ANCSA and the advancement and the preservation of our culture has been very beneficial. It sometimes hasn't been the healthiest approach, but it's been beneficial. There are certainly several elders. My grandparents are huge examples of heroes to me. There are women whom I've watched over the years, who have touched me in many different ways – Mabel Panigeo and Alice Hopson. My younger brother Poe is a hero. He exemplifies perseverance for me.

*What about Jake Adams' leadership in the sobriety movement?* It's an example of his commitment, not just to the Inupiaq community, but his commitment to the Native community as a whole, to preserving the culture, to keeping people healthy in order to do the job that has to be done. That's a good example of when you make a decision based on a community as a whole's health versus the individual choice issue. It certainly demonstrates his commitment to the community as a whole.

*Do you recall what it was like when ANCSA passed?* At the time I was pretty busy being a kid. I remember sitting around the kitchen table and my parents talking about it with some aunts and uncles. There would be these big family gatherings where there was a lot of consideration being given to: "Where are we going to register? What are the important decisions to make? Where would it be more advantageous to register our kids?" I remember those discussions. From a kid's perspective, it sure seemed like a whole lot of hoopla over what at the time didn't really amount to much. In retrospect, it was pretty thoughtful on their part to think of those types of issues in making the decisions that they made. We're Arctic Slope shareholders and enrolled in Ukpeagvik Inupiat Corporation, the Barrow village corporation. I recall some of the discussions around where to enroll at the village level rather than discussions about where to enroll at the regional level.

I think in our region, it wasn't so much the effect of Arctic Slope as it was the formation of the North Slope Borough that had that most visible effects. The formation of the borough was hugely visible. The cause of the passage of ANCSA and the formation of the borough are one and the same – the oil fields, Prudhoe Bay.

*Your feelings about ANCSA?* It depends on which side of me you ask. I think that overall my feelings about ANCSA are that it is a very important tool that we as Inupiaq people can use to continue to maintain our culture in a fashion that we decide. But I don't think that we can do that by ourselves. I guess what I mean by that is ANCSA in and of itself created corporate structures. The Inupiaq people cannot solely depend on that corporate structure or its subsets to maintain and move forward with cultural enhancement activities and programs. There has to be a comprehensive approach which includes federal, state, and local agencies.

I wish we lived in an environment where the impacts of oil development weren't anywhere near us. When I look at the overall health of the Inupiaq community, while we had our social problems, I don't believe that they were manifesting themselves to the magnitude that they have today. I think that a subsistence lifestyle provided an environment where the community as a whole – and the interdependence of the community as a whole – fostered a healthier society. As human beings, we got along better. The indicators I am using are: level of teen-age suicide, teen-age pregnancy, domestic violence, alcoholism, neglect, and child neglect to name but a few. I can go on and on. We're all pretty familiar with the social problems of rural Alaska. I'm not sure that no matter how much money you throw at some of those problems, that there is a solution without going back to some of those core values, such as our sense of community.

People with a lot of good intentions, and certainly with their heart in the right place, have taken different approaches at trying to address some of those issues. At times these programs have the appearance of being disjointed and uncoordinated. Politics and money have had a real impact, just being able to get together and say, "Hey, we've got a problem, how are we going to deal with it?" Ownership is a big issue, boundaries are a big issue. You have competing interests in service delivery creating a sometimes volatile environment. So we need to build a consensus. Somewhere in all this lies an answer that maximizes the level of benefits available to our people. Everybody's trying to balance these issues. The real reward lies in the balance and ensuring that our elders and children are well cared for.

So how do I feel about ANCSA? (Laughs.) I'm not sure I can directly respond to that without really going to what I think the core of the issue is. Have the economic benefits of oil development compromised our culture to the point of cultural insignificance? I think that oil development in and of itself led to ANCSA, that it led to the formation of the borough. And when I respond to that question as a member of the Inupiaq community, sometimes I wish it didn't exist. Given the fact that it does exist, I think we are in a very unique position to proactively look at the benefits that we can derive as a whole, and to manage it as a whole, rather than these independent segments. I think we need to develop closer coordination between our organizations. I believe you actually see some evidence of those efforts going on today.

When I look at and consider ANCSA as a settlement of land claims, I think that it certainly has raised the standard of living of most Inupiat. However, that is more an outfall, not of the corporate structure established by ANCSA, but of the incorporation of the municipal government. When I look at ANCSA as an Alaska Native, from the point of view of an all-Alaska settlement, the establishment of the corporate structures has been beneficial in raising the standard of living for a select group of Alaska Natives, and I feel that speaks to the design of ANCSA. The fact is there are only a limited number of jobs. We are never going to be able to employ all of our shareholders. We may never be able to pay a kind of dividend that is going to substantially impact the standard of living for any individual shareholder. Yeah, we can make contributions. There's no question about it. There is a role to play. But as far as substantially impacting Alaska Natives, individually, ANCSA by itself is not the answer.

You talk about Arctic Slope and Arctic Slope's resources. Arctic Slope is a majority partner in subsurface resources, yes. We get 30 percent. The other 11 regions get the remaining 70 percent of that under Section 7(i) of ANCSA. The analogy that I choose to use today is that we're a majority partner, managing partner, if you will, in an ownership of subsurface estates. We're only as successful as the other 11 partners will allow us to be. We certainly are in a unique situation. The land resources selected by Arctic Slope have the potential to contain significant amounts of developable natural resources and provide economic benefit, not just to the Inupiaq community, but to Alaska Natives as a whole. When it gets down to the individual Alaska Native level and the benefit that that individual may receive, it may not be as significant as a lot of folks would like it to be. And the truth of the matter is, that's a fact.

There is an afterborn provision that was allowed by the '91 amendments that was exercised, yes. In my role at the corporation, I've had the opportunity to work and develop a computer model that projects what we estimate the number of shareholders to be in the future, based on our existing enrollments today. The growth rate of the Inupiaq community, the shareholder base, is just below that what statisticians call "population norms." But when you apply the growth rate as we see it today to necessary profits for growth in dividend distributions – it's significant.

One of the things about the Inupiaq community is that it is a sharing and giving culture. There's no question. The vote that allowed the afterborn program to be established and to continue clearly speaks to that point. I think that the executive management – to their credit – at the time the amendments were being considered were very informative with the shareholders in regards to just how quickly the stock would dilute, how quickly the valuations would go down and in presenting a number of options that were placed before the shareholders to select from. They approached it a number of different ways and certainly provided options. I think they were unbiased in their presentation, to the point that it allowed the community to vote its heart.

One of the things that I think it's important to note are the differences between the regional tribal organization, the nonprofit tribal organization, the borough, the city government and the regional corporation and the village corporation. It would be a real shame if it got so segmented that the actual services that were received by the residents got diluted to the point that they're ineffective. I think it's important to recognize the differences in their responsibilities because when we start talking about the clash, it's not just in services but in the way services are delivered, the way you structure a program. Whereas on the state side, there are certain criteria and structure you've got to meet in order to provide services. On the tribal government side there's a lot more flexibility in the way you can structure services.

Arctic Slope Native Association Ltd. – Jake Adams, Oliver Leavitt, and Joe Upicksoun – approached me about resurrecting ASNA when I worked as the fuel manager for one of the ASRC's subsidiary companies. The experiences and the opportunities that I had as the Executive Director of this organization were to take this principle and apply it, to basically take it from the idea that ASNA should be the vehicle to capitalize on federal program dollars earmarked for our people and design a system to provide quality services. At the time these dollars were being managed by the BIA's Fairbanks office and the services were extremely limited if not non-existent. So basically we took it from a $50,000 grant from ASRC. Within a year we had a proposal together to run all of the BIA services for all but two of our villages. It kind of created a real opportunity for ASNA to answer the question: how do we structure this so that we have effective programs for the people?

My philosophy has been that the Inupiaq community is in a really unique situation, and it is directly tied to oil and ANCSA. We're somewhat different from the other regions. The opportunities are somewhat different. The ability to capitalize on the economic gains that ANCSA can provide is a little bit different just because of our geographic proximity to the oil patch. It provides a great platform for establishing ourselves economically so that if properly managed, those resources can develop a corporation that is no longer geographically or industrially limited. You can then take the resources gained from that growth and preserve the things that the Inupiaq people feel are important. If culture continues to be prominent and important to our shareholder base, we then have the economic ability to ensure that we preserve that which is important to us. But, if we continue to be dependent upon the oil industry, and if we continue to be dependent on Alaska, we may not have that much versatility. It is my hope that we are never put in a position where we have to compromise our cultural integrity and our cultural values for the sake of economics. The regional corporation provides us with that opportunity. ANCSA provides us with that opportunity. That is where I'd like to make my contribution.

Do I have a long-term vision? Yeah, that's about it.

On one hand, the borough government has done a lot as far as documenting the land use patterns of the Inupiaq people and the various communities. It's done an exceptionally good job in and around the areas where there is the highest potential for oil development, around Nuiqsut and Kaktovik. The region as a whole has been extremely effective in taking the various tools from the state and borough government to capture the kind of dollars necessary to conduct that work. While at the same time the leadership has focused some of its energy on the corporate side and developing the infrastructure necessary to facilitate development and economic growth, all the while enhancing the individual standard of living. Realizing the full social and economic potential to allow the Inupiaq people the opportunities to continue in the development of our culture is my long-term vision.

Arctic Slope is in a position where 20, 35, 50 years down the road, it is not inconceivable that we could become a major developer of areas outside our region. Then we are not in a position to have to compromise our cultural values for economic gains. ANCSA is pivotal to that point. We can't afford to look at ANCSA by itself. It is a piece to a larger picture.

If I could turn back time and I were in a situation where the choice was do we do it or not *(create for-profit corporations)*, I would say not do it for the reasons I talked about earlier in our interview. But, it's done. There's nothing we can do about it. So do you look at your cup as being half empty or being half full? I want to move forward and I want to take what tools we have as a Native community and maximize the effectiveness of those tools. I think that we're at a point in our struggle for cultural survival where we can't afford not to, and a lot of people call me an optimist. Well, so be it.

There's no question in my mind that ANCSA is a critical piece for making the economic independence a reality. I think it's a critical piece for the Inupiaq community to sustain itself and to continue to develop. It provides us an opportunity for us to continue to develop programs in the areas of language preservation and to work toward reviving some of the values and the principles around the activities that really brought about the essence of culture for the community. Without that economic independence, I'm not sure that we could continue that course over the long-term. ANCSA is a critical piece of making that happen.

One of my personal goals for the future is to be a part of the policy-making group of individuals for the Alaska Native community as a whole. As far as goals for my children – I just want them to be healthy and happy, regardless of what they do and where they go. I certainly want them to continue with their ties to the Inupiaq community, but as long as they're happy I suspect that the Inupiaq community is pretty well ingrained in those kids. They're not going to go too far, and if they do, they're going to come back.

***REX ALLEN ROCK, SR.,*** *was born on August 7, 1960, in North Pole. He was raised by his grandparents Allen and Frances Rock and grew up in Point Hope in Northwestern Alaska.*

*A whaling captain, Rock spends as much time as he possibly can maintaining his Inupiaq subsistence traditions. He is also the President of Tikigaq Corporation, the village corporation of Point Hope, and he serves as Third Vice President on the Arctic Slope Regional Corporation Board of Directors. Rock works to incorporate his Inupiaq values into his work with both the village corporation and the regional corporation. For Rock, there is no "I" in the corporation; it's all "we."*

*Rock is an avid basketball player and learned to play the game outside – often in subzero temperatures – because it was before the village had a high school or gymnasium. Currently, he is the head basketball coach for Point Hope High School. He was interviewed January 20, 1999.*

**O**ur culture's real rich as far as whaling goes. There's so much respect for the bowhead whale. Basically, that's what our community's based around. What I've learned – what I grew up with and maintained – is sharing. You don't get the whale. It comes to you. That's what I've been taught.

I was born in North Pole and then adopted out to my parents, Elijah and Dorcas. Elijah is from Point Hope; Dorcas is from Barrow. But I was raised by my grandparents from the git-go, Allen and Frances Rock, and I grew up in the Village of Point Hope. I've been there almost all of my life.

*How was your school?* I wouldn't say it was that good back then. High school had just gotten started in '76 or '77. We had a classroom building. We did what we had to. We had a basketball team back then, and we won quite a few games without having a gym. I think everybody thought it hard to believe that we practiced outside in gloves. There's a good story when we played Kotzebue at UAA. They beat us by 50 the first night, and then the second night they beat us in overtime. (Laughs.) We didn't have any gym, so we weren't used to shooting inside. The second night we got it down. Later on, it got better because we started more building. In 1980, we built the high school and the gymnasium.

*Did you learn Inupiaq?* My grandparents spoke it quite a bit, and then they spoke English quite a bit during the day. They owned a lodge there in Point Hope, and a lot of polar bear guides would stay there. My grandparents would speak Inupiaq at night, but during the day they basically spoke English. I was told by my grandfather that we had to learn to speak English. So what I learned of Inupiaq, I basically listened at night.

I went to the University of Alaska Fairbanks for about three and a half years. I was in and out of Fairbanks and visited with Howard Rock quite a few times when I was a lot younger, nine, 10, 11 years old. I visited him at the *Tundra Times*. He was my uncle, my father's brother.

My grandfather was a well respected whaler in the community. He got a whale every year, fed the people. I grew up around that, basically was taught our Inupiaq values, what they are, who you are, where you come from, that sort of thing – just basically believe in who you are.

Our culture's real rich as far as whaling goes. There's so much respect for the bowhead whale. Basically, that's what our community's based around. What I've learned – what I grew up with and maintained – is sharing. You don't get the whale. It comes to you. That's what I've been taught. There's just so much respect for the whale. Nothing's left on the ice. Once it's landed, everything is taken. Things like, you put the whale's skull back in the water. That, in itself, asks for the spirit to come back next spring. And you still do that to this day. A lot of things we do are not written, but passed on.

A few years ago I got asked to run for the village corporation board. I went ahead and did that – reluctantly – because I liked life as it was. But my grandfather and grandmother told me, "You work for the people and not for yourself." And that's basically what I've done. That's basically who I am and what I am. I said to myself, "Well, I'm going to have to sacrifice some things. I'm just going to have to do what I feel is right, what I've been taught."

I knew it was going to get hectic if I did that. I took it and after a few years was asked to run it. And I've been running it for about six years now. I'm the corporation president. I've basically taken all those same values that we do up on the ice, and tried to pass it on to the people who are in the corporation.

There is no "I" in the corporation, it's all "we." And if you can pass that on to the people that you have, everything's going to work smoothly. That's how I feel. We have a real decent board at Tikigaq. If you look around the table, there are a lot of whaling captains. Because they are well respected.

We've had to educate them into the business world, but even in the business world it takes a lot of common sense. And they have that. You go out whaling, those people are well respected. And what they say is what you do. And that goes right on to the boardroom.

There's a lot of respect. And if you're honest and up front with them, everything will go smoothly. It's just those same values I bring in from out there on the ice, whaling. You drop everything from during the year. You might have some squabbles. But all that is dropped during whaling to land the whale, which means so much to the community. If we don't get a whale, the village is not going to function. There's just so much culture behind it. You can feel the tension in the air if there's not one landed. Once that's landed, it's gone. It's like somebody burst a big balloon.

As I said earlier, we try to pass on to our people in the corporation the working together. Because when we're out there, we work as one. We want to pass that on in the corporate world. Then everything will be just fine. It's a growing experience. But it's been fun. I've enjoyed it. I've always kept those values with me.

What I've found out in the corporate world – there's just so much emphasis on "I," "me." It's just not the same. When you're out whaling and you tell somebody you're going to do this or they're going to do it, you trust that they're going to get it done. And the corporate world's just a little different. As far as corporations go, I had mixed feelings. I didn't want to get involved because I knew that at times it can be ugly.

*Was there a point when you were growing up that you had a sense of being an Alaska Native?* From the git-go. I think from when I was nine, 10 years old, my grandfather would sit me down on the ice. He talked about the whale, why he got it, how he was so lucky. And he just told me, "This is what you're going to be. This is what you're about."

And I got reinforced when I sat down with Howard Rock, too, because he told me to go and visit him every time we were in Fairbanks. He would say, "What your grandfather does is a lot more than what I'm doing." Howard told me, "He feeds the people. He could go on and do other things, but he sacrificed himself because of the family, the Rock family." He could have been out there doing pretty much what Howard was doing, but he stayed home to take on family, whaling, feeding the people. That's what I remember was real important.

*What was Howard like?* Real quiet. But when he talked to you, he was straightforward. He didn't beat around the bush. He just kind of told it like it was. Then, toward the end, he visited quite a bit in Point Hope before my grandfather died in 1971. I'd sit with both of them, listening. I read the book on Howard Rock, *Art and Eskimo Power*, and there were parts where there were a few squabbles between them and things like that. I don't think he would like that. Because at the end when I saw those two before my grandfather died, they were real close.

*Your Native hero?* I guess my main hero would be the whaling captains. No specific one, but who and what they are about. That's my hero. Because they're not about themselves. They're about the people.

*It must be hard to describe the feeling of "we," not "I."* When you've grown up around it, it's pretty easy. You never lose sight of that. I've got pictures in my office of my grandparents and their parents. You just look at them every day. And I guess I realized it a few years ago when I got my first whale. I knew they were right when they tell you it's "we," not "I." You go out and find out all year long that you've got to feed the people. You're working for the people – all year long. There's more work if you get a whale than if you don't. It's good. It's happy work.

*When the guides would come in, did you see a big difference in cultures?* Yes. My grandfather always told me I could do anything I wanted, be anything I wanted to be. I'd fly out with some of them. We'd go get supplies in Kotzebue. I used to fly with Don Johnson, who was a big guide out of Kenai. I knew I wasn't supposed to, but he'd fall asleep, and I'd fly the plane. I'd wake him up, and he'd say, "Follow the shoreline. Wake me up before we get there."

I just looked at it as a business. My grandfather would say, "Hey, we got to make all the money we can for getting supplies and stuff for whaling."

*Was there a clash of cultures?* I think the first taste of that came – some ugly things happening – when I became head coach. We had a bunch of teachers who tried to get something going to fire me the first year. They said, "You haven't graduated from college yet. You're showing the young people here that you don't have to go. You don't have to move on. You're a terrible example."

I let them speak, and I waited until they were done, and I said, "That's your side of the story. My side of the story is that you're telling me not to respect my whaling captains, my hunters, the people who are out there. That we're nothing, that what you are is something."

And I told them that was a crock. I said, "These people do so much more than you do." Back then we did have a superintendent that supported me, Shirley Holloway. She's the one who managed to get me to coach. And I was pretty happy about it because I got my first year, and I've been doing it 11 years now. But that was a wakeup call that that's still out there.

I still feel, and I tell kids today, if you're going to go out of the village, you've got to know who you are, what you are, feel good about yourself. A lot of kids get lost because they go out there away from the village, and they expect to be part of what's going on there.

And by the same token, I've been trying to tell my people when the kids come back, there is this jealousy factor. But they're the same people. Even our own people need to learn to accept them instead of being jealous. Instead of being afraid that this kid's coming back to take my job, we have to open our arms and say, "Here, come on in. You went out there. You sacrificed, and if you feel strongly you want to come back and work for your people, get in here."

That's what I see out there, too much politics. It turns your stomach at times. A kid goes out there, they work their butt off, they get their degree and then they come back, and then our own people make it hard on them. That's got to stop. We have to learn how to get past that.

*Discrimination?* There have been so many times. I got to see some things there at the university. I took a class with Bill Demmert, a history class. Once, he had us pick things that we wanted to write about. Some of us decided to research shamanism. We talked about how they moved on in the spirit world or how they could move from one spot to another, that sort of thing, things that I had heard. And then, you're in a class with 300 some students and then to have the majority of the class – white – start laughing when you talk about this. We put a stop to that real quick.

Today, we still see it. Sometimes we go to restaurants, we'll see other people get waited on first. Little things like that. But I've taught my kids not to take it. My own kids will get up and say, "What's going on? We've been here longer."

My son Rex Allen Rock, Jr., is in his first year at Columbia Basin Junior College now. I wanted him to go to a small college in a small community first, get used to the idea. It's in Washington. He got his first whale last year. I was real happy because he took on what I passed on to him. People would go up and grab him, "We're so happy you got a whale."

96

He said, "No, it came to me."

I said, "Yeah. He got what I taught him." I was pretty happy.

My daughter Raquel is a sophomore in high school, and we have two younger boys. Ryan is eight and Reese is four.

*How do you feel about the Alaska Native Claims Settlement Act?* Just like I mentioned, I have mixed feelings. When I took the course from Dennis Demmert, Roger Lang spoke about things like – "We had to take what we got. But that didn't mean we accepted it." I find that true. You have villages who have board members with no education, people who are respected in the community but with no business background, making business decisions. And our people are so trusting. Our village got burnt, and we were in Chapter 11 for awhile. We're out, and we're doing great now, but there have been little things like that. They're so trusting. It's scary. I told them you can't have blind trust. You have to have common sense. A lot of them – I know this is true in my community – feel it, but they won't speak up. You've got to let it out. It's not disrespectful if you do so.

I'm glad the Alaska Native Claims Settlement Act happened. I feel we're so much further. You listen to the Hawaiians, and we're so much further than what they've done. We might not have done everything right, but it's not over yet. We're still working.

*Do you recall when it passed?* I don't think so. Nobody really told us, until I got in high school in '74. Then I read *Alaska Native Land Claims*, and that's where we learned we were now shareholders. OK, we didn't know. We had no idea. When I was going to school, no one said we should get a business degree and come back and help. Nobody pushed that.

It's kind of amazing because I listen to John Oktollik because he was on the first board. And he tells stories about how his first meeting was. There was nothing there, no paperwork. He had to draft an agenda. It's real fun to listen to him about how the people were. It's pretty amazing what they did in so little time, what they've accomplished. He's done so much for Tikigaq. He hasn't been given enough credit. He's been there since the beginning, and he's still on. He has a lot of history.

*What about ASRC?* It's kind of mind boggling because with the village corporation you see what you've got, then you see their numbers, and say, "Holy Smokes. This is a whole new ball game." You look at the subsidiaries they've got. They've come a long way.

*What about adding those born after 1971 as shareholders in*

*ASRC?* I'm real happy about it. If you wanted to go the "I" route, you wouldn't like it. But it's not about that. It's about "we," the people. That's what it's all about. I just hope we never lose that ability. If someone doesn't have something, they're taken care of. It's part of the community. I just hope we never lose that.

What I don't like to see is our borough paying people to go help the elders. In the village, your parents would tell you, "Go over and check to see if they have ice for water." And you just did that. Now, the borough's hired people to do it, and you've lost that. That's what I don't like. I did that with my kids, but a lot of people didn't.

My grandparents would say – if somebody was in need of help – "Go get ice, and do it now!" Or, "Maybe you better go dig the porch out." Just help them. You did it. They would thank you. You knew that there was something else that would happen, that you'd get blessed or something. You were supposed to do it now, not in 10 minutes. Now is now.

*Is there a clash between concern about the bottom-line and culture?* Our shareholders feel a lot differently. When they tell you they own it, they mean it. For instance, shareholder hire: We could have more on the bottom-line, but we hire more shareholders than at times what's needed. We try to educate the shareholders and give back to them. We're doing a water and sewer project, and we could have made almost twice what we're doing now, but we want to get our shareholders jobs. We'll sacrifice that to get them training. You can have the best of both worlds. We've got a partner in this project, and they weren't used to that. Rather than looking at the bottom-line, we've had to educate them, "Hey, this is what we want."

*Scholarships?* Yes, we just established them. *Dividends?* We did for the first time last year. *Did Point Hope add those born after as shareholders?* Yes.

*Goals?* It's pretty scary. Our goal is to have our corporation self-sustaining, and we're going to have to look elsewhere besides the Slope – down this way in Anchorage or down in the Lower 48. We've formed a new company, and it's called TES, Tikigaq Environmental Services. We're hoping that that's going to be a springboard. We're going to grasp on to that and maybe some tourism. But we've been real patient in doing tourism. We had our shareholders accept it two years ago, but we've really been taking our time because we want to have it controlled. We want to control tourism so it doesn't bother the hunting and everything else that goes on. When they go out bearded seal hunting or walrus hunting, it's right there on the beach. It's not 20 miles away. So we need to definitely to control tourism.

And it's kind of challenging. It's pretty scary because of the oil, the declining revenues. And I think all the villages on the Slope feel the same panic. We're forming a new company with all the villages as one. We're going to be doing something soon. ASRC will always take care of itself and be here, but the village corporations need something to sustain ourselves. So that's what we're going to do – Point Hope, Point Lay, Atqasuk, Ukpeagvik Inupiaq Corporation in Barrow, Nuiqsut, Kaktovik and Anaktuvuk Pass.

*Your personal goals?* (Laughs.) Mine are pretty simple. I told my wife I realized I was put on this earth to help kids. I've kind of accepted that I'm just going to be there for kids. The only goal I ever had when I was younger was that one day I'd be the president of our village corporation. I've been there, done that. Then, I wanted to be head coach. I've been there and done that. One day maybe I would like to try a political office. I've been asked to run many times. I do want to stay close to kids. So many of the kids call me "Pop." I really love those kids. They mean so much to me. They are a bunch of good kids there.

You have television nowadays, bingo – so much time is not spent with our kids. If they do spend it with them, I'm hoping that it's quality time. I've seen so many kids nowadays that have no respect for the elders or certain people. And it's because of that. People say, "We used to respect our elders."

And I say, "Yeah, if you stay home and tell your kids and discipline them to show respect, they'll do it. You're the parent. You need to be that."

Some people aren't doing that. They're just having a good time, doing their own thing is what they want to do. You've got to make that sacrifice, be there for your kids. You have to take care of them. It's your responsibility. It's no one else's responsibility. Too many times we blame the education system. They say it isn't doing much for our kids. Well, hey, what are you doing for your kids?

Drugs, alcohol, TV, they all come into play. We used to do so many things before, together. We didn't have TV, so we went out and built caves, tunnels, stuff like that. Sliding together. We did a lot of things together. You hardly see that. Kids are home watching whatever.

*ASRC in the future?* They'll play a big part in Alaska. It depends on who they've got in succession plans. I don't think that's there yet. Those things worry me. Jake Adams and Oliver Leavitt – have they passed that down? To me, that's what's scary. There's got to be a plan. My hat's off to them. They've done some amazing things. But, still, they need to plan for succession.

*Are there misconceptions in Alaska about Native corporations?* Yes. One of the biggest ones: we're all rich and it was all handed to us. Those guys have had to work, and they've come a long way. Some of them have been lucky by hiring the right people. Caring people. They sacrificed to make it go. People don't know that. They think it was just given to us. That's not true.

# *Bering Straits Region*

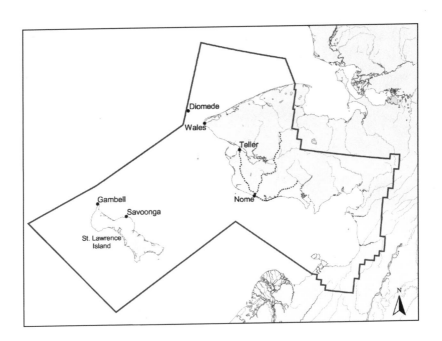

 **AUSTIN AHMASUK** *lives in Nome and was employed as a Land Technician by Sitnasuak Native Corporation, the village corporation for Nome, when he was interviewed. Austin and his wife Maricia now have three daughters, Adelaine Marie, Senora Noelle, and Kerry Nagitaagna.*

*Ahmasuk was born July 7, 1972. He has a Bachelor's Degree in Rural Development, with a Land Management emphasis from the University of Alaska Fairbanks.*

*His parents Harold Ahmasuk, Jr., and Janet Jesfjeld Ahmasuk met when his mother visited Nome as a tourist. She went to Nome on vacation to view totem poles and met Austin's father when she complained to him that the community had no such attractions.*

*Ahmasuk is a shareholder of Sitnasuak Native Corporation and through gifting, hopes to become a Bering Straits Native Corporation shareholder. Austin and his wife, who is originally from Mountain Village on the Lower Yukon, would like to move out of Nome into the country. He was interviewed February 8, 1999.*

When I came back to Alaska, I had a change of heart, and I guess the atmosphere at Fairbanks really made up my mind. I told myself, "I think I want to be involved with Native politics someday." I also told myself, "I want to work for a Native corporation." And that's where I am right now, and I'm really pleased with where I am. It's about the best job I could possibly think of right now.

I'm one of seven children. I have four brothers and two sisters – three older brothers, one older sister, one younger brother and one younger sister. I was raised here in Nome. Pretty much from the outset I was involved with my family with anything that has to do with the outdoors – hunting, fishing, camping and things of that nature. So very early on, I took part in all the activities attached to Native ways and lifestyle, other than the language. I know the language a little bit, since I heard it every day when I was younger.

My early years, there was a lot of working with older people, learning from them, watching them. One thing that really sticks with me was watching those older people do what they did out in the country. And then, finally, years later, learning what they were doing as I was watching them. Oftentimes, what elders know can seem a little trivial to someone who doesn't know what they're doing or what they're talking about. For instance, if you ask an elder: "How do you go fishing? How do you cut up a walrus? How do you hunt walrus?"

Oftentimes, they'll just say, "Go do it." Without that experience I had when I was younger, I wouldn't understand that inherent knowledge that they had by just saying, "Go do it." It means a lot more than just, "Go do it." It means prepare for how it was traditionally prepared for. Cutting up walrus or any animal is a process that takes a lot of knowledge, knowing where the joints are, that kind of thing. I'm very pleased as a young person to have witnessed those kinds of things, and I'm practicing them today.

Shortly after high school I went to college Outside to South Dakota for two years. I got kind of homesick, I guess, and came back to Alaska and went to Fairbanks. Immediately after high school I thought I was going to be a Civil Engineer, but after several years in that program and coming back to Alaska, I really had a calling within myself to be involved in anything that had to do with Native people. And so I switched my major from Civil Engineering to Rural Development with a Land Management emphasis from the University of Alaska Fairbanks.

And so it took me seven years to finish school. I took a semester off here and there, taking classes fairly leisurely. But I finally graduated from college in '97 and got a job here in Nome with the village corporation in the land department. The things that I learned in school directly relate to my job that I'm in right now, which is working as a Land Technician for Sitnasuak Native Corporation. I also am to some extent an ANCSA technician, helping shareholders understand some things about ANCSA or the land department or the things that the land department does here for the village corporation here in Nome.

One of the bigger things was getting married and having children. My wife Maricia and I have two daughters. My wife is from the Lower Yukon, Mountain Village, and we share many of the same interests. It's very good to have that kind of support from your wife and from your family. My oldest daughter, Adelaine Marie, is nearing three years, and my youngest, Senora Noelle, is one year.

I guess that's pretty much my life story in a nutshell.

My father's name is Harold Ahmasuk, Jr., and my mother's name is Janet Ahmasuk. Her maiden name is Jesfjeld. My mother's a Norwegian from South Dakota, so that makes me a half-breed mutt. My mother had moved to California for a couple years, working as a laboratory technologist and wanted to take a vacation in Alaska. If you can believe this – she came to Nome to see totem poles. And so she was kind of upset that there weren't any totem poles here. She was a typical tourist. As the story goes, my dad proposed to my mom on the first day. And so they struck up a relationship between here and California via the mail. Things finally culminated a year or so later, and they got married. My mom's been here since 1970.

The thing here in rural Alaska – some people come up for the darnedest things, and some of them at the onset don't know why they're here. But then 20 years later they figure out this is a pretty good place. My mom's content that way.

My father was married before, and so my older siblings are from a previous marriage.

*Your education?* I was very fortunate – very, very fortunate – to have grown up here in Nome. At the time that I was going to school, there was a very good curriculum at the local public high school. My high school education was very broad. I took a lot of math, a lot of English and all the sciences. The only thing that I know I was lacking in was computers, and at that time in Nome computers weren't a real hot number. I had very little computer experience. When I got Outside and I was going to an engineering school, I was thrust into computer programming classes. I was floundering. So when the professor, at the beginning of the semester said, "Look to your left, and look to your right. One of you three is going to flunk." I was the one who flunked. (Laughs.)

But fortunately, I made it up. I did real well in my other classes, math and science. But, like I say, when I came back to Alaska, I had a change of heart, and I guess the atmosphere at Fairbanks really made up my mind. I told myself, "I think I want to be involved with Native politics someday." I also told myself, "I want to work for a Native corporation." And that's where I am right now, and I'm really pleased with where I am. It's about the best job I could possibly think of right now.

The main vehicle for success in college is having a good base of peers that you can rely on. One of the advantages of Fairbanks is that they're highly devoted to rural student success. Rural Student Services is an arm of the institution there that helps rural students focus their college career. I feel that was very influential in my success and in my changing my degree. I believe the average age of the student at Fairbanks when I was going to school was 30, and so you meet all walks of people across Alaska. If you meet 100 people that are really devoted to going to school, and they're all interested in the same things – that's Native politics or being involved with anything to have to do with Native lifestyle – it's very helpful. It's a tremendous resource to talk to people from all over Alaska. You can hear and listen to people that you never thought you would. When I heard about Southeast or Southwest Alaska – I wasn't sure how different it was until I went to college and met all these diverse groups of Native people.

*Why did you go to college?* Looking back, I can easily answer that question and say my college career, my degree, has really given me a boost as far as my income goes. But in choosing to go to college, I guess I was just primarily interested in furthering my education. In high school I was also aware that without a college education I probably wouldn't be able to have the income level that I have right now, which is not exceedingly rich, but it's fairly comfortable. And so that was certainly an influence in my choosing to go to college. Another thing is in rural Alaska there is a tremendous need for an active voice for Native people. Maybe my initial decision to go to college was thinking, "Well, if I do something good for myself, get an education, maybe I can help other people." I guess I'm trying to do that. I'm involved with the legislative sessions, offering testimony regarding subsistence or fishing or what have you. So, having that college background – it certainly has given me an edge as far as being able to voice concerns that I've heard.

*Did your parents influence your decision to go to college?* They pushed me to excel or do my best at whatever I did. I think my mom was probably a pretty good influence there in going to school. And my father was a very influential person as far as encouraging us to keep your nose to the grindstone, do the best that you can and don't get involved in too many hare-brained things. It was a very good mix, getting an education from both sides of the world, really, my mom on the one hand and my father on the other.

*Discrimination?* Yes, there was some discrimination, going to school in South Dakota. But nothing that anyone would really get fighting mad over. I felt some discrimination, especially when I would tell other students about the scholarships I was getting and the kind of money that my village corporation was giving out for scholarships. There was some animosity toward that kind of thing. Other than that, there was nothing that I can really say was gross discrimination. But there was a tinge of it there.

I've always asked my older brothers about that. My older brothers are much older than I am. They're in their 40's. When they were younger, I think there was a very large amount of discrimination, racism towards Native people. When I was going to school, it was pretty well toned down. But there definitely was segregation of students. I guess it was along the lines of race. When I was going to school, some of my student peers made fun of Native people. But it wasn't anything long-lasting. My parents have told me that when I was in junior high or so, they had to get on some of the teachers for saying some racist things, discouraging Natives from taking a math class. I don't remember the specific instance, but there was one teacher who said something like that.

*When did you have a feeling of being Native?* It was very early on. When I was younger, I was primarily interested in going out in the boonies or whatever, so it was very early on.

My grandparents who passed away a number of years ago – they were very, very nice people, as most Native people are. They were reindeer herders who lived out in the country all their lives. They were very knowledgeable about anything that had to do with being Native. When you're younger, those experiences you have with older people – it's very hard to forget. When you're a little kid, some of the things you experience with older people are scary. Maybe your first experience with going hunting is a scary experience. But there are things that old folks who've lived out in the country all their lives can do for you to teach you about yourself or about the country or what to do in the country that will help you.

When you get older those things become ingrained in you. I also know that when you get older, things change. What an elder said 20 years ago or did 20 years ago, you reflect on, and maybe today the circumstances are different, but you apply what they taught you. Maybe you're not going to do it the same way they did it 20 years ago, but you're going to apply what you learned.

Going out in the country with elders is very useful to you as a person. Here in the Nome area people rely on the ocean for subsistence. The Seward Peninsula here – everybody relies on the ocean. People go boating – going 30, 40 miles out in the ocean – and then go after walrus, which are very strong animals. The one thing that I remember about being young was my first time going up to walrus. There were a number of men, much older men, and me and my brothers in the boat. I was the youngest one, and I was sitting right in the middle of the boat. We were going after walrus, and we got fairly close to these animals. When you're young, they seem like they're 30 or 40 feet tall. Get up close to them: it was very, very frightening. Grandpa was sitting there next to me. And one thing he said to me after we got the walrus on that little piece of ice there: "Did you see the mama? Did you see the baby go with the mama?"

I didn't see it, but I said, "Yeah."

I guess, looking back on that, Grandpa was in his 70's, and he had 70 years experience going out on the ocean. And for a man like that with a little boy like me – he wasn't scared. But he knew I was scared. And maybe he tried to ask me if I was even aware of what was going on. Course I wasn't aware. It was a typical thing for an older man to do that kind of thing, always looking down to the young person, trying to teach them something, any little thing. His name was Harold Ahmasuk, Sr.

*Your Native hero?* I really never thought about that. If I were to pick maybe the most influential Native person in my life it would probably be my father. With the tremendous experiences he's had, he is my primary teacher. But it's old people. If I were to pick one person, it'd be my father. But I'd rather pick an aspect of people, and I think it would probably be old people.

*Your feelings on the Alaska Native Claims Settlement Act?* ANCSA is a very highly pivotal point in Native history. And for one, it was an exchange of title between Native people and the United States government and the State of Alaska. So that part was very pivotal in our history. And the land exchange, the money exchange, the creation of corporations – today if you asked any Alaskan, Native or non-Native, what an ANCSA corporation means to them, oftentimes, what you find out when you talk with people is that a majority of them think that ANCSA corporations are synonymous with Natives. My particular feeling about a statement like that is that it's not necessarily true. The Native corporations try to represent Native people, but I think the fact of the matter is that a Native corporation is not necessarily synonymous with Natives. So my initial feeling with ANCSA is that when there was a strong oil push and people were starting to talk about the question of title in Alaska – the question that I ask myself is what were the processes that Native people had to go through in giving testimony?

What I've often heard from people who just want to talk about the Alaska Native Claims Settlement Act is that they wonder why only 10 percent of the state belongs to Native people. That's a big question that enters my mind. Being the first people of Alaska, we only own 10 percent of the state, and the eventual bureaucracy it has created with the Native corporations can sometimes lead to things such as issues of Native trespass on Native land. That's an irony that really has me perplexed.

That's the pessimistic approach. Not all people think the same way, and I think there are examples of Native corporations that are truly aware of Native claims and so manage their corporation business purely for the benefit of Native people. One example I can think of is a corporation near Illiamna that manages their corporation so it's not top heavy and with minimal administrative staff. They take the opposite approach of many corporations that focus on development. In fact, I think it sold all of its land to the federal government as a wildlife easement. And so, the actual corporation doesn't even own the large conveyance it was promised in the original act. But their subsistence land is protected in that way. Certainly, not all Native corporations think the same way or act the same way or carry out all their corporate practices in the same manner.

ANCSA's extremely complicated. We live in a complicated society. That's why I believe there are tremendous differences in the way ANCSA is applied as far as assets, equity or shareholder desires or concerns.

It was a tremendous asset that Native people had that they gave up. As far as how the act was created, it was governed by a bureaucratic process. And in that process there was a lack of communication on the part of the federal government. In the beginning, some land selections were totally miscommunicated. Perhaps the people who made the original selections couldn't speak very good English. As far as that goes, for those people, it was a tremendous mistake that was made. The process, I guess, was more the mistake. If Natives received 90 percent of the state or 100 percent of the state, maybe people would feel differently about it. I guess the mistake lies in that Native people gave up their aboriginal claim. But that doesn't necessarily mean they gave up who they are. We didn't give up our aboriginal rights. We didn't give up our aboriginal hunting rights or fishing rights. And that certainly has stood the test of time since ANCSA.

*How do you feel about the creation of corporations?* The biggest foulup is that many people think that the Native corporation is synonymous with Native people. As I'm sure you're aware, ANCSA corporations are generally not synonymous with Native people. Native people primarily just want to be left alone. The thing about corporations is if the bottom-line is to attract development or things like that, those ideals are going to clash with how I feel Native people think. There are things associated with development that certainly clash with how Native people do their business as far as hunting or fishing is concerned. So there is a potential clash between corporations and Native people.

In a village corporation, I see a clash between corporations in this area and Native people. I guess my desire to work with a Native corporation is that I'm definitely in touch with Native people. I work with shareholders and primarily deal with things that shareholders are concerned about.

The clash results from the fact that Native corporations own the land that people need for subsistence. The fundamental driving force in a village corporation concerned with a hefty profit margin or even an incremental profit margin is the bottom-line. If their largest asset is resources, tourism, what have you, the driving force for that corporation to develop itself will clash with Native people. Let's take an example. Someone lives 30 miles up the coast, or maybe they camp 30 miles up the coast. If there's a coal resource there that the corporation would like to develop, there's the clash. There's the clash between the corporation – between the onset of development and subsistence lifestyle.

*How do you feel about the people who worked on ANCSA?* I really don't know anybody who worked on ANCSA. But from what I loosely know about those people, I think they honestly tried to do their best. Of course, you hear stories of people who – non-Native people – took advantage of Native people as far as land selections were concerned. One of the driving forces in Native lifestyle is definitely land. So as far as how the selections were made in the early years, unfortunately I don't have that connection with our selections, other than reading through our own corporation's minutes. From what I witnessed here in the Bering Straits Region, a good majority of people who were involved with developing ANCSA had very little experience with even conducting a meeting. And so in the early stages, I think there was a tremendous learning process on Native peoples' part to become businesslike in their dealings. Maybe 50 years ago, there was a direct relationship with the federal government. Nowadays, land management decisions are made by Native people themselves. But that process has taken a long time to learn. Some areas in Alaska are probably further behind other areas in Alaska. So I guess my initial reaction is that at the beginning stage there was a tremendous learning process for everybody and more than likely mistakes were going to be made somewhere.

It's very unfortunate that our Native people were probably not as educated as they are nowadays. Maybe they could have really benefited from education prior to ANCSA.

There are many facets to a Native corporation. For Nome, we have a land department. We have the parent corporation. We have its subsidiaries. And so there are many facets to the ANCSA responsibilities that we deal with. It's a good place for anybody to learn about ANCSA and Native corporations.

*Do you think those born after the act should have stock?* Yes, I think they should. I've gone the alternate route and asked for gifted shares. Some people are going to inherit shares. For me, I guess, what I'm coming from is if you increase the shareholder base, you necessarily decrease the voice that one individual has. But it's a two-edged sword. If you continually increase the shareholder base, you get a wider distribution of ideas for the corporation. You can achieve the same goal by gifting shares. As far as that's concerned, if a group of shareholders within a Native corporation really rallied together and really want something of concern regarding the Native lifestyle, I think they'll get to the table.

*How do you feel about the fact that some corporations have been very successful?* For one thing, I think it's great that there are some of those corporations that have a fair amount of political power. One interesting thing I heard is that the first people the governor calls on Native politics are the presidents of the Native corporations. I don't know if that's true or not, but it's kind of enlightening because there you go again, the rest of the government, the rest of the world thinks that Native corporations are synonymous with Native people. If a particular Native corporation has a fair amount of political power, I think there's a check and balance. In the case of our corporation here in Nome, I think there's a strong tie to a particular concern within the Nome area, and that's salmon. And so our corporation has devoted a fair amount of time and resources to the chum stocks of the Nome area. In fact, we've been one of the more vocal advocates of increasing chum stocks, which I'm a part of. I'm being paid by my corporation to represent Native people's voice at the table.

My personal goals are to raise my children as best I can and try and keep our family – and not just my immediate family, but Native people – being Native. I guess that sounds kind of funny, but one of the things that I like to see is people showing respect for nature and people showing that they care about their neighbor. I guess one of the best ways a person can achieve those two things that I just mentioned is being true to what they say. In the long run, I don't see myself working for the village corporation in Nome the rest of my life. Sometime in the near future – whenever I get my student loans paid off – I really would like to tone down my workload and move out in the country. That's been a goal of mine for quite some time now – to live out in the country.

My wife and I share the same mentality, same ideals, same interests. We both someday would really like to move away from the town here and go out in the country. We'll see, though. Things always change. It's a hard decision to make.

One thing is when you become involved with Native politics, it seems like it's a never-ending job.

Goals for my children are to show them what I learned as a youngster and that is to get them involved with anything that has to do with the outdoors like I did. I try to do that as much as I can. Even though it's 30 below out, take them outside. Not for too long because they can freeze their lungs. But take them outdoors, even though it's cold like this. And hopefully try to teach them the kinds of things that I was taught, which is eating Native foods, preparing Native foods, going hunting, whatever. Hopefully, I can rely on some elder people to teach them. I certainly don't think I could teach them everything that I would like them to know. I think giving them a tremendous experience with other different people is very important for them – let my older brothers or my younger brothers teach them certain things. Maybe that will help them strive for education, learning more.

*A vision for ANCSA?* I hope there are further amendments. Tribal advocates are saying one thing, IRA councils are saying another thing, city governments are saying another thing, state government is saying another thing, BLM is saying a completely different thing. So when it first came about, there was a question of unclear title, and there had to be a payment made to Native people. Well, I think people today are questioning why there was an unclear title and the amount of payment that was received. I guess my short-sighted hope, and the only one I can really think of right now, is that people make amendments to ANCSA and try and touch a little bit on what the purpose was of ANCSA. There was a definite purpose, and that purpose was to try and better the life of Native people.

I like to think optimistically about it, but I think that in saying that I'm probably a minority in the eyes of other Native people who think that ANCSA was a mistake. For all the reasons that we've talked about earlier, ANCSA is a mistake. But then for all the reasons we talked about earlier, ANCSA can be a tool for Native people. It's all tied to the part that Native people play in whatever process ANCSA brings about. If there were not an ANCSA, there'd be another process that Native people would have to go through. But there is an ANCSA, and there is a process that people can use to voice their concerns.

ANCSA corporations – regarding their political power – they're special corporations. They're not just there for the buck. Certainly, our corporation has devoted a lot of time to Native issues. ANCSA corporations are pretty much governmental institutions that people can use for similar purposes that they would go to a government. Though ANCSA corporations are limited in the realm they can deal with, they certainly can be used as political tools. And so I guess my hope for ANCSA is a hope that ANCSA can bring about a certain amount of freedom. In that freedom, there's free use of hunting land. To some extent, ANCSA corporations are somewhat protective of their own land assets against their own shareholders. So my sincere hopes are that Native people can use ANCSA as a tool for the betterment of their own lives.

*Are you in favor of the repeal of ANCSA?* I am and I am not. For one, I think I would be stepping on the toes of people who are much older than I and with much more experience in government if I were to say that ANCSA is a big mistake and what some corporations are doing right now is a total mistake. But what I gather from older folks is that prior to Statehood, there was a large amount of freedom, and there was not so much competition, not so much development. Maybe as far as subsistence was concerned, life was very much better. Certainly, a repeal of ANCSA would bring into clearer focus the very, very big issue of subsistence. That would be a very strong point for Native people to bring to the table.

*JAYLENE Z. WHEELER was born on January 31, 1976, in Nome. Wheeler attended Mount Edgecumbe High School in Sitka for two years and then graduated from Nome Beltz High School in 1994. While still in high school, she attended the Rural Alaska Honors Institute at the University of Alaska Fairbanks.*

*Wheeler has attended UAF and is working on a Rural Development degree. Upon completion of her degree she may pursue studies in environmental or natural resource law.*

*She is a founding member of YANIC – Young Alaska Natives (18 to 30 years old) Initiating Change – and has been involved in numerous youth-oriented programs since high school. A more recent endeavor includes participation in the Eighth Inuit Circumpolar Conference in Nuuk, Greenland.*

*Wheeler is an enrolled member of Nome Eskimo Community. Because her father gifted shares to her, she is also a shareholder of Sitnasuak Native Corporation, the village corporation for Nome.*

*She ran for the Sitnasuak Board of Directors once, and although she was not elected on her first try, she plans to run again in the future. She was interviewed November 19, 1998.*

A friend I met in Greenland during ICC this past summer saw the dancing and the singing as a healing process – I mean a sense of identity, spirituality, everything. I think that's the purpose that it served years ago. You see, it's quite clear that some people use it for those very reasons today. When I was at UAF, I danced in the Inu-Yup'ik Dance Group. It was a mixture of Inupiaq and Yup'ik songs. Two of my friends – one is from Wainwright, the other from Nunapitchuk – were the main drummers. They are my age and they taught us the songs.

I grew up in Nome, and I was raised there basically my whole life. My dad spent most of his teen-age years in Tanana, but his mother originally came from what used to called "Jabbertown," a place right outside of Point Hope. And my mother grew up on Little Diomede Island and in Teller. So I've got family all over the place – some in the Interior – because my dad has seven sisters and most of them married into Athabascan families. I also have a lot of family in the Nome area – Teller, Little Diomede, and on St. Lawrence Island. My mom's birth mother is from Gambell, but my mom was adopted out when only a couple of months old. So, by blood, I am both Inupiaq and Siberian Yupik Eskimo, as well as Caucasian.

My maternal grandparents are Paul and Theresa (Omiak) Soolook, both originally from Little Diomede, and now living in Teller. And then my grandparents on my father's side are Floyd and Martha (Stein) Wheeler. My grandfather passed away, and my Grandma Martha lives in Fairbanks.

There's a road that goes to Teller, so every summer I go up there to visit my grandparents and other family and friends. Teller is pretty small; it has only about 250 people. There is a road to this community, so it's easily accessible in the summer. Teller is located near the ocean, and on the other side is Grantley Harbor. We'd go fishing and camping at Nook, which is located right across the harbor. So this is what I grew up with in the summers when I was younger – fishing and camping at Nook.

In regards to schooling, I went to elementary and about half of my high school years in Nome. For two years, I attended Mt. Edgecumbe High School in Sitka – not because I had to, but because I wanted to. Both of my parents went to school at Mt. Edgecumbe. They had no choice in this because there weren't really any high schools in the communities that they lived in. So I went to high school down in Sitka for two years, and that was a really good experience because I got to meet people from all over the state. And, to be quite honest, I think the quality of education down there was a lot better than what I had back home. I think I benefited greatly from schooling in Sitka. For two summers, in '93 and '94, I went to RAHI, Rural Alaska Honors Institute.

I went to UAF for two and a half years, and now I'm just going back to school again after taking a year off and working at Kawerak. I have one younger brother named Tudor. He's sixteen. And that's it. There are just two kids in our family.

I'm part Caucasian, but I don't think it's by blood that determines who you are – it is what you grow up with and how you choose to present yourself to others, what you value. Even though someone might be full Native by blood, that doesn't necessarily mean that they show themselves in the way people used to in years past. And I think that's just because we're not isolated in our own communities and our own cultures any more. It is such a challenge these days because we're living amongst many different peoples. And that's not to say that we can't borrow other ideas or values from different people of different backgrounds.

I was sitting in my Environmental Studies class a couple weeks ago, and someone, a Caucasian, was talking about the "Alaska Native Community," and it was almost like he thought he was speaking on behalf of me. And I told him, "You know, you need to be careful about how you choose to word what you say. And more importantly, you also need to be careful in what you choose to believe. Just because one person tells you that 'this is how the Native people feel,' that may not be the truth."

Look at what was going on prior to Election Day. There were ads on the TV where a Native – who probably got paid a lot of money – was up there saying he was in support of the "English-Only Initiative." That was a big thing. Sometimes you have people say things that other people don't necessarily support. And so you have to be careful.

People just have to be careful in speaking out and choosing to call themselves leaders if they're really not doing it for the benefit of the Native community. Western culture – in terms of personal gain and recognition – isn't always easily applicable to our ways.

One of my friends that I was just talking to yesterday was all excited about getting recognized in his region as having things to contribute. And he's done with his degree and he's making a lot of money. I told him, "Just don't let that get to your head. I told you a couple years ago that we needed to work together to keep each other humble."

Because that's one thing that we're supposed to do. He's Athabascan, and I'm Eskimo, but I'm assuming that it's a common thing from a long time ago – to keep humble and to remember that you're not just speaking for yourself when you're in a leadership position. Our conversation made me think about these issues. You're speaking for the community. And I'm just afraid that some people forget that.

When I went to Teller, I'd go camping and fishing with my grandparents, so it was a multi-generational activity. That was about the extent of my subsistence activities. Nome is different from Kotzebue and Barrow because there are a lot of non-Native people that live there. So as I grew up, it was easy to question the validity of being Native. You didn't see it demonstrated in the schools much, other than in your bilingual class. I did take bilingual, and that was in elementary school. But I didn't get to learn the language. You can't learn a language by studying it just a couple of hours a week.

I practice different kinds of cultural activities. My

118

grandmother and my mom taught me how to bead and do a little of the sewing when I was seven years old or around there. My grandmother still teases me about this sometimes. I was watching her sew slippers, and I wanted to sew slippers so bad. And so she cut out felt, instead of using skins, and let me sew. You could stick two fingers in between my stitches. I still bead once in awhile, but not that much.

And that's the other thing, too: When I was in high school – probably my senior year – I was really trying to make the decision as to whether I should go right off to college. I knew that higher education was important, and at the same time, I was kind of wanting to go and live with my grandparents for awhile in Teller. Although it would have been ultimately my decision, when I went in to talk to the high school guidance counselor, he really discouraged me from doing something like that – thinking that it was going to put me behind. "It would be better to go off to college right away," he said.

I'm still trying to get through with college, but every time I'm pre-registering for my classes, I think, "Should I take off a semester and just go be with my grandparents?" Because I figure if all of us are going to school, who's going to learn the traditions, like sewing and dancing and the language especially?

These are things where it's really hard for young people. We have a lot of people pushing us to go and get a higher education, and then we have all these people in political positions, where they're trying to defend Native rights, like subsistence and sovereignty and the right to use our own language. We also need to remember that we have to encourage people to stay back home also, not only to live in the rural communities, but also to learn the cultures and traditions.

I was talking to one of my friends who was saying he didn't really feel like college was for him. He enjoyed being at home hunting and providing for his family, helping his grandparents haul water. Because you've got to remember in a lot of rural areas there isn't running water, so people have to pack their own ice for drinking water or wash water or whatever. By talking to him, it made me realize it's OK if people choose to be back home, as long as they are productive.

So I try to bring up that point when I can because some people just don't feel whole when they're away from what they're used to. That sense of community and knowing people and cultural activities, things of that nature. This person who I was talking to just happened to be a young man, and I knew he was going through a lot. So I told him, "Don't worry about going to college if you feel like you can be productive back at home, learning, so you can pass on some of that to people even younger than you. Putting back into the community, that's just as valid."

One of the concerns that I've talked about with my friends, through YANIC *(Young Alaska Natives Initiating Change)*, is considering how much we've gone through in such a short amount of time. It seems like we've adapted relatively well in terms of 8-to-5 jobs, things of that nature that weren't so common even 50 years ago. However, it does seem that a lot of the jobs that are out there in rural areas are secretarial positions, clerks, or health-related – roles that seem to have been traditionally held by women. You've got to think about what this must mean for a young male or Native man's sense of purpose.

When I was at school in Fairbanks, State Senator Georgianna Lincoln came and talked one time. She was speaking to this very issue of young Native men because they have the highest suicide rate. Even in my home area, this is an issue. So that really concerns me. Georgianna was saying we need to support one another more.

*Did you experience discrimination?* Yeah, not always outright, but I knew it was there. And you can't help but feel that way when you grow up and you don't see your own culture in the school. Just recently, in the last couple years, Native Programs at the Nome School District has put up pictures of elders in the schools. Simple things like this help youth reaffirm and further develop their identity.

I remember clearly one situation where a friend of mine, who just happened to be Caucasian, was telling me how she didn't think we should be hanging out any more. We couldn't be friends. And I said, "What's up with this?" And it turned out that her mother didn't want us associating with one another because I was Native.

And I thought, "You know, you're in the wrong place." Her family was originally from Minnesota.

Nome is real interesting. There are four tribal governments that are based there – Nome Eskimo Community of which I'm a tribal member, Solomon Traditional Council, Council Traditional Council and King Island Native Community. So those are political units within themselves, which are separate, but they are starting to work more with the city. There are definite partnership opportunities and ways of bridging ideas and people together, especially if you're trying to get a community building of some sort. When I was working in Nome, I started thinking more about tribal-corporate-city relationships.

*When did you have a feeling of Native identity?* I always knew it. I felt like I had it at home. I had that strong sense of identity a lot of times when I was at home or when I was with family or close friends. It's kind of hard to describe. I always feel it when I think of my grandparents, visit with them in person, or talk to them on the phone. Oftentimes when I was younger, it was outside of my family and close friends that I felt it was harder to comfortably express my identity.

When I was in Nome for high school one semester, I took an Alaska studies course. Well, they – the instructor and the reading materials – talked about Alaska Natives in the past tense, like we didn't exist. All we covered was one week on Alaska Natives. It wasn't contemporary issues. It didn't talk about us still being in existence. When I started encountering those kinds of things, I thought, "This is wrong. There need to be more people getting educated and writing our histories even though we're primarily an oral-based people."

When I went to RAHI I had a Native studies course, and I learned some of the political relationships between the tribes and the U.S. government and the duties the federal government has. I thought these are things that are in writing. It's a matter of pushing it for our benefit. I could explain it in the phrase that one of my friends said, "You don't have to be anti-white to be pro-sovereignty." If you look at some of the arguments of the sovereignty issue, some people think it is racially driven. But it's not. It's a political relationship between the tribes and the U.S. government.

Do you see what I mean? These are things that people fail to recognize and respect. I've been thinking this really needs to change. There needs to be a requirement in all schools in the state to teach students about this political relationship, as well as about the diversity of Native people living in Alaska. Especially in high school, people need to learn that these political relationships exist so they don't ask, "Well, why do you get free health services? Why do you get help in college?" Issues like these often cause conflict between non-tribal and tribal members.

I've come to the conclusion that part of what's really hurting us now is that there's a lack of understanding, a lack of awareness. And when you're ignorant, you can't make good choices, whether you're in the Legislature or you're a part of the voting community, voting on issues like the English-only bill. And it's come to the point where within the Alaska Native community, aside from the fact that I think there are differences in corporate and tribal perspectives, that we can't just remain working with our own people any more. We need to think of ways to teach other people some of our own ways. Or, at least get them to appreciate and respect the way we think and the way we believe.

*Native hero?* There are a lot of people that have influenced me. Lots. In fact, my friend and I were just talking about this last night. He was saying how there have been many people who have helped him learn and get to the point he is at right now in his life. Because you don't do things on your own. So I think that's another quality of how we are supposed to be. You don't make it anywhere on your own, but with the help of other people in your community, especially your family. I think within my family my mom was a very big influence on me.

My mom passed away from cancer last spring. Above all, she's probably the one person that has taught me the most on how you're supposed to treat other people. Not like coming out and saying, "This is how you're supposed to be," but role modeling. And that's something that is very important in any culture, how you treat others.

Someone that has passed on that I've been thinking about with the Inuit Circumpolar Conference is Eben Hopson. He's called the "ICC Founding Father." Prior to ICC being established, Eben had this vision of bringing together people from all over the circumpolar North. Initially, it was Canada, Greenland, and Alaska, but later on in the '80's, Chukotka became a part of it. But he had this vision of trying to create an Inuit homeland. ICC goes beyond geographical, cultural, political and language boundaries. Because of our commonalities – the importance of subsistence activities, protecting the environment, cultural integrity and others – we've found ways of communicating, regardless of whether we speak the same language or not. That's pretty powerful. And although we all have our own forms of government now, we have found ways of working together. That was and still is Eben's idea, and it's so powerful to me.

An Inuit Circumpolar Youth Council associate of mine from Greenland quoted Eben throughout a paper he presented to the Eighth ICC General Assembly this past July. And I thought it was a real good reminder to the people about what ICC was created for and what it could be doing today. These are the things that we need to stick to. And I guess this brings me to the third person that inspires me, Henriette Rasmussen. She works for the International Labour Organization office in Geneva, Switzerland. She's from Greenland, and I've been told that she is one of the first Inuit women to work at such an important international position. I met her for the first time in 1994 when I was a senior in high school and participating at an indigenous youth conference in Copenhagen, Denmark. When I met her I was just really impressed.

I thought, this lady has managed to go to a totally different part of the world and not only advocate for Inuit rights, but also other indigenous peoples around the world.

And then I saw her again in '95 in Nome during the Seventh ICC General Assembly. After the charters arrived in Nome with all of the people for ICC, they had to go through customs at the Rec Center. But we were talking, and I thought this is really neat. We could keep seeing each other at these different functions, and maybe I'll actually get the nerve to say, "I want to be in your spot someday, maybe." I think it's important to know that there are people out there that can still maintain those values you grow up with, use them at work, and teach them to others.

And, of course, elders. Sometimes, I think they get frustrated with young people because they don't think we spend enough time with them. But I think the elders – you can't forget to recognize them above all.

It was funny – that's one thing that I think I miss the most from back home. A couple of weeks ago I was thinking about how being here in the city, you don't see as many elders around. Anyway, I had walked down to the Post Office in the Sunshine Plaza. It's right down the street from where I stay, and I saw an elderly woman walk in. And she was struggling with a couple small boxes. I took care of what I needed to do, and I walked over to her. I grabbed her boxes, stuck them up to where I was at the window, and she just looked at me, surprised. To me, that was just something to do. That's just something you learn. I thought, I could adjust to living in the city if I saw more of what I experienced or felt at home.

This is kind of beside the point, but the elderly woman was not Native. I don't know what she was. It was just like showing some of how we are. So that made me feel good. But living in the city is definitely hard. I think I'm relatively lucky in the sense that I chose to come here and try out school. Here in the city there's a lot of Native people that don't have the opportunity of being in a rural area, but both urban and rural Natives can carry and practice similar values – but sometimes it can be a real challenge.

A friend of mine and I have baby pictures of each other. She grew up in Nome through part of her childhood years. And then, her family moved to a community in the Southcentral region because of her dad's job. We were talking on the phone. I can't remember how the topic came up. She said, "Don't you think people would rather work an 8-to-5 job – if they could?" We had been talking about limited employment opportunities in the village, and how many people still rely on hunting and fishing.

I think we were talking about subsistence. And I was really angry. I got my thoughts together and said, "There are people out there who are happy with the way that they live – off the land. Maybe there are laws passed that say when they can do it or limit what they take. But that's the people's livelihood, their spirituality. That's what a lot of people want their kids to learn."

Some people feel like they've made it in life if they've got a good 8-to-5 job and are making lots of money. But for some people, that's not important. What's important to them is just being able to hunt and fish and other subsistence-related activities. These activities provide food, promote a sense of community, and teach people important values that you can't always learn in any other way.

I told her, "It's funny that you're bringing this up." I said, "I'm going to have to share this story with you." And you know, a long time ago, and still today, we learn through stories. We teach through stories. I told her, "You know, for people at whaling communities like Savoonga and Gambell, whaling is a big thing. It's not like people decide one day, 'OK, I'm going to go out whaling.' You prepare for it all throughout the year. You're cutting and drying skins, and then repairing the boat. Young men are being taught things about hunting through role modeling. There are different activities that are done at different times in the year, both in whaling and with other hunts. That's how you're thinking. It's kind of cyclical."

*How do you feel about ANCSA?* Technically, I'm an afterborn. But before I graduated from high school, my dad gifted me a quarter of his shares in Sitnasuak Native Corporation, the village corporation in Nome. Because of his efforts to include me in SNC, I now benefit

124

for higher education scholarships. But, I'm taking a federal Indian law class through UAF, and the last couple of weeks I've been struggling with a required written assignment. Part of it has been kind of frustrating.

A Klamath Indian woman from Oregon made a presentation to our class about the Klamath termination policy. She was talking to us about their experience, and I started seeing parallels between that policy and ANCSA.

But in regards to ANCSA and a class I took my freshman year on Alaska Native Politics, one has to question the intent of policymakers and other individuals outside of the Alaska Native support network – both then and now. My instructor for Alaska Native Politics used to continually ask us throughout the class, "Is ANCSA termination in disguise?"

I never really understood exactly what he was trying to say because I didn't, at the time, look at it from the perspective of what's happened to other indigenous groups in the United States.

But if you look at what ANCSA's done to us, it has drastically impacted land "ownership" issues, both among people and local governing mechanisms. People born after 1971, in more cases than not, are excluded from the decision-making process of our village and regional corporations because most tribal governments don't have a real land base. This also causes challenges. In some situations, I think village corporations have transferred title to the land to the tribal government, IRA or traditional council.

ANCSA and the corporate system have divided us. Although we come together during different forums, such as the Alaska Federation of Natives and the Alaska Inter-Tribal Council, I think our way of thinking is really being challenged right now.

And then, since I was born after 1971, I have to speak to this, too: People born after December 18, 1971, aren't entitled to shares in the corporations. This is a direct cut on tribalism. At the Second Annual Young Alaska Natives Initiating Change meeting held in conjunction with AFN, John Borbridge from Southeast spoke to this very issue. He helped get ANCSA passed. He was telling us that the land claims issue was based on aboriginal title. At least in my mind, it wasn't meant to separate people just because of a birth date or an age. Generally speaking, people born after the enactment of ANCSA have no shares in a corporation, no say in who gets to be on the board, no say in various other land issues. So that's part of it.

The whole corporate structure – it was never based on what people really wanted or expected. It's too easy to get people thinking about making money or a profit when you mention a corporation – and the Native corporations weren't just set up for profit motives.

A friend and I – he's from the Interior – were talking about these types of issues one day, and he helped me understand the "bigger picture." He was saying that back in the late '60's and prior to ANCSA, the goal was to come to a land settlement. Even though they tried to have provisions in there for the protection of subsistence, it never passed. So land issues were the big thing. I think it's safe to say next came learning the political system and the corporate world, how these operate. Some of the village and regional corporations have gone into bankruptcy and then got back on their feet again. Bering Straits Regional Corporation was one of them. So we've learned from that era.

Going back to Sitnasuak. The corporation has a foundation, and I'm very happy for that. Although Sitnasuak currently provides only financial support for higher education students, they are looking at expanding their program. Just because of how the corporations are set up, what they're based on, it's scary unless the Native community is real careful. Merely making a profit year to year is not going to help us survive into the 21st century.

I gave a presentation on ICC at the AFN Youth and Elders Conference last year and talked briefly about a video produced by Makivik Corporation out of Canada. It's called, "Capturing Spirit: An Inuit Journey." It addresses the changes we've made in blending both modern and traditional ways and suggests that we consider what I might call the "healing process." There seem to be many things we need to talk about that have happened in our past. In doing so, we gain strength and can move forward. These are things that cannot necessarily be pursued by our corporations alone – but by a concerted effort of all people. We're basically in a period of redefining our identity.

I actually ran for the Sitnasuak board, not last year, but the year before. I wasn't sure that I'd even get on. But I thought, well, I might as well try. There was a lot going on in my family, so campaigning was not my priority. I looked at the total votes, and my friend's mom beat me out by about 4,000 votes. That's not a lot – only like 400 people. And so, I was thinking this is pretty exciting.

Older people shouldn't be threatened. One of my friends said,

"There's room for everybody." Some people think, "Oh, this young person is going to take my job." That's not how it's supposed to be. We're supposed to make room for all showing an interest in helping out the Native community. In the Western way, you start looking out for yourself and not so much for helping people get good opportunities, too.

Even though I'm only 22, I think, "Yeah, I'm doing some pretty good stuff with and for youth." But when opportunities come up for me to travel, I think to myself, "We need others getting worthwhile opportunities to learn, to get involved and to feel welcomed." And now it's like we need to start taking care of and including more of our own people. One of my older friends from back home pointed out that it's easy to get overwhelmed with everything that needs to be done. She always carries herself very well – very happy, encouraging. And she said, "You know, I can't wait until you young people take over some of this. It's hard. It's hard work, real challenging."

Going back to the corporate-tribal stuff. I want to see a better bridge established between the corporations and tribal government. I worked for Nome Eskimo Community during the summer of '95, and since then I've been learning about Sitnasuak Native Corporation, I've really seen that this needs to happen. This relationship has to grow. It has to develop. But people have to get involved. Even though corporations are relatively new institutions to the Native community, they are there. If we don't use them to our benefit, it's going to cause problems. We must keep faith in ourselves and utilize existing systems we now have to work in – developing new models where necessary.

*Your goals?* My younger brother Tudor is graduating from high school in May 2000. I thought it would be kind of cool for us to have a goal to work on together. I want to go to law school, and I'm very much interested in studying natural resource and/or environmental issues. So, law school will come when the timing is right.

Going back to the challenges we face, a friend I met in Greenland during ICC this past summer saw the dancing and the singing as a healing process – I mean a sense of identity, spirituality, everything. I think that's the purpose that it served years ago. You see, it's quite clear that some people use it for those very reasons today. When I was at UAF, I danced in the Inu-Yup'ik Dance Group. It was a mixture of Inupiaq and Yup'ik songs. Two of my friends –

one is from Wainwright, the other from Nunapitchuk – were the main drummers. They are my age and they taught us the songs. They knew all that stuff. But it really made me think of how we could really teach each other. We could benefit from working more closely. That singing and dancing is a very important thing.

I'd like to end by sharing an experience that a close friend of mine mentioned to me shortly after he helped out with an Interior tribal consortium meeting. He was asked to lead the meeting for one day. There were 80 some people there, and the meeting went very well, with elders observing and guiding the process. At the end of the session, one of the elders raised both of his hands in the air, demonstrating his overall impression and confirmation of the day – that he was happy. Even though we're faced with many challenges and issues, there are good things going on in our communities.

# *Bristol Bay Region*

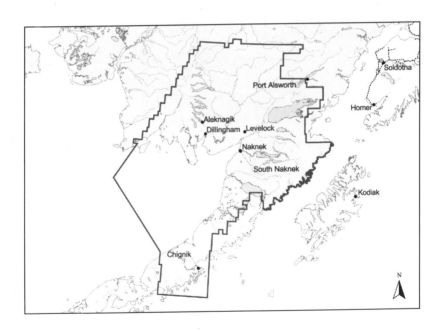

**BRAD ANGASAN** *was born January 2, 1972, about two weeks after passage of the Alaska Native Claims Settlement Act of December 18, 1971. Angasan is a shareholder in Bristol Bay Native Corporation because his mother has gifted some of her shares of stock to him.*

*Angasan lived in the Bristol Bay village of South Naknek until he was five years old. At that time, his father Trefon Angasan moved the family to Anchorage where he accepted a position with Bristol Bay Native Corporation. Although Angasan grew up in Anchorage, he maintained his ties to his village and participated in the Bristol Bay salmon fishery every summer with his father. After graduating from West Anchorage High in 1990, Angasan attended three years of college in Colorado and then returned to Alaska because he felt he was losing touch with his Sug'piaq Aleut culture. He graduated from the Alaska Department of Public Safety Academy in Sitka in 1993. He was married, and the couple moved to Levelock where Brad worked as a Village Public Safety Officer. The VPSO program is administered by the Alaska Department of Public Safety to maintain law enforcement in rural communities.*

*In a letter to Governor Tony Knowles, Angasan described the difficulties facing VPSO's. "In my short time of just under two years, I have worked seven deaths, four alcohol-related. . .The Legislature claims not to have enough money to give VPSO's a standard starting pay of $14 an hour plus geographic differential. Please try to imagine what your life would be like if the city you lived in had only 10 to 15 police officers instead of 100 to 200. If Fairbanks only had five policemen."*

*Angasan, his wife Annette and their daughter Spirit Snow live in Dillingham where Brad accepted a position as VPSO program manager for the Bristol Bay region. Angasan served as a member of the Rural Governance Commission, named by the governor. He was interviewed August 31, 1998.*

**I**t stripped our family of its structure. With structure you have frame, walls, windows. When my dad became involved with ANCSA, our family structure crumbled. And 20 years later we're finally getting the windows up. Our family structure is once again healthy, but with a lot of consequences. No longer are my father and mother married.

I was born just a few weeks after ANCSA. I grew up in the village of South Naknek until the age of five. And because my father had taken a job with the Bristol Bay Native Corporation, we moved to Anchorage. This was, for a five-year-old, a particularly rough time to be leaving essentially the womb of the life of your village, a very close-knit community. Having to leave that was very stressful.

This was also about the time that my parents got a divorce. I was about seven years old. We had lived up here, and I was living with my mother. And I would bounce back between my father and mother, spend the summers with my father in Bristol Bay, in the Village of South Naknek, commercial fishing. I'd spend about four months out of the year with my Angasan family. I'd come back to Anchorage and go school. And I did this up until my high school graduation. And it was about then I realized that I had to get out and see life on a broader scale.

Pretty much at the drop of a hat I went to school at Western State College in Colorado. I had very limited financial resources, the majority of the money coming from the Alaska state student loan program. I didn't want to end up to be one of the unfortunate residents of the village who didn't have the opportunity to get out, see life.

Ultimately, my decision has been to move back to the village, but with the experience of getting out and meeting people and getting a post-secondary education and having that opportunity. And I really didn't want to end up wondering all of my life what's America like? I know people that are 30, 40, 50 years old that have never left Alaska. Maybe that's something to be proud of, but what if they just didn't have the opportunity? I didn't want to end up like that.

Four years ago, I ran into – literally – my childhood sweetheart, Annette. She is a young lady that I had a crush on since I was eight years old. After a very quick month of courting we eloped. My father didn't like that too much. I came home one day and said, "Dad, I'm married." And he was very sullen for about a year, until the birth of my daughter, Spirit Snow. And that is amazing right there, the life that we produced into this world, the impact that she has upon my family. It's allowed me and my father to bond a lot better. It's just amazing.

About two years ago, I took a job as a Village Public Safety Officer in the Village of Levelock. I have a lot of emotional feelings about the VPSO program – a lot of good ones, a lot of bad ones. The bad ones are from the failure of the Legislature to provide adequate funding for the development of the VPSO programs throughout the state.

Incidentally, I gave some testimony to the House Finance Committee last year on the VPSO program. I was so appalled and amazed that some of these legislators had no idea what a VPSO was. Their idea was that a VPSO was either a security guard or a medic. And, just to let you know, as a VPSO, 90 percent of the job you do is police – community policing. You become the police officer in the community. The other 10 percent of the job is divided up between search and rescue, fire and medical and preventative programs. Ninety-seven percent of the job is alcohol-related. Ninety percent of the crime is alcohol-related. And that's a pretty conservative level. It's amazing how much alcohol has saturated the villages. This burdensome cloud is rained down upon the village and holds the community to a lack of thriving, apathy. It's a really ugly disease, alcoholism.

As a VPSO, I've seen some drug abuse, but not too much. It's out there. Don't let me fool you by saying that I haven't seen too much.

More recently, I was nominated and appointed to the Rural

Governance Commission. It's a 22-member board of people appointed by Governor Tony Knowles to figure out what is going wrong with our tribal government system and its status with the State of Alaska. Why isn't the tribal governance system thriving? What's wrong with it? What can the State do to improve their position with the tribal governments throughout Alaska? The federal government has recognized tribal governments within the State of Alaska, but the State has not.

Right now, I think the real big issues that Alaska Natives face, the young Alaska Natives, are the issues of subsistence, local law enforcement, the right to tax, just to name a few. The deal with subsistence: You know, you hear the idea that we don't want the federal government to come in and take over subsistence. A lot of people don't realize that the federal government already manages subsistence game. However, the subsistence fishing is maintained by the State. And, the problem right now is that the State cannot find a happy medium between Alaska Natives, non-Alaska Native rural residents and sportsmen, who pay a pretty hefty sum of money to the State of Alaska to come in and hunt, take game. That's a disgrace. I mean it's terrible. Although sportsmen throughout Alaska contribute a lot to the local economy, we cannot lay the fate of the Alaska Natives as well as the rural residents – their fate – in these people's hands.

And, if we continue to elect legislators who have lived in Alaska for 10, 12, 13, 15 years, and have never set foot in a rural village – a real village – then they're going to succeed in slowly getting rid of the Alaska Natives. It's a slow death. You're taking away all the rights. You've taken away the right to land. You've granted Native allotments, and you find out that your Native allotment's in a national park, and for the good of the country they take your Native allotment away because it happens to be a prime source of economic development. It's a real sad story. That would be my experience, my family's experience. And we're just one family out of thousands of Alaska Natives.

You can only bend so much before something happens – some kind of chain reaction, whether it be a political revolution of some sort, or some kind of a backlash. And last year, we as Alaska Natives bent so far before we started to get some light focused on us with the Native March. I wasn't able to attend, but I was able to listen to it on the radio, watch it on TV. Such a beautiful thing to happen but such an unfortunate purpose for being there – standing up for our subsistence rights.

The Alaska Natives have taken a lot from the Russians, and then finally America, the United States. They've given up everything. Their entire land. Traditionally, there was no land ownership.

And so far, the United States government – Westernized cultural upbringing – has succeeded in getting rid of those traditions. Our traditions are now in books, rarely practiced and rarely seen. It becomes more of a novelty than an everyday way of life, which is very, very sad. And I can't knock this Westernized style of living because I drive a relatively new car. I wear cotton clothes, eat canned food. But I also refuse to pay four dollars a pound for beef in my village. I am a subsistence hunter. It's in this order: I am a husband, father, hunter, Native and then a resident of the United States. Because if everything fell down behind us, around us, Alaska Natives are still going to continue to self-govern. No matter what. You can put all the printed paper you want in front of us, but we'll still self-govern.

I'm the oldest of three children. I have one sister who is 22. She just gave birth to a very healthy baby girl two months ago. And I have one brother who's 14. My sister – she's a very talented young lady. She works for the Bristol Bay Area Health Corporation. Ironically, she's the one that started getting me involved with the AFN Youth Convention. She was about 11 years old, and to be a part of the AFN Youth Convention, you have to be a certain age. Well, she would sneak into the convention, the AFN Youth Convention and claim to be a delegate. And they'd let her. She'd lie about her age. She did this for about five years. She became highly active within her youth core group and was an AFN youth chairperson for two years. And this opened my eyes, really.

She now lives in the village of Chignik and is a traveling health aide. She is married to a wonderful Aleut named Harold Odomin. He does an excellent job taking care of his family. And they have an incredible family structure. I think this is due in part to the fact that they do not drink or do drugs. They maintain a healthy lifestyle. He, too, probably more so than I, is dependent on subsistence hunting and fishing because he's in a more isolated area of Alaska, down on the Alaska Peninsula. And, instead of paying four dollars a pound for meat, he probably has to pay six dollars a pound.

*Did this focus on a healthy lifestyle stem from your past?*

Absolutely. You know, I was just having a talk with Marlene Johnson from Sealaska, and she was telling me how fun my dad used to be in the '70's and the '80's. It was a fast-lane type lifestyle that I think a lot of people were involved with at the start of the ANCSA corporations, unfortunately. It was the fast-track, going out, drinking your booze, doing your drugs, the socializing – Anchorage-city socializing. These people spent 90 percent of their lives in their rural village, and all of a sudden they were overwhelmed by our miniature "big city." And that was limited to the bar. I hear these stories of all these bars that don't exist any more, like the Monkey Wharf and Montana Club and how wild and crazy they used to be. And, these capitalists, the bar owners, they really took advantage of the Alaska Natives.

*Was it taking a toll at home?* Oh, big time, yeah. It did. It stripped our family of its structure. With structure you have frame, walls, windows. When my dad became involved with ANCSA, our family structure crumbled, and 20 years later we're finally getting the windows up. Our family structure is once again healthy, but with a lot of consequences. No longer are my father and mother married. My mother lives down on the Kenai Peninsula with her husband. They live a healthy lifestyle, but with an incredible lot of damage, as a result.

You know, many people think Westernized lifestyle is inevitable. Maybe it is. I don't know how much of a part ANCSA played in dissolving of my family. Don't get me wrong. My family is actually very strong, has a very strong family structure. But it took years to get it to that point. My entire family, every one of my uncles and aunts, all 10 of them on one side of the family, have been affected by drugs or alcohol. I've seen it in my family. As a VPSO, I see it every day. And there's not much you can do about it, not when there's a lack of funding for the preventative programs. And, it's because, like I said earlier, we are continuing to hire, elect legislators who have no business being there and dictating the lives of Alaska Natives, voting on these super sensitive issues of subsistence.

*When did you have a sense of being a Native?* Children can be very, very cruel. Growing up in the city of Anchorage, your identity when you first get here is you're an Alaska Native. You know no racial barrier when you're growing up in a village. And you come to Anchorage, and you hear the racial slurs. I don't know how many times I heard "Klut," which is a derogatory statement to Alaska

Natives. Terrible words like that, many others, "salmon cruncher," something a kid would say. I grew up with these words. I remember being little and going home and telling my mom that I wish I wasn't Native, that I wish I was white. Very sad.

In high school, 90 percent of my friends were white. I tried my hardest to fit in as a white person, to live like a white person, to be part in all of the white people's activities – going to parties, getting drunk, acting like a fool, delving into forms of drug abuse, marijuana. There were things that I didn't think were fun, but I did because my friends were doing it. Say we were driving along with a bunch of friends, and somebody would see a drunk person walking down the road, and they happened to be Native. My friends would poke fun at them. Very painfully, I would be part of that, and I would poke fun at them as well. I did not want to, but for the fear of rejection from my peers, I did it. And I'm sure you've probably heard that a lot.

People call that "peer pressure," and for the longest time I'd never really believed in peer pressure because when you're in school, and the teacher's telling you about "peer pressure," you're looking at a white teacher who's telling you that these are white kids and they're "peer pressuring" you. I never really believed in that. I thought it was kind of racial. I started getting involved in these activities of smoking marijuana. It's something that I'm very embarrassed about, but I think it was an absolutely essential learning experience for me. It's very painful because no longer can I say, "I didn't do that." But I can say, "I've done that. And believe me you don't want to do it."

*When did you have a positive sense of being Native?* Well, actually when I was little. My dad would sneak me these Bristol Bay delegate buttons, AFN buttons. I was very proud of these because they said, "Bristol Bay Native Corporation – BBNC – Delegate." And the word "delegate" sounded like such a powerful job. It was just an amazing job. He would give me these buttons, and he'd type my name onto the little placard, and I would wear these buttons. I was very proud of that. I was very proud of the Alaska Federation of Natives. When I said the name it sounded very powerful. And it is indeed a very powerful organization. Something to be proud of – that we are united in a very powerful structure.

Later on, the positive influences started happening the last two years of high school when my Native youth group teacher, actually one of the Polagio girls from Dillingham, wanted me to get involved in the Native Culture Club. And I was very reluctant because I didn't want people to poke fun at me. It wasn't the cool thing to do. But then I did go to a meeting, and I saw that these were people that were just like me. They were Natives.

As you're growing up, if you wore a certain brand of clothes you were cool. And if you didn't, you weren't cool. And you didn't want to hang out with "uncool" people. And these people that went to my school – some of them wore the same clothes I did. Some didn't. The ones that didn't wear my style of clothes, I didn't like. That was horrible. But around that time, I started to identify with their personalities rather than their style of clothes.

*The Native Youth group?* At first I didn't like it because it was change, and something I wasn't good at was change. I developed this womb-type comfort with the people that I had socialized with. But then they started talking about things that I could identify with, like certain Alaska Native issues – hunting and fishing. I'd always been proud of being a fisherman because fishing was something I had done all my life, and my earliest memory with a fishing boat was when I was three years old, going out on a little bow-picker, CWF-23, with my mom and dad. It was just one of the most wonderful feelings in the world.

I started recognizing that these people were similar to me. Their families left the village. They came to Anchorage because Anchorage was where the economic development was, then I started becoming friends with these people. I started becoming defensive with my other friends who were knocking my Native peers, making fun of them because they looked "funny," talked "funny" because they had an accent. A year or two before I would have said, "Yeah, he sounds funny. He talked like a Native." Now, it was like, "What's your problem? He's alive. He's human." Those were my first identifiable positive experiences with being Native.

*Do you have a Native hero?* Yeah. My Native hero, absolutely, 100 percent all the way, would have to be my dad. He's totally self-made. He was a young, burly guy growing up in the village who became active in Alaska Native issues facing his generation and my generation. And he wanted to be part of it. And he did. He got involved. He's a Vice President of Bristol Bay Native Corporation. He's on a number of boards. He just served his last term with the Alaska Board of Fish. He's a very busy person. He's given up a lot of time for his job, a lot of time with his family.

He is the voice in my Native region of Alaska that you hear

when something is not working right with Alaska Natives. He's the one that people turn to. And I realized that about probably my freshman year of college in Colorado. Mom sent me one of the articles he had written in the *Anchorage Times* before they sold to the *Daily News*. And it started dawning on me, man, my dad, he's a pretty powerful person, a lot of pull here, a lot of ideas. And he would write little articles: growing up in the village, subsistence life in the village. The *Anchorage Times* back then advocated for Alaska Native rights because they allowed people like my dad to be guest columnists. Unfortunately, he doesn't do that any more. I know he won a writing award – a small award. But to me it was like a big trophy because I started becoming more and more proud of my dad and what he was doing and what cause he was fighting for, the Alaska Native cause – survival and sustaining future life for the Alaska Natives, not only in Bristol Bay, but throughout the state of Alaska. We're all linked. We're all Alaska Natives. And whatever right we're going to have to give up, my neighbor in Barrow is going to have to give up.

*What are your feelings about ANCSA?* I don't want to label myself a victim, but I was born January 2nd, just literally days after the cutoff date, December 18th. If anything, I'm probably one of the oldest "new bloods." I guess that was the word that they used in the early '90's – "new bloods" or "descendants of ANCSA." ANCSA created an incredible amount of dilemma for the Alaska Natives. The corporate system is based on assets. Basically the corporate system is designed to fail, with the asset being the land. Native corporations' holdings – the land – that's a terrible gamble for Alaska Natives.

We literally took people who were independent as subsistence hunters and fishers, gatherers of wood from the village. They had no idea what the corporate lifestyle was like, and we put them in these big jobs. They had no idea what they were doing. All of a sudden, overnight, these guys went from chopping wood, smoking fish to sitting in an office building with thousands and hundreds of thousands of dollars at their hands. And they had no idea what to do with it. And we call this "job opportunity" now. Native corporations that weren't so successful, didn't have very much influence, failed miserably, and almost at the expense at the very soul of what Alaska Natives have right now, and that's the land.

That's a very terrible situation to put a group of people in. The lawmakers come in say, "Hey, we want to set something up for you and we know it's going to work." Maybe the very first developers of ANCSA probably had the very best intentions. They probably wanted Alaska Natives to thrive and maintain control of their land and their people, but some places it didn't work. It wasn't working. And just now some of the corporations are finally starting to dig their way out. And that's not just limited to the regional corporations. That goes all the way down to the village corporations. And I know village corporations that were literally abandoned because they were failing so miserably. They were in the red, big time. They were trying to operate. Nobody wanted the job. Terrible.

I have about five shares gifted to me by my mother. My daughter has 22 shares gifted to her by her grandparents. And my wife, she's older than I – she's a full-blood stockholder. She's got a hundred shares of stock.

It's really weird how you were allowed to register under different corporations, no matter what region you were from. I have relatives that live in Bristol Bay that registered in CIRI, the Roehl family. My friend Jason Metrokin: He's a Koniag from Kodiak. He's a Bristol Bay shareholder gifted to him by his grandfather who grew up in Kodiak, but was still allowed to register under Bristol Bay.

*Should stock be created for those born after December 18, 1971?* I've heard a lot of argument about this. And I really don't think it's necessary to adjust for the future generations. The idea of gifting and willing stock is a really efficient method, and I think we ought to stick with that, rather than having to expand and degrade the stock, allowing the children to be shareholders. It's unfair that we as children born after December 18th are not shareholders, but in order to keep the integrity of the stock, I think it's essential that we continue on with the method of granting, gifting and willing stock.

*Is there a clash between corporations and Native culture?* Absolutely. You cannot base your culture on money. Money makes, unfortunately, the world go around right now, but we can't identify who we are by the amount of money we make. If we are a corporation that failed miserably – we had to liquidate everything – we're still going to be Alaska Natives. We have no value financially. We're human beings, and to isolate your culture on an economic value is impossible. It doesn't make sense at all. That's ridiculous. We don't have a choice but to try to operate our corporations as Alaska Natives.

I'm very angry about some of these corporations that hire non-shareholders, non-Alaska Natives for the really good jobs. For my region, where we're pumping out young adults that are going to get their post-secondary education and are not being fairly looked at, that's not fair. Alaska Natives who are from their regions and are shareholders have first priority. And I've heard that some of the corporations don't do that. I'm not one to judge, but that puts the idea in my head that the possibility of me not being hired is there. And that's a scary, scary situation. And I don't like to think that way.

*Personal goals?* The tribal government system is evolving almost at an hourly rate. We've gotten issues: The subsistence issue is one of the biggest, if not the biggest, issue we as Alaska Natives are facing today. I have found employment through my regional corporation's nonprofit, the Bristol Bay Native Association. I really enjoy working there, working in the social services, the tribal government operations. And if I can continue on in preserving the future and allowing my daughter to grow up in an Alaska Native community, operated by Alaska Natives – self-rule, self-determination – then I will continue to do that for her generation. Then when it's her time, she will continue to do that for the next generation. That is my goal – to allow my daughter to grow up in a good tribal organization. And then keep this perpetual.

The focus now is more on tribal. Our Native corporations are pretty healthy at this time. And I'm sure if the Native corporations were failing pretty miserably, then that's where I would be at right now. But right now, the danger zone is the tribal government system, the right to self-rule.

I believe that Alaska Natives living in the rural Alaska communities, absolutely should be left alone to continue their own form of tribal government. Because if they are not allowed to do that, then who will? The State of Alaska certainly isn't going to spend the money to send somebody out there to perform daily tasks of living. That'd be too inefficient. They wouldn't think of doing something like that. And actually, I think the State of Alaska is stabbing themselves deeper in the heart whenever they try to get rid of the tribal organizations throughout the state. I've heard representatives say one government works efficiently, 226 impossible. Well, yeah, but if these 226 are ruling their own, then the one government has no business taking part of that. Alaska Native tribes are very efficient people. They know how to live their lives efficiently. People who don't live there, I mean, have no right in making decisions for us.

I was appointed to the Rural Governance Commission by Governor Tony Knowles to find out why the 226 tribes throughout the State of Alaska are not working in sync with the State. What can the State do? What can this commission do to establish a boundary for the State of Alaska to follow? As commissioners, we've already determined that tribes do exist in Alaska. It will be up to the administration to follow and implement that.

I understand that there have been commissions in the past that have said the exact same thing we are saying. But we can no longer ignore the Alaska Native community. They have to recognize tribal government in Alaska. If they fail to do that, then I don't know what the State of Alaska is going to do because we as Alaska Natives will continue to live, continue the right to self-management no matter what. I will still hunt. I will still live in the village no matter what rule or paper they put in front of me. I'll still be a fisherman.

*JASON METROKIN was born on April 29, 1972, in Anchorage. He is an Assistant Vice President at the National Bank of Alaska, Corporate Relations Department in Anchorage. His work takes him to many rural communities, and it gives him an opportunity to learn more about his Alaska Native heritage as well as current issues facing rural Alaska. Previous to his current position, Metrokin completed NBA's Management Training Program. After that, he spent two years as a loan officer in Ketchikan.*

*Metrokin grew up in Anchorage playing hockey. He continued playing hockey through high school and college. He currently plays for several adult league hockey teams and makes time in the summer for the Midnight Sun Running Team, softball and other outdoor activities.*

*Metrokin's mother, who is non-Native, is originally from Massachusetts, and his father, who grew up in the Bristol Bay community of Naknek, is the President of Koniag, Inc., the regional corporation for Kodiak Island. Jason inherited shares in Bristol Bay Native Corporation when his grandfather Walter Metrokin died.*

*Metrokin graduated from Service High School in Anchorage in 1990 and graduated from North Adams State College in Massachusetts in 1994 with a Bachelor's Degree in Marketing. He was interviewed July 15, 1998.*

**A** corporation down in the Lower 48, or a non-Native corporation in Alaska: if they don't like their corporation, shareholders can sell their shares. And they can get out. But as a Native regional corporation shareholder, this is their life. If they have a problem with their regional corporation, yes, they have voting rights. Yes, they have their say. But they just can't pick up and sell their shares and get out. That's not a possibility.

My mother is from Revere, Massachusetts. My father is a Koniag shareholder. In fact, he's the current Koniag President. I'm not a shareholder of Koniag. I'm a Bristol Bay shareholder through inherited shares from my grandfather, Walter Metrokin. His 100 BBNC shares were basically divided between myself, my sister and one of my cousins. So we each have 33 1/3 shares. My sister is 29, four years older than me. She was born in Kodiak and raised in Anchorage. My father was a commercial fisherman during his youth, but then he got involved in the National Guard. He was in the National Guard for 30-plus years.

I was born and raised here in Anchorage. My family background is kind of interesting. My mother is from back East, my father was raised in rural Alaska. Then, once my mother moved to Alaska, she moved to Kodiak with her parents as a Navy dependent. She met my father, and they started their family in Kodiak where my father was a commercial fisherman, as were his father and his father. So, that's the background, which isn't my background at all. Mine's quite different. Just before I was born they moved to Anchorage – my mother, my father and my sister. They have been here ever since. People have asked me recently a little bit about my background, and they take the name, the last name, Metrokin, and they just assume it's from Kodiak or Bristol Bay. Well, it is. But that's not where I'm from. I was raised here in Anchorage under the city lifestyle.

So upon graduating from college, I decided to move back to Anchorage where right after college I got a job with National Bank of Alaska in the management training program. It was an interesting experience because I have a degree in marketing, and I never thought that I would become a banker. That was the last thing on my mind. But I had heard through the grapevine that working for a bank was kind of interesting because you could really use that background and take it anywhere you wanted to go. So I thought it would be a good place to start.

I went back to Kodiak quite a bit, actually. I still have some relatives there. At the time of my childhood, I had quite a few relatives in Kodiak, both on my mother's and my father's side. I'd go about once a year or so. It was just for vacation – visiting relatives and fishing in the city of Kodiak. It wasn't until recently, working for NBA, that I got a chance to go back and see some of the villages of Kodiak Island, which was really interesting.

I attended North Star Elementary School here in Anchorage and Hanshew Junior High, then Service High School. I always had a sense that I was Alaska Native. The last name is a familiar name to some people, and there was the interaction with my relatives, who on my father's side are Alaska Natives.

To be honest, I would say I really didn't have a true sense of being an Alaska Native until I started working for NBA and traveling. I'd never been off the road system, other than someplace like Kodiak. Then I got a chance to start traveling and talking to people from other places. That's when I got a sense, hey, these people are a lot like myself, whether they were born in the village or born in the city, there are some ties there. You kind of have a sense of family, even though you may not be related to another person. I guess it was just knowing what my family did as they grew up, knowing where they were from, knowing the people they knew, the lifestyle they had. Although I didn't have that growing up, I still had a sense that it was part of me – the traditions, the foods, the way of life. I was never brought up knowing what subsistence was or knowing what different cultures

Alaska Natives had. Nor did I even know the various regions of the state, other than, there's the North Slope, the Interior, the Chain – the geographic regions.

I wasn't aware of the various Native corporations. I wasn't aware of ANCSA, other than I knew I was born after 1971, therefore I wasn't involved in the act, so to speak. And I can't say I blame that on anyone. You know, my parents were the type to say, hey, this is your lifestyle, coming from Anchorage. You have your friends, your local family. You do what you want to do. It's kind of interesting because I think eventually they thought I would learn about this type of stuff. Which I did, and I was happy that I did. They never pushed me one way or the other.

*Did you experience any discrimination?* No I definitely didn't feel any discrimination. I think that's because I was kind of caught in the middle with my Alaska Native background and my – I can't say typical Anchorage person background, but a lot of people in Anchorage just seem a little closed minded as to what goes on outside. *Did you hear any racist comments?* Oh, yeah, regardless of someone's race, although mean comments weren't ever made to myself. A lot of people don't even realize that I am Alaska Native. Just like any other race, there are people who are racist. That's unfortunate, but that's part of life.

I think it was because I really didn't have any close ties with other Alaska Natives. Even if I did, I probably didn't know about it growing up. I just thought, hey, this person is from outside of Anchorage, or this person is from Anchorage, or this person is from the Lower 48. They're all the same to me. Now, I take a look back, knowing what I know now, and I would think it would be a little bit different if I had been brought up in a lifestyle a little bit more close to rural Alaska. It was kind of ironic that more of my friends who are non-Native spent more time out in rural Alaska than I did, whether it was fishing or hunting or traveling. I always thought that was kind of funny.

I grew up playing hockey my entire life. In fact, I still have a copy of an article from the *Tundra Times* when I was in high school. In 1990 Barbara Crane wrote a story on me playing for the Alaska All Stars Hockey Team, traveling around the United States, going back to the National Tournament in New York – and then, also being Alaska Native, a Bristol Bay shareholder. That was a pretty big article and a nice photo. I think they did a great job, and it was just kind of out of

146

the blue that they did an article on me. But I would always think back to that article. Why would someone do an article on me in the *Tundra Times*? What is the *Tundra Times*? At that time, I had no clue. I just knew that I was Alaska Native, and possibly someone was interested in what Alaska Natives do. I was doing something somewhat special. I was a hockey player, traveling around the United States.

I went to school in Massachusetts to play college hockey. I went to North Adams State College. I did not have a hockey scholarship. It was a Division III school, and at that level they really don't give out scholarships for athletics, but I wanted to play and I knew I was at a level where I could not play Division I, like University of Alaska teams. So I wanted to make sure I was on a team where I played a lot, and plus got an education at the same time.

My degree is in marketing. I worked in Anchorage in the summers at Anchorage Golf Course, which is close to home. It was just kind of a summer job where my buddies worked as well, and we had fun.

I did receive some scholarship money from my regional corporation. My whole life I kept hearing, hey, Alaska Natives have opportunities within their own means to get scholarship money, employment opportunities, things like that. Why should I take advantage, being one quarter Aleut? Do I really qualify for those types of things? Should I qualify when maybe there's someone else who would benefit from it more than I? At the same time, it is my tie to my history, my family history. So the requirements for scholarships were that you fill out an application, you write an essay, you get letters of recommendation. Those things aren't difficult, so why not try? I think I received probably a scholarship of maybe $500 a year. Every bit helps, and I received student loan money from the State of Alaska to help me though college.

I inherited stock the year my grandfather died when I was in grade school. Some of the things I inherited were stocks, some stocks he had as an Alaska Native living in Kodiak. Some of those stocks were Native corporation stocks. That's all I knew. I knew that I received a quarterly dividend from Bristol Bay. At the time, hey, a couple bucks in your pocket every quarter of the year – it was kind of neat. You put it in the bank or you spent it or you did whatever. My parents never told me what to do with the money.

Really, I don't know a lot about Bristol Bay. From the business side I know a little bit, just because they are a customer of the bank,

NBA. I keep going back to my knowledge prior to working for the bank, and it was very minimal. It was my current position that really educated me on the various subjects of ANCSA, ANILCA, land rights, Native corporations, Native businesses, tribal politics, things like that. This is just from the last three or four years that I started learning about this stuff. There is my tie with my history, my community, my family. My tie is the knowledge. What does it mean to be an Alaska Native? Those are some of the things that go along with your race, your background.

To me, Native culture is everything and anything that myself or anyone as an Alaska Native feels. My Native Alaskan culture is very different from someone else's Alaska Native culture. I believe it's the lifestyle, the traditional foods, the interaction with your community – and your community could be the State of Alaska or your village, it doesn't really matter. It's your language and your geographical background. I know a few words in Aleut not because someone really taught them to me. I know them because they're on bumper stickers or someone says, "Camai," when you walk in the door. In the Alutiiq Region or, as I travel with the bank, I pick up words, whether they are in Yup'ik or Aleut or Tlingit.

I think I do have a sense of what it means to be an Alaska Native. As I mentioned before, it's as of late that I got this sense. I don't hold any grudges. I don't feel bad about not knowing my family history or the state's history, the Native Alaskan history until just recently. I just had to take the fast track in the last couple years to catch up, but it was kind of interesting.

We had a seminar at the bank, and after the seminar, we had a lunch at the bank. Our keynote guest speaker was Rosita Worl. She is a very prominent Alaska Native from the Sealaska Region in every aspect – culture, history, politics, you name it. She tied all this together – the Native corporations, ANCSA, subsistence, tribal politics – all the things we talked about. Having her stand up in front of a group of business people, and say that she's been around the Native Alaskan lifestyle her whole life was very impressive. Even she said she doesn't know everything there is to know about ANCSA or these various things that we spoke about. It was really important because here I am trying to catch up as fast as I can, not only because it's interesting to me, but I'm getting paid to do it. It was comforting.

ANCSA is a confusing act. Still today, people are arguing over what it means, what's right and what's wrong.

*Do you have a Native hero?* I'd have to say I recently filled out an application for Leadership Anchorage Program, and one of the questions was do you have a mentor, and if so who is it? I said, yes, and I didn't answer the question "so and so" is my mentor. I just described who this mentor was. It was my father, the first person that popped into my mind. I figured that he is my mentor – being an Alaska Native, the closest Alaska Native person to me, and a business person like myself, and a person who has taught me most of the things I know. I've learned a lot as of late on my own or through other people, but most of my knowledge from Alaska Native culture, history, so on and so forth is from him. I think the biggest thing that I admire about him is his background, being an Alaska Native, raised in a village in Naknek and Kodiak. At that time Naknek was a fairly small community.

*What are your feelings about ANCSA?* Knowing how much of an impact it had on so many people in Alaska and beyond, and having a job where ANCSA was something I needed to know about, led me to believe that this is something important. Not only because it's part of me, but it's also part of my job, part of other people's jobs. No other state that I know of has something like this. It divided the state into the 12 ANCSA regions in an effort to try and bring people together, Native people.

Every region has their land, their people, their village corporations, their regional corporation, their nonprofits, so on and so forth. They're very diverse. I can't say whether it was a good idea.

I don't have much knowledge about those who worked on the act. Every once in awhile I'll read something. I started learning about ANCSA and some of the other public laws that have come out from the Alaska Natives Commission Report. For someone like myself, it's very overwhelming.

I never grew up in a surrounding where alcoholism is a problem or that I was exposed to other people who had a problem with it. I guess that maybe goes back to the fact that I wasn't born or raised nor did I live in a village where it's a smaller group of people, and you may be exposed to more problems.

*Should ANCSA have created corporations?* I'm kind of indifferent. As a business person myself, I'm very interested in the corporate hierarchy. At that time, to expose a group of people to this corporate hierarchy, I don't know if that was a great idea. Now the corporations are doing, for the most part, very well. Native people have definitely learned how to deal with it. At that time, 1960's, early '70's, I'm sure that there were at least some people that had an educational background in regards to business or some exposure to corporations. For the most part, I just don't think Alaska Native people at that time had a good grasp of how corporations should work, how they can work, how the shareholder and the corporation can benefit. I think it's just in recent history, the past five or 10 years, a lot of people are beginning to understand how this whole thing works. I guess I am saying that the corporation route may not have been the best way to go, but I don't know what other options there were. I wasn't around at the time. Obviously, the Native leaders at that time chose to go with this route, chose to be part of this act. How can I second-guess them?

I think ANCSA is very important. From my perspective, if I was being very naïve, I could say that I'm a shareholder of a regional corporation where I receive quarterly dividends. What kind of impact does that have on me? Well, very little. To someone else, this may be their only source for employment. This may be their only sense of culture or family. So, I can't say for me individually that ANCSA plays a big role in my life, because it doesn't. In my job, it plays a much larger role because some of these Native corporations, regional or village, are customers. They are people I deal with on a business level, therefore, this is like a "need to know" type of thing. So I think there are a lot of different levels to ANCSA. There's the personal level, there's the family level, there's the business level, there's the corporate level. It's a pretty broad spectrum, I think.

It seems like every subject of ANCSA is at least two-sided. There are always arguments. Younger generations – this whole "afterborn" or "new Native" subject – how can someone who was born after 1971 be a shareholder in a corporation? They're not an original shareholder, obviously, but if new shares are distributed to new Natives, afterborns, then that's the way they can play a role in that corporation. Is this going to dilute the shares of the corporation? Sure, it's possible. Will this new generation of Alaska Natives have the same ideas and the same beliefs as the original shareholders? Maybe, but maybe not. They have a different educational background. They have a different lifestyle. They have a different viewpoint on the history of Alaska. These may be the people that run those corporations in the near future. So I think that there's kind of a sense of uncertainty from elders – original shareholders – on the future of their corporation. Beyond that, if they start issuing shares to the younger generation, is their share going to be worth less? Are they going to start getting less as far as distribution? That's possible, too. I can see if this is the only source of their income or it's a very huge part of their personal economy, they might be worried.

*What about the corporations that have created stock for those born after 1971?* It doesn't affect me, that I know of. Take, for example, one of those regions that has issued new shares. It's a different stock as far as voting rights are concerned and things like that. I can't say if it's good or bad. I can see, say a shareholder from the Arctic Slope Regional Corporation – they get certain voting rights, certain shares, certain dollar distributions on a monthly, quarterly or annual basis. For the corporation to issue new shares to the new generation coming up, I would think that that has a fairly good-sized impact on that original shareholder or elder. If I was a person who did not have stock in a corporation, it would probably make me feel better to have stock. As a new Native, an afterborn, I would think that is important. That is their tie to their community. When I say "community" that includes the regional corporation, the village corporation, the region itself, the village, all those ties.

I can say that I would feel probably better about myself if I were to receive shares from my regional corporation – if I didn't have them already. At the same time, I've never really taken advantage of my position as a shareholder. I didn't know the issues. I didn't know the people. I didn't know who was running as a director. I'm not from Bristol Bay. I'm not living in Bristol Bay. And if I were living in Bristol Bay, and if I were a voting shareholder and someone from Anchorage who has never lived in Bristol Bay, has never spent more than a few days in my region voted, I would think I'd be upset. I can see it from other people's eyes, too.

You cannot compare the standard corporation that you would find elsewhere in the United States with an Alaska Native regional corporation. There's just no comparison, other than the hierarchy. A corporation down in the Lower 48, or a non-Native corporation in Alaska: if they don't like their corporation, shareholders can sell their shares. And they can get out. But as a Native regional corporation shareholder, this is their life. If they have a problem with their regional corporation, yes, they have voting rights. Yes, they have their say. But they just can't pick up and sell their shares and get out. That's not a possibility. So I think that that's really why there's so much dissension in some regional corporations in Alaska. Because it really hits home, some of these issues. They can't just back away. It's no mystery. I don't think any regional corporation is immune to dissidents. Some of the village corporations have family members fighting amongst themselves. I strongly believe that business and politics should not be co-mingled.

*What about the political clout of the regional corporations?* As a multi-million dollar corporation, you need to have a lot of clout. At the same time, for an individual shareholder to go against that corporate, political clout is very difficult for one person. I'm sure that's probably why a lot of the dissidents band together. They try to get a snowball effect going. If they can convince their brother shareholder, their sister shareholder, whether it's true or not, they can get that snowball building. If it gets big enough maybe they can compete with this political clout or compete with the majority of the shareholders.

When you're talking dollars, regional corporations rank very high. When you're talking political clout, they rank very high. When you're talking, being in the spotlight, being in the public eye, they rank very high. I think all those go hand in hand. It makes me feel good, as if I'm a part of something that's very big. It also makes me sensitive to the fact that these large corporations, with all the politics, all the money – someday this big rock could just fall out of the sky. Things have been up and down for the past so many years, but just like any other corporation, they can face bad things. What those bad things are could be anything, the shareholders, the natural resources.

If you were to ask me if Alaska Natives should have chosen ANCSA or the reservation lifestyle, the reservation lifestyle is out the window as far as I'm concerned. I believe this was the better choice.

When I visit a village, I do take the time to sit down with the tribe – the tribal leader, tribal members – and talk to them. I think the tribes play a very large role in the community. There may be a clash between corporations and tribes. I think the reason there might be such a clash is that a regional corporation has to put the well-being of all tribes or villages in that region first and foremost. From a tribal level, their priority is the village or the tribe.

*Personal goals?* Being at this stage in my life, not being married, my goals change often. One of my main goals is to move up the corporate ladder. I don't have any timeframe. I can't say the sooner the better, because why would you want to move up a corporate ladder without a sense of where you're going, the background, the experiences? I've been able to move at a fairly good pace anyway. I've been promoted to my current position as Business Development Officer in Corporate Relations where I actually deal with rural Alaskan business development. There are a lot of communities out there that do not have an NBA branch, but those communities are customers of the bank or there's potential for those communities to be customers of the bank. So that is in a nutshell my job, to go out and promote the bank and make sure that the existing customers are satisfied and at the same time, bring in new business. I would say that the majority of my job duties relate to Alaska Natives.

I do deal with the village corporations very often, as well as some of the regional corporations. From a village level, the dollars aren't there like they are with the regional corporations. I think as time has gone on, village corporations have grown immensely. At the same time, just as the tribes have had their differences with regional corporations, I think they do with the village corporations, as well. Creating village corporations gave the villages a sense of ownership, a sense of being a part of this whole act. It gives the village corporations a sense of some empowerment on a local level, and also a way to deal on a professional level with the regional corporations. Where you have your village corporation president dealing with a regional corporation president, it kind of levels the playing field a little bit.

I would hope to see the Native community of Alaska – this may be a far-fetched idea, but I'd like to see the Native community agree on more things. Some people will say, well, that's impossible. Through the course of this interview we've talked about many things that people just do not agree on, whether it's voting rights or shares or the structure of corporations or the access to land, down the line. But I think it takes a lot more communication among the people involved. I think it takes a lot more education. That's probably the biggest thing. I'd like to see Alaska Natives become better educated and more united on some of the issues. Everyone needs to keep more of an open mind and definitely take the time to look at both sides of the story. The framework of ANCSA was set. Now the corporations, both regional and village, and even the tribes for that matter: they are a part of this evolution of ANCSA. We wouldn't be out there teaching our own people about ANCSA if it wasn't important to us.

# *Calista Region*

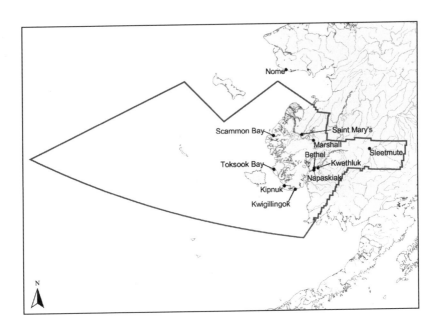

 **ANDREW GUY** *serves as Vice President/General Counsel of Calista Corporation. He was born June 6, 1962, at Bethel Native Hospital and grew up in Napaskiak. Both his parents are Yup'ik, and Andrew is a shareholder in both Calista Corporation and Napaskiak, Inc. Guy graduated from the University of Alaska Fairbanks with a Bachelor's Degree in 1981. He completed law school at the University of Colorado at Boulder in 1995.*

*He and his wife Minnie have four children, two boys and two girls. The family lives in Anchorage, but would eventually like to return to live in the Calista Region.*

*Guy is very active in Native affairs and has served on the Calista Corporation Board of Directors and the Napaskiak, Inc., Board of Directors. In addition, he has served on the Board of the Alaska Native Justice Center, and he is a member of the Alaska Bar. He was interviewed September 22, 1998.*

**I** keep thinking about my experiences, especially in law school where most of my classmates would compete – even take a critical case out of the library and maybe "misplace" the book where someone couldn't find it. That kind of environment is akin to a business environment. But here I was, willing to share my work and my outlines, that kind of stuff. And that's the same thing that we have in our villages – people who are in our corporations. They haven't lost that ability to work together, even though they might be from different villages or different regions.

I was born at the Bethel Native Hospital. I grew up in Napaskiak, which is about six miles downriver from Bethel. I had three brothers, two sisters. My parents, Paul and Sophie Guy, and siblings are still in the village. My dad's originally from Kwethluk. My mom's from Napaskiak. I am the second oldest, but I was the first son and first grandson on both sides.

We had a small house, basically one room with a divider. The kids would sleep together. It was a typical large family, Native village life or house, I guess. Right now there are about 350 people in the village. I'm practically related to everyone in the village – almost everyone. *Was it a traditional lifestyle?* I would say so. At the same time, it's a very religious village, too. The religion is Russian Orthodox, which allowed us to incorporate a lot of Native practices. One big example is Slavic, the way it evolved to the way it is now. It's a Russian Orthodox Christmas. It's a blending of Russian and Native. There are a lot of Russian Orthodox villages in the area, including Bristol Bay. Napaskiak – except for a family or two – it's all Orthodox. The other families are Moravian, but their kids are becoming Orthodox.

And back when I was a boy – I don't know if it's like this in the other villages – but they'd get all the boys together a few times a year and talk to them about the facts of life, how to comport oneself, how to act in the wilderness, all that kind of stuff. I think they still do it, but not as often as when I was a boy.

I was speaking Yup'ik before I was speaking English. The first teacher I had was Native – in the BIA system. He was helping us make the transition. We picked up English pretty fast. And by the time we were in the second grade, we were able to have a white teacher. I didn't really think anything about it. It was just something to be used at school. My parents understood that we had to make use of the language because that was what was the medium for teaching everyone back then. Nowadays, we have immersion programs where you are taught in any number of languages.

My mom hardly ever speaks English still. My dad's a fairly good speaker, but at home they always speak in Yup'ik. *Are they both full Native?* Yes.

Wintertime, there was schooling. Springtime, the people would start going off to spring camp. They'd be taking their big *assingaq* – that's a big sled – with the boat and then take off with the dogs. Then, they'd come back after breakup in the boat. Summertime, start preparing for fishing, that kind of stuff, berry picking. Falltime, about the same kind of stuff. Preparing for school.

We didn't have running water or flush toilets. In fact, during the majority of my childhood, we'd get our water from rain. And wintertime, we'd go down to the river and get ice for melting. I did a lot of that – picking ice. It was good exercise for the kids anyway. I think I was in fourth or fifth grade when I first saw a TV. "Sesame Street." Our BIA teachers had a television set, and they'd allow a certain number of kids to come in and watch TV. We had it at home probably a year or two later. I was just real curious, eager to see something like that. That's the adaptability of kids.

*Food?* We never went hungry. Plenty of food. *Ahgutaq* has always been my favorite. I just love Eskimo ice cream. Salmon, too.

I don't get tired of eating salmon in all its forms and all the ways that we prepare it. Ducks, geese and that kind of stuff. At the BIA school we'd have those lunches. I think that's why I don't like milk nowadays. The BIA milk wasn't very good. It was something to gulp down. Most of the kids were obedient – they'd eat the food that was prepared for them. *Even if they didn't like it?* Yeah. I know some of the food that I didn't like or didn't like the smell of, I'd just hold my breath and gulp it down.

*Did you have a sense of being Native?* In the sense that we had white teachers, I knew that I was a Yup'ik. It was just normal, who I am. It didn't make me feel any higher or lower or anything like that or that I was a minority in the sense that we use the word now. I was in the majority almost all my life out in the Yukon-Kuskokwim Delta.

*Do you have a tie to your culture?* Language is a big part of it. Even here in Anchorage, I still speak it. At home, even at work here. Then, there's the hunting seasons. That's when I get really homesick at particular times of the year. Spring hunting, fall hunting. In summer – fishing and picking berries. This is the first summer I didn't pick berries since I came here to Anchorage. I have to learn where the berries are here so I can do that. It's expensive to go home to do all that kind of stuff all the time. But I prefer to have food that I'm familiar with – store it in the freezer and have it over the year. You know, food is a big part of that tie. Then there's my family, most of whom are back in the villages.

*Education?* I went through the BIA system up until the sixth grade. We had very good teachers. They prepared us very well. I moved on to Bethel, which had the Bethel Regional High School for junior high and high school. *Was it a shock to leave your family?* At that young age it was. I remember I'd cry every night for about a whole month. But after that, I never really got homesick any more. Even when I went down to the Lower 48 – anywhere I traveled, I didn't get homesick.

My dad wanted me to have a good education. I was going to skip two grades, and he didn't like that. And in retrospect, I'm glad he did it the way he did because I got to participate in sports. If I had skipped two grades I would have been too small. I remember they did a test at the high school, and my lowest grade level was ninth grade level, and that was at the time I was a seventh grader. And my reading was at the college level.

I started reading at a very young age. I got started on comic books. My dad likes them. At the BIA school we had a row of books, maybe three shelves high on one wall. By the time I left the village, I had almost read all the books. Most of the books were about history. That's what got me interested in history, too. In fact, I majored in it for awhile before I changed to another major in college. I think a lot more should be taught about our own history. I didn't have anything of that. The only history I was exposed to was Western history: Columbus discovered America, that kind of stuff. The only Native history that I got was from the old people talking about the old days whenever they got together. That's when I really listened, too, nowadays even.

I went to the University of Alaska Fairbanks. I stayed in Alaska because it was the only school I could afford. I paid my own way with help from my dad the first two years. So I was kind of limited in my choices. Plus, Fairbanks had a dorm and Anchorage didn't have a dorm back then. That's why I went there. Even so, back when I was going to school, the university was rich in oil money, and the School of Business Management, which was my major, was one of the leading schools in computer applications for business purposes. So I think I came out ahead in that respect with my business administration major. I was there all four years. After my second year, I started learning about obtaining scholarships. And I think that's one of the biggest reasons I stuck with it that first year and a half year especially. Because here I was shelling out my own money.

I'd get really homesick about hunting, the village life basically – people gathering for men's basketball, that kind of stuff.

As I was nearing the end of my undergraduate work, I started thinking that a bachelor's degree wasn't quite enough for the world today. So I started looking at the options that I had for graduate work. I considered an MBA, but I was getting tired of taking business courses. And then I looked at law, and to me it seemed like an excellent fit between business and law, especially considering the Native corporations that we have. That was a goal of mine, to be involved in ANCSA corporations.

At the school in Fairbanks, some recruiters came. I got application forms from some schools even though they hadn't sent recruiters. So I just took those and filled out my applications. I think there were seven schools I applied to. Back then, I remember hearing that you needed to apply to as many as you could because in all probability you'd be rejected by most of them. *What happened?*

Well, I got accepted by all seven. So that's when I started dealing – who wants me more?

I narrowed it down to three schools. Then I narrowed it down to Willamette in Salem, Oregon, because they gave me a full scholarship. But when I got down to Oregon and spent the whole winter there, I found that I couldn't handle the constant rain. So I started looking for another school to transfer to. And the school I decided on was the University of Colorado at Boulder. And that's where I finished up my law school. The climate is a lot more akin to here in Alaska. They also gave me a full scholarship. I wasn't about to move, even though I didn't like the rain, without a similar deal.

*Did you experience discrimination?* In Fairbanks, not really. There were other Natives from my region and other Natives from the rest of Alaska. And there were other races, too, but they were friendly. I got along well with all of them. I had friends with all the ethnic groups. Oregon, Colorado were another matter. They had local boys or kids that didn't like people of color, I guess. There was discrimination, or feelings expressed by what I call "rednecks."

One time, I was in a restaurant with two classmates. One is a Scandinavian type – white, blond, blue-eyed – and the other friend of ours is half-Japanese. And you could tell she wasn't full *gussock*. So we were eating at a restaurant, and these four guys – you could tell they were local farm boys – came and sat close to us and made a rude remark to our Japanese friend. I got mad and went and confronted them. They apologized. Well, the one guy apologized, the one that had made the remark. And we left it at that.

*Alcohol problems?* It's still a problem all over the region. You see people staggering around – and mostly men, hardly any women. The women seem to keep the family intact. My dad drank, but not often or even, I guess, in a really drunk kind of fashion. And he quit drinking when I was a young boy still. My grandparents: I never saw them drink, nor my mom. I guess I was brought up by a sober family.

*Native hero?* Actually, there's this guy – I never knew him, but I read about him. His Native name was *Ohyaquk*, which is translated to "neck." I think that's the correct name anyway. You've probably heard about Sequoia, who developed the Cherokee written language in about a decade or so. I'm not familiar with just exactly how many years. But this guy developed the Yup'ik written language once he became aware of the fact that it could be accomplished. He developed one within a matter of years. It didn't depend on the

English alphabet or any known lettering system. He developed it on his own. He's from the Lower Kuskokwim, that region. He really impressed me. He was a genius.

The thing is, we don't use the lettering that he developed now. We use the English alphabet to write out Yup'ik, the written Yup'ik language that we have now. There's basically two types, the old way, which is how the Bible was written, and the new way, which is what I learned. But I learned how to read the old way, too, back before I went to high school.

In my village, there was a guy that was a very good archer. His name was *Inista*, which translates into "someone who hangs stuff." Maybe it's in reference to the fact that he was a very good archer.

*What do you think of ANCSA?* I think we could have done better. But I understand that people who were working on this back in the early '70's or late '60's were limited or were working with the tools and the knowledge that they had back then. They got a good deal, considering that this was completely different from any other type of settlement that had been reached before. So I don't begrudge them anything. They accomplished what they set out to accomplish, and that was getting land and money for the Natives. The structure, I believe, could be improved on.

Well, the way I look at it: We had these Native organizations that are tribal entities that were in existence from way back. And they were totally ignored during this whole process. The way I look at it: this ANCSA is a settlement for individual Natives, although they're grouped into common regions. It's basically a settlement for individual Natives. And that's what creates a lot of the tension nowadays because the tribal entities have been totally left out.

I'm not really informed on the people that played a role in getting ANCSA. But I know that my uncle was one of those people, Phillip Guy. I've never talked to him about what he did. I've never asked him. Someday maybe I will.

*Was it a good idea to create corporations?* I don't think it was a good idea, just for the reason that the majority of the Natives were not a corporate kind of people. But I think they have to allow for a process or an entity that could develop the economic base for the Natives. Because economic development is what drives the world. In that respect, I agree with the focus on economic development. But I think it should not have been the main focus, for us, anyway.

*What about your village corporation?* Yes, it's one of those fairly good corporations. We've had dividends for the last 10 years or so. I got on the board about three years ago myself even though I live here in Anchorage. It's Napaskiak, Inc. Our biggest enterprise is the village store. And we're renting buildings to teachers and stuff like that. We have a big stock and equity portfolio. We've joined with a group of other villages, including Calista, in some region-wide and even now statewide projects. The dividends have been about 100 dollars a year.

*What about those who criticize Calista?* Well, they got into too many projects that they couldn't follow up on. And I think a large part of that was that we did not have this background in business which, I hope we now have addressed. I don't feel bitter about what Calista experienced. I feel disappointed about the opportunities that have been lost because of those losses. Because, I think, with the expertise and knowledge that we have now, we could do so much with what has been lost. But I'm a realist, so I'll go with what we have now and build upon it. It's a corporation that has recovered and is on its way toward being a good corporation in the financial sense.

*What about the young people born after the act was passed?* I think they really ought to be included – everyone. In fact, when I was a director for awhile at Calista Corporation, that was one of the things that I pushed: for Calista to include the "PANs," as I call them, the Post-ANCSA Natives. The board has placed it as one of their goals – enrolling the Post-ANCSA Natives. But they also understand that it can't be done overnight. Their goal now is to begin the process in 2001.

*What do you say to those who say I've never gotten anything out of my Calista stock?* I've never gotten anything out of my Calista stock, either. But that doesn't mean I'm going to work against my own corporation. I can't really persuade those people otherwise if they have such strong feelings about Calista. A lot of it has to do with events that were totally beyond our control, the fact that a lot of them can't get into any position that could afford whoever that person is some control over what happened. In the board of directors' case, a lot of that depends on the shareholders and who they trust to be sitting on the board.

I don't think negativism comports with being what a Native is, so essentially you can say negativism destroys Natives.

We've turned the corner, and I think our "sick days" are over. We do have a lot of projects – viable projects – that we have going, including our projects with our villages. We have a very good relationship with our village corporations. *Hasn't 7(i) made a big difference for Calista?* We gave up a whole lot of land to get that percentage. You look at the number of people we have: we got a whole lot less land than Doyon did. The way I look at it, we gave up land in order to be able to participate in the wealth of the lands of the other regions. Plus, you've got to realize that Congress fully recognized that the different regions would have different resources. They did a good job, I believe, in the fact that it benefited Calista and a whole bunch of other regions. That was the purpose for it.

*Is there a clash between the corporate focus on profit and culture?* There definitely is. That's why I am critical about the structure of ANCSA, the way it was set up. As I said, the main focus should not have been the corporate – economic development – aspect of it. But now, I've said and I've heard other people say that ANCSA is a sleeping giant. The corporate world: in mainstream Western society, you have these competitors, competing, going for business, driving the other people out of business, that kind of stuff. And I think the Native corporations, including the village corporations, got into that mode, which is totally contradictory to our culture. Or, I guess you could say our ideals of working together. But now, I think a lot of people who are in the corporations are starting to realize that our cultural ideals and corporations might not be mutually exclusive. We can have these Native corporations working together to enhance our lifestyle.

I keep thinking about my experiences, especially in law school where most of my classmates would compete – even take a critical case out of the library and maybe "misplace" the book where someone couldn't find it. That kind of environment is akin to a business environment. But here I was, willing to share my work and my outlines, that kind of stuff. And that's the same thing that we have in our villages – people who are in our corporations. They haven't lost that ability to work together, even though they might be from different villages or different regions.

Actually, I didn't like to hang out with those very competitive people. I had a few friends, and most of them were from the other Native groups – Indians from the Lower 48, Guam and Hawaii and the Philippines. Most of my friends were from those groups. *Did you get good grades?* I remember, the first year in Willamette: apparently, we had the highest number of minorities entering that class. During that first semester, white people were starting to grumble that we had too many minorities. Well, we went along and had our first finals. We only have one exam at the end of the semester. After the grades were posted, there were three of us in the top 10, and one of us was the highest in the class. That stopped the grumbling very fast. *Who was the top student?* An Indian friend of mine. *Were you one of the three?* I was one of the three, yeah.

*What about the clout that some Native corporations have today?* I haven't really thought about it, but as long as that clout is being used for the betterment of our Native people, I'm all for it.

*Your goals?* I don't see myself living in Anchorage all the time. Well, eventually I'd like to move back to the region, especially to my village. Because I would like my kids – two boys and two girls – to experience both worlds: not only the Anchorage life here, which to me is totally Western unless you make a concerted effort to practice your Native practices like hunting, fishing, that kind of stuff.

Not only that, village life is so much different. That is what I would like my kids to experience, too. It also helps them to speak the language. Right now, two of my kids are going to school – one in pre-school. But the language that they use all the time is English. My wife is from a village about 25 miles upriver, Kwethluk. We try to talk Yup'ik at home. But even during that time, they play with the kids around the neighborhood who only know English. So they're getting a big dose of English as opposed to Yup'ik.

*Do you have a vision for Native people?* The economic development aspect of ANCSA: we have to look long-term. Right now our culture might be totally geared toward – for most of the time – subsistence activities or commercial aspects of that like commercial fishing. Looking at the population boom that we're experiencing – just looking at the long-term trends – I think we have to prepare ourselves for the time when that part of our lives won't be such a big part, fishing and hunting and gathering. There's only so much we can do with natural resources. We have to plan for other endeavors: economic development. Jobs are what I look at as part of the answer.

**GEORGE OWLETUCK** *was born on March 13, 1965, in Bethel. He was raised in Marshall, a small village of about 300 people in the Calista Region.*

*Owletuck is a shareholder in the Native village corporation for Marshall, Maserculiq, Inc., as well as Calista Corporation. He served on the Maserculiq Board of Directors for four years. He went to St. Mary's Catholic High School and in 1983 graduated valedictorian. In 1986, he completed Aerospace Ground Equipment Mechanic Technical School at Chanute Air Force Base, Illinois. He received a Bachelor's Degree in Education from the University of Alaska Anchorage in 1995, and he has attended Gonzaga Law School.*

*After working as an intern in the office of Alaska Senator Ted Stevens, Owletuck worked for the Cenaliulriit Coastal Resource Service Area in St. Mary's, handling coastal resource management issues for 50 villages. He recently was the Natural Resources Director of the Alaska Inter-Tribal Council and is a vocal advocate for Alaska Natives' subsistence rights. He was interviewed August 3 and 4, 1998.*

T he reason I remember is because on the line, it said: "What percentage Native are you?" Blood quantum level. I knew that I could put in 100 percent Native, and I'd get away with it. But since I was taught to be truthful, I put in 50 percent Alaska Native. It stands on that record to this date. So that's why I remember ANCSA passing – because it had to deal with my identity. Who am I? Am I Alaska Native? Or, am I some mixture thereof?

Our family was raised in Marshall, Alaska. My parents are Alvin and Agnes Owletuck. My sisters are Clara – Shorty – she's now married to Moses. They have five children. Linda is my next older sister. She's married to Wesley. They have two kids. I'm third in line, the eldest son. Next are two brothers, Alvin, Jr., and Robert. Robert is married, and they have two children. My youngest sister is Rena, who is married to William Andrew. They have six daughters. And we lost one brother in 1986. Arthur, the one we lost, was born after 1971. Everyone else was born before 1971.

I grew up in a little village of barely 300 people. We went camping a lot. For spring camping we went with our grandparents, Irene and Vernon Evan, our Uncle Gabe and his wife Theresa and their two daughters. Camille and Agnes Boliver, our aunt and uncle and their children, went with us, too. They had five kids. And then the Fitkas went with us. We were all related to the matriarch and the patriarch of our family, so the whole clan went out to spring camp. We hunted muskrats for food. Ducks, geese – all the spring waterfowl were coming back. Our dads would teach us how to skin and stretch furs. We'd shoot the muskrats and skin and stretch their furs. Then we'd dry them and sell them on the fur market that spring after we returned from spring camp.

Summer camp was living in a tent in the woods for the sole purpose of drying fish. And we went with a different family to a different location, up the river. This was more of a neighbor family than a "family" family, but they were related in some way to my grandmother, so in a sense they were family through that distant relation.

So we spent six years – every summer – just living in a tent until TV showed up in about '76 or '77. And then we started living in the village and smoking our fish. It used to be no one would stay in the village and smoke their fish. They'd all leave the village to smoke their fish. Now many people just stay at the village. Just a few families go out camping nowadays.

Fall time, the women and the kids stayed home. The men and the young men went out fall camping for geese, ducks and moose. We had two different fall camps: One for waterfowl and another one for moose.

Winter was for school, of course. So when my dad went to winter camp, we couldn't really go until Christmas break. And he had his own winter camp for trapping, snaring beavers, to skin and stretch the furs to sell.

And the following spring, the cycle repeated itself. It was all cyclical. We were in tune with the land and the seasons for the animals to harvest. Those were the happiest times of my life. We were in a pristine environment – the wilderness.

I remember going canoeing. I was about eight years old, and I had a nine-year-old cousin and a 10-year-old cousin, and we all went out in his dad's canoe for hours. We were the men in our respective families. We took care of our families though we were just children. We would have guns, and we'd handle those weapons like any other adult. We were in a canoe traveling all evening and all night into the early morning hours, all over the country in the sloughs and the lakes, hunting muskrats. You would normally think twice about leaving kids in a canoe, but they trained us early to be careful. We caught on at an early age what a life-and-death experience it is to be living out in the woods.

My parents came from a generation where they punished them

for speaking the language. So in order to protect us, they primarily spoke to us in English and spoke to us in Yup'ik secondarily. So the younger we were in the family, the more they spoke English and the less they spoke Yup'ik. My older sister knows more Yup'ik than me, and I know more Yup'ik than the younger ones behind me. I understand more than I can speak.

Irene Evan and Vernon Evan: Vernon is our grandma's second husband. My dad's dad died. His name was Charlie Owletuck. So Vernon and Irene had a son Gabe, who was my dad's half-brother. And the Bolivers are our grandma's first husband's daughter. Agnes and Camille. Agnes and my dad are sister and brother.

*The effect of television?* This new generation that's been brought up in the last 20 years is more sophisticated than we were. We just came out of the woods, and they've been exposed to American and international culture all their lives from television. All we had was our own culture.

In those days, communications were so primitive – there was a lack of telephones, a lack of TV. We pretty much had public television and that was it. We didn't have bathrooms in the house before we moved into a three-bedroom house. Late at night we'd be watching TV, and if anyone would have to use the honey bucket, my mom said we'd have to turn off the TV because she thought the guy she saw in the TV would see us. The generation before us didn't really understand about TV. They thought it was a window into another world where not only did we see them, but they saw us (laughs).

Eventually, she got over that. TV became understood as to what it really is.

*Alcohol problems?* Yes. Our village was typical of every other village where there was no law enforcement except for tribal or council enforcement of law and order. As a child, from a very young age, I remember people yelling and screaming outside of our house in pitched battle. Three, four, five, six young men, of course, and young women, highly intoxicated. Screaming and fighting.

I've seen, as a young child, a man who was our neighbor. He and his brothers were fighting. He came in with a gash on his forehead. His brother hit him on the head with an ax. So my mom had to sew him up – stanch the blood flow first, sew up his gash And then I watched him eat. My mom forced him to eat. And he was a 200-pound, 6-foot tall young man in his prime, and my mom's 5 feet and maybe 125 pounds. My dad's bigger than her, but smaller than that young man. But in those days, our code of conduct was different than nowadays. We would never disrespect our elders. So, though this man was highly intoxicated and potentially dangerous, they still had that code of respect for elders. Our parents didn't fear for us kids or themselves. But when those young people were out – all night long they'd be yelling and fighting. So my introduction to alcohol and the use of alcohol was to see people stumbling drunk in the streets, fighting, drowning. Only later in the '80's did we see suicide.

I'll be quite honest with you. I was adopted into the village. I'm half Irish and half Yup'ik Eskimo. And the elders in the village would point at me and say, *"Gassay'aarr-aq."* That means, "Look at that white boy." And it hurt me very deeply. I didn't know who my natural parents were. I had an identity crisis. So in order for me to be accepted into the group I would hang out with the older boys, and the older boys were making home brew, and I would drink with them (laughs). Due to this identity crisis, I drank a lot in my youth. Fortunately, I finally found my natural mom and my natural family and pretty much got over that identity thing.

What really brought me back to the Yup'ik community and destroyed those ghosts of those elders who were pointing at me as a child and saying, *"Gassay'aarr-aq,"* was after I graduated from college, I moved to St. Mary's where my mom is originally from, my adopted mom. That's where I went to a Jesuit Catholic high school. So they knew me from '79 to '83. And they also knew my mom from the generation before me. So when I came back from college – rather than taking a cushy job in Seattle or Washington, D.C., or Anchorage or Juneau, I took a job out in the village. I brought a job out to the village from Bethel. It was a state job. We were under contract with the Association of Village Council Presidents in Bethel to use their office and administrative expertise to run this state program that originated from federal funds, the Alaska Coastal Management Program.

Out in Southwest Alaska, it's Cenaliulriit Coastal Resource Service Area, which is about 50 villages. Cenaliulriit means "people who work together along the coast." In that job, I represented the villages' coastal resource management issues. I took that job out of Bethel to St. Mary's in August of '95. The mayor and the chief elder of the village, Andrew Paukan, were at a dinner we were having for an elder who had passed away. They held a feast in honor of her memory, and I was invited to this feast. They sit the men first, the Yup'ik people, because men hunt and fish. They feed the whole village. It's proper.

So I was sitting with the elders, which is a great honor in itself. And I'm young. At that time, I was only 30, and Andy Paukan, who incidentally taught me Yup'ik in a classroom setting in 1980-81, my second year of high school in St. Mary's Catholic High School, told me, "When we start drumming this fall, you come drum with us."

I was shocked. I was stunned. I was speechless. I couldn't say anything, and I couldn't refuse. It was a direct order. I said, "Yes!" And I was told later by a wise lady – Lilly Afcan who lives in St. Mary's – "Those elders don't just ask anyone to drum with them. And you should drum with them." My oldest sister Clara said Lilly Afcan is wiser than most elders, and she is considered to be one of our wisdom-keepers.

So we drummed four nights a week for two and a half hours a night from October, November, December, January, February, March and April – seven months out of the year. I learned at least 30 Yup'ik drum songs that winter. And in order for us to be properly established as a drummer, we need to be introduced to the group and accepted by the entire Yup'ik community as one of their own.

Lilly Afcan's dad is another one of the three elders in our drumming group – there were 10 drummers. I was the youngest. Her dad is John Thompson, Sr. My Eskimo name was after John's dad. So John and his daughter, Lilly, were responsible for sponsoring me into the community. At the potlatch, which is in February, John introduced me to the crowd, and Lilly was behind me. That introduction is a means to say that I'm one of them. They do this for children normally. But I didn't get it done, so I was an adult when they did it. But they had to do it for me to be properly established as a drummer and as a dancer.

So that really was closure into my identity crisis – 25 years later. It really meant a lot to me. I was in tears when they did that. My parents were all proud, of course.

The young people nowadays have turned to our culture, our Yup'ik dancing and drumming, to embrace their own identity because they're a cosmopolitan people now. They've been raised on television. I've been in foreign countries, and I've seen young people raised on that same TV, people in Japan, the Philippines and the villages, who pretty much have the same values. And the values are what the commercial market puts on in their commercials.

All those young kids: they like Nike. They like all these commercial things. They all have the same value system. So the young people in the village – and this is my speculation because they've been raised in the age of television – they've turned to their own culture and embraced it by dancing and drumming, as establishing their unique identity. My observation is we're in a global village now from TV, and everyone has the same value systems or pretty much similar value systems, which originate from marketing products on television.

My age group: we weren't really interested in dancing or drumming. We were interested in embracing Western ideas. We were emerging into the Western world at that time in the early '70's. The world was coming to us slowly, and we were embracing that and turning our backs on our own culture to supposedly succeed in this new culture, the Western culture. So we didn't value dancing and drumming as much as we should have. The older people danced, and we didn't. We were the generation between the old world and the new world. We're like a bridge. Our formative years were before television.

*Education?* First of all, I remember reading comics at three years old. When I went to first grade, the teacher wrote the word "Bill" up on the chalkboard and asked us, "What's that word?"

I knew the word. "It's 'Bill.'"

"See Bill run. See Bill run fast." That first grade book was too easy for me. I couldn't stand those first grade books. The second graders would come to me and ask me to help them do their math. So, by the end of my first grade year, I was reading third grade books.

At least through eighth grade I was never with my age group. I was always doing my own thing. My seventh grade year I lived in Boring, Oregon, and went to school down there. It was a great culture shock to get there from a remote village in the wilderness, and it was an even greater culture shock to get back to the village because I could see the village with new eyes. I could see the village as an outsider looking in.

So when I did eighth grade in the village, Marshall, I knew I couldn't give up on school. More people in those days dropped out of high school than finished high school. And for good reason – you didn't need education out there because we could get everything we needed from hunting and fishing. We really hadn't established a cash economy yet. So there was low expectation for us in terms of educational achievement.

I wanted to go to a good school, so I went to St. Mary's Catholic High School. In school, they put us through a rigorous curriculum. They gave us critical thinking education. And I have a Bachelor's degree in education now, so I know the difference between public school and private school, and what we got at that private school was a prep school education that only the elite of America get. So I did very well in St. Mary's. They graduated me the valedictorian.

I went to UAF, though I had virtually guaranteed entry into Harvard and Stanford. Based on a National Education Development Test I took my sophomore year, the principal announced to the whole school that I and another student, who was a teacher's son, made the top 10 percent in the nation on the NEDT. So she tried to convince me to go to Harvard or Stanford, but I declined and went to Fairbanks.

After two years at Fairbanks, I didn't feel I was doing very well. And it goes back to my identity problem. I didn't really know who I was or what I wanted and didn't care. So I went back to the village, and I was a janitor for the city for about seven months, and then I joined the Air Force and moved overseas, came back four years later and went to college and did very well.

The Air Force opened my eyes to the international arena, specifically living in the Philippines for two years, Japan for a year and a half, Thailand for three months. I had that perspective to compare America to, and I had that perspective to compare our village to.

*Discrimination?* I saw it in the military, and I felt it. It was very insidious. The way they promote people in the military, pretty much the "good old boys" got the best positions. Like the NCOIC, the non-commissioned officer in charge, he'd be a good old boy. Although, they did promote minorities, and I saw minorities in leadership ranks. It was the lifers – we called them the lifers – who got those leadership positions who were minorities.

After that experience, I went to UAA and got introduced to the concept of institutionalized discrimination. I don't want to speak ill of UAA because I'm a graduate of that school, but they did have a problem. And I saw it at UAF in the early '80's: Natives were invisible. We had a feeling that we weren't wanted there. It hurt us.

174

It hurt us young guys.

My heroes are Gandhi, Martin Luther King and Elizabeth Peratrovich. Gandhi kicked out the British from India and returned India from a colonial country to an independent country after he got kicked out of South Africa for trying to remove apartheid. Martin Luther King, we all know his story. Elizabeth Peratrovich: she introduced a bill before the Alaska Territorial Senate to stop discrimination against Alaska Natives. When she introduced that bill, one of the senators stood up and said: "Who are these people, barely out of savagery, who want to associate with us whites of nearly 5,000 years of recorded civilization behind us?"

And when it came time for Elizabeth Peratrovich to speak before the Senate, she stood up and said, "I would not have imagined that I, who am barely out of savagery, would have to remind gentlemen with nearly 5,000 years of recorded civilization behind them of our Bill of Rights." These people stood up for what they believed in.

I got all A's in education courses. I wanted to graduate this time. I met my natural family, and I resolved my identity crisis.

I requested to work in U.S. Senator Ted Stevens' office, and they put me there in the summer of '92, along with his college interns. Being former military, an older student and one who worked in his Anchorage office as a volunteer, I knew how to get the job done. All summer long, I just cranked work out. And at the end of that internship, the senator said, "George, what are you doing this winter? Are you going back to Alaska?"

"Yes, sir, I'm going back and finishing up my degree at UAA, Senator."

"Well, talk to Barb in our Anchorage office and see if we can get you a job."

"Yes, sir." So he hired me on the spot.

So for the next two years I worked part-time as paid staff in his office in Anchorage, full time during the summers. And during the summers, I went to school part-time. And then the spring of '95, I worked as a legislative intern in State Senator Lyman Hoffman's office in Juneau.

I wanted to work for Yup'ik people, Yup'ik Eskimos. I wanted to be in the village. I wanted to go back.

*Do you have any other Native heroes other than Elizabeth Peratrovich?* I think my dad, Alvin Owletuck, Sr., is one. He was ordained a Catholic deacon, the first ordained Eskimo deacon for the Diocese of Fairbanks about 23 years ago. He's a very humble man. He's got an eighth grade education, but he's very community service oriented. He's served on the village corporation board of directors. He ran the fish processing plant when it first started up and did a good job. People really like him. The ladies, especially, tell me how sweet he is. He's got a sense of humor. He just had heart surgery, and three days later he was walking all over the hospital visiting sick people (laughs). And the day before he couldn't walk. I had to wheel him around in a wheelchair. So he's got that tenacity. And, of course, he raised myself, three brothers and three sisters, and he always held the highest standards of moral, ethical conduct, both from a Christian standard and also a Yup'ik Eskimo standard. So amongst my heroes, he's one of them.

William Paul is another one. I believe he was the first Alaska Native attorney. And he took on the fishing industry in Southeast Alaska. I'm very impressed by the man. He just did so much good for Native people during that time. He made a lot of powerful people angry at him, and they turned against him and tried to tarnish his name and reputation. So I could see how taking on powerful interests could be detrimental to your personal lifestyle. He had a hard time making a living because he was blacklisted. He's one of those guys – and this is why I admire him – he's not willing to accept the status quo, to toe the line. Neither was Elizabeth Peratrovich. They were willing to take on powerful interests on behalf of Alaska Native people regardless of the implications to their personal situation. There's always backlash, and they were willing to accept that.

I don't know as much as I should about ANCSA. I just know what the result is. And I have a peripheral exposure to the history and the players. I know that Congress and the State of Alaska were opposed to sovereignty of tribes. It's part of a termination policy, an assimilation policy where the greater society is trying to assimilate what they called the "heathen savages" in those days to be "productive citizens." I think the fact that Congress and the State of Alaska dealt with these new state-chartered corporations instead of, let's say, traditional councils or tribal government entities, was an effort to terminate tribes as sovereign governments and assimilate tribal members into society. And what better way to accomplish that than to force them to create these corporations that they'd have to learn how to run like every other corporate entity in America?

176

So I have a beef on one hand with the structure of the settlement. It took away from tribal governments. I guess the bottom-line of my beef is that we weren't really prepared to run corporations.

*Do you remember when ANCSA passed?* Yes, I do. I had to sign paperwork. The reason I remember is because on the line, it said: "What percentage Native are you?" Blood quantum level. I knew that I could put in 100 percent Native, and I'd get away with it. But since I was taught to be truthful, I put in 50 percent Alaska Native. It stands on that record to this date. So that's why I remember ANCSA passing – because it had to deal with my identity. Who am I? Am I Alaska Native? Or, am I some mixture thereof?

*Are you a Marshall village shareholder?* Yes, we've done very well in the past 20 years selling salmon to Japan, and we've had sound management. There was no mismanagement. We're fortunate in that respect. Our village corporation is still solvent. We still have a large amount of principal. And I learned the details of the corporation because I served on the Board of Directors for four years. It's Maserculiq, Inc., which means "the place where the fish spawn."

*Your feeling about the more successful corporations?* That's the best thing that could have happened to the Alaska Native community is those corporations that have succeeded. Because they're able to gain the ear of policy makers and effect policy. Money talks. So the intent of ANCSA worked in respect to those companies. And I like that.

*Is there a clash between corporations and Native culture?* Native culture – we were taught to never waste, and our first catch of any animal was distributed to the elders in the village. So we weren't so possessive about things. We weren't so self-interested. But when the profit motive came along, the bottom-line – and serving on the Board of Directors I could see, we make decisions based on the bottom-line. And sometimes those decisions, in the short run, aren't beneficial to the community or beneficial to individuals in the community. But based on the bottom-line, it's beneficial in the long run. So there's a certain conflict in the philosophy of the old ways and the corporate philosophy of make money or die.

*Can ANCSA be used to reach goals in the future?* I think so. I have to thank Calista Corporation for finally setting up scholarships for students within its region. And when I was in law school last fall, that scholarship money came in very handy. So I think educating the young through corporate scholarships is a great benefit to shareholders. Another thing is students come to our corporate offices and get work experience. College graduates come to the office and get work experience. I've even seen law school students come to our Calista Corporation office and gain extremely valuable experience. Andrew Guy is an attorney for Calista. He's a friend of mine from college, UAF days. He's very supportive of young people, especially young people to come work for him to gain that experience. So sure, the corporations are helpful in that respect. Education is very important.

*Do you have a vision for the Native community for the future?* There are so many things we could be doing. I think what's most important to us out in the village is the opportunity, the ability, to live off the land – hunt and fish. There's one problem – as Western culture has encroached into our villages, more and more of our freedoms are being taken away. There are restrictions on hunting, restrictions on fishing – punishment for hunting, punishment for fishing out of season.

My vision is that management authority is removed from centralized bureaucrats in Anchorage, Juneau and Washington, D.C., and that authority is delegated to the communities so that the communities could police themselves, regulate their own hunt. I'd like to see that. It's the arrogance of man to think we can manage creation. But we could manage the way we use the resources. I think that's more appropriate. Right now, the management decisions are being made by biologists from outside, with some input from villagers.

I just had a teleconference this morning with the Yukon River Drainage Fisheries Association. There were Fish & Game fisheries biologists, also members from the mouth of the Yukon all the way up into the Interior. And they were giving reports on subsistence catches, salmon in the river, the numbers. And the model of management is changing for the better, where they are allowing local participation in the process, which is good.

There's a challenge for young people in the villages. They get out of high school and pretty much have no opportunity in the village. I know some start to get into alcohol, get on the river in a boat, intoxicated. They have too much time on their hands. They need an opportunity to get out of the village and succeed in whatever they wish to succeed in, whether it be military or technical school or

178

college. I hope that our education system out in rural Alaska can improve to such degree that instead of just teaching the kids the basics, they need to emphasize career development. And we need to set up career paths – both nonprofits and profits – to cultivate these young people. So I hope we can accomplish that because statistically, of each age group, the young boys die off. And the young women, they have no one to take care of them because statistically their peers are dying, male peers. So some go on to college, get educated and marry non-Natives.

The corporations have a duty to their shareholders, not only fiscally, but socially. When we're in our posh nonprofit or profit corporation offices in the city, we lose touch with village people, and we need to remember where we came from and try to reach out and help the village people.

The feds and the state have created this culture of dependency. And my own observation is this: People weren't allowed to make decisions in the village. Before they made decisions, they needed permission from either the feds or the state government agencies. And I've seen meetings where federal or state government agencies are coming to the villages, and there's a question that the village needs to decide. The village won't decide. They'll ask the federal or state agency bureaucrat if it's OK for them to make that decision. That really bothers me.

And the policies that were imposed upon the Alaska Native community over the past 50 years were such that the result is a culture of dependency. In the early days, they weren't allowed to make decisions. They weren't even allowed to speak their own language. Their mouths were washed with soap. And those kids became adults, and, as a result, they had their healthy fear of bureaucrats. And the result was a sense of powerlessness. And this sense of powerlessness is destroying everyone. Our society's being destroyed by this sense of powerlessness.

We will reverse that. We're going to have the villages make their own decisions. We're going to have the villages involved in management, where the federal and state agency people must consult with us, rather than we consult with them. It's going to take decades to accomplish, and it'll take a new generation to witness this transaction so that they grow up and see that their elders are making the decisions, not the state government bureaucrats or the federal government bureaucrats. So we've got to show the young that they can make a difference.

We might use buzz words like "sovereignty" or "subsistence," but the bottom-line is self-determination. We will make our own decisions. We're not going to toe the line of the establishment. We're not going to follow the status quo like sheep or like cattle with nose rings. That day is over.

What people who talk about subsistence often don't understand is that it isn't just a lifestyle choice. Alaska Native societies depend on hunting, fishing and gathering for nutritional, physical and spiritual well-being. Immersing oneself in the wilderness of creation instills a growing awareness of the Creator and the laws of nature over a lifetime of living the hunting, fishing and gathering lifestyle. This acute awareness conveys the sense that the Creator has established a balance in nature to sustain the food chains in the web of life.

Alaska Natives, indeed indigenous peoples, maintain cultures that live in harmony with the environment – Creation – to preserve this delicate balance in nature.

*DEBORAH VO was born June 24, 1967. She is from St. Mary's on the Lower Yukon River. Her maiden name is Alstrom, and she is the youngest of 10 children. Her grandfather on her father's side was an immigrant from Sweden, and he ran trading posts up and down the Lower Yukon River. Her paternal grandmother was from Scammon Bay. Vo's mother comes from a large, traditional Yup'ik Eskimo family and she grew up in Fish Village on the Lower Yukon River.*

*Vo graduated at the top of her class at St. Mary's Catholic School, and then went on to Our Lady of the Elms, a private Catholic college in Massachusetts. She has a Bachelor's Degree in Marketing and Business Management, and she is pursuing her Master's Degree in Business Administration at Alaska Pacific University.*

*Currently, Vo is serving as the Executive Director of the Alaska Inter-Tribal Council.*

*She is a shareholder of Nerklikmute Native Corporation, the Native village corporation for Andreafski. Andreafski is a former Townsite that was annexed into the City of St. Mary's. She is also a shareholder of Calista Corporation.*

*It was in St. Mary's that she met her husband, who immigrated to the United States when Saigon fell in 1975. They have three children, sons Joshua and Jesse, and a daughter Brittany. The couple currently live in Anchorage, but Deborah misses her home village a great deal. She was interviewed August 24, 1998.*

T he Calista Region: You know people say it's the poorest of the poor who live out there. But I think it's the richest in terms of its culture. In that sense, it makes it a very prosperous region because it's been able to hold onto its language, its dance, its song. It makes me feel really good about being Yup'ik Eskimo because we're so culturally enriched and so close to the land. You can see that in our song and dance. In the way we express ourselves. It's genuine.

I'm from St. Mary's on the Lower Yukon River. My maiden name is Alstrom. I'm the youngest of 10 children, a very large family. We're one of those type of "half-breed" – I guess you call it – mixed-blood families. My grandfather was an immigrant from Sweden, and he ran several trading posts up and down the Lower Yukon River. He had three sons, including my dad and his twin brother. They're identical twins. They grew up on the Lower Yukon doing the trading post business after my grandfather passed away. Both stores are closed now. Both my dad and his twin were Bush pilots in their younger heyday. My mother came from a very large, traditional Yup'ik Eskimo family. Her father was a reindeer herder. Most of her family were wiped out when the TB epidemic struck, back in the '30's and '40's.

The youngest of 10, my goodness, I was thinking about it the other day. My oldest sister and I – my oldest sister's 48, and I'm 31. I really didn't grow up with the first three or four older brothers and sisters because they were already out of the house when I started to remember.

I had a very happy childhood. We didn't have television until I was in the third grade. And we didn't get telephones until, I think, I was in the sixth grade. So a lot of my free time was spent playing outside. Playing games you don't see kids play these days. We basically roamed the whole Andreafski Townsite. It was our back yard. It was a lot of fun. No TV. I think that was so good because you got to do a lot of things with your friends and family that you don't see today. No video games. So there was a lot card playing, Monopoly, outdoor games, like lap game, hopscotch, kick the can.

My grandmother on my father's side came from Scammon Bay. His father came from Sweden. His mother – her roots are Scammon Bay area. My mother's side, she grew up in Fish Village, which is on the Lower Yukon River. And it's no longer a village. It's just like a ghost fish camp now. Her dad was a reindeer herder. He came from a very large family also. Her maiden name was Afcan.

We had our share of alcoholism in our family. As I grew older, progressing from grade school on to junior high, you have the same pressure, such as smoking marijuana, experimenting with marijuana. And when you get into high school, of course, the booze was always there if you wanted it. You knew where to find it. But in the early '80's, something clicked and just went wrong. That's when they had all the suicides. My brother is a statistic of those suicides. All these young people that were dying – it was always alcohol related. And it seemed like it had become a norm, a normal thing to die an accidental death or one that was self-inflicted. And it's not normal. A lot of young people committed suicide.

*What was it to be an Alaska Native?* My parents never spoke our language, the Yup'ik Eskimo language. It wasn't until I was in the fourth grade that they started the bilingual education program in the schools. I excelled in that program. I could write it and pronounce the words. I could spell it. And I know the phonetics, everything. But if I sit down and have a conversation, I call myself a "tight tongue" because it wouldn't come naturally. It was kind of like something I always wish I had, but I didn't. Because language is so important. We'd pick up from my parents once in awhile when they would supposedly tell secrets or something. And they talked in Yup'ik. If you pick up a key word, then you know the gist of their conversation, what they're talking about.

I got very involved in Eskimo dance. In fact, I traveled with a dance group out of St. Mary's for a couple of years. We'd go up to Fairbanks and perform at the Festival of the Native Arts, at the museum.

Sometimes, I was mocked by other kids because of the way I grew up. Mocked that my family weren't "Eskimo," mocked that we were *"gussack"* or white people. We never paid attention to that because we knew it wasn't the truth. (Laughs.) *Why did they say it?* I don't know. Jealous. (Laughs) My mom used to tell us, "Don't pay any attention to them." So I've experienced racism both in the village amongst my own people and outside of the village. *Was it painful?* Yes.

I think that's really important, your basic values you learn right at home. We're a church-going family. We were hard-core Catholics growing up, so religion played a big part in our upbringing. There are several large Catholic families in St. Mary's. Sometimes I wonder how my family kept their sanity, despite the alcoholism, because my father drank a lot. We had a good, strong mother who never drank and made sure her kids were up for school, had food in our stomachs, clothes on our backs. And we're there at school, always doing our best. That's all she told us, always do your best.

It was a positive feeling (being Yup'ik). I think there were just periods when the media was too focused on the alcohol-related suicides among the youth in the early '80's. I mean, there was nothing good to say about Alaska Native youth, except that they're just killing themselves off. That was a very difficult time. I didn't like it. And it was exposed. "A People in Peril," remember? As good as it was, the series just, in itself, hurt a lot of the young people. Our family was featured in that. There wasn't anybody in that series you didn't know who they were. Because you knew who they were, their families. You either went to school with them or they were your cousins or something. You don't air out your stuff to the whole community, worse yet to the whole state. It was a good series. It woke up a lot of people to what's going on out there.

My girlfriend and I graduated at the top of our class. She's a teacher now. She's been teaching for about eight years now. I went to a private women's Catholic college run by the Archdiocese of Springfield and the Sisters of St. Joseph in Massachusetts. Our Lady of the Elms, but they just went coed. I was so disappointed.

I knew I wanted to go to college. I always had that goal. My sister has a Bachelor's degree in education. My brother is in education also. He teaches. And there's myself. And there's my other brother. He has just a couple more years to complete his Bachelor's degree, but he's home raising his family.

I got support from my parents and I had good teachers. There was a lady there by the name of Julie Sheldon. She was a teacher at the mission. She just recently passed away, a couple weeks ago. She had a brain tumor. It was amazing she survived four operations. Elms College was her alma mater, and she's the one that encouraged me to apply.

Some of my best years were just living it up there in Massachusetts. I had some wonderful friends and met so many wonderful people down there. Wonderful experiences. Different culture. Different East Coast living. So uppity from the village. (Laughs.) It was a big change. And the good thing about it, too, was I was so far away. Whenever I got homesick I couldn't just hop on a plane and leave. I was down there; I had to stay there. But I was determined to finish, and I did. My degree is in marketing and business management.

I met my husband in St. Mary's. My husband is Vietnamese and he immigrated to the United States when Saigon fell in '75. I think we share a lot of similarities in our growing up, even though we're from two different countries. It's the way we were brought up. It's amazing.

He was the store manager for Alaska Commercial Company. We have two sons. Joshua is eight, and Jesse will be three in October. I am expecting a daughter in less than a month, a couple weeks.

I've lived on and off in Anchorage for awhile, and this is the longest I've lived here, since '96. Thank God my very best friend in the whole wide world other than my husband lives here. She's just a two-minute drive away, and she's my childhood chum. We grew up together. And we're always talking to each other on the phone or visiting. So it's good to have that connection. My dad practically calls me every day.

We try to go to all the cultural events here in Anchorage, bring our kids. It was so funny last fall we went to the museum. They were having traditional storytelling. We went down and the museum was packed. Marie Meade was telling a story, and some of the chants that she used – she sang them in Yup'ik. Just some of the things that she said, I think that only Yup'ik people would understand that's supposed to be funny. So we're like the only ones that are laughing (laughs). So we try to do that. I try to get home at least once a year. My oldest son goes home at least once a year. Because that's where he grew up. He grew up in the village. He's very close to his grandparents and cousins out there.

Gotta have the food. I get these cravings so bad. Gotta have it. Like the fish, the dried fish, the *ahqutaq*, dried pike, moose meat, you know stuff that we grew up with. Just got to have it or else something's missing.

*Do you have a Native hero?* I never really thought of that question. The only person I really admire in terms of a hero and my role model is my mother. I just admire her strength, perseverance. My God, raising 10 children. Patience. I would say it would have to be my mother. If I told my mom, "You're my hero," she'd just like shy away and kind of chuckle, make some remark under her breath. (Laughs.) But I think it would be my mother.

There are a lot of Native women that I admire, elderly women in the village. I admire their qualities, their compassion, their humility. Never a bad word that comes out of their mouths. They don't talk about other people or anything. And there's just a simple "peace" about them when you're around them. A harmony. And you don't find that very often when you're in the presence of someone. And if you were to meet these old women you'd be able to feel it. They don't speak English, but they talk to you, and it's amazing.

*Discrimination?* Here in Anchorage. It's the worst I've ever felt it before. I think it was more before I realized you need to be more assertive. You know, being assertive is kind of like being bossy and rude in our culture. And I wasn't raised that way. When I visited Anchorage and went out shopping: you're waiting in line, and you get skipped over or something. Pretty soon, it's like: "I was next. Help me. I need help." You can feel it. I guess you'd have to experience it – when you're being ignored or not acknowledged. There's just some kind of air about it that makes you uneasy, uncomfortable.

If the East Coast was closer to Anchorage, I'd live on the East Coast rather than Anchorage (laughs). The fact that there is no preference in fish and game taking for subsistence users just goes to show how out of touch they are with their neighbors that live right next door to them. And it's not thousands and thousands of miles away. It's the same state, my God.

Your church, your family. I think family is so important. I think that's why they always talk about the deterioration of the family unit. It's true. Parents are not being consistent. Not only telling their kids about values or showing them by actually living them.

I really never started to learn about the Alaska Native Claims Settlement Act until I was about 14 or 15 years old. We had a class, I think, when I was a junior in high school that just devoted a whole semester to learning about the law itself and what it did. My first impressions were not very good. I was angry that we had to give up so much for so little. I wasn't too hip about the idea of getting money for land. Land is everything in the Yup'ik culture – in all Alaska Native cultures. If you don't have land, you can't survive. Just the idea of getting, I'd call it "paid off," and these corporations formed. The thing that really angers me is giving up your tribal rights to hunting and fishing. Boy, oh, boy, if that wasn't put in there maybe I'd be saying something different now. But giving up that status that just left the people powerless because that's all they knew. They didn't know anything about corporations. What's a shareholder? That was just foreign, foreign stuff. I think many of the shareholders – well, they're getting older now – but the few of us that were born before '71 have a better understanding of the whole corporate structure – shareholders, what their rights are.

I belong to a small Native village corporation called Nerklikmute Native Corp. There are 84 shareholders. St. Mary's never used to be a united St. Mary's. Andreafski is where I'm from. Andreafski used to be a townsite. Back in 1980, we became annexed into the city of St. Mary's, something I think that a lot of people didn't understand. So St. Mary's has a city council, which is a municipal government. It has two village corporations, two tribal governments and an independent school board. So, you can imagine, it can get pretty schizophrenic out there when you have one person that sits on these boards trying to make a good decision. (Laughs.)

The village corporation didn't do a lot. When they first started out they got into some bum deals with – I call them crooked lawyers. We lost some key parcels of land within the Andreafski boundaries to an outside company. That was poor decision making, information that was provided to the board at that time. But now, ever since then, we've been very successful with our financial portfolio. We're now starting to expand – a little. We're building a new Post Office out in

St. Mary's, and we're going to be looking at some other real estate ventures, hopefully tapping the eco-tourism market. Because what we're seeing right now is outside big game guides are coming in, just recently within the past two or three years, bringing people up the beautiful Andreafski River. And sports fishermen, are being guided by people that don't live there in St. Mary's. They're bringing them in. And none of this money stays in the village. It goes out with them from wherever they came from.

We've had a couple dividends. I mean that's not important, but more importantly I think it's gotten our shareholders involved in understanding what is a corporation, what are the roles and responsibilities, getting them to pay more attention to how to interpret the financial information that comes out in the annual reports. So it's been more of a learning experience.

*Calista?* I'm just not a satisfied shareholder, haven't been for a long time. I just think they lack leadership. It is very difficult to get the same old board members out that have been there forever. A majority of the shareholders do not understand the voting process, the proxy process and what they do when they vote their rights away to a committee to vote on behalf of them. I don't think they realize the power that they put into other people when they throw their vote away. I think people do not understand the power of the vote.

Increasingly over the years, I've seen a large number of shareholders at Calista showing no interest in annual meetings, in voting. And this past year was a sign of that. A couple days before the annual meeting, they did not have a quorum of the shareholders. People were not turning in their proxies. So they had to set up booths over at the hospital and Brother Francis Shelter to solicit proxies. They barely, barely made it, I think by six-tenths of a percent over the minimum needed for a quorum. It goes to show the very strong lack of interest on behalf of the shareholders in what's going on with Calista and a lack of interest in who's running for the board. There's a message to send. Let's hope they've gotten it and understood it.

I've heard bits and pieces of information about ANCSA. I hear names like Willie Hensley, John Borbridge, Emil Notti, Paul Dixon, who else? Those are mostly the names I associate with it. Oh, these people are getting old (laughs). I hope they don't say that about me in 20 years, "Oh, she's getting old." (Laughs.) What I always heard about ANCSA was that was a really good thing when it first started. Alaska Natives wanted to protect their hunting and fishing rights, something that was true to the heart and core to the Alaska Native Claims Settlement Act. But as everybody threw in their hat and had secret meetings behind doors, it turned out something totally different. It angers me. They said Alaska Natives were at the table when this thing was put together. Then why did they ever give up what they were so dearly holding on to? I mean how could you give up your right to self-govern yourself, your inherent tribal rights? That's just crazy. That's insane. And poor. I think people didn't understand that's what they were giving up. *Not everyone would agree that ANCSA meant giving that up.* But you know people always come back and use that against us: ANCSA says all tribes gave up their rights and land. It's always this brick wall that gives the other guy ammunition against any Alaska Native tribe that tries to do something good for the community, to take back that self-control.

*Would the situation with subsistence be different if it weren't for ANCSA?* Oh, I think so, too. Definitely, we wouldn't be in this 18 years later after ANILCA passes, the State of Alaska can't even comply with it. It's just ridiculous. And again, the power sits in a few who hold the power.

Sometimes I wish I could get rid of my stock. I would have gotten rid of it a long time ago. *Both your region and village stock?* Definitely my region. My village, I would hold on to. Because I think the main difference is, with our village corporation, we really make sure that the information we give to our shareholders is well understood. Communication is really important. With the regionals, a lot of people say, "Oh, they're just dissidents." Somebody's not getting the message, or somebody's interpreting the message wrong. Dissidents want to make a change, and change is always very difficult, as human beings, to deal with. Because human beings have that natural resistance to change.

*Is there a clash between for-profit corporations and culture?* There is a strong difference in philosophy. I grew up in a culture that was family- and community-oriented. We share everything. You go out and you catch, and you share. Corporate culture – no matter what flavor you put in it – it's always the bottom-line that counts. And that's something that's just totally different from the culture you grew up from in the village. So I think it was very difficult for people to understand. How do you make this deal and that deal and not care about the other guy? Without hurting their feelings? I don't know what to call it. Eskimo people are not aggressive. It's not their nature to be aggressive. That's something you have to have if you're going to survive in a corporate culture. You have to be aggressive. That means stepping on other people, whether it hurts them or not. That's something that's just not in our culture. If you're going to hurt someone, you just up and you leave. You walk away from it.

*How is your village succeeding?* Being a little bit more aggressive. (Laughs.) More aggressive in their thinking, and I guess the approach that we can't be left behind. If we're going to do something, let's do it now. I think they take a more aggressive approach before an outsider comes.

*How about the success of some of the other corporations?* I think it's very good. They have rich land resources. They are able to use them wisely. That advantage of having the resources on their land, i.e. ASRC got the oil, Southeast got the timber, Cook Inlet here, they diversified, they've looked beyond what's here. The way they think in terms of business, that it's just not something that's local. I like the way they've expanded their thinking into globally. I think that diversification is what makes CIRI very successful.

Leadership has a lot to do with it, too. You've got to be real risk takers. Depending on who's at the helm of the boat and how willing they are to take a risk has a lot to do with where they want to take the company. Business savvy.

*Does their success help Native people in general?* I like to call it the frosting on top of the cake. When you slice a cake, sometimes it's dry underneath, or sometimes it's not baked, and it's kind of soft and soggy. So it has the appearance of making Alaska Natives look successful, but underneath, there's still a lot of down-to-earth social ills that are just eating us away. Outsiders may say, "Oh, those Natives, they've got lots of money. They can solve the problems." I think that isn't true because the money doesn't get to where it's needed. I've never seen a dividend out of Calista except maybe once. But corporations that give out quarterly dividends, I think it has created a dependency – corporate welfare dependence type of mentality. They just rely on that dividend like it was the only source of income, which it is I'm sure for many. But that doesn't mean you can't go out and find a job or get an education. And that welfare dependency mentality, I think that the government created it – forced it on us. It's something that we can't get out of. It's something that we never wanted in the first place, but it was forced on us. Now they're trying to fix it – welfare reform.

*How about those born after 1971?* I think it's sad. I think they have as much right being a shareholder – being a part of it – as any of us that were born before '71. Because this is a generation of young adults that are smart. They're bright, and they're ready to take risks. They're more firm. They're just more up to date. They're more open to speak their mind, to say whether they're dissatisfied or not. They're the movers and shakers coming up. They really are. Because I see some very bright young people coming up.

In my second life, after my kids are all grown, maybe I'd like to go to law school. That's something that may change. Who knows? Here? I'd like to put some stability in this organization. The Alaska Inter-Tribal Council was formed by tribal governments, for tribal governments. Tribal governments need to take responsibility for this organization. It's theirs, and they make it what they want to make it. It's very much at an infancy stage and it's challenging. I enjoy the challenge this organization has put before me.

I want to build infrastructure in this organization to put in a good financial system, a good human resources system, a good communications system – a good networking system so that I can communicate on a daily basis with tribes and other agencies. Those are three things I'd really like to build in here and make sure they are solid. Because people are your number one resource, but you've got to have money to make the clock tick. Putting these systems in place is very important to me right now.

When I say its membership needs to take responsibility, I mean they need to get more involved. They need to participate. They just can't be a select few doing it all for them. If issues like subsistence, self-governance, economic development are important to their communities, to the future of their children, then they should be able, at the local level, to make that a priority and become involved. Because when you're out in the village, you hear about these things and you think, "Gee, that's so far-fetched from where I live and what I do every day, how could it ever possibly affect me?" And if you've lived in the village all your life, thinking that, it's hard to change that mentality.

*Can villages and tribal governments work together in the future?* I think they can work together. I mean a lot of the village corporations have their offices right there in the village sitting right next to the tribal government. So there is an opportunity that needs to be tapped. The tribal governments have access to numerous pots of money, and vice versa with the corporations that have the business and financial backing. I think there's a collaboration there. I'm sure some already do, but I think the potential there is even greater.

I have a vision for my children. I think it's because of the way I grew up. It's so very important that your children know that you love them. Tell them you love them, you respect them, so that they learn respect for themselves. Discipline them. A lot of people think discipline is hollering and smacking your kids, but that's not what it's all about. It's about guiding your children, helping them make good decisions, and how that's going to impact, not only their lives, but other people around them. Good family values are so important. Pay attention to your kids. They're growing up in a world that's very difficult for them. So much information out there. They've got the Internet, they've got cable, they've got video games. You wipe that all away, and it's very important to stick to love and respect, who they are, and give them the attention they need. It's so easy for parents these days to flick a TV on and let the TV babysit them. Or give them a few bucks here and there and go out to the arcade or go to the mall and hang out at the mall. The mall becomes the babysitter. It's dangerous. Protect your kids. My whole mentality has changed since becoming a mother. Now I know what my mom went through.

My hope for the Alaska Native community is that I want them to be the healthy, prosperous people that they were once. They can. They will be.

Our cultures are so rich. You can see the pride in our song and dance. It's time to regain it. This new generation coming up, they've got tons of energy. These young people, they're like a different breed. I talk to my niece. She's in her 20's and she's a Stanford graduate. The things that come out of her head are amazing. She's a smart, bright young woman. It's like nothing can stop them. They want something, they hunger, they'll go out and get it.

If I didn't have the childhood that I did, I don't think I'd be the person I am today. My older brothers and sisters – they grew up when they had no electricity or plumbing. I grew up when there was electricity, just starting out with television and telephones. To go from no plumbing or water in your house to have running water and plumbing, it's just amazing the amount of difference it makes! The change that it did in terms of your chores. I remember we had to pack water. Then when you got running water in your house, you became lazy. One less chore to do – pack water, carrying wood. It still goes on in the village because a lot of the villages don't have plumbing or running water. A lot of them melt snow and ice during the winter when the creeks freeze up. So you learn the ethic of hard work. Everything is so easy today. My mom always says, "It's so easy. Microwave. Turn on the gas stove." When you had to make kindling and start the stove early in the morning – wood stove, get up and make kindling and go out in 30 below and pack wood. My mom did her laundry on a scrub board and had to wring the cloth diapers.

The Calista Region: You know people say it's the poorest of the poor who live out there. But I think it's the richest in terms of its culture. In that sense, it makes it a very prosperous region because it's been able to hold on to its language, its dance, its song. It makes me feel really good about being Yup'ik Eskimo because we're so culturally enriched and so close to the land. You can see that in our song and dance. In the way we express ourselves. It's genuine.

# *Chugach Region*

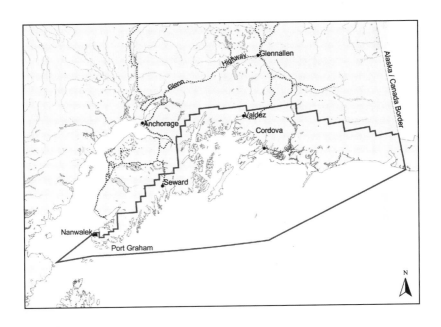

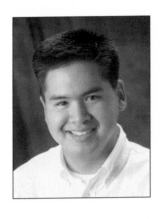

***JAMES W. LABELLE, JR.,*** *was born February 2, 1973, in Anchorage. He grew up in Port Graham and Anchorage and is an enrolled member of the Port Graham Village Council. During high school, he held a number of youth leadership positions. He later joined the Marine Reserves.*

*LaBelle inherited all of his great-aunt Nadine Ageenya's Port Graham and Chugach Alaska, Inc., stock when she died. He was elected to the Port Graham Corporation Board of Directors in 1998.*

*LaBelle lives with his girlfriend Rhonda Wolf, and they have a son, Anthony. She also has a son Cody from a previous relationship who lives with them. LaBelle has worked as a camp counselor for Cook Inlet Tribal Council and as a program staffer and site director for Campfire. He enjoys working with children and is particularly interested in programs for Native children. He is employed by Chugach Alaska Corporation, as the Shareholder Outreach Coordinator, and he has worked for Chugachmiut, the nonprofit arm of Chugach Alaska, under a grant from the U.S. Department of Education to develop a cultural curriculum for schools in the Chugach Region. He was interviewed November 17, 1998.*

197

**W**hen I was younger, I thought, "Why can't they just say, 'Here you're a shareholder,' and give me that document?" For me, it was just being recognized that I belonged. That was an important part to me, that sense of belonging to the community and the region. I'm a shareholder and I belong. But it's more than that now, I realize. But the basic idea of that is still there – belonging. So we need to find a way to recognize our young people as shareholders.

I was born in Anchorage. We lived here for a couple of years and then moved Port Graham when I was about two years old. We lived there about three years. My dad was President of Port Graham Corporation there, and my mom was a pre-school teacher. And then my dad got a job working for Chugach Natives, Inc., that was the name back then. It's now Chugach Alaska Corporation. So we moved back to Anchorage. Actually, I guess he worked for ARCO first. He was a Human Resources person at ARCO, and that was only for a year or two and then he decided to take a job with Chugach.

I've lived in Anchorage pretty much since. I attended Lake Otis Elementary, Wendler Junior High and East High School. Then I decided to join the Marine Reserves, so in '92 I went off for Basic Training. That was about three months and then another four months of military training after that. Then I came home after my training was completed.

I was involved in a lot of leadership activities in high school –

president of East High's Native Culture Club for a couple of years, president of Native Leadership Council out of Cook Inlet Tribal Council, which is a weekly meeting of Native students around Anchorage. I was on AFN Youth Council for about three years, and president of a Junior Achievement company in high school. (Laughs.) Yeah, I was really interested in leadership-type activities.

A lot of that had to do with the influences I've had in my life. Both my parents, James and Susan LaBelle, and two of my uncles, Derenty Tabios and Willie Hensley. So it was almost natural for me to be interested in leadership activities.

I have an older brother Kurt. He's three years older than I am. And I have a younger sister, and she'll be 18 next week.

*Did you have a sense of being Native as you were growing up?*
I did, mostly because of my family – my parents and my uncles and frequent trips back to Port Graham during the summer as a kid. It was really important to my parents for us to identify ourselves as being Native. So that was instilled in us at a young age. So I did identify as being a Native. And in town, there wasn't a lot of Native activities, of course.

I did attend a Native summer camp for kids every summer. And my parents wanted me to experience the AFN conventions as a young kid, and I enjoyed it. I attended the convention probably every year as a kid growing up, not to mention attending Chugach annual shareholder meetings.

As I got older, most of my friends were non-Natives throughout elementary and junior high. And then I got to high school. I knew I was a Native, and I identified as a Native, but all my friends were non-Native. When I was a freshman at East High School, they had a Native Culture Club. They had a study skills class for Native students through the Johnson O'Malley Program. So I took the class at the suggestion of my counselor at the time. It was really good because it was a really small group, and we were all Natives. I got to know quite a few Native students. And so I was invited to attend a lunch-hour meeting of the Native Culture Club, and from there I really enjoyed it. I felt more of a sense of belonging to the Native community. So that's where I spent most lunch hours. I attended all the meetings, and I was really getting interested in their activities.

I guess I can kind of point to that time. I really felt a sense of belonging because I was with my peers, and they were Natives. And from there, it just kind of blossomed.

They were having elections for Native Culture Club, and at that point I didn't really know a whole lot of people in there. I thought, "What the heck, I'll give it a shot. I'll run for vice president." I later became the president. And so that really started a chain. Being involved in Native Culture Club, I was invited to the weekly Native Youth Leadership Council meetings at Cook Inlet Tribal Council. And by then I was real confident and really enjoying leadership. I think in my tenth grade year I was elected president of that council. And then the following year as well.

And that council led me to the AFN Youth Convention, which was actually in Fairbanks that year. I think it was '88. Same thing there. I grew up in Anchorage and I didn't know a lot of my peers from my region, the Chugach Region. So in the caucuses, I was getting to know my peers from the Region. And they had an election for someone to be the representative for our region on the AFN Youth Council, and so I just said, "OK, I'll give it a shot."

Even if I hadn't been elected, I would still have been involved. So from there, with each little thing, my confidence grew more and more. Self-esteem was going up. It was just a great time of my life, and I can really look back and see how one thing leads to another.

I can kind of look back now and see how those little things have made me who I am today. And I didn't really realize that until probably when I was doing my Marine Corps training, which was really a stressful, hard time for me. It was seven months of training. It was very intense for me. Very. But, out came that inner strength that I had, the way I was raised, my parents and family.

*Do you have a tie to your Native culture?* I do have a tie. I identify myself as first, the son of James and Susan LaBelle, but also where they came from. My dad grew up in Fairbanks, but his mom was from Kotzebue. And my mom grew up in Port Graham. So I identify myself as being their son first, and then where they're from, which I kind of claim just by being their son. And then, I'm a member of the tribe. I'm an enrolled member of Port Graham Village Council. So I identify myself with that tribe. And, then even broader, I'm part of a region, the Chugach Region.

Right now I'm working at Chugachmiut. They received a grant from the U.S. Department of Education to develop a cultural curriculum that we hope the schools in the Chugach Region will adopt. It's a history, heritage and language curriculum. I was working on the local level in Port Graham for about eight or nine months, and now I'm back in Anchorage and working on the regional level. But working on the project has made me realize that there's so much more. Sure, I can identify myself with being from a certain family from a certain place, but there's more to that culture that I need to explore personally myself. I don't know the language. I go to Port Graham often to visit relatives and go fishing, but I know there's more to it. We say "subsistence," but you really can't define "subsistence" because there's so much to it. There's more to culture that I need to find out for myself, having grown up in Anchorage.

*Do you have a Native hero?* Well, I kind of like to think of my parents and my uncles as my Native heroes. I look at the era they grew up in, and they tell me stories of them growing up, and going to high school in boarding schools. Really, what they had to endure made them the people they are today. So I really have to respect my family – all Natives who experienced the same thing – Derenty Tabios, Willie Hensley. Derenty is my mom's brother, and Willie is my dad's half-brother.

*Discrimination?* Oh, yeah. Like I said, all my friends were non-Native. I remember at a young age: I was six or seven. Somebody called me a name. I think it was "Muktuk" or something. I really didn't know what it meant, but it hurt me at the same time because of the context in which they said it. It was not very nice, obviously. So I went home and told my parents what this other kid called me, "Muktuk." And as I was telling them, I started crying. It really touched me. It was the first time I had experienced that kind of prejudice. And probably, starting from there is when my parents taught me about prejudice and why people try to put down other people. I forget exactly what they told me, but they kind of explained prejudice. From then on, I was kind of prepared. My parents taught me how to act. They taught me not to act like those other kind of people that are prejudiced.

There were a couple of other small instances after that. But I was taught pretty well how to handle that. And kids at that age, they don't really know what prejudice or racism is. I could just remember that one particular time because it was the first time.

I didn't graduate from East High. What I tell students is that it's nice to have all these extra-curricular activities and it's a sense of belonging and comfort and camaraderie, but you can overdo it, which I did. I didn't realize it at the time, because when I was a teenager it was just so important for me to be involved in almost everything in terms of Native youth leadership. I really got behind because I didn't focus on school as much as I should have.

So that led me to an alternative school, kind of work at your own pace, SAVE (Specialized Academic Vocational Education, a work-study program). This was my senior year. And then I had lost so much ground on my school work that it would have taken me awhile to complete my diploma. And I wanted to experience the Marine Corps for some strange reason. Actually, it's not a strange reason. The experience was a strange thing, but I only wanted to experience it because my dad had served in the Navy, my Uncle Derenty in the Army. And my Uncle Kermit, my dad's brother Kermit LaBelle, was a Marine. He died in Vietnam, and that's probably the main reason why I wanted to experience the Marines. I never knew him. He was 19. I think it was '68 or '69. He was three or four weeks from coming home when he died. So my dad talked a lot about him because they grew up together and they were real close. So I thought it was kind of like a legacy. I wanted to honor my dad and my uncles who served in the military. Being 18, it was almost natural.

To get back to SAVE, I saw how long it would take to graduate, so then I decided to attend UAA's Adult Learning Center. They have a diploma program. And I graduated faster than I could have at SAVE or East High.

I was 20 when I came home. At that point, I didn't really know what I wanted to do. I wasn't quite ready to commit to going back to school. And I just wanted to find a job, make some money. So I'm 20 years old, I'm single. I needed a car (laughs). So then when I came back, I probably didn't work for a month or two. I took it easy after seven long months. But then, I was broke and I was living at my parents' house.

So I went to work on the Slope for awhile as a janitor. It was just a job. It was good money. After nine or 10 months, I decided it's not what I really want to do. I wanted to work in town in Anchorage, maybe possibly go to school. So I came back to Anchorage, and I ran into an old high school friend, Rhonda Wolf. We eventually started dating, and then we had our first son the following summer, Anthony. It was unplanned, but I don't regret it. And we're still together. It struck me that I have a responsibility now to my child.

If I'm responsible for anything, I go right for it. I had to find a job because I was unemployed. I decided, "Well, what kind of work do I want to do?" I knew that I didn't have any skills or training for a skilled vocation. And that's not really what I wanted to do. So I was thinking, "What do I enjoy doing?" And I always enjoyed being around kids, just how kids are with me. So I applied for a summer position at Cook Inlet Tribal Council for a camp counselor, for Camp Shana Kahata. But it was only a summer job, and that was the summer my son was born. And then the summer ended and it was time to look for another job. So I took a real low-paying job as a barista, a coffee slinger. And it was just to pay bills and buy diapers. And I was still living with my parents.

I was looking for other opportunities, so I applied with Campfire, and at Campfire I was with any kids that are enrolled. I enjoyed it, but I really wanted to go back to working with Native children, and I had never thought about it before, but I was looking in the paper and I saw that Chugachmiut, which is our regional nonprofit, was hiring for the Youth Action Coordinator position.

I worked for Chugachmiut for two years. It was really what I was looking for. I got a lot of good training, good experience. I was a little burned out. It required a lot of traveling, a lot of time away from home. So I thought, "Well, maybe it's time for me to move on." Plus, there were some budget cuts coming up. My program was going to be cut.

So then I packed up the family and moved to Port Graham because I heard about the Department of Education grant that Chugachmiut received, but the councils themselves were going to administer it. This was a good time to maybe make that move to Port Graham. It was a good change, and I needed to be in the village. Then I got really busy working on the curriculum development project, and I really enjoy it. I went from working with youth to working with elders, working with recognized experts, local resources. This is what I'm doing right now. I'm working on the regional level.

*When were you elected to your village board?* I got on last April. My boss gave me the day off to go to the annual meeting. So I attended and listened to all the financial reports, how our companies did, our store and fuel sales, and just our overall operation. And then the time came for nominations for the board. I had been nominated the year before and I had declined. While I was living in Port Graham, I learned quite a bit about what our corporation was doing.

We're kind of at a crossroads. Our natural resources aren't

bringing in as much as they used to. Our fisheries are in a decline, especially since the oil spill. And our cannery burned down in January. But there are plans to rebuild that. And then our timber – it's just a really bad time. The market's not there. The price of timber is not what we would like it to be. In our timber operation, the contract ended with Klukwan, who was doing all the cutting for us.

So we're kind of at a turning point that I saw back in April. But with all the new tourism activities in Alaska, and particularly Prince William Sound and Lower Kenai Peninsula, I thought, "OK, I'm pretty educated now on the operation of our company, so I will run this year." I got on, which was a total shock to me. I didn't expect to get on, being so young. I'm only 25. There's another young person on the board, and she's about 20. But the others have mostly been 40 and older.

I inherited my stock from my great-aunt, Nadine Ageenya. She had no children of her own. She has many, many great-nieces and nephews. I guess at the time, most of them were born before '71. There's probably about 30 or 40 of us, all of whom are my second cousins. And my mom was the only one who was really close to her in her late 70's. My great-aunt decided to will me her stock, just me. My sister hadn't been born yet. My brother was born. He had stock. And she filled out the will when I was just a kid. She died when I was 17 or 18. I didn't know that she willed me her stock. It was a big surprise to me.

Before that, in leadership activities in high school, I had talked a lot about the issuance of new stock to new shareholders born after 1971. Even though I inherited mine, I still would like to see that happen. I know it's happened in other regions, but my village and my regional corporation haven't decided to do anything and they haven't really talked about it. But they are talking about it some now.

Even the older directors feel it's real important that we recognize those Natives born after 1971 because they are our family, too. No decisions yet, but there's a lot of talk about it. It's just a matter of how do we work that out. And Chugach is still going through bankruptcy.

I was just at a village corporation board meeting last week, meeting with our financial people, looking at all our passive investments on the market and different stocks and how they've broken it up. And based on the revenue that's come, we declared a dividend this year of five hundred dollars, which was the same as what we got last year. And it's from our permanent fund revenues. I thought that was pretty good, considering what the market's been doing.

*What are your feelings about ANCSA? Was it a good idea to do it?* I think all the intention of doing the right thing was there. I think there was too much pressure from the state, from oil companies, to have it pass so that oil development could happen. I know they started years before it was passed. I know there had been a lot of talk about it before. But, then there was the big oil discovery and now it was rushed. It's kind of hard for me to talk about it because I wasn't even born yet.

*Was it a good idea to create for-profit corporations?* I'd like to say yes and no. No, because if the money and the land title had been given to the village councils that might have been a better system. That way, every Native born into a tribe or a community could have enrolled into that tribe or community and everyone would have a say. Being a member of a tribe, you have a certain amount of say. And everyone is enrolled.

I think in some instances it's good that the profit corporations were established. In a lot of cases, it has meant a lot of jobs and training for our people, and it has led to education.

Port Graham's permanent fund is about two million eight hundred thousand dollars, and that's all invested, broken up into different areas. We have a good combination of investments. Port Graham Corporation has not yet developed a foundation or scholarship fund, which is the first important thing that I wanted to discuss as a Port Graham board member. I feel it's important that we support the education and training of our young people because someday they're going to be back in the village, and someday they're going to be running our village corporation or our regional corporation. We need to invest some time and money into our young people because it will only help us in the long run. I've presented that, and we've discussed at the board level that we need to have a scholarship program or foundation program and even support for a vocational training program. Those kind of skills we know will help better our community, as well.

Chugach, through the Chugach Heritage Foundation, applies for grants, and awards scholarships. They also have an intern program. Port Graham does not, but they will.

*Is there a clash between culture and a focus on profit?* There could be, but we're a very small region, and we're a very small village. Just living in Port Graham for a few months I've learned that what one entity does really affects the other entity, the village council and the corporation. And they really get together a lot and they communicate, and they try to agree on what's best for the whole community – not what's best for the corporation, what's best for the council. There's always a middle ground, and they try to reach that middle ground of agreement. And, as for the region, they've got the Chugach Heritage Foundation.

*How does your sister feel about adding shareholders born after 1971?* She has the same views that I have. Her views are really simple: it's not fair that just because she was born after a certain date that she's not entitled to receive stock in our corporations. My dad inherited his mom's stock. My dad had enrolled in Chugach and Port Graham. My grandmother's stock came from Doyon, which he gifted to my sister. So she is a shareholder now of Doyon from my grandmother's stock.

*Goals?* First of all, myself. My immediate goal is to continue to support my family financially. So my immediate goal is to make sure I have a good job. And I also want to go back to school. I would like to go full-time, but I'll start off with a couple of classes.

Actually, my girlfriend has a son from a previous relationship, and he was just two years old when we got together. And that was five years ago already. So I've claimed him. I'm his dad. His name is Cody. And then there's Anthony. So my goals for both – I have to include them both – are to raise them in much the same way that my parents raised me. But knowing that it's a different time than when I grew up, I also want to teach them about today's world. My parents did stress education a lot. Now, after high school, and being a teenager – I know how smart my parents are, let's just say that.

I want to instill the same values in my kids that my parents instilled in me – hard work, education, being honest, having integrity, pride in being who they are – not just as a Native, but pride in themselves as a human being.

*Goals for ANCSA?* At the village corporation level, we need to look at other operations besides passive investments, besides our own natural resource development of fish, timber. We just need to find a way. If we don't know internally, we need to go talk to people who know about developing other operations – tourism, for one as an example.

We still have the cannery that we're going to rebuild and try to have completed by the end of next year. It burned in January. I was there, and I see that a lot of credit has to go to all those people who fought the fire. In the community, people really depend on a combination of their working in the summer in the cannery and doing subsistence and trying to balance that. And the cannery was a real big provider, not just for Port Graham, but for Nanwalek, the neighboring village, which is just a few miles away. So it really was an economic disaster. The Small Business Administration is going to help us finance the new cannery.

For the village, we want to find a way that's feasible for the corporation to recognize our younger Natives as shareholders. When I was younger, I thought, "Why can't they just say, 'Here you're a shareholder' and give me that document?" For me, it was just being recognized that I belonged. That was an important part to me, that sense of belonging to the community and the region. I'm a shareholder and I belong. But it's more than that now, I realize. But the basic idea of that is still there – belonging. So we need to find a way to recognize our young people as shareholders. And as long as I'm on the board or even not on the board, even if I'm just going to attend an annual meeting or informational meeting, I'm going to voice – we need to recognize our young people. We need to have education and training programs.

*MATT MCDANIEL was born on September 2, 1976. His father's family is originally from the Cordova area. His parents divorced when Matt was six, and he grew up with his mother, a non-Native, in Anchorage and Palmer. His father is on the Lands Committee of the Eyak Corporation, and his uncle, Jim McDaniel, is a director of the Eyak Corporation Board of Directors.*

*McDaniel can trace his father's side of his family back to his great-great-grandfather, Chief Makari, a chief of the Prince William Sound Aleuts.*

*He was labeled as dyslexic when he was in grade school and always felt that he did not have the aptitude to succeed scholastically. That changed, however, when he was a high school sophomore and a coach suggested that he might be able to get a diving scholarship to college. From then on, McDaniel focused his attention on his school work and sports and wound up being awarded a full scholarship to the University of Alaska Anchorage in diving.*

*McDaniel grew up knowing very little about his Alaska Native heritage, but has worked hard in recent years to learn as much as he can. He is employed as an intern at Chugach Alaska, Inc. He was interviewed February 18, 1999.*

**A**nd it's really sad because a lot of the culture came with it, and a lot of assimilation. I'm a prime example of it. It's really sad to think that there isn't a home country for me to go to. There isn't something like an old Italy that I can go to and learn culture and language. There just isn't. It was here, and now it's gone. I'm the person that got assimilated. All I can do is just read and learn and talk to elders. And that's really sad because I don't know near as much as I could or should.

My family is originally from the Cordova area, and most of them are shareholders in the Eyak Corporation. My dad is involved with the corporation and has worked with the corporation for awhile. He's on the Lands Committee right now, and my uncle, Jim McDaniel, is one of the directors on the Eyak Board. So my family has some background in the Alaska Native Claims Settlement Act and the village corporations. But as far as I go, around the time I was six, the family was separated. I ended up growing up in Anchorage and going to several different schools in Anchorage and in Palmer.

I have a lot of contact with my father and uncle, and they are very proud of their heritage, and they have made me very proud, too. I have some lineage of Chief Makari. He's my great-great-grandfather. He's a chief of the Prince William Sound Aleuts.

I do feel a tie to my culture. I just found a book that was made about 50 years ago that has Chief Makari in it. I'm learning more about it as it goes along.

My brothers – I try and get them more involved in Native issues, but it's really tough. When you're not around the Native part of your family, you pretty much have to search for yourself what being Native's about. And I think there comes a time in most people's lives when they wonder what they're about and where they come from. And that's what I did, probably my sophomore year in high school. And ever since, I've been interested in what happened.

And as soon as I learned about ANCSA, I was very disappointed, but very interested in all the problems that came with it. There are a lot of problems.

My mother is non-Native. She grew up in Alaska and she met my father in Cordova. My grandfather worked for the FAA in Cordova. My parents met in high school. I have two younger brothers. One is Josh McDaniel. He's 20. He is going to UAA, and he wants to become an engineer. And my other younger brother is Nicholas. He's 16, and he's going to Palmer High School.

*You had to learn about Native issues on your own?* I did pretty much. I talked to my dad, and I talked to my uncle, but mostly my Native education was at the university. I had to actually go out and research and find out exactly what happened. A lot of different people came into the classes, and I heard their points of view. With politics, there's a different side to everything, so it worked out real well where we could chew the meat, spit the fat and make a decision on our own.

I went to a lot of different schools because my mom was raising three kids alone. So we moved around a lot. I was always the new kid in school and getting in fights and things like that, which has made me do things like – Tae Kwon Do and wrestling, and I've boxed. That's something that has made me the person that I am now.

*Sports were important to you?* Oh – sports – I wouldn't be here today without sports. I wouldn't be in school. Shoot, I could be in jail for all I know. You want me to talk about sports? Sports turned around my life. They found out I was dyslexic when I was in the first grade, and I ended up getting held back a year. I got a label that said, "You have this learning disability." All the teachers and everyone around me: I don't think they quite understood what it was about because they just said, "Well, you have this problem and you're not going to work real well with the system. Here are these easy classes.

210

We're not going to really challenge you that much." And they do that with everybody who gets that label. They still do. It's kind of disappointing. I was just barely getting through school by the skin of my teeth because I just didn't think I had what it took. I mean everyone around me thought I was incompetent.

And then I started sports. I started in the eighth grade. I got talked into joining the wrestling team, and I started winning a lot. I was real talented – in diving, too. I joined the diving team. I just found something I was good at. Then, my sophomore year in high school, I got fourth at State for diving, and my coach didn't know anything about the dyslexia, and he said, "Have you thought about diving in college?"

And I said, "Jeez, no one's ever said anything like that to me."

So then I went to the counselor, and I said, "What do I need to do to go dive in college?"

And he said, "Well, you need to take all these classes, and you need to bring your GPA up so you can qualify for the Clearinghouse eligibility requirements."

So here I am with about a 2.0 GPA and a bunch of classes that I wasn't supposed to take. So, for the next two years I had to get honor-roll grades and take nothing but required classes. It wasn't very much fun, but I got through it, and I just barely ended up with a 2.5 and all my required classes and just barely got in the Clearinghouse. And I dove and won State my senior year and got a full diving scholarship at UAA. And I got to travel all over the country. It was just a dream come true. I had a lot of fun. It worked out great.

I went to UAA on a diving scholarship and got housing and tuition. And yet in the elementary grades, they said, "You are incompetent." They said I had a learning disability, but they just didn't challenge me. I look back and wonder, what if that coach hadn't said join the wrestling team that year? Who knows what I'd be doing right now?

As soon as I found out I could do really well, I was somewhat upset at the entire system. It was all the work I had to put into it and barely got into college by the skin of my teeth. Had I waited another semester, I might not have made it into college because my GPA was so low that even with honor roll grades for two years, it was just a lot to bring my grades back up. Luckily it worked out.

Sports were very important to me. It was my life. I used to do labor jobs over the summers in high school so I could pay for diving camp. And I'd go to diving camp. I had recommendations from colleges all over the country because all the scouts and the coaches were at the camps. They'd have a practice, and then they'd take a break and switch people in and out. But I figured I had worked five hours for every hour I was there, so I dove 12 hours a day. And the coaches thought I was nuts. The other kids were there getting babysat. And I left there with a videotape and a bunch of recommendations, and I had offers from different colleges. It worked out great. It taught me a lot. It's taught me about how to be competitive within yourself.

Before I went to the diving camp, I was working minimum wage in a warehouse, actually, in a freezer. I must have weighed all of a 120 pounds. But I love thinking about that time. It was actually one of the best times I ever had.

I dove all through junior high and high school. I also did Tae Kwon Do and I was real successful in that. It's pretty much the same principles of diving – a lot of spinning and kicking and things like that. Wrestling – I wrestled for about five years counting junior high.

My degree is in organizational management. The target date is this fall, but who knows? I'm very close. I can see the light at the end of the tunnel.

*You've received scholarships from your corporation?* They're paying my tuition and fees now, and they're paying for work. I couldn't ask for more. But that's another thing people don't understand. I've noticed that when people find out that I'm Native, for some reason they think, "Oh, boy. He's got a full ride. They throw rose petals in front of him when he walks through the door." But the fact is, I've been going to school for four years and owe 20,000 dollars out of my own pocket. Sure, I'm very appreciative. I've gotten a thousand-dollar scholarship from my village corporation, Eyak, for the past three years. A lot of people think, "Gosh, Natives have all these benefits, and they can go to college for free. How come they aren't all doing it?" Well, it's not that easy. We work just as hard as everybody else.

When I got my scholarship at the university, I knew that I wanted to get a degree, and I wanted to win nationals. At the time, I had so much confidence, I believed that anything was possible if I just worked hard at doing my very best. I wanted to set an example for my family and everyone around me. I cared a lot about what people thought about me, especially people in my family and people close to me. I went to the university after two years of trying to prove everybody wrong – that I can actually accomplish something, that I can do well in school, that I can win State and I can do things. I put a lot of pressure on myself to dive and perform.

It's a lot of pressure to deal with because it seemed like when you're coming in straight out of high school, you don't have any money – if you screw up and don't perform and lose your scholarship, you can't afford to go to school. There's nothing you can do. So there was a lot of pressure to prove everybody wrong and keep my grades together. If you get below a 2.0 and drop below full-time, you're not eligible. Some classes are just not very easy. And it was real close for the first semester.

Luckily, I got through the first year, but it was really tough and really scary, especially going to practice. I had to dive on the high dive and learn new dives every day. I smacked during most practices, which is what most divers have to do. It was a tough experience. I didn't have a choice. I wanted to stay in it because my goals were real set in it. But the hard thing to deal with was there were days I didn't want to do it, and the fact was, I didn't have a choice. There was no other way to finance my education, even working over the summer. And with the scholarship, it was still not very much. But there are a lot of good things that came out of it, too. I had an experience of a lifetime, and it's made me who I am today. I'm very disciplined now, and I can look back on hard times and realize I can get through it.

*How did you feel about being an Alaska Native?* It was the same type of thing as my dyslexia. I felt like I had something to prove because the Natives are just so misrepresented and misunderstood. It's a different type of society. It's parallel to the capitalistic society of me, me, me, me. Natives work together. There's so much more of a spiritual side. I've heard that we're a cultureless society, and I look around. In my own life, I think, "Gosh, I crave culture." And that's part of the reason why I want to know so much about my history.

The only spiritual experience I can think of is that I prayed to God to win State. I said, "If I win State, I'll go to church for a month." I wanted to be reasonable. I didn't want to give Him a promise I couldn't keep. So I won State, and I went to church for a month. That was in '95. God helps those who help themselves. That was the whole thing. I practiced and I practiced. What that meant to me was that every minute of the day, I had to be doing my very best. I couldn't be making any excuses for myself.

*How did you feel about the stereotypes of Natives?* Natives are very identifiable. That's the biggest thing: When certain non-Native people see a white person on the street, drinking, they don't think, "Oh, that dang drunk white guy." Nobody thinks that because they can relate to him. Natives are different. But then, again, most of those people didn't have to get assimilated into a culture that is totally foreign to them. They're dealing with something completely different, and something they don't understand. And for people to put judgement on something they don't understand is very ignorant and very upsetting.

I used to brag about how I was Native and didn't quite understand what it meant to be Native. Now, I see the responsibilities that come with it. Every once in awhile I'd hear a joke or something about Natives. It'd really hurt me, and it seemed like they didn't mean any harm by it, but it hurt. It definitely hurt. And then a week later, I'd look back, and I'd say, "Gosh, why didn't I say anything?"

*When did you feel a positive sense of being Native?* I went to a pow-wow, and I just felt a great sense of pride. I think I must have been a freshman in high school when I went with a friend. I was with their family. And I said, "You know, this is really great. But how can I call myself Native if I'm only a quarter Native?"

And then they said something to me that I'll never forget. They said, "You're only as Native as you are in your heart."

And ever since then, I've felt very good and confident about myself and proud of that part of me. I'll be completely honest: There are some people that are hardly Native at all that I would consider more Native, more proud of being Native, than certain half- or full-blood Natives. I don't think some people understand what it means to be Native. I don't even claim to understand, but that's what I'm trying to do is find out what's going on.

I had always wanted to work for the corporation. That's been another thing that's really odd – my dreams are just – everything's coming. When I started college, I thought I wanted to work for the corporation. And here I am, I'm a management intern, and I'm graduating. It's working out.

*A Native hero?* When I think about it, it would be my dad, Dan McDaniel and my uncle Jim McDaniel. They are the people who got me interested in my culture and my values in the Native community. I've always looked up to them as role models as what a Native person should be.

*How do you feel about the Alaska Native Claims Settlement Act?* I believe that ANCSA was an act that the sovereign Natives of Alaska really didn't have a vote on or a choice in. A lot of the Natives didn't vote on that. All of a sudden they found out that their rights as a sovereign people, their rights to subsistence – everything – got moved into corporations. Their entire culture, their language, their rights got assimilated into this corporate structure. It was a quick fix to deal with the Natives out here.

And it's really sad because a lot of the culture came with it. I'm a prime example of it. It's disappointing to think that there isn't a home country for me to go to. There isn't something like an old Italy that I can go to and learn culture and language. There just isn't. It was here, and now it's gone. I'm the person that got assimilated. All I can do is read and learn and talk to elders. And that's too bad because I don't know near as much as I could or should.

And that's another thing that I'm so upset about: I'm really disappointed that even though there's so much Native business out here with the 13 regional corporations, you would think there would be some type of requirement for graduation to just have a 15-minute insert in one of the classes of someone saying what happened during ANCSA. I remember in the sixth grade, I learned about how the Russians came in and lined up the Aleuts to see how many people a bullet could go through. But I never once read anything about ANCSA. I never once heard anything about the Alaska National Interest Lands Conservation Act. I never once heard anything about any of that until I heard it from my father and my uncle on my Native side. And then it wasn't until I took some Native policy classes at the university that I followed through on the Statehood Act and then up through ANCSA and the 1991 amendments.

And it's disappointing when you hear the media misrepresent Natives when they talk about why Natives have certain rights. I've been upset more than once with the media. It's just that people are not educated. No one's ever made them sit down and listen to why Natives have what they have. I didn't even know until I took some elective Native policy classes.

I felt like my family went through a lot with ANCSA. I almost felt betrayed. I understood that it didn't happen to me, but it happened to my family and what my family left me, as far as being a shareholder. It's very important and it's something we need to hang on to for generations to come to make sure it isn't lost because after these corporations are gone, that's it.

Speaking of the culture, my grandmother, Vi McDaniel, is the last person in my family to speak Aleut. I can see the language dying. On top of that, I've talked to other elders, saying, "You know a beautiful language. Why don't you speak it? Why don't you write it down?" And the problem is that years ago, they were shamed out of it. They used to get hit at the boarding schools for speaking their Native tongue. And the teachers would not speak a word of the Native language. The kids had to sit down and listen to teachers speak some language they've never heard. And then when they'd try and say something they'd get hit. And they'd just have to sit there. It's ridiculous. Why did they need to learn all this stuff? It didn't help them in their hunting. They didn't need to know how to write up memos. They needed to know how to take care of their families, do subsistence, how to hunt. It was completely useless to them.

*Do you hear your grandmother speak her language?* Yes, I try to get her to talk every once in awhile. But she just gets worn out. She has trouble breathing.

*What do you think about the corporations?* I think the corporations were highly undercapitalized when they first came out. And on top of that, they dropped these corporations in the Natives' laps, and the Native people had no idea what to do with it. They weren't educated in the business way, and lo and behold there were all these problems. They're trying to compete in a market that they don't understand. And, of course, they don't do very well. They lose a lot of money.

But times are changing. People are getting educated, and corporations are starting to take more care of their shareholders. People are coming back and working for their corporations.

Our corporation is coming out of bankruptcy because we've gotten out of volatile markets – timber, canneries. We're paying our debts off, and that's great. Every time a job opening comes up, I do my best to contact as many shareholders as I can about it because we really want to get our shareholder hire up. A lot of times I'll find someone that's very educated and qualified, but they're not willing to relocate. That's another problem with these contracts that are all over the country – it's tough to relocate a lot of people.

*What do you think about the amendments to ANCSA?* I'm not as well versed on the amendments as I can be. As far as shareholder stock goes, that's a very interesting topic. When they said, "OK, only these people born before 1971 can have stock in the corporation," what they did was they took away the identity. They were saying, "Well, you're a Native. And you're not." They really did. This is something that I've talked with other people about. In my case, I was born in '76. It's not so much the status, it's more like, "Why do you get this? And why don't I?" We have the same blood quantum. I don't understand. I guess I understand, but I don't.

It messes with Native identity, and that goes back to everything being transferred – the rights, the culture, everything – into these corporations where you're not Native unless you're a shareholder. You don't get these benefits if you're not a shareholder. You don't get these dividends unless you're a shareholder. Well, why not? Kind of silly. But then again, if everyone got redistributed shares, then the value of the stock just gets devalued.

*Do you believe you'll be a shareholder someday?* I do, especially since I think my family – that side – understands that it's the mission of my life to make life better for the shareholders. I truly feel that way. I want to help the shareholders.

Another thing that bothers me about it is, after a couple of generations the stock gets split up and split up and after about four or five generations, there's nothing left. Who's got voting power? Who's getting dividends? Who's getting benefited? And I really hate the idea of putting our Native stock on the open market or getting outside investments.

*What about the corporations that have added young people?* From what I understand, the corporation needs a vote on that issue. I think it'd be beneficial seeing how – you look around and there's a new generation coming through. The funny thing about it is, this generation didn't go through what the generation before us had to. And I think understanding what they went through, what those people fought for is very important. So people know what they're dealing with. It's more than just a business. It's everything.

*How about the success of some of the corporations?* I'd like to see the Native community be more politically powerful. I think sometimes the public's a little scared of that. As I said before, I just wish the public was a little more educated about what's going on with these businesses. Because if you work in Alaska, sooner or later you're going to have to deal with Native businesses. Or, if you're hunting and fishing, you're going to have to deal with Native subsistence issues. I mean, we're all over Alaska.

*Your personal goals?* My personal goal is I want to get my Master's Degree within the next year and a half. I'd like to get it by the time I'm 25. From then on, I just want to take every opportunity that comes my way and do my best. That's all I can ask for myself. I'd like to be involved in the politics side of it. There are some issues that I still need to become better versed in. There's a lot more knowledge I need to get before I'll feel like I have a good understanding of what's going on.

*Do you plan to marry?* Yes, I do. That would be nice. *Native or non-Native?* Yeah, I have thought about that. That type of thing is – I'd love to do the politically correct thing, which would be to marry a Native person. But marrying someone is a difficult issue. It's real tough. I would like to see the blood quantum stay up. Not that that it even makes a difference. It's kind of weird how we care so much about blood quantum, and then at the same time, we get mad because it just doesn't make a difference. I'm only a quarter Native, but my heart is in the Native community.

*Your vision for ANCSA and the Native community in general?* My vision? I'd like to see shareholders get involved in their own corporation. I'd really like to see them get educated and get involved in their own corporation and take care of what their families fought so hard for. It's real important. A lot of the top positions require a lot of business experience, and we need people that are qualified. Otherwise, we'll just destroy the corporation. We can't just turn a profit, but we have to keep the shareholders in mind. These corporations are becoming very powerful, and part of that has to do with economic conditions. But we also have good leadership and we're starting to figure out what's going on.

# Cook Inlet Region

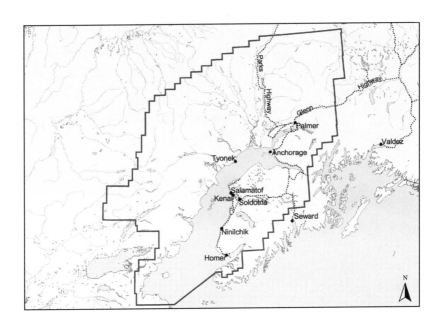

 **DORIS HUNTER-WHITLEY** *was born June 1, 1962, in Soldotna and spent the first eight years of her life on the Kenai Peninsula. She moved to Anchorage when she was eight. She went to work for a flight service company in Anchorage after she graduated from high school and has worked there for the last 19 years. She is currently one of the few female operations managers within the company nationally.*

*Hunter-Whitley is a shareholder of her village corporation, Salamatof Native Association, Inc., and CIRI, and she serves on the Salamatof Board of Directors. With her involvement on Salamatof's Board, Hunter-Whitley represents the third generation of a long line of Native activists. On her father's side of the family is her grandmother Rika Murphy, first Chief of the Kenaitze Indian Tribe, first president and chief of Salamatof Native Association, a member of CIRI's interim Board of Directors and one of the originators of the Alaska Native Health Board. Other family members include her great uncle, Harry Mann, a member of Salamatof's first Board of Directors and active until his death; and her three aunts, Laura Jean Murphy, active until her death in 1989, and Mary Ellen Perrizo and Hazel Felton, both of whom have been active on the Salamatof Board since 1975.*

*Her father, George N. Hunter, Sr., worked alongside his mother before ANCSA was passed and was a member of Salamatof's first Board of Directors. During the drafting of ANCSA, he made several trips to Washington, D.C., with Native leader George Miller, Jr., CIRI's first president and president of Kenai Natives Association. Other active family members include her great aunt, Julia Mann, who served on Salamatof's first Board; cousin Irvin "Bud" Witbro, who served on the Kenai Natives Association Board for 15 years; and cousin Bernice (Mann) Crandall, who serves on Salamatof's Board.*

*Hunter-Whitley lives in Anchorage with her four children. She was interviewed October 1 and 9, 1998.*

In September 1997, they called me and said there was a board seat open and would I be interested in applying for it? And, of course, being single, working about fifty to sixty hours a week and raising four children, I didn't think I would have the time. I wanted to wait until my youngest child was ten. But something that day made me think about it. . . As I wrote the letter to apply for the seat, I got excited and began looking forward to a chance of actually getting on the board. And it turned out that I did.

I was born in Soldotna and raised for the first eight years of my life on the Kenai Peninsula. I moved up to Anchorage when I was eight. But the times I remember in Kenai before moving to Anchorage were a lot about my grandparents, Rika and Ray Murphy. They both played a big role in my life then, and even though my grandmother is gone, she's still present in my life in many ways.

I went to kindergarten and first grade in Kenai. We lived poorly. We lived in several different houses – a few without running water, one without electricity. I remember a lot of hand-me-downs. I think that's why the best times were going to my grandparents' house. I looked at it as a little castle. My grandparents had a lot of pride. They loved us kids a lot. We were always a close family. I remember my aunts watched us a lot at my grandparents'. My mother Judith Kent-Hunter made a good home for us no matter where we were. My father George Hunter, Sr., was a fisherman.

He provided, I guess, the best that he could for us until my mother ended up leaving him when I was eight and we moved to Anchorage. I started school there. I remember being on welfare for awhile. I have two brothers and two sisters – a brother and two sisters older than myself and one younger brother. We were pretty close growing up. We're even closer today. We had our normal childhood fights – that happens – but we've stayed close through the years.

It was very tough. There was always a lot of love, but it was much different from how I live today. In some of the places we lived, our bedroom was the living room. There were no "bed" rooms. It was a room, and that's where everybody slept. We stayed in one place where we packed out our own water from a lake. I remember my mother forever boiling it and straining it through a cloth. She made the best of everything, though. We knew we didn't have as much as other kids, but she didn't let us feel that way.

It was very hard. My father was an alcoholic. That's why my mother ended up leaving him. She actually sneaked off with us kids when I was very young. This was a very difficult time for me because I was a "Daddy's girl" up until that time.

My mother definitely wanted all of us kids to be in school. No matter where we moved and picked up, that was one of the first things she did. We had to make sure we got re-enrolled in school. One time I sat down and figured out I went to ten different schools in my thirteen years, including kindergarten. She was very adamant about making sure wherever we lived we went to school. When we moved up here, and she was on welfare and we moved into low-income housing – even then, it was the same thing. I remember being very scared one time to go to school, and she had to go to work. I didn't want to go, but she walked with me and made sure I got there. Education was important. She wanted all of us kids to graduate. She didn't press the issue of college. She would be happy if her kids had an education and were able to support themselves once they got out of high school and left home.

My mother was and still is my best friend. She always provided for us, even when my father couldn't.

*Your education?* Just through high school. I graduated from 12th grade in 1980 in Washington, which was one of my two years out of Alaska. I spent one year in high school in Washington, only because my mother and stepfather had moved down there. Then my dad became ill the year of 1980, so immediately after graduating, I moved back to Alaska and spent his last couple of months with him. He died in August of 1980.

I had every intention of returning to Alaska after graduation. That was quite a change because I had gone to a high school in Anchorage where my graduating class was going to be 400 people. Then I went back to Kenai for a year and a half and was going to graduate with close to one hundred students, and then I found myself in a little town in Washington, where I ended up graduating with twenty-four students. So it was quite a shock, quite a difference in high schools although my mother's family, who lived there, made us feel quite welcome.

*Were both of your parents Alaska Native?* No, just my father was. My mother is originally from Washington and moved up here with her family in 1953 and met my father when she was 13, very young.

*Did you have a sense of being Native?* I didn't understand honestly any of that while I was growing up. I mean I knew certain things we did, certain traditions that we had – the canning of the fish, smoking fish, the smokehouse, just a lot of things I remember as a child that we did. But really, to say that I felt a sense of being an Alaska Native, that didn't happen until – actually until quite a few years later in high school when I started kind of understanding the meaning of what had happened and what was going on. And that was years after the Alaska Native Claims Settlement Act passed. So I wasn't tied into all that. I probably would have been more so had my parents stayed together because my dad was very active in that. But because they separated and my mother was not the Alaska Native – not that she ever talked down about my father or anything – it just wasn't brought up like I know it would have been had I stayed with my grandmother and my father.

*Did you experience discrimination?* No, I can't say I did. When I was younger, I felt "poor." But it had nothing to do with being Alaska Native. I felt that was more due to my father's alcoholism. I can't say I felt discriminated against. I think more than anything, I just kind of felt deprived. I wanted a nice home. I wanted a bedroom. I wanted certain clothes. But, I looked forward to the times when extra money would be there and our father would take us to get an ice cream cone. Something that simple. That meant a lot.

I do remember at one point the low-income area we lived in

Anchorage was quoted as the "poor" neighborhood. That's where the "bad" kids lived, the "poor" kids. But that didn't stop me from having different types of friends who had nice homes. They didn't really discriminate against me because of that.

I remember being picked on in almost a friendly manner. They were trying to tell me it was time to get some new clothes because I'd had the same ones that I wore continuously. I didn't have any other clothes. That was kind of embarrassing. It hurt my feelings. I talked to my mother. I said that it was noticeable that I was wearing the same clothes. I was in elementary school at the time, and kids can be very cruel in elementary school. She understood that, so we went out and bought some used clothes for me. We shopped at thrift stores and garage sales. In fact, to this day we still like to bargain hunt at garage sales. It's kind of instilled in our blood, I guess. Of course, now, I don't do it as often as I did then. It's nice to be able to shop for my children at department stores.

My mother knew when something hurt me bad enough and she did something about it. She was always there for all of us kids, no matter what. And she always stayed very good friends with my father and didn't let us say one bad word about him. She made sure that we wrote to him and wrote to our grandparents when we were away from Kenai. So we remained in contact with them.

I had some sense of being an Alaska Native through high school, especially when I went back to Kenai for the '78-'79 school year. I do remember my mother talking about a lot of excitement when the Alaska Native Claims Settlement Act was starting. She remembers there being some anticipation about the possibility that people would get their own land and possibly some money. I don't know if I remember that or I just remember her saying that through the years.

When I graduated from high school in Washington and came back up here in 1980, there was talk about CIRI giving out a check. I heard we might get a share of some money and land that the villages would get. I remember my oldest brother was ready to quit everything he had ever done and sit back and wait for this hundred-thousand-dollar check that was coming down the wire (laughs). My dad had a talk with him and told him, "That's not how it's going to work. Don't stop living your life right now, waiting for this to happen."

This was after my dad stopped drinking. I must say in his

defense that he beat his alcoholism. My parents did not get back together, but he became more involved in our lives. He did a lot of work with Sohio, which became BP. He would talk to us about that, show us pictures of Prudhoe Bay. He had been up there in different stages of the pipeline. He was only 44 when he passed away. I know there would have been a lot more that he could have shared with us kids had he been around. Before he passed on, he started to give us a sense of pride in our heritage. He and my grandmother had signed us up as shareholders in Salamatof and CIRI.

So I remembered that, and I started to get a sense of being an "Alaska Native." I never felt that we had a lot of special treatment. That didn't come until I learned about the medical care. As I had kids, I realized what medical and dental bills can amount to. It did have a big impact on my life. But when I was younger I didn't realize how much. Back then, I just thought, "OK, Alaska Natives. There are some things coming down the works," but I didn't stop doing what I was going to do, which was finishing high school and finding a job.

After graduation, I lived with my sister. That's also where my father was staying in Anchorage because he needed to be close to the hospital for his chemotherapy and radiation appointments. I stayed there with them and decided to get a job and help out. My Aunt Mary Ellen, my dad's sister, called because her husband worked for Western Airlines. She said they had some bottom-level positions opening up in this flight kitchen that made all the meals for Western Airlines and some other airlines here in town. She asked, "Would anybody be interested in going to work there?"

My sister and I just looked at each other. Since she was more involved in running my dad back and forth to his appointments, and her husband was working, she wasn't interested. I was single and needed money, so I said, "Sure, I'll give it a shot."

So I went in for an interview and got hired. I started out washing dishes (laughs) from ten at night until six thirty in the morning. I stood in front of a big machine, scraping dishes that came off of the airline trays. I was scraping food into a huge garbage disposal and running them through a dish machine and taking the clean ones out and starting the process all over again.

I did that for about three months and then got moved to another department. I had no intention of staying there at that time, but I moved up into different positions of actually assembling the meals onto the plates. So I was working with the clean dishes and the "good" food this time, and I felt this was a step up. The money at the time was good for me. I had worked a waitressing job in high school in Washington for two dollars and sixty-five cents an hour plus tips. And the tips were maybe a couple dollars a night. No reflection on the waitress, of course. You have to understand what it's like in a small town. They left a dime or a quarter. That, to them, was a tip.

So when I started working in this new job and I was making eight dollars an hour, I felt rich at that point. As the paychecks started coming in, it was nice be able to buy myself stuff and give my sister money for staying in her house. I got laid off one time and went to hostessing at the Northern Lights Inn. But it wasn't too long before a new company took over, and my boss that was my boss at Western Airlines offered me a job with this new company.

On a personal level, I ended up getting pregnant and having a little boy in 1981. He is a wonderful son, but it was very tough at the time being single. There was not a choice for marriage, and I don't believe in abortion so that ruled out those two options. I was eighteen and had him, and I was still living with my sister. We found out at the same time I was pregnant that my older sister who lived in Florida was also pregnant. Shortly afterward I found out that the sister I was living with was also pregnant. This all happened the same month that my father died. It was one of those stories that you look back on in awe. We all had our babies in May, just days apart. And my dad's birthday was in May. It was almost like God had taken something away from us, and so he was going to give us something back. It was pretty amazing.

I raised my son alone until he was five. And it was wonderful. I tried to give him everything I could since I didn't have a lot when I was younger. Then I had a daughter in 1986, again unwed, without the option of marriage. My son's name is Shane, and my daughter's name is Shawna. I raised them both alone until I met a man in 1989. I married him in 1993, but it was a very brief marriage. We had two children, Kevin and Kassidy. In 1995 I divorced and continued to raise my children. At work, I gave it my all, and promotions just seemed to keep coming over the years. I was working my way up through the company. Eventually, I was made Operations Manager, which is the position I'm currently in.

Our company is a huge multi-million-dollar business, and there are only few female Operations Managers. So it was a big accomplishment. It took eighteen years to reach this goal, but I think it's better when you go into a job to have worked your way up and have experience behind you. Of course, I never had a choice. I had to keep working, but I got to work in every different department until I got to where I am. That gives you a broader view of the whole business and how to handle people. Right now I manage about ten supervisors who supervise about 150 employees. We have about 350 employees altogether here in the unit in Anchorage. In the summer, we go up to about 440.

It's been a wonderful job and still is. There are still plenty of challenges. I have learned so much, especially over the last three years since our new company took over. They have a lot of supervisor and management training programs. They're looking ahead to the future and the vision. There is a lot of team-based management where it's not just one person's decision any more, you have to get together as a group and a team and you work at goal-setting together. For the most part, it's been a great job and experience.

For quite awhile, my aunt, Hazel Felton, and my aunt, Mary Ellen Perrizo, have tried to persuade one of us Hunter girls to get on the board of our village corporation, Salamatof Native Association, Inc. They both are board members. My grandmother was very, very active in Salamatof. My father was one of the first original board members. My other aunt, Hazel's and Mary Ellen's sister Laura Jean, was very active on the board for many, many years, too. So it just seemed right they would try to get one of us girls to step in there and take a seat and get the experience and knowledge it could bring. It's a whole different outlook than a day-to-day type of business.

In September 1997, they called me and said there was a board seat open and would I be interested in applying for it? And, of course, being single, working about fifty to sixty hours a week and raising four children, I didn't think I would have the time. I wanted to wait until my youngest child was ten. But something that day made me think about it. I didn't have a feeling that I really had a chance of getting it, but I thought I might as well start putting my name in there now so it could be heard in later years when I would run for a seat. As I wrote the letter to apply for the seat, I got excited and began looking forward to a chance of actually getting on the board. And it turned out that I did.

I've been on the board almost a year now, and it's been

something totally different from the everyday side of going to work and making a living. I'm learning a lot. For one thing, I had no idea how a board of directors worked. I'm learning some history, which is wonderful. I've even started checking out some books and looking on the Internet, trying to find things about Salamatof and Cook Inlet. I'm just trying to learn more now so that I can pass that information on. I didn't feel that I got a lot of information when I was growing up. I want to pass that on to my children and even on to my brothers and sisters. I have one brother who pretty much is aware of a lot of the Native issues, but my other brother and my two sisters are not. It's nice to be able to share this knowledge with them.

The seat goes up next May. I hemmed, hawed about trying to run for it. But now, I know that I'm definitely going to. It can be time consuming. You do have to put some effort into it and be an active board member. You don't just go, sit at a meeting for three or four hours and then walk away from it. You constantly keep your eyes and ears open for something that might benefit Salamatof. So it's been a whole new focus for me.

My brothers, sisters and I all had 100 shares each in CIRI and Salamatof, and when my father died we each received an additional 20 shares.

Salamatof has been very successful. It's a small corporation with only 129 original shareholders. We're getting a good return on our investments as far as the stock market. We've invested in land, and we've developed some of it. We're making plans for further development. It's exciting. We're able to give dividends to the shareholders, not like CIRI, but I think in time and with the right strategic planning, the right kind of mindset from the board and shareholders, eventually it's going to grow. Dividends – last year it was 320 dollars for the year and then a bonus of about 260 dollars.

Some shareholders, of course, don't think it's nearly enough, but I think this is where there needs to be a mindset that in order to make money, you have to invest it. It doesn't make sense to take this whole pie and split it up. I think that was the mindset for the people who wanted the money now – the same issues that CIRI has dealt with, those who say, "I'll just take my share now." But in order for a corporation to grow and be successful – not just for the current generation, but generations to come – assets can't just be taken and split up with everybody taking a chunk and leaving nothing.

For a few years, we've had a bonus. There are a lot of

wonderful programs that Salamatof and its nonprofits have. Besides awarding scholarships, Salamatof has created jobs. There is a shareholders' park that's at Spirit Lake down in Kenai. That generates jobs in the summer time. There is also a summer youth program where they have supervisors work with youths and teach them some skills, such as construction and carpentry.

We own a building that is leased out for office space and another building that is a pre-school for the Kenaitze Indian Tribe. Overall, we have been successful with our property management.

There have been some good decisions made in the past years. I cannot take credit for those years, but there has been and still is good direction by the board. It shows with the growth.

*A Native hero or heroine?* My grandmother, Rika Murphy. She has been recognized by many as a great Native leader. From the beginning, she was active in the formation of Salamatof as an ANCSA village, and she was the first Chief of the Kenaitze Indian Tribe. She was Salamatof's first president. Many meetings were held in her own home. Under her leadership, the Kenaitze Indian Tribe went forward as a traditional Indian tribe to claim its place in history. She was named honorary Chief of both Salamatof and the Kenaitze Indian Tribe for all her dedication, hard work and perseverance in establishing and holding the corporation and the tribe together. She is also going to be honored for all her early work as an original member of the Alaska Native Health Board in an Alaska Native heritage ceremony to be held this month. She tried to keep Native culture alive, and she passed on a lot to her friends and family.

I just wish I had learned more about her Native roles sooner instead of waiting until this point in my life to do it. It wasn't really until I got on the board that I realized there was this whole other part of my past that I hadn't explored. I would love to research back when she married my father's dad and how that all came about. I know her great-great-grandmother came from Russia. So there are just a lot of things there that I'd like to research, and I plan on doing it someday.

*Your feelings about ANCSA?* Of course, I have to go by what I've read or heard and not by personal experience, but as far as getting the textbook information on it, I believe that it was only right. As I understand it, the government wanted the land and the Natives were saying, "Hey, wait a minute, this is technically our land."

So it was understandable that something had to be done to transfer money and land back to the original Native people. What

I've read so far has to do with how they settled on which land, as far as CIRI getting land and the village corporations benefiting from that also. Personally, I would have to say it was necessary, and I feel those who chose to do something with it and make something of the land or the profits of the land would agree. I'd have to think that the land has catapulted some regions and some villages into good profits, enabling them to give back to the people not only through jobs and dividends but through land itself.

My brothers and sisters and I all have parcels of land. And as for my father's parcel – instead of Salamatof dividing the total amount of land between each of us kids – they went ahead and allotted his as one piece and let us decide what to do with it. We've kept all of our land so far, and his land is actually the best parcel. It's about thirty-two acres, and it's located on Arrowhead Lake in Kenai. It's a wonderful piece of property, and we're trying to go there more and more often. In this aspect, it's meant quite a lot to be able to have that parcel of land. Without ANCSA, we wouldn't have it.

This land was from our village. Salamatof surveyed 129 parcels of land valued at 60,000 dollars apiece and let the shareholders choose the land. The elders in our village were first in line to pick out their parcels, and the allotment continued by age. My oldest sister received a real nice piece of property that overlooks the Kenai River on part of it. My oldest brother picked a parcel of land that was up near my grandmother's and my aunts in North Kenai. My sister Rika, brother Neil and I opted to select land that was close to each other, and we picked our father's in the same area. So it's about 160 acres of land that in some way connects or is very near each other. My father's and mine both surround Arrowhead Lake.

I saw mine last summer and visualized how I could make it a peaceful family retreat. My brother, just last weekend, has poured the foundation on my dad's parcel to build a cabin for all of us to go in the summer time.

For us, it's been wonderful. We've been approached about selling the land, and we have not considered it at all. It just means a lot to us. I know my sister was able to use her land for collateral to partner in a company, so that was a huge benefit to her. I know some of the other Natives who have sold their land, and that's maybe what they needed to get on their feet and get started.

So, all in all, in my personal opinion, I feel it's been a good move. And I know at Salamatof we're getting money for some resources that are on the land. There's always logging to be done. Salamatof has built a shareholders' park on quite a large parcel of land. In all of it, it has come back to the Native members, and that was the whole intent of ANCSA.

I think I mentioned earlier that I went to the library to read about ANCSA. Of course, there's just dozens of books on it, and you don't really know which one to pick and which one's going to give you the information you're looking for. Although they were interesting, I think for somebody that doesn't want to bury themselves in books, it would be nice if there were a simplified version of how it all came about and who participated in it. I did take the initiative to get some books on it and start reading some, but it was a complicated issue.

I hear how much Roy Huhndorf did when CIRI was just starting out. I know that all had to do with land development and knowing what to do with the resources we were given and investments. But as far as when it first happened and who was involved – I don't have much insight on that.

*Creation of corporations versus a reservation?* In my opinion, seeing where we are today, I feel corporations are a good idea. I know there are those who would disagree and would think that the reservation – having their own laws and their lands – would be better. When you look in this day and age – it seems unlikely that that type of governance could continue on forever. I'm sure there are a lot of elders and a lot of Natives who want their own reservation and to have their own laws. But eventually, I feel with continuous change, we all would be living under the same laws. Under a different system, I don't think we would have as much as we do now in the way of opportunities.

Our corporations have been able to help develop nonprofit organizations. There are a lot of programs that exist in nonprofits that can help Natives when they're in trouble or need scholarships, job training, housing and medical and dental care or any other kind of health programs. I don't know that it would have all been here had we opted for reservations only and not corporations.

There are a lot of benefits for the less fortunate, but I have an issue with the fact that those who choose to work so hard to get to where they're at don't have a lot of benefits. I had the drive when I was younger to move ahead. I wanted to strive and make a good life for myself and my children. That closed some doors for me along the way. For example, as I went to look for a home through the housing program, I made too much money at that time. Even though I was a single parent and received no child support, I felt most things were there to benefit those who didn't work. But those who had the drive to go forward kind of got a door closed on them. I just don't think they should shut out people who do decide, "Look, I have ambition. I want to earn a good wage. I want to make a good home for my kids, but I may also need some help."

I had a goal to own my own home by the time I was 25 years old. That probably came from having so many rented homes when I was growing up. It didn't happen until I was 26. But it was still a wonderful thing. So I've been buying my home now for ten years. It wasn't a big elaborate home by any means. It was a fixer-upper. So I looked into remodeling programs through nonprofit organizations to see if there were any programs that offered help. There weren't for me. If you made this much money, sorry there's nothing available for you. I had lots of water problems, flood damage and different things that my insurance company couldn't help me with, and I turned to some Native programs, but they also couldn't help out. I have had to do the repairs and finishing on my own.

I know Southcentral Foundation has a wonderful Headstart Program that I would have loved to put a couple of my children in. But there, again, because of an income, which I didn't feel at that time was that much, I still did not qualify for the programs. This was even though I was single, raising four children and received no child support. It can be a little disheartening. It's enough to make you want to sit back and think, "Should I be working this hard if other people (who are not working) are getting the same things I'm working fifty and sixty hours a week for?" But I could still answer that question with yes. It gives me a sense of accomplishment.

I'm happy for those who can use the benefits and get ahead by doing so. I don't judge those people for that. The programs are there, so take advantage of it, is my opinion. But at the same time, it would be nice for those who are striving to get ahead to receive some help.

I didn't want to get on a soapbox about that.

*Is there a clash between business and culture?* I believe there is a place for both of them. There are some things as a business corporation – profit-making – that you can do to actually keep some of the heritage and culture going that you maybe wouldn't be otherwise able to do without a certain amount of money. It may be in the way of museums or archeological digs. Or, just the education and the programs you can get involved in. I didn't know too much about my culture or even a lot of the Native dances, but I enjoy them. CIRI puts on an annual potlatch my kids and I go to. That has to cost some money to put something like that on. Now my kids look forward to going each year. They like the dancing and the friendship cloth. They are getting something out of it each time we go.

Profit-making companies are keeping some heritage alive. Whereas, if it had been a reservation that didn't survive, the culture would also be lost. I do believe Native corporations have an obligation to keep culture alive.

*Your goals?* My career goal is to continue on in the company where I am now. Having made it to Operations Manager, I've been asked to move forward, but I'm still challenged enough and like the interaction with all the employees. I'm not at a point to move up any further and lose "being out on the floor" to sit behind a desk. Also, in the last year since I have been on the Salamatof board, and I came back from this retreat and I'm reading these books, now one of my goals is to learn more about ANCSA – CIRI and Salamatof in particular. From our retreat came some good short-term and long-term goals – a lot of shareholder involvement. It's really exciting. So that now is what has changed for me in the last year. My goal going forward is to continue in building my knowledge and getting to know the shareholders of Salamatof. It's been real interesting so far.

On a family level: My 17-year-old all his life has wanted to be an astronaut, and then at the very tender age of about 14 found out that if your eyesight isn't nearly perfect uncorrected, then you cannot be accepted as an astronaut. He was devastated. He had been going to ROTC. He's a 3.7-grade-point-average student. National Honor Society. Community service. He was doing everything he could to get his foot in the door for certain colleges and then to go on to NASA. It's still his goal now to work for the aerospace industry with NASA. He's going to go to college to be an electrical engineer and eventually work in the aerospace program. I encourage him to continue in that direction. Hopefully, with all the scientific changes, they'll eventually be able to have people work in space who don't have perfect uncorrected eyesight.

He's a very bright, wonderful young man. I know he's got a bright future in front of him. My goal will be to get him through college. He will be able to get scholarships – I hope from CIRI,

Salamatof and others. We've already gotten started on our paperwork. He's already picked a college – the Rochester Institute of Technology – it's up there as far as the cost, but he's pretty determined to be accepted and graduate from this college.

I'm going to help him every way I can. If I have to dip into my retirement that I've been saving, I will do it only because I look on it as an investment. Whatever I pump into my children now will come back to me since they're going to be our future. I know that. It's the same way with my mother now. I know she feels she instilled in us the knowledge that eventually we will be the ones taking care of her. She invested in us, and she'll get a good return on her investment. And that's what I tell my kids – I want a good return.

My 12-year-old daughter Shawna is really undecided about her future. I always joke and say she's 12 going on 18. She's a lot like I was. She's opinionated. She's got a broad view – a different way of looking at things. If she could she'd run an animal farm and collect all the stray pets. She claims she may become a veterinarian, but if she doesn't, I'd like to channel her in my direction and maybe get her attention in the things I'm doing – whether it's sitting on the board or just getting interested in it. My goal for her is that whatever she decides to do, that she do it to the best of her ability. I will support her always. She's a wonderful daughter with a bright future.

And then Kevin, he's my eight-year-old little boy. He wants to be a teacher in the winter and a librarian in the summer. He's another straight-A student. Shawna is, too, but I have to pull it out of her.

Education, I prioritize highly for my children. A "C" – I can't say it's not acceptable, but they want to say, "Well, that's average." Yes, if that was the best they could do that would be fine. But I know what they're capable of. If they bring home a "C" and I know they could have gotten a "B," then I push them in that direction. I wasn't pushed to my potential in school, and I want better for them.

Kevin has a hunger to learn right now. And he loves books. He loves school. He loves everything having to do with school. He doesn't ask for a toy when we go to the store. He wants a notebook and a pen. (Laughs.) So the child must have 15 notebooks and pads of papers and a Daytimer. He's probably the only eight-year-old with his own little Daytimer and address book. My goal for him would be to keep his hunger for knowledge and to be a teacher. He's also got this huge, huge heart and he tries to accept everybody. So I would want him to keep that – to never lose it. I know the world can harden a person real easy. I don't want that to happen to him.

And then there's Kassidy Laura-Jean. She's my five-year-old. She'll be six in a few days. She dreams of being an entertainer. I often thought it would be neat to try to get her into cultural dance because she loves to dance. I'd like to see her grow up to follow her dreams. I'm going to get her into chorus at our church because she loves to sing, and she loves to get up in front of an audience. She sang to me and her aunties on a high stool in Auntie Hazel's kitchen with a turkey baster as a microphone. She sang Celine Dion, and we cracked up. She's a good singer. She's a good entertainer, and she's the one that brings the rest of the family together. So my goal for her would be to continue entertaining because she loves to make people laugh and smile.

I am proud of them and I'd like them all to have a sense of where they came from and what options are there for them. I'd also like them to go back to our land. I told them now that it's being built on and that every summer we're going to make it a point to go there for a week. When we went to our land for a week last summer, they absolutely loved it. We saw moose. We saw black bear. We went four-wheeling. They took rafts and boats out into the lake. We built it up like a little homestead. We hand washed clothes and had a clothesline hung. We invited people out to have dinners with us where we all just sat around and visited. It was all outside. There's one little tiny moose camp shack that my brother built, but other than that, it's all open. And we chopped and hauled our own wood. We stayed out there pretty much the entire week, although I have to admit we went to town twice to take showers. Other than that, I washed my daughters' hair with lake water – twice. It was a great experience for them. It was roughing it for a week, but it was something that brought us close together. I'd like to see them continue doing that and not lose that sense of the land and what it's like to be out there and be together. It's far enough away from the town that they can just be them, the family.

I would hope even after I'm dead and gone that they would continue to go back there with their kids. We're big on family. And this is one way to get the family together for some peace after the hectic pace of our lives.

I want to thank God for my children and my entire family. I was baptized Russian Orthodox when I was 18, and at that time didn't really have a relationship with God, as far as being able to thank Him for my blessings and talk to Him. But now God is very much a part of my life. I do try to go to church every Sunday. Even though it's not the Russian church, it's very important for me to instill the faith of God in my children. They go to Sunday School. In fact, my youngest kids are in a Christian school. I think this will provide them with a good foundation to grow upon.

I also would like to thank my parents, grandparents, stepfather, sisters and brothers, aunts and uncles, family and friends for their love and support throughout my life. There may have been hard times, but I believe that is what makes us who we are – stronger and wiser people, able to enjoy and cherish the good times in our lives.

I remember praying when I was a little girl about my parents making it through an argument or a fight or something that made me feel bad. It was reassuring for me. I still pray to this day, and I still thank Him at night and wake up in the morning and ask Him to guide my family, my children and me through the day.

**GLORIA R. O'NEILL** was born on April 21, 1969, in Soldotna. She grew up in Soldotna, but spent her summers in the Bristol Bay area as her father participated in the world-class salmon fishery there.

O'Neill has a Bachelor's Degree in Sociology and Business from the University of Alaska Anchorage. She is the Executive Director of Cook Inlet Tribal Council, Inc., which administers programs to perpetuate and enhance the cultural heritage, social and economic well-being of CIRI shareholders and other Alaska Natives and Native Americans within the Cook Inlet Region. Previously, she held marketing and public relations internships with the Anchorage Telephone Utility, the National Bank of Alaska and the University of Alaska Anchorage.

O'Neill currently serves as a board member of the Alaska Federation of Natives and The CIRI Foundation. She was among the first group of Leadership Anchorage participants and was named to the Alaska Journal of Commerce's *"Top 40 Under 40"* individuals within Alaska.

She has one daughter, Ravynn Faith Nothstine. O'Neill shares in raising her daughter and teaching her about her Yup'ik and Inupiaq background with her former husband Greg Nothstine.

She is currently working on her Master's Degree in Business Administration at Alaska Pacific University. She was interviewed October 19, 1998.

**M**ost importantly, I believe the shareholders can receive great opportunities from all the resources, not only from what the for-profit corporations have to offer, but also from the nonprofit corporations, the health corporations and all of the subsidiaries within this structure . . . You can be an Alaska Native and do anything you want to do or become anybody you want to become.

I was born in Soldotna, Alaska, on the Kenai Peninsula. My mother's originally from Pennsylvania, and I think she moved up here in the '50's. Her father was involved in the oil business at the time, so she moved up here at a young age and has stayed ever since. My father is Yup'ik, and he was born in Levelock, Alaska. My grandmother, his mother, was born in Sleetmute. And his father was a full-blooded Irishman from the San Francisco area. When my father was in eighth grade, the family made a decision to move to Kenai for the simple reason that my grandfather didn't want to send the kids to boarding school to finish their education. He wanted to keep the family together.

My father and mother met in Kenai High School and married right after graduation. I have one brother, who's 30, then myself and a sister who was born three years after me, and then the baby of the family is now 20 years old – my little brother.

I grew up in Soldotna and spent my winters there, going to school. My father would take us back to the Bristol Bay area in the summers. We had a little cabin in Naknek. My father's been a commercial fisherman in the Bristol Bay area since probably the day he started walking, and he continues to be to this day. Most of what

I learned of my family values and traditions came from the Native side of my family – my father's side – just because my mother's parents moved away when I was very young. My father had an extensive family, both in Kenai and some in Anchorage, but the majority of the family lives in Bristol Bay. That's where I really got a lot of my influences from.

I always tell this story: I remember being on the boat over in the Bristol Bay area. I think I was about three and a half years old, and we were over in Naknek. We went up the Kvichak River because every year after fishing we always would go up the river to clean out the boat. We were at a village, and I don't recall the name of the village, but it was past Levelock on the Kvichak, and I was following a group of little kids from the village and thought that I could keep up with them. We were jumping around on the boats and all this stuff. They all were running in front of me and they jumped onto the skiff. I thought I would try, too, to catch the skiff. But I didn't, and I fell into the river. I remember watching fish swim by me. I have this vivid memory of trying to grab ahold of the bottom of the skiff. Then I don't remember anything else after that but waking up in the cabin of my father's boat. Apparently, Auntie Judy from Naknek swam in to get me out of the river.

So I have a lot of interesting experiences over in the Bay growing up as a small child. I grew up around the water, around boats most of my life.

As I was in the Bristol Bay area in the summers, I would help out babysitting with my cousins, aunts, relatives over there. Then I started going fishing with my father at the age of 12. And then I said, "Well, you know, I think I want to be more independent," knowing that my father was extremely traditional in the sense that the boat was the man's work. I thought I would show them all up and go work on my own in the cannery. So for a couple years there I worked with my grandmother in the cannery as a bull cook. It was the Petersen Point Cannery, and I got a lot of good experience.

I went to elementary school at Tustamena Elementary School, and that's down in the Kasilof area. I went to junior high at Soldotna, and I graduated from a nondenominational Christian school.

I would say that while growing up, one of the most significant things I learned was the work ethic. My grandmother – in the '30's, I believe – and all her siblings went to the Holy Cross Mission. In the mission they learned how to work. They grew a lot of vegetables up there. That was a part of their everyday routine. Because of the strong work ethic she learned from the missionaries, she taught that to my father and his siblings.

As a result, the work ethic continued with us kids. I remember waking up in the morning, and it would be 20 below and we would get up to cut a cord of wood, just to learn how to work. Or, move wood. But, you know, thinking back on it, that was an extremely good experience for me. Or, I'd go moose hunting with my dad, and he would make sure that I was walking softly. He taught me how to walk and carry all of the guns and everything else as he walked ahead of me. And I think that taught me a lot of discipline. Not only that, it's through those experiences, I came to really appreciate the environment in which I lived at all times. So I basically had a very loving family growing up. I'm still today very close with my parents.

Probably the most significant person in my life was my grandmother, Pomela, who was my father's mother. She really wouldn't talk about many of her experiences, but she told me a little bit. She was just an amazing woman. She had thirteen children. A couple of her children passed away. But, you know, she never said a bad word about anybody. No matter what she experienced in her own life, she always had a very positive outlook. So she really taught me a lot about love and what it is to be myself.

*Did you experience any discrimination?* I have to say not really. Probably because I'm so many mixed bloods. I really didn't feel a lot of discrimination. I always felt a lot of love with my family. I mean there were always a couple of comments when some people knew I was Native, but really no, I didn't encounter a lot of that. And really, I was going to a high school where I was one of eight in my class. There were two other Alaska Natives in my class from Port Alsworth. And so, I was really sheltered because of the school I went to, probably.

It's interesting you asked me that question because after I finished high school, I went to Clarion University because my mother's from Pennsylvania. So I wanted to learn a little bit about her background. I went back East and went to college back there and stayed with my mother's family, which was extremely interesting because I learned a lot about where she came from and that side of my family. But, then, after the first year, I really didn't feel like I fit there. I really wasn't happy. So when I came back to work in the cannery, I just decided to stay. I said, "I'll go over to meet my big family over in Dillingham." So I lived there for a year, and I was 19.

I was very well accepted because everyone knew who I was related to. It wasn't until I came to Anchorage that probably I experienced discrimination, but it was more reversed than anything. It wasn't really anything that people said. It was more just a subtle undertone. But, you know, I always felt that I know who I am and I know how I was raised. And I really believe in not only who I am, but what I'm doing for Cook Inlet Tribal Council and for the Native community in Anchorage. So I always let that stuff kind of roll off my shoulders. But as I got to know more and more people here in the Native community here in Anchorage, it doesn't really even present itself any more.

I always knew that I was Native because my father is Native. I never really thought about how much I am Native, how much somebody else is. It wasn't even a question as I was growing up. In my family we never talked about stuff like that. We were just always accepted. And it wasn't until I had to go down to the BIA and get some sort of certificate, and people asked me, "Who are you?" that I really even started thinking about it. Any more, I just tell people who I am and where my dad comes from.

I worked over at the Kanakanak Hospital over there, run by the Bristol Bay Area Health Corporation. It was a really neat experience. I worked for awhile as an administrative assistant, and then I wanted to become an EMT and work with the Fire and Rescue Squads. We would get up in the middle of the night after we got a call. And we would go to whatever emergency was happening at the time, which were pretty significant emergencies that I was able to assist in and really learned a lot and saw a lot. And then I worked for about six months with all of the nurses and doctors, and I was given an opportunity to watch about six or seven births and help in that process, too. I was able to travel to a few of the villages there with the Bristol Bay Region.

I think when I was 19 or 20, I said, "Okay, what am I doing with my life?" I had one year of school, and I was over there in Dillingham, and there's really not a lot and I knew I needed to finish school. So I moved back to Anchorage, and I started going to school full-time. I worked at the same time, full time, as a receptionist. And I did that for a couple of years.

I would go back to the Bay in the summers and work. But in 1992, I started here at CITC full-time, and I worked my first job in

242

Summer Youth, and then I worked throughout the company the last six to seven years – as a counselor, the business development specialist, as General Assistance coordinator, Child Care Programs. I've worked in mostly all the programs CITC has to offer and administered most of those. So, in a sense, I feel like working here at CITC, I was given a real "natural" internship in the sense of knowing the programs and understanding those programs.

But, as I worked, I finished my Bachelor's Degree in Sociology and Business. It took me awhile because of having a baby and getting married and a lot of other stuff in between. But I've started on my Master's Degree in Business, and I'm nearly completed with that now.

I have one child. She'll be four January 2nd of this year. Her name is Ravynn Faith Nothstine. She is just like her mother in every sense, but ten times more independent (laughs). But Ravynn comes from a really rich background. My ex-husband Greg Nothstine is from the Nome area, actually from Wales. And his family has really gotten back in touch with their culture, even his family living here in Anchorage. And so she knows how to dance. And she dances with her dad's group, and that's the Kingatmiut Dancers. She's really close to both sides of our family and really has a strong understanding at such a young age of who she is. That's the way Greg and I would both like to raise her. We just see so much potential in her. She's a really, really smart little girl. I could go on and on about her forever.

Her Inupiaq name is *Ahklaseak (Ak/laasiaq)*. *Ahklaseak* means "little polar bear." Her name was given to her by her grandmother Sophie Nothstine and was the late Helen Senungetuk's name. Helen, like Sophie, was originally from the village of Wales. It is said that Helen was found suckling her dead mother's breast during the flu epidemic that wiped out whole villages in Northwestern Alaska in the early 1900's. I've also been told that Helen was a creative, friendly and beautiful person that everybody enjoyed being around. I believe when you are given an Inupiaq name you inherit many of their attributes, and this is what I hope for my daughter *Ahklaseak* – that Helen's vivacious, caring and intuitive spirit lives on through Ravynn.

*When did you have a sense of being an Alaska Native?* I don't know if I ever thought about it. Like I said before, my father's family really had a strong influence on my development – learning traditional values and things like that. But I would have to say that I always felt like I was so fortunate that I had such a rich background and diverse cultures. Having the ability to understand where my mother comes from and her background and also living my father's culture was probably – I always saw as more of a gift than anything. I don't even know how to put it into words. It was just always knowing. I never thought of it being a certain group of people or another group of people. I just knew who I was and my family as a result of that. I felt like I was very fortunate to come from such a diverse background.

I'd have to say my grandmother was probably the most significant role model in my life. Listening to her stories gave me more of a sense of pride in who I was. Her name was Pomela Peters. She passed away in 1992.

*What about ANCSA?* I would have to say that I think the Alaska Native Claims Settlement Act has been extremely beneficial for the Native people of Alaska in comparison to the reservation model that the Lower 48 has – where they have reservations instead of corporations. It's really interesting to look and understand the magnitude of services that each region offers its shareholders or the Alaska Native people that live within those regions, compared to going and getting services at a tribal office at a reservation in the Lower 48. We have so much more here than many of the Native people in the Lower 48. And so I think that the model, from my understanding and what I know of ANCSA, has been positive in many aspects. And not only that, the for-profit corporations themselves, on the whole have been extremely successful in all of their endeavors. I mean look at CIRI. It is a very successful for-profit corporation. And I feel that it pays its shareholders well.

In order to survive in this world, you need to understand the basics of business – whatever you do. If you go and open a checking account, you need to know how to keep your checking account balance. And I think ANCSA and the development of the for-profit corporations have given the Native people a little more education in what it is to be shareholders in a corporation. It's probably given shareholders another avenue or opportunity to understand business. And, of course, as we live in this democratic, capitalistic nation, we need to have a good understanding of that in order to thrive and be successful as the Western society sees it.

Most importantly, I believe the shareholders can receive great opportunities from all the resources, not only from what the for-profit corporations have to offer, but also from the nonprofit corporations, the health corporations and all of the subsidiaries within this structure. I mean resources in the sense of social services, educational grants, dividends, low-income houses. You can be an Alaska Native and do anything you want to do or become anybody you want to become. Because the resources are there, I believe, you can become very successful.

Within CITC, we have "cradle-to-grave" services, so to speak. The annual budget for CITC runs around 10 million dollars, and we have about 148 employees. We have child-care assistance for babies when they're born. We have burial assistance, as their families may need some financial assistance with paying the cost to bury the deceased.

We also have an in-patient treatment facility, which we call the Ernie Turner Center. It's located here in Anchorage and it is very successful treating individuals who have entered and completed the in-patient program which runs about thirty days in length. Those individuals on the whole have abstained from alcohol. So we have high success rates in that area. We also have out-patient programs and continuing care programs. Within the Ernie Turner Center, we really focus on family values because we believe the family – just like a village – is the core to that individual's existence, especially in Native families. Family is very, very important. So, if the individual is seeking to get well, the family needs to support that individual.

We also have our Welfare-to-Work services, which are extremely successful. This is a new program. It's probably been in operation about 18 months. With all the welfare reform and all the big hype and federal legislation being passed, we thought it would be best if CITC were to specifically design and operate a program for Alaska Natives within the Anchorage community to transition them out of welfare to work in four weeks. Within the Anchorage community here we have approximately 1,600 open cases at any given time. That means 1,600 Native families are receiving welfare. We're about 35 percent of the entire Anchorage caseload. And we're probably about 20,000 total population out of 250,000. So, on the average, there are more Alaska Natives on public assistance when you look at the statistics in comparison to the general population.

Most individuals – 97 percent of our caseload – are single mothers who for some reason have been on welfare for varied amounts of times and who are really looking at changing their lifestyle and becoming self-sufficient.

We always say that we're here to give a hand up, rather than a handout. And we have the resources available at CITC – from basic computer training to child-care assistance so people can become self-sufficient.

Another one of our departments – newly formed – is Family Services, and we offer child-care assistance. It could be in the form of transportation, clothing, tools, other work related services.

A new program that's really exciting is EVAG, the Emergency Voucher Assistance Grant Program. And those are housing grants made to eligible applicants who are at risk of becoming homeless. We served a number of individuals within the community this last year. This is a partnership with Cook Inlet Housing Authority. Another program we have is the Elders Program where we serve hot meals – lunch meals – Monday through Friday to seniors who are 55 and older at the Senior Elderly Housing Complex.

The elders get together at noon. We have regulars, and that number is always increasing. It's really just the elders who are active and go to the lunch site by themselves. Within that, we have potlucks and bingo games every once in awhile. We do fun things with the elders. And we also provide the elders with case management.

There are just so many reasons why people come here. What we try to do is be there to help them. We're not interested in acting as if we're a federal bureaucracy – "You've got to fill this form out and that form out and this form. And this is where you're getting this line of money." We're trying to make all those lines of money that we get into the agency as invisible as possible so that we provide seamless services here. And we've come a long way in doing that.

And, of course, we have a big emphasis on family preservation. We teach many different classes – parenting skills to anger management to surviving the workplace. The classes can help individuals or give them tools so that they can become self-sufficient and stay that way. And then we have general social services. If we can't help them here, we refer them to the agency in town that can. So we really try not to have any of our families fall through the cracks.

We have an expanding Education Department. We provide academic instruction to improve achievement at various schools within the Anchorage School District. We're in Bartlett, Dimond, East Anchorage High, and then Clark Middle School and two elementary schools, Wonder Park and Tyson. And we really looked at where to put tutor-counselors in those schools. We studied, not

246

only the demographics – there was a high Native population – but what was the retention rate? How were the Native kids doing in school? So, as our funds were starting to dry up, we really wanted to make the best use of our resources in the community. So that's why our tutor-counselors are in those schools.

We have an in-school youth program, which offers employment opportunities and supplemental learning opportunities within the traditional school year. And then, we have the Summer Youth Program, in which we provide youth employment opportunities to 100-plus youth from the ages of 14 to 21 every summer. We're everywhere, and we just recently hooked up with Southcentral Foundation, and we run as one program.

Right now we're talking about the Tribal Education Center where what we will do is offer college students prep courses in math, English – the courses you have to take before you can get into the required courses. We offer this on-site. We have professional teachers offer those classes. And then we also offer some of the basic college courses, like English 111 and so forth. We have a full computer lab.

And all of our programs, with the exception of our higher education scholarships, are offered to everybody within the Native community. So if you were from Calista Corporation, it wouldn't matter. We serve everybody.

We also have individualized tutoring in academic counseling and scholarships for higher education. And if you want to go to a technical school, we have grants.

Lastly, there is the Alaska Native Teachers for Excellence, which is a new program we started. We're in our second year. We're working with The CIRI Foundation and the Anchorage School District to increase the number of Alaska Natives and Native Americans to be hired within the school district as certified teachers. So this has worked very well.

We also have some really fun things that are coming up. We just opened up a coffee shop, and it was our first welfare-to-work entrepreneurial endeavor. Some of our welfare-to-work participants run the coffee shop directly themselves. So that's done quite well. We've even turned a small profit. Not only is it self-sustaining, but it's giving people the skills they need to go out and work. It's the Coho Cup, right there across from the new Native hospital.

I believe culture is so important to our Native community and very important to CITC, and it is a part of our mission. And so what we've done is we've implemented a new program. It's called Cultural Education. And we have Native artists, whether they're dancers or singers or people skilled in skin sewing, beading or story telling or what have you. We have a pool of Native artists that we send out to the local schools, to the prisons to day care centers, whoever requests it within the community, and we give a cultural presentation. That's to increase awareness of the Alaska Native culture and to preserve it. We pay the artists a nominal fee.

We do not get any money from CIRI. To really leverage our resources and to provide the optimum quality of service to the Native community, we have one accounting department which serves all the CIRI nonprofits. So you don't have duplicate services in each nonprofit. CITC runs those centralized services for the region. We just started this a couple years ago, and it's going full swing right now.

It's interesting because I really believe that things I've learned from business school brought up the level of understanding of coming into my current position – knowing we needed an operational plan for computer services, knowing we needed one for accounting. And with our Ernie Turner Center, we have not only federal and state grants, but we have to sustain ourselves with third-party monies, either insurance or Medicaid. It helped knowing that we needed a full business plan to ensure that center's success because if we can't keep the doors open, the community loses.

I think that it's really imperative these days to have some sort of business understanding as you run nonprofits. Because the resources are becoming more and more scarce, but yet our population is growing tremendously. And we have such a responsibility to the Native community. Understanding that trust responsibility is very important, but so is really understanding how to run efficient operations and making sure your money goes as far as it can in serving as many people as you can.

I really feel that CIRI's taken a leadership role to make sure that happens among its nonprofits.

So, overall, yes, I think the Alaska Native Claims Settlement Act has been very good for the Native communities, just in the sense of the resources that it's brought to each of our communities. And now, along with federal and state grants that we receive, we also have the for-profit corporations. And most of them are self-sustaining and

248

generate money and in many cases, there are dividends that do go back to shareholders.

*How do you feel about the fact that some people born after 1971 are not shareholders?* I understand financially why it might not be in the best interest of the corporation to open the rolls and dilute the shares of the stock if for some reason a Native corporation like CIRI were to make everybody born after 1971 shareholders. But then again, I think that it's important that individuals born after '71 have an identity. And a lot of the young people we see here know they are Alaska Natives or descendants of Alaska Natives, but in some cases they don't know what village their parents are from. Or, they don't know if they're Yup'ik or Tlingit. But they know they are Alaska Native. Some of the shareholders in the various Native corporations know how to relate to each other as shareholders. Whereas some of the younger generation – they don't even have that identity. So, I have really no strong feelings either way. I feel that if you have stock and you pass on or gift stock, you can gift it to your children or leave it to your children in a will. It's really imperative, though, that descendants of Alaska Natives understand or learn where their family's from and who they are and more about ANCSA and the impact that it's had on the Native community of Alaska.

*You have CIRI stock. But if you didn't have stock do you think you would feel left out?* No. I've always had the opportunity to work in Bristol Bay in the Native health corporation and here in the nonprofit, so I've always known from a young age of the services that are available. But sometimes people do not understand that services are available to them. I think the services carry much more magnitude than the stock.

I think it was a good thing that in 1971, corporations were created. Again, I just go back to my earlier point. It has given many Alaska Natives opportunities not only, for example, leadership roles they can play in these corporations, but also it's just brought a lot more resources to the state. In order to be heard in the Western world, you need to be economically viable and strong. And, I think, collectively, the Native corporations across the state are economically viable and strong. And that's why when we go back to Washington, D.C. – not in all cases, but in most cases – we're listened to and we get things done.

If you didn't have that in this day and age, with how business is, I don't think you would have that strong voice. And that's very important to have in making any type of change. Going into the 21st century and protecting our resources, you have to be very innovative and creative and have a lot of business sense to run a nonprofit.

*Your goals for the future?* Immediate future, I'm really focused on concentrating my efforts here at CITC. I think that there are a lot of things that we can do that I'm really excited about in the future. I want to ensure its success, taking this organization into the 21st century, making sure it's strong and viable and always – forever – trying to increase our base so that more resources flow to our Native community here in the form of services. And then also, in the very near future, I want to finish my MBA. After that, who knows? I love working for CITC and love the positive results that we can bring to the community. It warms my heart when I go and sit in a classroom of welfare-to-work recipients and watch the growth over a couple of weeks and the changes that we can help people make in their lives. Not do it for them, but help them make in their lives. It's very gratifying. And so I'm very passionate about our mission and what we have to offer and really hope to grow that in the future.

And then, for my child: Well, of course, I want her to be everything. But most significantly, I would like to pass to her the skills that were passed to me by my parents. I talked about my grandmother a lot, and the things that I learned from my family, and I want to always expose her to her rich, diverse background and make sure that she always knows who she is. I want to let her know that she can accomplish anything that she sets her mind out to accomplish. Having those opportunities available to her is what I hope for her in the future.

Something significant happened to me. Friday, there was a prayer breakfast for the Alaska Native veterans, sponsored by AFN and the AFN Sobriety Movement. I went to the prayer breakfast with my chairman, Patrick Marrs. We were just so fortunate to sit at a table full of elders who attend our lunch program. The elderly man sitting next to me, who has such a rich history and background – I've heard him tell stories – turned to me and said, "I'm very proud of you."

# Doyon Region

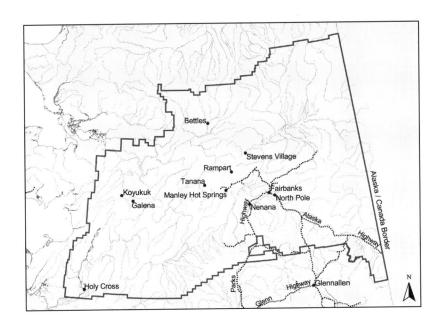

*DAWN N. DINWOODIE grew up in Fairbanks. Her mother is Athabascan from Stevens Village on the Yukon River. Her father is Scottish, and he has lived in Alaska most of his life. Dinwoodie was born May 16, 1968. She has a Bachelor's Degree in Business Administration from the University of Alaska Fairbanks. She graduated in 1992.*

*After she graduated from college, Dinwoodie had an internship with the Alaska Permanent Fund. She then worked for the Tlingit and Haida Central Council, developing a community loan fund to help tribal members in Southeast Alaska start businesses. She then was the Marketing/Development Director for Koahnic Broadcast Corporation, where she helped to develop KNBA, the first urban Native public radio station in the nation. She recently accepted a position with CIRI as Community Relations Specialist.*

*Dinwoodie serves on the Doyon, Ltd., Board of Directors. She was elected to the board in 1994. She also serves on the Alaska Federation of Natives Board. She is married to Rodney Worl, and the couple live in Anchorage.*

*Her passion is moose hunting and camping with her father in the fall. She looks forward all year to heading home to experience the spirit of the fall time, especially the colors. She was interviewed October 26 and 29, 1998.*

W hen I first started, I thought, "I don't want my dividend to get smaller." I was an intern in Doyon's Shareholder Relations, so I was involved in the committee that was studying the issue to enroll children born after 1971. When it was time to vote, I thought: "Darned if I'm letting my nieces and nephews not be involved." I was a total turnaround. There was no way I was going to leave them out. There was no difference between me and them. They were just born later.

I grew up in Fairbanks. My mother is Athabascan. She's from the village of Stevens Village. It's on the Yukon River. It's about 20 miles upriver from the Yukon Bridge when you drive up the Haul Road. And my father is mostly Scottish. And he's been in Alaska for a long time.

When I was younger we would go to Stevens Village to visit my grandfather and relatives. Even though I grew up in Fairbanks, I still felt very connected to my family because of the way my mom brought me up. She made sure that we were always around our family.

I remember when we were younger, we used to go to the village. I remember driving up the road, and my grandfather would come down from the village in his boat and pick us up and take us back up to the village. My grandfather died when I was 12, and I remember going to his funeral in Stevens. I remember his funeral very vividly. I don't know why. I remember strong images of people and things that I did when I was in the village when we went there for his funeral. And, he didn't smoke, but he had weak lungs. I come from family that has a very big problem with alcoholism. My grandparents – both of them had problems with alcohol. They were both alcoholics. And my grandmother died before I was born because she was an alcoholic.

When I think about my family and my relatives and all of Stevens Village, I cannot think of one person not affected by alcoholism. Because of those problems, my mother grew up in children's homes. She probably spoke Indian until she was five. Her Indian name is *Tlaaheelno*, which means "eldest." She has a younger sister and a brother.

When she was five my grandparents moved to Fairbanks. From the stories I hear, when my grandfather lived in the village, he trapped. And he had a very successful trapline. And I've heard that he even could hire people. I have an uncle who told me that my grandfather was a very good hunter and trapper. There's a story about him, and he told me the story when he was trapping wolves that he actually ran down a wolf with snowshoes on. He was very strong. These are the stories told to me by my family.

Even though my dad is Scottish, he has been the biggest influence in my life and educated me about my Native culture. He hunted with my grandfather. And he has a lot of Native friends. He knows a lot of the stories and ways. He's told me things about my family that my mother couldn't tell me. And that's mostly because she grew up in children's homes. It's very interesting with my parents. There was a period in my early 20's where I was adamant about questioning everybody about my family history. And with my father, it was easy. He knew a lot of stories. My mother's difficult years in the children's home has had an impact on me.

Probably in my early 20's, I started searching for anything about being Athabascan. And in the '80's being Native was definitely not cool in Fairbanks. But now, when I go back to schools, I see such pride in young Native kids. They have Native culture classes. There's a big difference now. There was no outreach to Native students when I was in high school. You don't want to be Native in these schools. It's not acceptable. In my school, in the period I went – this is my experience.

I remember in elementary school when all these kids came up from Texas and Oklahoma for the oil pipeline. Overnight, there was this trailer park out of nowhere. This whole subdivision went up in what seemed like minutes. Our school couldn't handle the kids, and it went to double shifts. They didn't know anything about the Native culture. And there was no education. The schools could barely handle teaching them, let alone trying to introduce them to Alaska and the Native culture.

But I remember kids teasing me because I wore mukluks to school that my grandma – my grandma's sister made me. We call her "Grandma" in the Native way, but she's technically my grandmother's sister. And I remember I felt very different because I was Native. In the school I went to there were few Native students. And it's mostly because we lived outside of Fairbanks. And that's where the new development came in because it's open land. So the school I was going to was mostly white. And I don't remember any discussion – anything – about Alaska Natives when I grew up. Nothing.

I love to tell this story because it's hilarious. I remember I had just gotten out of high school. So I got this job as a maid at the worst rundown hotel in Fairbanks. (Laughs.) And I was making seven dollars an hour. I thought this was pretty great. But I'm not paying rent with it and I'm thinking, "Wow! Lots of money here."

At the beginning of the summer, I thought, "Well, I'm going to go to college." And I have this tendency to not give up. I hate starting things and quitting them. So I thought, "Well, it's only this summer. I'll just tough it out." There were some nice people that worked there. But the end of the summer came, and for a few moments I was thinking, "Well, maybe I won't go to college. Maybe I'll just work. This money thing is kind of nice."

So I remember this one morning. It was August, before school. And I was at home, and my dad just got up. We have a wood stove. He is putting wood in the fire. And I was just sitting there, kind of waking up, and he's checking the fire. And he turns to me and says, "So, have you enrolled at the University? Are you ready to start school next month?"

And I think I got maybe three words out, and he knew exactly where I was headed. (Laughs.) I still remember him going berserk. I think I said something like, "Well, I was thinking about maybe w–" I maybe said "w," and he just blew his top. He was ranting and raving. It was hysterical because my dad – he's just woken up. He just went berserk in – like – two seconds. And I just said, "OK. I'll register tomorrow." (Laughs.)

When I think back on that moment – it was a pivotal point in my life. If he hadn't said anything, I would have said, "Oh, great. Maybe he doesn't care. I'll just go get a job. Who cares? Dad doesn't care. So maybe I'll just go work and be a maid or something."

At that moment there were two paths. I didn't really care which way I went, but did he! I just remember sitting there and thinking, "He really, really, really wants me to go to school, so I better go to school."

The next day I remember I drove to the University, filled out all the paperwork, applied and was going to college in a month. And I thank the Lord for my dad for sending me on the right path. I've told him this story. My dad and I are very good friends.

I have a nephew in Fairbanks, and he's in his last year in high school. And I just know how important it is for people to let him know what his choices are after high school. I have a different role in his life as an "auntie" than his parents. I feel very strongly about my nephews and nieces because in the Native way, these are my sister's children so they're my children. And I consider them as my children.

When I was in college, as with every young person, it was a time of learning and growing and finding out about my culture. I took a Koyukon Athabascan language class from Eliza Jones from Koyukuk. I loved that class. I felt like I was home. That class did wonders for me. I learned so much from Eliza. She moved to Fairbanks with her husband, who worked for the state. Dr. Krauss with the Alaska Native Language Center recruited her to record Athabascan Koyukon. She's finalizing a Koyukon dictionary right now. She really inspired me to learn more. It was so different from any other class. Sometimes she'd say, "Well, let's stop doing this. I'll tell you a story." And then that's where we really learned. She would tell us stories her father would tell her. She'd tell stories about growing up in the village.

In this class I learned things about the culture that I didn't know growing up in Fairbanks – like it's taboo for women to say the Native word for "bear" because "bear" is such a powerful spirit. Women are very powerful because women give life. There were a lot of what you'd call taboos – *hutlani*. When I was younger, I didn't understand why – I always thought, "Women's roles are so restricted. Why do they want to hold women back?" But it wasn't that at all. They had ways of doing things to honor the earth, to honor the spirits and to honor women. And these rules were designed because women's spirits are so powerful. It would clash with the bear spirit. Two very powerful spirits. Child-bearing women couldn't eat bear meat. They couldn't look at a bear. They couldn't say the Native word for bear. There was another word women would use, but it was a different word than men would use. Women had to use another indirect word that meant "black covering." In the Native ways, you are indirect when you speak.

In the old days when men would go hunting, you never go out the door and say, "I'm going to go shoot a bear." Because in the Native way, everything has a spirit, and bears know what you're thinking because the word is so powerful. Everything people did was to honor and respect. So when you leave, you say, "Well, I'm just going to go out and look around." You're respecting the bear, and you're respecting their spirits.

My grandfather's sister, Hilda Stevens, had such a good memory. She remembered everything. With some of the elders – because of Christianity – they chose to forget cultural beliefs or stories. Auntie Hilda was a gold mine. I kick myself when I think about not spending enough time with her. She remembered Native names, people, things, stories, everything. When I was in Juneau I would go back to Fairbanks and visit with her and ask her questions. One time she told me my grandfather's Native name. And I wrote it down, and of course, I can't say it. But she was telling me how to say it, so I was trying to say it, and I couldn't say it right. And she said, "What's wrong with your tongue?"

And I said, "Well, I think it's too white." (Laughs.)

I took Alaska Native history and Alaska Native languages. And I had a minor in Alaska Native studies. And then the year I graduated, I was elected as Outstanding Student for the Alaska Native studies program. I took an elder's class. That's a wonderful class. They bring elders from the villages, and they live on the campus for six weeks. It's traditional learning. They tell you stories, and you listen. There was a paper and journal, but the major focus was on learning the oral traditions from elders. We had two Yup'ik elders and two Inupiaq elders.

The two Yup'ik elders were wonderful. Paul and Martina John

and his daughter Theresa John from Toksook Bay. He spoke very limited English, and he spoke in Yup'ik, and his daughter translated Yup'ik to English for him. And he was wonderful. He told us the first time he saw a white person was when he was nine. I'd never met anyone that lived so long without seeing a white person. There were a lot of funny stories about when two cultures come together, how they get things mixed up. Funny things like not knowing what coffee grounds are or drinking tea for the first time, these kind of cultural encounters.

And then the other two elders were Inupiaq. And they were very different because they had been involved in the "white" culture for three generations. They were from Kaktovik. So it was two really different perspectives – one very recent contact, and one group who had been in contact for a longer period.

I was active in volunteer projects in college, and I still am today. I always blame my mom because when I was growing up she was busy in the Native community. We were always driving somewhere to help somebody. That's what I remember when I was little. And I tell people I grew up in a car. I remember going to the airport a lot to meet people coming in from Stevens Village. There's a joke about old beat up cars with lots of people in it – you know it is a Native car. That was us. We always had a lot of Native people. We were always driving somewhere, going somewhere, visiting, driving people to the airport, picking up my relatives and grandfather. Before he died, he would stay at our house. My uncle would come and stay with us. My dad had a friend who was a taxi cab driver. He was a nice guy. His name was George McCoy. He would tell my dad that his living was driving people around, and one day he passed my mom nine times on the roads!

I moved to Juneau after I graduated. I got an internship at the Alaska Permanent Fund. I studied real estate investment that summer. After that, I got a job with Central Council Tlingit and Haida Indian Tribes of Alaska. That was very exciting, my first job out of college. It was to start a community loan fund to help tribal members in Southeast Alaska start businesses. Moving from Fairbanks to Juneau was like night and day. Native cultures are a lot alike, but to be immersed in the Tlingit and Haida cultures was very rewarding for me. There are a lot of similarities, but there are a lot of subtle differences in the way we do things. The Tlingit and Haida people were very good to me.

The project I started is still going, so that's a good thing, and I traveled a lot to the villages. The traveling allowed me to experience and learn the culture and help people in remote locations. I did that for three years, and I got married. My husband is Tlingit. We moved to Anchorage after we got married. I look back fondly on my Juneau days. College was a growth time for me, and moving to Juneau – away from my family – was another huge growth for me. Learning a new culture was very exciting. I have such respect for the Tlingit and Haida people. The Alaska Native Brotherhood, the Alaska Native Sisterhood, those groups started in the early 1900's. They had their first Tlingit lawyer in the early 1900's. They are very progressive, politically savvy people. They knew they had to fight to keep their land, and they knew they had to learn a different way to do that.

I loved the Southeast Native foods: the seafood, the cockles, the herring eggs, the gumboots. I was in heaven with the Native food down there – the sockeye. I still love my Athabascan food. Moose meat, I still get cravings for.

We got married in July of '95. Rodney (Worl) is enrolled to Klukwan and Sealaska, and I'm enrolled to Doyon and Dinyee Corporation, which is the village corporation for Stevens Village.

I was on the Stevens Village board for about a year when I was in college. And I got elected to the Doyon board in '94 when I was living in Juneau. When I was elected I think I was the youngest female board member elected to Doyon. I think John Sackett and I tied for the youngest board member at age 27. He served on the board when it first got organized.

*Is the village corporation successful?* I'm sure there are small successes here and there. Dinyee is not one of the financially thriving village corporations like Klukwan, which is a very well known village corporation. We are in tourism. It's a small corporation. You have a limited number of people to be on the board and everyone is related. Mostly, the corporation relies on 7(i) money from other regions. I thought I had something to contribute. I was politically naïve, but very full of desire to be involved and make a difference.

The important job of the Native corporations is to protect the traditional lands of the village or region. Stevens Village is a well known statewide leader in protecting their traditional lands because the pipeline runs right through it. The village corporation sued to protect the village and the land from the pipeline.

I ran for office in '94. Two years earlier, the corporation shareholders voted to distribute stock to children who were born after 1971. Our shareholders felt very strongly that young people need to be involved. We cannot leave them out. Doyon did three years of research, study and disseminating this information to the shareholders before the vote. And, at one point, it was like 50-50. Half the shareholders thought, "Nah, I don't want to do it. I don't want my dividend to get smaller."

The other half thought, "We can't leave our kids out. They're our future."

By the time we got through this three-year process, I think that vote passed by 75 percent. When I first started out, I thought, "I don't want my dividend to get smaller." I was interning in Doyon's Shareholder Relations, so I was involved in the committee that was studying the issue to enroll children born after 1971. When it was time to vote, I thought: "Darned if I'm letting my nieces and nephews not be involved." I was a total turnaround. There was no way I was going to leave them out. There was no difference between me and them. They were just born later. So, the vote passed by a big margin, and when I ran in '94, basically it was the vote that we want our young people to be involved. That's how I perceive my election of why I'm on the Doyon Board.

*Your Native hero?* My mother is my hero because she overcame alcoholism. She was unable to be with me in high school. I took care of my younger brother with my dad. It was the three of us. I admire her strength. It takes time for people to heal. We are friends now.

OCTOBER 29:

What I was thinking about after I left the last meeting was that Doyon's mission includes the culture of our people – not only business. We balance the two. And a big part of our cultural preservation is subsistence.

Politically, we've been active in promoting and preserving that; socially, we've done it with programs. What I was thinking about is: the issue we face in the future is that more of our young people are growing up in urban centers and not knowing or understanding rural life, village life or what subsistence is. And I was thinking I felt very fortunate because I grew up outside of Fairbanks and I grew up "urban," but I was very fortunate to have a father who lived a subsistence lifestyle. And it wasn't a choice. My father had a humble income, and we grew up eating subsistence food. We liked it, but we had to because that was just how my dad got by. There were four of us, and in a Native family there's always extra – so there were actually four kids and usually two or three more. My mom was always taking care of other people's kids.

This is one of those peak rabbit years, and I haven't seen this many rabbits for a long time. But when I was growing up, I remember being seven or six and looking out the window and seeing tons of rabbits. We used to snare them all the time and eat them. I got sick of them actually. There's a lot of funny stories about rabbits and our family. When my sister was little, she saw one of my dad's snares. I don't know how old she was. And a rabbit was in it. She tried to let the rabbit out, and the rabbit bit her. He got away. He was saved, but he bit her. And then we had to take her to the doctor. And she had to get rabies shots. (Laughs.) But she remembers distinctly – it made a noise when she approached it.

My mom had this way of skinning rabbits. She would tie it to a broom, and the kids always had to hold the broom on each end, and she'd peel it like you'd peel a banana. We grew up eating a lot of moose, bear. I remember my dad would go out hunting, and he'd come back. And I'd go outside and look and see what he got. A lot of fish. In the summertime my dad ran a fish wheel with my grandfather on the Tanana. This is one of those things, when you look back, you think, "God, how did my parents do it? How did they raise us?" It's amazing what my father did. He had a full-time job, and then in the summer he ran our fish wheel. And he'd make strips of dried fish, and he'd go downtown to sell them for extra money.

Before I was born when my mother was pregnant with me they were living in an apartment building in downtown Fairbanks. It was old and dumpy and my father hated living in the city. And he decided he was going to do anything to get out of that. And the only way to do that, he decided, was to move the family to an island on the Tanana River. And he saved enough money to buy a piece of land. That was the only way he knew he could save enough money. And my mom didn't want to go, but eventually she went out there. And they had a wall tent. Wall tents are pretty common in the Interior. And they lived on the island for a summer. And he'd drive his boat back and forth to get to work.

My dad bought the land I grew up on Chena Small Tracts. It's right on the Chena River. Before development, there was more open land. We spent a lot of time outside. Watching TV and being inside – for us – was not an option.

And my dad – the way he was able to build a home for us – he bought a trailer. He built a wannagon on it. We lived in that. And this is amazing to me, too. In one summer he built a log home for us – in addition to working a full-time job. He had help. We had relatives that would come out and stay and help him build. But I remember him – he worked all day long and then he'd come home and work all night. I remember watching it go up. And I remember the first day we moved into it. I thought it was the biggest house in the world – you know, coming from a trailer. And it was actually a small log cabin. (Laughs.) But to us, it was the greatest thing in the world. Dad still lives there. All of us kids, obviously, are grown and moved out.

Those are important memories to me because I think they were valuable experiences for me growing up in understanding who I was and subsistence and my culture. For me, to be on the Doyon board, I think those were important things for me to experience and understand.

And I wonder what our future will look like when we have more and more kids growing up in the urban areas and not understanding what subsistence is. Maybe they've never been to their village, and maybe their whole life is shopping at Carrs or going to the mall.

I think there are a lot of good programs, though, that are helping to bridge that gap, as with Southcentral Foundation. Cook Inlet Region, Inc. provides an amazing array of services for Native people. They could provide all these services and say, "This is for CIRI only." But that's where I have a lot of respect for this organization that strives to promote Native culture and Native people. Their services through Alaska's People, the Alaska Native Heritage Center, Koahnic Broadcasting: they all serve Alaska Native people.

I grew up in ANCSA. I don't remember my mother enrolling me. I was too young. My husband is nine years older, and he remembers his mother (Rosita Worl) coming to the kids and saying, "Should we enroll to Klukwan?" And talking about enrolling to Sealaska. He was old enough to remember that.

With my father being from Montana, when we were young, we

went to Montana quite a bit to see my grandmother. And so I never asked anybody, but I wondered why Lower 48 Indians had reservations. I knew we were different. I knew Alaska Natives were different from Indians in the Lower 48. But I never questioned it when I was little. I just remember driving around Montana and thinking, I wonder why they call themselves "tribal members" and I'm a "shareholder"? And I wonder why they live on reservations, and I don't live on a reservation?

I grew to understand how the Alaska Native Claims Settlement Act was different. I took a college course at UAF. The professor was Dennis Demmert. He's a Tlingit from Klawock. We discussed the legislation. I loved that class. For me to finally look at it and read it, there were a lot of "aha's."

"Oh, that's why they did that."

So I highly recommend that young people go through the act and read it. Study it and understand it.

Right now, I'm going through this period in my life where history is really important – especially Native history in Alaska. I have a couple of books I'm trying to read. I just think it's so important for young people to know Alaska's history and Alaska Native history especially. To know that the Alaska Native Brotherhood started discussions about land claims issues in the early 1890's. That's important to know. And to know who Elizabeth Peratrovich was. I didn't know who Elizabeth Peratrovich was until I moved to Juneau, until I was in my 20's. And when I finally found out who she was and read about her, I was shocked and very proud that this woman – Alaska Native woman – fought for equal rights for Alaska Native people in the 1940's.

Through my reading, I found out that when James Wickersham was our representative in the Territorial days, our U.S. Representative in D.C., he won at least two elections because of the Native vote. That is so important for people to know. And that people actually tried to restrict Native people from voting because they knew how powerful the Native vote was. There were laws that said you had to prove you were a citizen to vote. And if you didn't write and speak English, you weren't a citizen. It's important for young people to know how hard our ancestors fought for us to be where we are.

Some people think that the Alaska Native Claims Settlement Act is not living up to what it was supposed to be. Or, it doesn't fulfill our needs. I agree that the Alaska Native Claims Settlement Act does not fulfill all the needs of the Native people.

When I was growing up as a Doyon shareholder – what I knew was that I had 100 shares of stock in Doyon. And Doyon was Athabascan. It represented to me where I come from and who I am as an Athabascan. And I understood the business part of it. And when I was going to college, I got a business degree. And I always thought, "When I grow up, I'll get a business degree and work for Doyon." And I think that was very common for young people. The Native corporations – young people knew about them. Doyon was always there. The newsletter's always there. I think it's something that's always present in people's lives. And it's something that they can relate to. And it's where they see role models – it's where they see the presidents and the CEO's and the board people. So it's easy for them to identify with that.

I remember in college when I was in my second or third year, I wanted to intern at Doyon very badly. In fact, I went to an annual meeting – our annual meetings are in March. And I knew the person that was in charge of the intern program, and I found her at the annual meeting, and I told her that I really wanted to apply for the intern program. And this was in March. So, I was months ahead of the application date. So, I did finally get a job there that summer, and I got it with Robin Renfroe, the person that I talked to at the meeting. And one of the reasons that she told me she wanted to hire me was because she was very impressed with me thinking that far ahead and coming to her at the annual meeting. And I've always considered Robin a mentor in my life. She's a Vice President at Doyon right now. I learned about what Doyon is, what they do. I was involved in the 1991 Committee, which looked at the issue of enrolling the children.

That was my first real job in college. I took it seriously. I did a report for Doyon. It was my project that summer. It was outlining the services in the Interior for Native people. And I interviewed I don't know how many people. But it was compiling Fairbanks Native Association, Doyon and Tanana Chiefs services. And basically Robin needed this report because people come to Doyon for everything: "I can't pay my rent." "I need help with my children." And she needed that report as a resource to direct them to the right agency.

I was very proud to work there. Robin was incredible. She was just very patient. She was an excellent role model. She really mentored me and took the time with me and encouraged me. And I really can't say enough about her. That's what I expect from Doyon – to turn around and help the next generation out. Because of Robin and people like her, I feel that it's important for me to do the same and when I can I turn around and I look to see who needs my help, just like Robin gave me a hand. I feel it's my duty to turn around and do that for others who are coming behind me.

*Was it a good idea to create a corporate structure in ANCSA?* Now that we have the corporations, how could you say they weren't a good idea? To me, the corporations are successful in many ways, but there is always room for improvements. I think there's a misunderstanding about what the corporations were intended to do. That's why so many people call Doyon for so many things. And what I admire about our corporation is that our shareholders' needs are very important. And if they call us asking something that's not related to Doyon, they get help. They're not turned away. Shareholders know that we really care. I can't answer that question because I never grew up on a reservation and I didn't grow up in the Lower 48. So I wouldn't know otherwise. But what I do know from traveling down there – I personally think that the Native corporations were better than the reservations.

One example: I traveled to the Pine Ridge Reservation in South Dakota when I lived in Juneau. I went down there because they had started a micro-loan fund, and I was going down to study it for the work I was doing in Juneau. I don't have a comprehensive view of reservations. I'm just talking about this one experience. But I was really shocked at how differently they lived. And I was only there a week. It's a poverty-stricken county. From what I can see, there's not a lot of subsistence activity. People rely a lot on government food. They call the food "commods." The Lakota Fund, the nonprofit I was studying, was doing a lot in the area of helping people start businesses. They were helping low-income people. It's a thriving organization still. But I was just surprised at how different it was down there.

We were talking about Native foods, and I asked one of the ladies, "What kind of Native foods do you have?" And, you know, if you ask someone in Alaska, it could be an hour-long discussion, maybe a week discussion, I should say. And she said, "Well, we have a berry dish." So I didn't say anything because I thought she was going to keep going. But she didn't keep going. That's all she said.

And we did go to some people's homes. The Pine Ridge

Reservation is two hours from Rapid City, so it's like the villages in Alaska. You rely on a lot of foods that are preserved for a long time. But what I saw was they didn't have the subsistence that we have in Alaska. That's what it looked like to me was the difference.

I'm obviously getting back to subsistence because that, I think, is who we are. Subsistence is the Native culture. And I feel fortunate I grew up that way. I grew up in the subsistence way.

I think if you look at statistics, and I've heard this at conferences, that Native corporations are wealthier than tribal entities in the Lower 48. When I lived in Juneau, I went to a lot of economic development type of conferences. But there's a lot more to Native corporations than business. Business is obviously the driving force, but we're in business because of our culture. For us to provide the cultural services for our shareholders, we have to have solid profitable businesses. So there's always a balance. I know at Doyon when we look at business opportunity, shareholder hire and profits are the two leading issues in any business decision.

Doyon is in a catering/security business because of shareholder hire opportunities. It wasn't seen as a high margin business, but it has been profitable.

*Do you know much about the people who worked on ANCSA?* Yes, I actually work with them. (Laughs.) I've heard Morris Thompson and Willie Hensley interviewed about ANCSA. I think the early founders have taken criticism about ANCSA because it has not fulfilled everyone's needs. In my humble opinion, I think the Native leaders did the best that they could at the time with what was given to them. Obviously, they didn't have a lot of money. They weren't a financially powerful lobbying group. But I think, given the situation, they did a good job. A lot of them were faced with situations they'd never faced before. Some of these were people were in their early 20's. I couldn't imagine being in my early 20's and having to fight these types of political battles.

ANCSA did not address subsistence for Native people. I believe that was left out because the Native leaders were told the legislation would not be passed with it in. So later, the Alaska National Interest Lands Conservation Act of 1980 was supposed to provide subsistence protections, but it hasn't worked out that way.

I can't imagine any 20-year-olds today – maybe they're out there – that could do what the leaders did at that time. I think they were facing monumental decisions. And the elders, from what I understand, were relying on them. The elders chose them because they were the ones that grew up in the BIA schools. They were the ones that were reading and writing English, and they felt that these were the people that would best represent us.

I have a lot of respect for the Native leaders at that time. They were young, and they were facing huge challenges that they had to figure out.

There was one other thing that's always struck me about the Alaska Native Claims Settlement Act. Two or three years ago, a lot of the corporations were facing these issues with shareholders wanting liquidation. In our region, we had a small group of shareholders who started a petition to do a very large liquidation of Doyon that would liquidate half the assets. There was an elder who was a part of that group who was advocating with the group. Their position was basically, "Doyon needs to distribute more money."

I'm not going to speak for or against them. But what struck me about the elder was that this person comes from a culture where leaders give everything away. The more they give away, the wealthier they are considered to be. Keeping money and growing it, investing it, compounding it is not a part of our culture. Throwing the biggest potlatch in honor of your relatives is probably the most honorable thing you can do with your "riches," and keeping it is selfish.

So I thought, "If that's the way he grew up, looking at a corporation that has over 200 million dollars in assets right now, has a portfolio well over 130 million, it doesn't make cultural sense." Because to be wealthy is to give everything away to people you love in honor of somebody you love – sharing and giving. And the Western business concept of investing and compounding and re-investing does not complement the culture.

Doyon has been very progressive in terms of shareholder needs. The Shareholder Relations Department does surveys every couple years to track the pulse of our shareholders. What are they thinking? What would they like to see us do? And, I guess, listening to the shareholders is probably the best thing that I can do. The shareholders are concerned about mostly jobs and education – and dividends. I've run into a lot of shareholders who would appreciate a job that paid them a consistent income from Doyon more than a dividend. Because a job obviously gives you a lot more than a once-a-year dividend. That is definitely our goal – to provide more jobs.

I respect the opinions of our elders and strive to balance the two worlds of culture and corporate opinion. I grew up in ANCSA. I grew up with our culture, too. I think personally Doyon goes way beyond what a non-Native corporation would do.

We have a unique dividend policy. Our dividend policy is that 50 percent of our profits averaged over the past three years will be distributed as dividends and also as donations. I could be wrong, but I don't think any other corporation has that liberal of a dividend policy. That policy was actually developed by a former Doyon board member. We had a lot of pressure to do a big liquidation, and he came to a meeting and said, "Why don't we just do 50-50? That's what people want. They want us to be equal. So let's just do 50 percent to them; 50 percent re-invested back into the corporation." And when we say 50 percent back to the corporation, it's back to projects, businesses and other investments.

I think communication is a critical component of a strategic plan and shareholder relations. We've done a lot in the past three years to communicate more with our shareholders. We've gone from six newsletters a year to 12. We do a radio show called, "Radio Dialogue with Doyon" to reach more shareholders. We've done surveys. We've increased our community meetings. We've done a couple open houses in Fairbanks so people can come into the headquarters and visit so they would know this corporation is your corporation. What I'd like to see in the future is just continued dialogue with shareholders. They have a lot of good ideas about businesses.

What I'd like to see Doyon do in the future is – we have long-term strategic plans to have more natural resource projects in Interior Alaska. That will provide jobs to shareholders. That will provide dividends. We lease our land to companies to do exploration, but we'd like to have a large profitable natural resource project that will return money and jobs. That's one of our long-term goals. And that will be helpful for people in the villages.

A consistent challenge for Native corporations is to create successful businesses in rural Alaska. Board members need to be creative and seek solid partnerships to create jobs in villages. I would hate to see people move to Anchorage because they feel they have to. And a lot of people do. But I think we need to have that choice. I think we need to help people with economic opportunities in the villages. And I don't have the answer. I don't know what the business would be. There are tourism opportunities that Doyon has researched.

Doyon has experienced growth in the last couple of years. And we went through some internal planning to catch up with the growth with management. We are at the point now where we can start looking at new business opportunities.

I talked to some people with another corporation, and I was very impressed with their global view. They were getting into some projects in other countries and in the Lower 48. And I think that's an opportunity for Doyon – to look beyond the Alaska borders for business opportunity. I think we're coming to a point in our business where we can start doing that.

In the mid-'80's, Doyon was in severe debt. So it has gone from a company that was near bankruptcy in the mid-'80's to a company now that has over 200 million dollars in assets. What happened was, in the mid-'80's when we were having financial problems, staff was severely cut back and Morris Thompson was hired as the President. And, in the time since Morris has been the president, the company has grown. It's financially strong now.

I think the board is balanced. There's a good mix of people that have been on the board awhile. They were on the board when it was nearly bankrupt, and they helped to turn the ship around. And then there is somebody like me, who's been on the board since 1994. There are those two perspectives. And it's good for me to hear those stories about what happened and to understand how current policies and perspectives were formed.

I think the challenges the Native corporations face are how to include the younger generation. How do they perceive ANCSA? How are we going to involve them in the corporation? I think a big issue coming up is blood quantum. I think more and more Native people are going to have less and less Native blood. And an issue we're facing again at Doyon – for the second time, and some corporations haven't faced it once – is enrolling our "second wave" of new kids. We've enrolled them from 1971 to 1992. Now, we're looking at enrolling kids born after 1992. That's an issue on the near horizon for us.

We enrolled new kids in 1992, and a popular concern for shareholders was: "My dividend's going to get smaller." And it never has. Ever since we've enrolled new kids, Doyon dividends have never decreased.

Corporations can enroll children with different policies to

lessen the financial impact. And that's what we did. It's not the same stock as mine. It wasn't a hundred shares. You got 30 shares at birth, then 70 when you turn 18. So that lessened the impact. And it's "life estate" stock. It dies with them. It's not like my stock. I can pass my shares on to family members.

And I think for Doyon, the challenge we face is the oil industry. We have a drilling company. I just took an educational trip up to the North Slope. It was my first trip. We went to our five drilling rigs. To see to the rigs, to visit with employees, to get a better understanding of the business was really good for me. We met with some executives with ARCO and BP to hear their perspective on the future of the oil industry.

One of our strategic goals is expanding into non-oil industries. And we have with our tourism company. We have Kantishna Lodge in Denali Park.

I think the future, too, for the corporation – the non-business side – is our cultural preservation, promoting and protecting our Native way of life. We have to be secure in our business opportunities so we can do non-business things like the cultural preservation. Even what some people would consider political activity – we have to do it to protect subsistence and our culture.

Native corporations are maturing in their business development. In the early years, it was common practice to joint venture with a company for industry expertise and management skills. Corporations are maturing and now can turn to each other for joint ventures in the areas of tourism, natural resource development and others. I hope to see more collaborations and partnership amongst the village and regional corporations.

 **CARRIE IRWIN** *was born September 13, 1971, in Fairbanks. She grew up in Nenana. Her great-grandmother was full-blooded Athabascan from the Koyukuk region near Bettles, and her great-grandfather was Inupiaq. The Athabascan members of the family are Koyukon Athasbascan. Her mother is a non-Native from Texas.*

*Irwin is a shareholder of the village corporation for Nenana, Toghetthele Corporation, and Doyon, Ltd. She currently serves on the Board of Directors of Toghetthele and is the youngest person ever to serve on the Board. Eventually, Irwin would like to serve on the Doyon Board.*

*Irwin graduated from Alaska Pacific University in December 1994 with a management degree in International Business. She interned at National Bank of Alaska in the Community Development Department and has worked at Alaska Village Initiatives and Providence Hospital in Anchorage. She was interviewed September 15, 1998.*

I just came back from Kipnuk and Kwigillingok, which are very, very traditional villages out in Southwest Alaska. And we went from having fresh goose soup – and they're eating seal oil and everything else for lunch, and we go back to the office and they're speaking Yup'ik to each other fluently. And that's all they speak to each other. And then he gets on the phone, and he's speaking English to some guy in D.C. So I think that the people that are in these positions have an incredible ability to switch back and forth, really and to sort of straddle both.

I was born in Fairbanks at the Army Hospital on Fort Wainwright, which is where Native babies were born at that time. It was before they had the Chief Andrew Isaac Health Center there.

My family is originally from up in the Koyukuk region near Bettles. My great-grandmother is full-blooded Athabascan, and my great-grandfather was Inupiaq. It was a little different in that Bettles is one of the few places up there on the Koyukuk where there were both Eskimos and Indians living in the same villages. And so my grandmother is half-Athabascan and half-Inupiaq, and my grandfather was Irish. He came out of California to Alaska when he was 16 years old, I think. My dad and a few of his brothers and sisters were born in Bettles, and then they moved to Nenana later. So I grew up in Nenana, as did some of my dad's younger brothers and sisters, and that's where I was raised. So although we're from Nenana, we're not Tanana Athabascan, we're Koyukon Athabascan because of the relocation.

My mom is from Texas, so I am a quarter Alaska Native – an eighth Athabascan, and an eighth Inupiaq and was raised Athabascan. So I don't really know much about the Inupiaq culture. And I'm a Doyon shareholder; a shareholder of Toghetthele Corporation, which is the corporation for Nenana. I might have a couple of other cousins that are also shareholders, but for the most part, my dad and his brothers and sisters are not shareholders in the village corporation that I'm a shareholder of. And my sister and my other cousins were too young to be shareholders. So I'm kind of a lone wolf there in Toghetthele Corporation.

Our family was raised a pretty traditional lifestyle based on subsistence. We didn't do a lot in Fairbanks. Although where a lot of people see Nenana as not really a village because it's located on the road, we lived a very traditional lifestyle until I was in high school. We didn't have TV and telephone and all of those kinds of modern amenities until later, probably junior high or high school. So that was a little different, too, even though we were right there on the road system. It was very traditional, and we were very involved with the potlatches and everything that went on on the village side.

Nenana's a little different, too, in that it's pretty split between Native and non-Native, and I think at the time I was in high school it was probably about 50-50. And I think that's changed a little bit. There are probably more non-Natives there now than there are Natives. But when I graduated, about half of my class was Native and half wasn't. And I was born and raised there, went to school at Nenana from kindergarten through twelfth grade. When I graduated I went to the University of Hawaii my first year of college, and that was a huge culture shock, of course. And from there, I later returned to the University of Alaska Anchorage, and then I went to UAF and from there I went abroad to Japan for a year. I majored in international business, so it was a requirement of my program. I graduated from Alaska Pacific University in December 1994 with a degree in management in international business. I've been here in Anchorage almost four years now.

I have one sister. She's younger than me – about three and a half years younger. She now has her own Doyon shares because we let in people born after 1971. So she does have shares of her own in

Doyon, but not in the village corporation. We didn't let anybody else in the village corporation. In my dad's family, there are seven brothers and sisters, and of course, they all have like three and four kids. So I have a lot of family up there.

*Discrimination?* I can't say that I felt any discrimination because we mainly just stuck with ourselves. We did our own thing. And it's almost as if there's a village there, and then there's a city, and we just basically stuck with the village. Even the non-Native people that live there – at the time I was there – a lot of them don't live in town. They live out on the road system. So it wasn't really like there was any discrimination. I don't think I was ever subjected to it, and I think, too, with my family – my family was one of the largest families there.

*Was alcohol abuse a problem in the community?* Oh, yeah, that's in every village, and in Nenana, too. Most of my life, especially when I was younger in elementary school we had foster kids that lived with us a lot of the time. So we saw it all the time. And now, too, when I go home, I see a lot of the welfare people that live in "HUD row," as we call it.

*What encouraged you to pursue higher education?* I think my parents would have killed me if I hadn't. (Laughs.) My Uncle Mike Irwin was the first person in our family to ever go to college, and I was the second. I never even considered not going to college. But I think in Nenana, too, from the beginning, people were split out. It seemed like our class was either already designated as: these are the smart kids, and they're going to go on and do something. And these are the kids that nobody expects anything out of. There were 12 or 13 in my graduating class, and there were about six of us that took the harder classes that were offered. Everyone kind of knew that we would go to college. And then there were the other kids that I don't think anybody even ever cared about where they were going or thought about what they would do after high school.

We've thought about this a lot because we have the Howard Rock Foundation. We've gone through this over and over again, discussing the differences in education in rural Alaska and why I came out OK and why a lot of people don't. It did have a lot to do with my family. My parents had me when they were 17 years old. They got married when they were 17, and may have gone through school to tenth grade and later got their GED's. But I also saw my parents as very successful people. My dad – he's a very hard worker.

He's always worked on the North Slope or in construction. And my mom's now the business manager for the school district in Barrow. So even though they encouraged education, I never saw it as something that was absolutely necessary. I see that people are very smart and very successful without having gone to college. But my parents kind of drilled it into me that it was necessary for me. They both just turned 44.

That's another thing about my family. I'd have to say I am the oldest one not to have kids or be married. Almost everybody in my family got married and had kids when they were 16, 17, 18 years old. Even my sister, she has two kids already.

My grandma speaks fluent Athabascan and Inupiaq. But she never spoke it with us. I guess she probably did with my dad and his older sister and my Uncle Mike. It was used around us. I know phrases and certain words, but never used as sentences or any type of fluency at all. I remember when we were in elementary school. They used to have some of the elders come in and teach us a limited amount of conversation, but that didn't last very long. Other than that, it's mostly just what we know from hearing things here and there and just from knowing the songs and things like that – but never any type of formal education for sure.

*Did you ever feel any discrimination from Native people?* When I'm at home or in the Interior when I'm in Fairbanks, people know my name. They know the Irwin name, so they know I'm Native. But I've found that at this company it's a lot different because we work with Native people from all over the state who don't know my family and who don't know my name who just would assume that I'm not Native at all. Or, if I say I'm Native, they say, "Oh, you're from Nenana, it's not really a village." That kind of thing. So I have seen some of that. And especially, too, because, even at home, I get this because I like nice things. I like to go shopping a lot, and I like to dress up. You know, they think, "Oh, you couldn't possibly have come from a village" and that kind of thing. So I have seen that.

*When did you have a sense of being Native?* I never considered myself not because I was raised around my dad's family. I was raised as an Athabascan. I met my mom's family, and I visited them, and I've known them. But it's not me. It's a foreign thing, these people from Texas with their big hair and their Southern drawls. And I never considered myself anything but. I've always just known it. I think a lot of people put a lot of emphasis on – if you're mixed with "white" of some kind, you're not full Native. But I never knew anything else but that.

*Native hero?* I guess I'd just have to say Alaska Natives in general are just such resilient people. How can you not honor that and respect that? I think that's in general, but I don't think there would be any one person. I'd have to say my grandma for the traditional skills that she has and the things that she brings. But I'm just so much different from that. My goals and everything are so much different that I don't know if I have anybody like a mentor-type person other than following the footsteps of my Uncle Mike Irwin, who was the Executive Director of the Alaska Natives Commission and who was Commissioner of the Alaska Department of Community and Regional Affairs. He's a very successful Alaska Native person. And that's something to look up to and kind of follow his lead, but at the same time trying to keep my own identity without getting sucked up in his. But, a lot of times, it's the first question I ever get out of people – if I'm related to him. On one hand, of course, I want to be like that and I want to follow his lead, at the same time I want to establish myself as my own.

That's just a Native thing, too, to try and connect you to somebody. When I go home, if I meet somebody and I'm introduced and they hear my name, they automatically want to figure out who I am. If I say my name is Carrie Irwin, they want to know, "Well, which one's your dad?" And then try and figure out who you are by associating you with your family. So that's pretty normal. I had that happen downstairs actually. When I first had met Nelson (Angapak) from AFN, and he asked me who I was, and I told him my name and he said, "Who is your dad?" So I told him. And I told him Mike was my uncle. And he said, "Now I know you." And that's kind of how it is. Once you figure out who their family ties are, you know somebody that they know – then you know them.

*When did you become aware of ANCSA?* Probably in junior high. I guess we always knew about it because we knew we were part of Toghetthele or Doyon, and it was explained to us why are we a part of these organizations. Why do we care about Doyon and what Toghetthele is doing? So we've always been associated with that. And I think especially with the village corporation, the village council in town. We always interacted with them. We always knew they were there. And they sent us to AFN as youth delegates. I don't think it was ever really discussed.

*Do you know much about the act?* I do somewhat. And a lot of it has come just recently, as far as who was involved in it. The history, I've known. It's been a good topic for term papers and things because a lot of people don't really understand it. So I have done research on it and written about it before. And then I was always sort of primed for becoming a board member one day and sort of understanding what the role of the corporation is and what the role of the council is and the role of Doyon and Tanana Chiefs. My family has always made it known to me what my role is there and what they think our family should be doing when it comes to things like that. And you know my Uncle Mike was on the board of Doyon when he was real young. And getting involved with those organizations has always been a pretty big part of living there in Nenana.

I'm on the board of Toghetthele. I was appointed three years ago. We've had the same board members on the board since probably it was created. And finally, there was a resignation, and I was nominated and then appointed. And that lasted for about a year, and then I was elected at the following meeting – the youngest person ever on the board, and probably the only one under 45 right now.

And there's been sort of a – this is statewide – push to involve more young people and get them ready for when these other leaders are going to be moving on eventually. They can't stay on there forever. Who's going to take over when they leave? When I was put on the board I didn't know anything about being on a board. I didn't really know the details of the activities of what the corporation had tried in the past or what they were willing to try in terms of projects – economic development projects.

It's been really difficult because even though people say that they want to get more young people involved, they don't want to give up that seat. And it's very rare that you see young people on the board of directors of most village corporations because they have the same people that have been on there for 20 years. And a lot of them will hang on to that seat until they die. I'd have to say that a lot of them probably go because they get the 50-dollar check for showing up or whatever it is. They've just done it for so long that it's just something to do. But I haven't really seen – we have quite a few young Native people here at this company, and I don't think any of them are on their boards or have even really been approached to try and do something like that. My village – I have to commend these guys for realizing the importance of leading the younger people to take over what they've been doing. There are nine members on the board of Toghetthele.

*Do you hope someday to be on the Doyon board?* I do, and I have made my intentions known to them for the last two years. I submitted my name for the board slate last year and wasn't selected for the board slate, so I didn't pursue it. I figure that's the easiest way to get on. But, again, there's a corporation where a lot of the board members have either been on the board for a very long time or have been around in the organizations in Fairbanks for a very long time. They've worked for Tanana Chiefs Conference for 15 years or they work for Fairbanks Native Association. Although Doyon is one of the other ones that really is progressive in getting younger people in there. As you probably know, Dawn Dinwoodie is on the Board of Directors for Doyon. She's the youngest board member ever.

*Has your village corporation been successful?* It depends on how you define success, but I'd have to say no. With Toghetthele there were some scandals in the earlier years – probably until about 10 years ago. And I don't know all the details of it, but apparently a lot of money was sucked out of the corporation. This has happened all over the state. It's not just this particular village. It's happened all over. They went through periods of horrible management of the resources. A lot of it was just ignorance of business practices.

For the last five years, at least, they've been extremely conservative and basically have not done a single thing besides investments. And even the investments are significantly more conservative than what the "prudent man" conservative is. And they've basically just been hoarding it and holding on to it and making sure that it doesn't happen again. Another board member and I got them stimulated and thinking about some possible projects that we might be able to do that weren't so risky that the board wouldn't even consider them, but at the same time something to create jobs, to help develop the community, so that we're not just sitting around keeping our money in a bank and hoarding it. So we've sort of tried to move in that direction in the last couple of years.

Our future has a lot to do with Nenana's location. We have good timber, we're a transportation hub, we have the barges, the rail lines, the highway – all right there. It's great to see us actually doing something. And we also recently went through – I guess it would be called a "financial planning retreat" rather than a "strategic planning retreat." We had somebody come in and help us take a look at our financials and say: "Where are our pots of money? Where shall we put them?" Because at that point, they were keeping over a million dollars in cash. We could be earning interest on it. In some cases they're just so scared from what's happened in the past that they're not willing to try anything. You see all over the state people going through the same types of things.

We do pay an annual dividend. They range from maybe 70 dollars to 200 dollars a year, which in my opinion is a complete waste of time and money. And I think that a lot of corporations do this, and they're giving out a hundred bucks, which ends up being beer money for somebody. You're not making a significant impact on anyone's life. If we multiply that times 400 something shareholders, we could put that money into a language project. We could put it into some type of community development or economic development project instead of just throwing it away, basically. And the shareholders, of course, want the money. But they always want more.

It's kind of almost a blessing that we really don't have much. I've worked with a Southeast corporation very closely, helping them develop some of their different programs. They're continuously fighting about money. It's divided families. They have brothers and sisters that don't speak to each other. They have shareholders constantly petitioning the board for board recalls. And it's all because they have 30 million dollars in the bank, and they want a piece of the pie. And I have to say that at least because we don't have the money, we don't have those types of problems. We give out dividends, but I'd like to see us doing more economic development, creating jobs for people – not just any old jobs, but jobs that people will want to keep and stay in the village for.

*What about those born after 1971?* Quite a few of my cousins don't have stock. If they get any, it will be a gift from my grandmother or inheritance of some kind. I don't think it's made that big of a difference. With my sister, she doesn't have (village corporation) stock, and she's not considered a shareholder, but she still affiliates herself with Doyon and with Toghetthele and with Tanana Chiefs Conference. And I think that what the organizations give us more than anything – it's not about money, it's about an affiliation with other people in our region. When we go to AFN, we say, "We're Doyon." Or, "We're Nenana Native Council" or whatever we are. They're still tribal members, and they're still eligible for a lot of programs and things. I don't think that the stock itself makes that big of a difference. I haven't seen that it has in my family anyways. I only have one other cousin who's even of the age where she would be eligible for it. The rest of them – I don't see that it's hindered them in any way, to say the least. My sister can still get scholarships through Doyon. She can access the programs and services of the Native council. Most village corporations, if you can prove your parents or whoever are shareholders, you can still access the services.

*What about those corporations that have created stock for young people?* It was very impressive. It was a big leap for Doyon to take, and for the shareholders to give up. Because Doyon has paid out pretty good dividends – at some points in time as much as a thousand dollars here and there. And that was a big leap for shareholders to say that, "I'd be willing to take only 200 if my kids could be shareholders." Again, it's not about the money, because obviously we would get less money with more shareholders. It's just about an affiliation, and it's about being able to say that they're Doyon shareholders – whatever that means. We don't really get anything monetary out of that.

But, again, I think it has to do with the amount of money that it has. For instance, in these Southeast village corporations, you will not see – you are not going to see any of them standing up and saying, "Let's let another 2,000 in." Because their dividends are going to go down, and that's what they're looking at. That's the way they see it. So I think it was a very impressive step for them to do that, and I think a lot of corporations – regional and village corporations – are not going to be willing to do that.

*Was ANCSA a good idea?* I have to say yes and no. It obviously wasn't successful in the way that people envisioned it being successful. Natives didn't know anything about running corporations – multi-million-dollar corporations. That much was obvious. As far as the money and the land – that hasn't been successful. The amount of money: it seems like a lot. And to a person outside that sees that Alaska Natives have such and such million dollars and all this land, it sounds like we're pretty rich people. But as individuals, we don't really have anything. And most people have nothing but what they know of their land and what they can live on by subsistence. Most people didn't get anything out of it. And as far as the land goes, most of us don't even have the land that we selected – 20 years later. So I don't think that's been successful.

But, you know, there are other things that have come out of it.

We now have Alaska Native leaders in government. We have Alaska Native leaders that have business skills and know about the corporate world. And that's something that probably would have taken a lot more time to come if we hadn't been sort of thrust into these corporations back in the '70's. I don't think that would have happened. But I think they gave us a more powerful voice. We can stand up to the ARCO's of the world. We have some clout in Alaska if we pull together because we have the money and the land and the resources. So there are both sides of it, I think.

We did get something out of it. It wasn't a complete loss. I don't think it worked the way anyone told us it would work. And we certainly didn't get rich off of it.

*Would you have done things differently?* I don't know. As a Native leader, if I had been in their shoes? I'm sure I would have done the same thing. It sounds like a great offer. Sounds wonderful. Who knew that we'd get 70 bucks a year? Who knew that we wouldn't have our land to call our own 20 years later? You know, we have small timber stands, we have certain areas we can access, but we don't have what we thought we would have. So I can't say that I would have done anything different. It probably sounded like a great thing. (It's a problem with the) conveyance of the land, and because you have to have surveys on it and everything else that's required by the government. Until you do that, you don't own title to that land. You don't own that land. You do, but you don't. We don't have any land in the town. All of our land is outside of Nenana, actually. There might be a couple of sites in town, maybe some Native allotments.

I just think that what was conceived at that time and what they thought they would get is not what they got. You know, if people think that Nenana, for instance, is village land, it's not true. There are some places where that's true, like Tyonek, that's village land. But, also, there's a lot of it that's federal. There are mental health lands, there are all kinds of different people that are cutting in on the pie.

*Your goals?* My personal goals, I don't know that I want any specific title – like vice president of the company or whatever. I've gone pretty much as far as I'm going to go here at Alaska Village Initiatives. But I just see myself working for – whether it be a nonprofit or a profit – some type of organization that works with Native people. Whether that's a regional corporation, whether it's my village corporation, who knows? But I can't picture myself working for a non-Native organization. I can't see myself working for ARCO or even NBA or something like that – KeyBank. I can't picture myself in that type of environment. I guess a lot of it, too, there's not anyone in my family who's not involved in a Native corporation of some kind. My sister works at Tanana Chiefs Conference, that type of keeping in touch with what's going on in rural Alaska and being involved with that.

I have a friend who works at KeyBank. I know it's vital and it's important, but I don't see how it's making a meaningful contribution of any kind. And I guess that's what I need to see. And if I didn't see that here, I wouldn't stay in this position. And I had gotten to the point in my last position where I was sort of feeling that way because there wasn't a lot of contact with rural people or Native people. It was just sort of accounting type stuff and that kind of thing. So I just think that's really important to me. And I guess I'd have to say not even just Alaska Native. If I were to move to Seattle, I'd like to be involved with the Native groups there. So I guess it's just Native issues in general, both Alaska and Native American, even though they are somewhat different.

*Do you have a vision for the Native community?* I don't know what I would see the vision as. I think what will happen – and I was laughing with my dad about this because AFN is coming up, and he said, "Yeah, you know what they were talking about at AFN 20 years ago? Subsistence." It's the same issues that have been at the forefront for so long. I really don't see that changing any time soon. I guess I just kind of see the Native community just sort of plugging away, like we always have. I don't see us coming together to fight these issues or anything significant like that. I just see us sort of plugging along the way that we do.

*Does ANCSA fit into this vision?* I don't know if it does, other than just what maybe some of the corporations can give to the fight if we have a particular issue. If there's something Doyon can do to help in that, then they should. But I don't see anything more than that.

I don't see that anything new and wonderful is going to come out of ANCSA. I think it's going to be the same as it's been. Actually, if anything, I think that we'll see more liquidation of corporations, more of them going away. We've seen that more in the last couple of years, even just Akhiok-Kaguyak, which is now trying to liquidate.

And you see it especially with the elders. You know, they're getting older. They don't have much time left, and they haven't seen the results. They haven't seen anything come out of this big experiment. And so a lot of them – you'll see a lot of the dissidents are elders who want to see something come out of this before they die. If anything, we're going to see more people pushing for that. We've had petitions for how many years at Doyon now for a distribution of 5,000 dollars per shareholder, which doesn't seem like a lot, but when you add it up by 12,000 shareholders, that's a lot of money. If you keep sucking it off, and you keep sucking the money out of the company, eventually it's going to go away. It's a company just like anything else, it can go bankrupt. It can go away forever.

I think people kind of think of Native corporations as these perpetual entities, but they're not. They're run by shareholders, and they're subject to the whim of shareholders. I just see it a lot more lately. Working here, because we're statewide, we work with so many different regions. So I've seen things in corporations that have happened all over the state, and maybe a lot of people don't see it because they're just in one region and focused in one region, but you see it all over.

*Is there a clash between profit-making corporations and culture?* I think there is and there probably was, especially in the early years and for a long time. But I think now, the Native leaders that are on these boards are so business-minded – they're already leaders in the business community, and they have the skills to run a multi-million-dollar corporation. It used to be true that you had to hire people from outside to run your company. But that's not true any more. And especially with a lot of younger Native people going to college and going further than their parents ever went, I don't think that's the case any more. There are still some areas, maybe specialty areas, where outside assistance is needed: maybe in tourism, for instance, where the people in the company don't have as much experience in that area, a new industry. But, I think for the most part, they're already business leaders, community leaders.

*Is there a loss of culture with the corporations?* Not at all. I'm sure some people probably say that you have to do that, but I just came back from Kipnuk and Kwigillingok which are very, very traditional villages out in Southwest Alaska. And we went from having fresh goose soup – and they're eating seal oil and everything else for lunch, and we go back to the office and they're speaking Yup'ik to each other fluently. And that's all they speak to each other. And then he gets on the phone and he's speaking English to some guy in D.C. So I think that the people that are in these positions have an incredible ability to switch back and forth, really and to sort of straddle both.

I have a lot of faith in Native leaders today, but at the same time I think that people can get greedy. If anything, that would be the downfall of a lot of these corporations.

It can be very frustrating and you want to do something and you want to make things happen and go nowhere. It's very frustrating. That's why I said I don't see any drastic changes happening. I see us just plugging away. These things take time, a lot of time.

*Has there been progress in 30 years?* In terms of individual skills. But for my own village corporation I can't point to anything that they've done over my life that's made a significant impact on anybody. And maybe they've created a few jobs here and there, but for the most part the money creates one full-time position, and then we're paying lawyers and accountants. That's who has really made money off of ANCSA, the professional services providers, the accountants, the lawyers that are constantly working with the corporations. That's where the majority of the money goes. I'm sure that our accountants for my village corporation have made more from my corporation than I ever have or ever will. The only key to that is educating people in those areas. What can you do?

We're inheriting their mess (laughs). We're inheriting the mess that they came up with 30 years ago. Whatever they came up with, we now have to deal with.

# Koniag Region

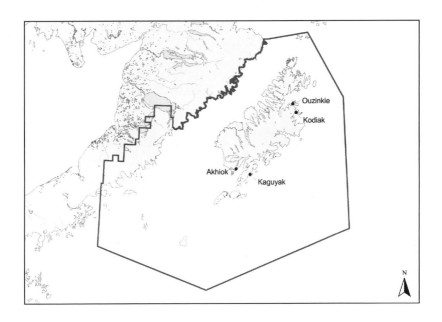

*SHARON ANDERSON was born May 16, 1969, in Ouzinkie and grew up in the Kodiak Island village. Both her parents are Alutiiq. She has a Bachelor's Degree in Rural Development from the University of Alaska Fairbanks. After graduating from college, Anderson worked part-time for the Ouzinkie School District as a Teacher's Aide, and also part-time as the Education Director for the Ouzinkie Tribal Council. She later moved to Anchorage and accepted a position with Alaska Village Initiatives. She then accepted a position at the Alaska Native Heritage Center and has since decided to seek other work.*

*Anderson is a shareholder in her Ouzinkie Native Corporation and Koniag, Inc. She hopes to attain a seat on her village board someday. She was interviewed October 22, 1998.*

A s more time goes on, more people are not part of the corporation and don't really share in the benefits, such as dividends. Perhaps in some regions where corporations don't do so well, it's really not that much of an issue. But, to me, I think it's still a way of excluding people if they're not part of a corporation. . . And there really shouldn't be division, especially within families.

I was born in Ouzinkie, Alaska, and raised there. Both my parents are Alaska Natives, both Alutiiq. I lived there until I was 18 years old and graduated from high school. I went to high school in Ouzinkie. Before that, the eleventh and twelfth graders were sent to Kodiak to the high school. But I finished high school in Ouzinkie. I was part of the first group of students to graduate from there. There were three of us.

I was just a "village" Native, I guess. I then went off to college at the University of Alaska Fairbanks and started out in the business program there. I did not complete that because I just didn't feel that it fit into what I wanted to do. I had an idea going to college of what I wanted to do with my life, and after three years that kind of changed and I had to switch majors. I switched to Rural Development and went another three years and completed with a Bachelor's Degree.

After that, I moved back to Ouzinkie because I couldn't figure out how to get a job. It was just a little too soon, fresh out of college to just go into the workplace. So I spent a year and a half in my community. I worked part-time for the School District as a Teacher's Aide and also part-time as the Education Director for our Tribal Council with their Higher Education and Adult Vocational Training

Program. I worked at that, and then I just kind of decided it was time to move on. There were no jobs available in my community, so I decided to move to Anchorage.

My parents are divorced and both remarried. I have an older brother and an older sister, and I have two younger sisters. My brother is currently living here in Anchorage with his family. My older sister lives in Ouzinkie. She graduated from Fairbanks and is a teacher with her husband. They have two kids. One of my younger sisters lives here in Anchorage and she has a degree in anthropology. My youngest sister Melodi is off at college right now, studying English.

*Both younger sisters were born after '71?* Yes, one was born in '74 and the other was born in '77. *How do they feel about being born after 1971?* It was brought up in high school. I studied a lot about the Alaska Native Claims Settlement Act in high school, and I started going to AFN then. During that time, they were talking about "after borns" and stock – because the whole idea was that you could sell your stock after 1991. There was a lot of discussion about that. I came home one day and asked my younger sister, Jean – she must have been about 12 or 13 – I asked her some questions. "How do you feel about being able to sell your stock in 1991? People can sell their stock in 1991."

She said, "That's not very good. We might lose our land."

And then I said, "You know what? You don't even have stock because you were born after this date. You don't have stock."

She got mad at me. But I wanted to make the point and said that it was just that there were people who were excluded. And she was one of them. She really had no say. I told her she had no say in our corporation. Our corporation funds school trips. They give out dividends. They have annual meetings. And I told her she was not a shareholder, and she could not participate in the decisions they were making about land issues, stock issues, financial issues that have to do with our community and our land around it. And she didn't feel very good about that.

Over the years, I don't think she was very vocal about it, but she always knew that she wasn't a shareholder. As the years went by, she was in high school and they would try to get money from the corporation for school trips. And eventually all of them weren't shareholders, and then the corporation had to ask the question, "Should we give money to these students who aren't shareholders?"

They do contribute funds for school trips, but I think they had to discuss it.

But I do know that my sister Jean understood it a little more than our youngest sister. Jean wasn't very vocal about it, but I do know that it affected her interaction with our regional corporation and our village corporation.

*Did you have a sense of what it meant to be an Alaska Native?* I've thought about that a lot. I came from a small community, about 200 or 250 people when I lived there. And when I was in college I thought about that. Because you're in a small community, and everybody is the same as you so you don't really think about being a "Native." When I went off to college I had to think about it more. So I thought about: When was the first time I realized that I was Alaska Native? And that has to do with stock also. I thought about the first time I realized that, and I think I was about six years old and at an annual meeting. They have drawings, and, as a shareholder, my name was in there. And I won a small camera. And I realized for the first time – for some reason, for being Alaska Native, I won this camera.

But I never really thought about being "Native" or "Alaska Native" until I went off to college. Before that, it was more of a concept because I had never really traveled all that much and encountered others. To me, there were Aleuts, Eskimos and Indians. And I was an Aleut, and there were Eskimos and Indians. I went off to college, and I realized there are Inupiat and Yup'ik, and there are the different groups of Athabascans. And that was the first time I really thought about being an Alaska Native.

*Was it a positive feeling?* Actually, it wasn't a very positive feeling. It had to do with going off to college and encountering these other Native groups who knew more about themselves – about being "Native" than I did. Being from the Kodiak area, I didn't really have a Native culture. And so it was very difficult for me to explain that I was Native. Because I couldn't speak my language. I didn't wear a kuspuk. I didn't necessarily bring my Native foods with me. And so it was difficult to define myself in this Alaska Native sense.

I didn't necessarily look fully Alaska Native. I didn't necessarily participate in Alaska Native cultural events. My problem was there was no way for me to show that I was Alaska Native, and I felt that I had to, to be accepted as Alaska Native. So that took awhile, and the search began in college for my cultural roots. Because before that I didn't really have to because everyone around me was just like me.

It's a slow process, and I'm still going at it. Because I didn't feel that I had to go back all the way back in history and find out who Alutiiqs were. Because I was "Aleut," and all of a sudden – I actually went to "Koniag" for awhile because it was my corporation. But it just didn't seem right. And a new term came up recently, which is "Alutiiq." It is different from "Aleut," and I choose that word. And some people say, "Sugpiaq." But to me, that's too much. It's a little too traditional for me because that's not necessarily my roots.

How I define myself culturally – I thought of things that I was proud of that I had that may not have to do with being Alutiiq, but things that I was proud of in my life. And that was the connection with my church, which is Russian Orthodox. It really has nothing to do with my Native culture, but that was something that unified all of us as a people. And, another thing was the water, the ocean. My father was a fisherman, and I actually was ashamed of that for awhile. And then I realized that I love fishing. And I love fish, and I decided that that was something to be proud of.

And I just started grasping at things that I felt good about. And these were just a couple of them. Also just talking to other Alutiiq people in school or at home. Just realizing that I felt comfortable with them and they were experiencing the same thing. They were searching for their culture.

I think one thing, too, that unified us as Alutiiq people were the people who attacked us, saying: "You aren't Native enough."

"You guys don't wear skins. You guys don't hunt seal or sea lions anymore. You don't get sea otters or sew skins. A lot of you don't speak your language."

And just feeling that it was something that a lot of us didn't have. And we just unified and said that we have to define who we are. Other people throughout history have been defining us, and we decided that we had to define ourselves. What I came up with: I always tell people I am Alutiiq. It may not be as understandable as saying Athabascan or Yup'ik, but it's what I define myself as. Since I, as an Alutiiq, define this as being Alutiiq, it's Alutiiq. It's more of a personal definition for each individual or group of people because it's too hard to define all Alutiiqs into one region.

There was an Elder's Conference, and it united all the people – elders from Prince William Sound, Kodiak and the Alaska Peninsula – last year. And they talked about being Alutiiq and realized how much the same we are. I think people are trying to come up with what it means and were trying to bring back the culture in some ways. But I don't feel that it's appropriate to go back to being really traditional. You're going into a new millennium, and you can't really go back that far. You have to work with what you have right now.

*Did you experience discrimination?* It was more inner discrimination than having non-Natives discriminate against me. I became more aware of it when I went off to college because I was around different sorts of people and there was some racism with non-Native people. But I think I really felt it more within the Native community itself at the university than with non-Native people.

*Did your parents stress education?* No, not really. We always wondered about that: Why did we all go off to college? Our parents did not stress going off to college. They didn't really even stress finishing high school. I think it was just something that was expected from us. They never really encouraged us, but they never discouraged us, either. My mother graduated from high school, but my father did not. I think he quit in about the eighth grade. And he fished, and so he thought, "Well, there's no reason for me to do this. I've been fishing since I've been 10 years old."

I don't know why my older sister went off to college. When I was younger, I always thought she was the smartest person I knew. She went off to college, and I thought it was great. She made the transition much easier because she was there. It was either UAA or UAF, and I chose UAF because I knew that her being there while I was there was going to make it easier for me. And the same thing for my younger sister Jean. I was at college when she entered college. And hopefully I made it easier for her. She also went to a pre-college program in Fairbanks. Actually, when she got there she knew about 20 people already who were entering college as she was. She was there when our youngest sister Melodi entered college. I think they spent about a year together, which made the transition better. We're all extremely close.

*Do you have a tie to your Native culture?* Yes, I do. It's more academic learning that brings me closer. And just talking to other Alutiiqs in and out of my region makes me feel more comfortable with being Native. And I don't feel as much any more that I need to show that I am Native. I'm more comfortable with myself than I was when I was in college. I'm a lot more confident and positive.

*Do you have a Native hero?* No, I don't think that I really do.

I can't really think of any stories that I might have idolized anyone. One thing is, because I was really involved in studying the Alaska Native Claims Settlement Act and I studied it a lot in high school and college, I was just in awe of the people who were involved.

Now, when I look back and I'm older, I can see problems with it. But I think it was very positive that they worked very hard. They were young. They were trying to get something that wasn't the reservation system. They were trying to keep as much as they could, land-wise. A lot of money is mentioned in ANCSA, but I don't see it today. And I don't know too many people who said they saw it back then. But I think they were trying to get as much as land as they could. And I think they did their best on ANCSA. And they just grabbed it. And the problems that we saw later – we just had to deal with them.

*Do any of the people come to mind?* I read a lot – Emil Notti – he was very young when he started AFN. And Willie Hensley. I knew he was very young when he was involved. I was reading this stuff. And I was heading off to college. I was thinking of how much they accomplished in their young age with ANCSA. I was thinking – being in my 20's – I was just amazed at how much responsibility they had, how much weight that must have been on their shoulders. I'm sure they must have felt it. I don't know how they felt about what they were doing and if they thought they were doing things right or not. But I was just amazed at how young a lot of the people were that were involved and what they accomplished. And just: how were they taken seriously at such a young age? It was just amazing.

*Was it a good idea to create corporations?* I never really thought about what the other options could have been. Obviously, the corporations have done well for some regions and have not done well for others. And you really have to work with the resources that you got. I think they work OK. I think the corporations work. They're not perfect. Not all. The cutoff was in December 1971 for the shareholders, and some corporations now have included people born after that date. And some corporations haven't. And that's an issue. I think the more you go into the future, the more the corporations don't make sense. I don't know what the solution will be. But I think that they were OK.

As time goes by, there are more Natives who are not part of the corporations. And they get the benefits of the land or even maybe some dividends through their inheritance. And so that makes it a little easier. But as more time goes on, more Alaska Natives are not part of a regional corporation and don't really share in the benefits, such as dividends. Perhaps in some areas where corporations don't do so well, it's really not that much of an issue. But I think it's still a way of excluding people if they're not part of a corporation. It may not mean much. If the corporation has no money, why should you be part of the corporation? But it's just more the principle of it all. To me, it's just a way of dividing people. And there really shouldn't be division, especially within families like that.

I think deep down, it still bothers people. I think about when I eventually have kids. They're not going to be part of the corporation, and when I have to split up my shares amongst my kids to make them part of it, then they have kids and eventually being a shareholder really isn't going to matter because everyone's going to have such a small piece.

*Are you familiar with any of the changes to ANCSA?* I remember some of the amendments – 1991 amendments – in which you couldn't sell your stock. And then there was a land bank issue. I don't know if people use it or not. And the idea of giving stock to people who are born after 1971 was another option. I think some regional corporations have done that.

*Are the changes good?* I think so. I was kind of scared when you had the option of selling your stock. I felt that a lot of people would sell it for the quick buck. I'm always thinking more long-term. Once they spend the money, it's gone. They have nothing left. Their stock may not be worth much, and they could have gotten a few dollars. But at least if they keep it, it still includes them in something.

And I think you should give stock to people born after 1971. I think it's a big issue in my village corporation because we give out dividends. And a lot of people don't want to lower their dividends by including a group of people that are larger than the shareholder base. So I don't think that it's something that is going to happen in my village corporation any time soon. I doubt they'll include people born after '71. *How about at the regional level?* I don't think that it has really ever been brought up. I don't think anyone really wants to bring it up. They don't want to talk about it.

*Have you thought about serving on your village board?* I've thought about, and I actually ran one year. I was 18 years old. I ran and didn't win, of course. But that's something that I will probably do in the future. A lot of the board members have been on the board for a very long time. Some of them have been since the beginning of the corporation, well over 20 years. Slowly, new people are getting on the board.

Our village corporation, Ouzinkie Native Corporation, does very well. We have a timber base, and we are a part of Koncor Forest Products. So we do very well as a corporation.

*How is the village doing as a community?* It used to be a fishing community, but there are not too many limited entry fishery permits left and, of course, fishing prices are low. A lot of people have sold their permits, just to pay the bills. A lot of people do odd jobs. They do construction in the springtime and throughout the summer. A lot of them actually do longshoring for the logging, done by our village corporation and Koncor Forest Products on Afognak Island.

But there's no real steady industry. You have to keep finding new ones to work in. When I worked in the education department of our Tribal Council something I thought about a lot is that people really aren't willing to leave their community. They're not willing to leave their wives and children to get training. And the women – if they go, they have to leave their husbands, their kids or take their kids with them. So the training option wasn't really open. The idea of a lot of people getting trained outside the community to do jobs within the community really wasn't realistic. I think some people are trying it, but it's difficult. Tourism is starting up in the community. People are starting to do charter businesses and bed and breakfasts to put a little money in their pockets.

*Social problems?* Our village has a problem with alcohol and drugs. I don't know how big of a problem it is because I've been away for about three years. But when I was there and I lived there, I thought it was a problem. And I sometimes think, I don't know if it's because when I was younger I just ignored it. Now that I am older I have noticed it. I know that the adults drink more than they really should. And I know that some of the kids have gotten involved in alcohol. And we didn't have a Village Public Safety Officer for a very long time. So there was really no way of catching them if the kids were involved. And if the parents were abusing it, then it just went on. There was no way of stopping it. I know there's drug abuse. I don't think it's as much of a problem as the alcohol problem. But I felt that was a problem in the community and hopefully the community and the people in it will decide how to deal with that.

They haven't come to that point yet.

I worked in Ouzinkie for about a year and a half in our Tribal Council. I enjoyed the job, and I felt I was accomplishing something. I could have kept on going, but it was part-time. I really didn't want to get involved in drinking. And that seemed to be about the only thing to do, just sit around at home alone or drink. It was like a "negativeness" in the air. It was just building and building inside of me perhaps. And I just realized that I wasn't very happy. So I decided to leave the community to get a full-time job and actually make a living and to support myself. I felt it was time to move on, so I did. I moved to Anchorage.

*Is there a clash between profit-making corporations and culture?* I don't really think that there is a clash. I grew up with the corporations. They've always been around. So I really can't imagine them not. In the beginning, when I was in high school, I started thinking more about cultural stuff, which also began with my studying about ANCSA. And so you're studying about this land claims, and you're asking: Why was this land claims going on? And you learn about land claims and indigenous rights. We didn't lose the land in a war, and we didn't sell it. I started thinking more about cultural stuff. But I didn't feel that the corporations – my village corporation and regional corporation – were doing all that much to preserve culture. I felt that they could have done more. But now, as time has gone by, the corporations and Native people themselves are trying to preserve the culture more and trying to preserve the cultural sites.

The corporations now are doing better, and they spend a lot of money in the area of preservation. Kodiak has a cultural center now in the Afognak Native Corporation building, which is a repository for things found in the Kodiak area. It's very modern, and it's very nice to see the cultural items, to get a feel of where I came from. It also adds to feeling good about myself, to be able to see what Alutiiq people did.

*Your goals for the future?* I do want to go back to school and get a Master's with a Public Administration, anthropological mix because I think this is something that could be done very well through a nonprofit organization.

I don't have kids, but you have to think about things that you want to pass on. What is good in your life and your culture that you want to pass on? A lot of it has to do with just being happy with yourself, feeling good about yourself without having to feel so negative about it. It doesn't necessarily have to do with culture, but in a way it does because I didn't know much about my culture. I had to learn about it.

For many years, my father was a fisherman. He did that all his life. But I was ashamed that he was a fisherman. Why couldn't my dad be a businessman? Why couldn't he be a lawyer? Why couldn't he be something respectful? And then I realized in college that – I was thinking, what's wrong with that? What's wrong with him being a fisherman? All the people in the Kodiak area are fishermen, and there's nothing wrong with that. He put food on the table. I guess when you're younger, you just don't see.

My mother didn't work. And some of my friends' mothers worked. And I thought, "Oh, my goodness, my mother isn't working." It seemed so bad to me. I thought, "My mom's a homemaker. She doesn't do anything." And then I realized, what's wrong with that? She raised us. We're all a close family. We all love each other. I don't think she did anything wrong.

I'm still learning about my culture. I want to pass on to my kids whatever information I do have. I want them to know about it and be proud of being Alutiiq. I want to tell them that I searched a long time and that it took me a long time to find myself.

And I think language is very important. There are not too many young Alutiiq speakers around any more. But hopefully there will be in the future. It's something that I want to do myself – learn Alutiiq. And I guess there are arts and crafts and cultural stuff that I'd like to do. I don't necessarily think that I would finish them, but I started taking Aleut basket weaving.

*ANCSA in the future?* I don't think I ever really thought about ANCSA in the future. To me, it has an effect on us today, but it's behind the scenes.

**KIM EATON-OLSON** *was born on December 8, 1970, in Bremerton, Washington. Her father Perry Eaton is originally from Kodiak and moved to the Seattle area with his family when he was a teenager. He attended a community college there and met her mother, a non-Native. About eight months after Kim was born, her parents moved to Anchorage, where she grew up. Eaton's father has held a number of leadership positions in the Alaska Native community, and her grandfather Hank Eaton played an important role in the passage of the Alaska Native Claims Settlement Act and spent much time in Washington, D.C., during the years that Alaska Natives lobbied for passage.*

*Eaton-Olson is an enrolled member of the village of Ouzinkie on Kodiak Island, but she is not a shareholder because her blood quantum is one-eighth Native.*

*She graduated from Service High School in Anchorage in 1989 and attended college in Denver, then transferred from Colorado to the University of Alaska Anchorage and graduated in 1994 with a Bachelor's Degree in Management. She was married on August 28, 1998, to Brad Olson.*

*Eaton-Olson was selected to participate in Leadership Anchorage in 1997, a program developed by the Alaska Humanities Forum with a grant from the Pew Charitable Trust. She is one of 16 participants who elected to remain in the program for the second year as a mentor.*

*Eaton-Olson is the Marketing Coordinator for CIRI's Tourism Department. She was interviewed September 1, 1998.*

**R**ural Alaska knows tenfold more about Anchorage than what Anchorage knows about rural Alaska. There are programs out there that bring students from rural Alaska into Anchorage – AFN, for example. But I think the programs are lacking that take Anchorage kids to rural Alaska. That exchange isn't there.

I have one brother Brent who is five years older than me. I was born in Bremerton, Washington, and my family moved back to Anchorage when I was about eight months old. My father was born in Kodiak and grew up commercial fishing. His family moved to the Seattle area when he was a teenager. He attended a community college there, met my mother. They married and lived in Port Orchard and Bremerton, Washington. He worked for Seattle SeaFirst Bank. About eight months after I was born, he requested a transfer to Alaska. He was transferred to the Anchorage office and relocated the family back here. So I pretty much grew up here. All I can remember is living here in Anchorage. I grew up with a great family life. We were all very close. My parents have been married for 34 years.

My brother and I attended colleges outside the state. My parents encouraged us to get an "outside of Alaska" experience. Both my brother and I thought we would never come back once we left. (Laughs.) I think it was the typical teenager thought: boring, nothing to do, and wanted to leave. Brent went to San Diego State, and I went to the University of Denver in Colorado, and both of us ended up coming back after college. Soon after I entered college, I realized that Alaska was a pretty wonderful place. My brother and his wife just had their first child, and I was just married a couple days ago. It's been a big summer for the Eaton family.

I have tribal enrollment with Ouzinkie, but I'm only one-eighth Native. My father is an Ouzinkie and Koniag shareholder.

*When did you have a sense of being an Alaska Native?* I'm sure it was pretty young. My father and my grandfather both have a great sense of pride in their Native heritage. I can't really remember a conversation of "this is your lineage" or anything like that. It was never a sense of "this is how we're different." It was just "this is who we are." I remember my father and grandfather both being very Alaska oriented, and I grew up with a strong sense of pride for the state. The Lower 48 was called "the United States," and the family joke was, "The rest of the United States is the U.S.A., and we're Alaska." My grandfather always had stories, and my dad's business interests increased my awareness.

*Why did you decide to go to college?* I was always an A/B student, and college was just the next step. I looked up to my brother and he did it, so I'm sure that had a lot to do with it. My parents never pushed us and said, "You have to." I guess it was probably instilled that it was the next step. It was the great adventure to leave home and go to college.

I spent my first year in California in a small private school and then I transferred to Colorado. I had some friends there, and it was an area I wanted to go to. I actually missed the seasons a little bit.

In Anchorage, I went to Service High School. *Did you identify yourself as an Alaska Native there?* No, I didn't. I really didn't identify myself as an Alaska Native until I left for college. Growing up, I dog mushed (sprint teams), and I looked at it as a sport and something that was different than what the majority of my friends did. But I never really announced that I was Native because of peer pressure, teasing at school and things like that. I never really wanted to admit to being different from the majority of my friends. Kids can be pretty cruel with the stereotypes of Natives. I just didn't play it up. I never denied it. I just would never announce it or proclaim it. *Did you feel inside that you were?* Oh, yes. And it hurt deeply to be teased. I regret it now, but no one wants to be an outcast or different or to be teased at that age. I still always kept a great sense of pride because of my father and grandfather and their influence.

*Were there many other Natives at Service High School?* I had no clue. I don't know if there were any groups. Even if there was a group or a club, I don't know if I would have gotten involved. The interesting thing now is, with my past experiences, I have worked very closely with high school students and college students. And I think things have changed. That's been one of the neatest things I've seen at the college and academic level – the groups, clubs and organizations. I think we're entering into a generation where cultural awareness and cultural pride is more prevalent in the education world and probably in the business world. "Cultural diversity" seems to be the "p.c." catch phrase. That was a neat thing to see: Going into the colleges and even the high schools and witnessing that sense of pride carrying down – and organizations are also starting that.

My mother's not Native, so my brother and I grew up with a very well rounded cultural awareness of all levels. Our parents were very careful with letting us make our own decisions and our own mistakes. Religion was never pushed on us. It was something we could do if we wanted to. Even cultural events or anything like that were our option. I think they really allowed us to choose our own path. I probably went to AFN once with my father but could never grasp what it meant at that point.

*A positive feeling of being a Native?* When I went to college, I discovered it was "neat" to be from Alaska. It was exciting and people wanted to hear stories about Alaska because it's still this great unknown to a lot of people: Do we use American currency? How much postage does it take? You know, the typical questions a lot of the people in the United States have that haven't been here. It was really neat. To be Native was accepted there, I felt. Maybe it was because at the college level, I reached a sense of independence and a self-confidence level. As your self-confidence increases, it's easier to confront your fears and confront people. You're more comfortable and self-assured. I will always remember going through sorority rush. I had put on the application that I was Alaska Native and I had dog mushed. I remember going to every sorority house, and everyone wanted to meet the girl from Alaska that had dog mushed. So that became a neat thing. I remember the Alaska "gang" at college stayed very close. There was a huge Alaska pride that we all carried. No matter what high school we came from, we all became immediate friends and grouped together and had a great sense of who we were and where we came from.

My grandfather is probably one of the best historians in Kodiak. He helped put together the new museum that was built a couple years ago. He has a great memory. I remember listening to his stories of him being a hunting guide and working with the tourists that came to Kodiak. Also, stories about Kodiak during the War and how things were then, and having military troops there. I don't remember learning about the ills of the community or the political structure or anything like that until much later, until I started asking. My dad and I talk about business a lot. I think we have become each other's confidants. It's interesting to hear his side of things and then actually work in the business and learn things as I go. It's great.

*Do you feel there are problems in villages?* Yes, I do. I think we have a lot of problems in rural Alaska that Anchorage doesn't know about. I believe the barriers that have developed between rural Alaska and Anchorage are great, and probably getting worse. Rural Alaska knows tenfold more about Anchorage than what Anchorage knows about rural Alaska. There are programs out there that bring students from rural Alaska into Anchorage – AFN, for example. But I think the programs are lacking that take Anchorage kids to rural Alaska. That exchange isn't there. I think Anchorage maybe takes more of a hit sometimes than it should from rural Alaska on political issues. Maybe the community of Anchorage takes the blame more, but sometimes it might be deserved due to Anchorage's lack of understanding of rural Alaska. Lack of knowledge about rural Alaska is too great. We need to bring back the Alaska unity between rural Alaska and urban Alaska.

*Do you have a tie to Native culture?* I think I do, not as great as I'd like. I worked in an engineering firm for three years where I developed an Alaska Native hire program. It was a training and educational program to hire more Alaska Natives. When I went into the workforce, I thought I would just be the average employee. But when they asked me to develop this program for them, it really brought me into Native culture in the business sense that I had not experienced. It was really wonderful. I was doing a project that brought me pride in my heritage. I learned more about the culture through a process, and it was a continual learning process for me, too, as well as educating the management that I was working with. I remember having discussions with the management staff because of feeling so strongly about the Native heritage or culture or having to do things certain ways – and they didn't understand that.

A funny example was: I wanted to have a cultural awareness seminar for the management staff. My thought was to bring in Rosita Worl or my father or someone of that stature to talk about the differences and the diversity in the workplace. I wanted an ANCSA background and history or something to that effect. And when I brought up the idea of a cultural diversity seminar for management, they thought I was going to bring in a dance group and then show the difference between a mukluk and an ulu. (Laughs.) So, needless to say, it was very interesting to work from that level. It really made me aware of where a lot of people probably are in their awareness of the Native culture. But I think it brought me even closer to my sense of pride.

And that's another discussion I had with the management staff. They said, "You're not going to be able to change their minds on how they feel about Natives." I didn't want to change their minds. I just wanted to give them the education to make a decision. If they chose to change their opinion, that would be great. If not, they had a greater knowledge to make an educated decision.

Another example: the managers had problems working with some of the student interns because they wouldn't make eye contact. They didn't realize that maybe they did not make eye contact with elders or someone of a more superior level because it was a part of the culture. Or quiet mannerisms. Management had difficulties understanding that, too. A lot of times it was difficult for me to explain the heritage and the culture and our mannerisms, but everything I did brought me more and more sense of pride. It was a great learning experience for me.

We designed a series of four to six training sessions – one-and-a-half-hour long sessions. And it went great. The first one was a history lesson. From there, we let the management staff build the sessions to what they wanted to know. We went over everything from workplace diversity issues to the ANCSA background. We discussed the regional corporations' background. They were pretty intensive sessions. And they loved it. The first session they came away, saying, "We never knew." That was the biggest thing, just the awareness.

It was a challenge, but that position awarded me a huge opportunity because of ANCSA. I would have never had that position if I hadn't been Native. I was in a position higher than many of my peers because I was Native, and I had an opportunity. Of course, I had to prove myself once I got that position, but I think it was an opportunity awarded to me because of what's happened through ANCSA and what's been done over the last few years by the people involved in ANCSA.

*Do you have a Native hero?* It would definitely be my father, mostly because he's my father, but it's neat to see what he's done with his life. I think he, probably like me, was awarded opportunities that probably wouldn't have been there if he hadn't been Native. He has worked for a Native-owned bank and Native corporations, and I think he's excelled very well – incredibly. He's always been my coach through life.

I believe Dad's been so successful because he's so well rounded. He's really able to see the big picture. Dad's able to see both sides of the Native/non-Native issue. And he's able to discuss either viewpoint. When we talk about things, very seldom is it from a single perspective. There's always a good argument for both. Dad's exceptional at explaining the pros and cons. He's always been like that through every aspect of my life, whether it had to deal with business or career aspirations or a problem that I had with a boyfriend when I was in the tenth grade. He'd always say, "Let's analyze the big picture and discuss the pros and cons. And whatever you do, whatever decision is made, it's going to be OK."

There are many people I would list who I look up to: Debra Call, Janie Leask, Julie Kitka. It's great to see the women in the Native culture succeed. That's been an interesting observation for me lately. I might be overanalyzing, but it seems like the younger Native generation has more females that are in the career fields than males. When I was in the engineering field recruiting for Alaska Native engineers, we were pretty even on the male-to-female ratio, which is very uncommon for engineers. It's mostly a male-dominated industry. But then, it seems like meetings I attend or groups I'm involved with, the majority are female. That's always intrigued me. The Native males in my age group, I really admire. I think that they're few and far between. And that concerns me, too, because I think we need a balance.

*ANCSA?* I don't think my generation does know much about it. I'll admit that sheepishly. I've read some books that my father has given me, but I don't think that we as a generation know enough about it. I know that what it has done has had a tremendous impact on my life and my family's life. I think ANCSA was a great thing. It was something that has developed a sense of Native pride in the state. I think it's evolving and improving. I don't know much about the people involved, either, just bits and pieces here and there. I admire them all tremendously and what they went through. And, from the stories I've heard, it sounds like it was quite the event.

*Was it a good idea to create regional corporations?* I think it was. Opposed to creating tribal corporations? There are pros and cons to both. I can only speak from my own experiences with the regional corporations, but I feel it's a good thing. It's been very positive. It has provided opportunity for the people. I think the only thing I can say against tribal organizations is that maybe the regional corporations have integrated the culture more than what the tribal organizations probably would have. There really isn't one Native culture because we're so diverse within the Native community. Tlingits, Aleuts, Eskimos and Tshimsians are all so different in their cultures that you can't have one Native culture. And I think that if there were only tribal corporations, it might have separated the cultures even more.

It was very interesting to me: for the last AFN convention, I invited the Leadership Anchorage group that I had been involved with to the convention. (That group's goal is to put new faces at the table in the Anchorage community – those new faces being a representation of every culture.) We have African Americans, Samoans, Alaska Natives, Asians, Latinos – really a great cross-cultural group of 20 people. And those 20 people came to AFN to observe. It was funny because I was proud and embarrassed at the same time.

When AFN gets heated – and it did that day – it gets very intense. There were "discussions" and people taking over the microphones, going over their time limits and being very aggressive. I've seen it before, and it's no big deal, but to sit there with people outside the culture, it was very interesting to feel my reaction. My father came in and talked to the group a few months after AFN, and he commented there is no one Native culture. We're so different that we clash within the culture. I didn't really think about it until I was around people from other areas of the community attending AFN that Anchorage is just a huge sandbox. There are so many different cultures involved. There's not just one Native voice. At no point can any one person stand up and say, "I represent the Native community." And I think that's a huge challenge. We'll probably never overcome that. But it provides for a challenging playing field. You have a few Native leaders who can't really sit at the same table together, leaders of corporations. Their cultures are both Native, but they don't cooperate.

It was funny. Everyone at Leadership Anchorage really

understood my feelings. We don't expect every African American to have the same opinion. Sometimes, I wish the Native community could do that. But then I really have to step back and look. I don't expect every Asian person to speak from the same voice and from the same culture. It's really been a fascinating adventure for me.

*Do you see a clash between profit and culture?* I don't. I think that the profit-making corporations make the Native community stronger. If we as a culture and people can come together and be successful in a profitable situation, I think that increases our credibility within the community and among people who don't know much about our cultures.

What better accolade than to have Alaska's people being successful in Alaska? And to be successful in business, in every industry that we have, oil, mining, timber, tourism – every major aspect of the Alaska community. If an African American corporation were formed and became very successful, what a great thing. Maybe by being successful at something, someone will look at them and say, "Wow, they're doing a great job. I want to learn from them, whether they be black, white, purple, brown or yellow." Maybe someone will take something away of their culture of what they're doing right.

I think there's another aspect of making profit from our culture. With the arts or crafts or dance, some might think there's exploitation there. My theory is you need to educate people and heighten awareness, and if someone is paying to see a dance group, they're going to take something from it and they're going to learn something. I have a huge concern that we're losing the artists of our culture. The younger kids don't want to grow up to be artists. If we can offer a livelihood from our culture, we might be able to preserve more of that. But there are pros and cons to everything.

When I went to recruit college students in rural communities, it was very hard for me to recruit those students because I felt I was viewed as coming to take their children. I was offering them an engineering education, which was so far from their Native culture. It was a very tough battle because I wanted to provide these students with an educational opportunity to better themselves and to make a great living. But then inside you think maybe one of these kids wants to grow up to be a great artist. You don't know what you're taking from them.

It's a tough battle. Do you offer an educational opportunity? Where's the balance? It's a real tough emotional pull inside to make that decision. I think it's tough for the rural students. Prime example is an Alaska Native scholarship at UAA. One of the requirements for entrance is to write an essay. One particular student's parents – we found out later – pretty much wrote his essay for him and really pushed him to go to this engineering program. Very shortly after, his parents decided they wanted him home. He got letters and phone calls from his grandmother and his mother – daily – until the emotional pull was just so strong, and he ended up leaving the program and going back to his community. The ties to the family are so strong within the Native community I think that really influences what they do.

The dean of the engineering program and I sat in a meeting: What do we do? Do we encourage this student to stay and better his educational opportunity? Or, do we tell him to go back to his family and his culture and his heritage? UAA had established a dormitory that was just for Alaska Native students. They tried to keep it a family atmosphere. They really tried to prevent the shock of moving to a bigger city. But it's just such a tough pull.

*Do the corporations have political clout?* I think it's inevitable. Any large corporation that does well will have political clout, no matter what state they're in. I think it's good. Having political clout as a large corporation helps the Native community have political clout because the corporations represent the people. I think it is a trickle down where a corporation that represents a culture and has political clout is going to help the culture have political clout.

*Your goals?* I want to stay in the state. I think it's a great place to raise a family. My career aspirations are to stay working where I am. I truly – for the first time – can say I absolutely love my job. I wake up every morning and love to come to work. And the people I work for and with are fantastic. When I first started working here it was neat to see the number of people who have worked here over 10 years. That has got to say something. I had not experienced that at my previous employment. Five years was unheard of at my previous employer. It was also great to meet people who had been working here so long and still had such great attitudes. At my first staff meeting, I was amazed at the communication level and what they told us. I think that has a lot to say. If you're happy and you're having fun, stick with it.

Through Leadership Anchorage, I've gotten more involved with community activities, and I'd really like to continue that.

Working within the Native community has given me such a sense of pride and self-worth. It just generally makes you feel great when you know you're working in your culture and your heritage. I really want to continue doing that.

Leadership Anchorage is a program formed by the Alaska Humanities Forum, which was given a grant from the Pew Charitable Trust. Pew awarded 10 grants to 10 cities within the United States that were of medium size. They've put together a one-year leadership training. We attended two seminars, one in Colorado and one in Arizona with the nine other cities, and then we did extensive training for the year here with just our group of 20. Just recently, 16 of us voted to stay on another year with this year's new class to be involved in the training. Our project is developing a community-based mentorship program. It will partner this year's class of "civic entrepreneurs" with community-based individuals.

*Vision for the Native community?* My vision would be to bridge the gap between rural Alaska and urban Alaska. I think that's one of the biggest problems, and it deals with everything from subsistence to tribal rights to sovereignty. It takes the whole gamut. There's a huge gap right now between rural Alaska and urban Alaska, and I think we've got to come together.

*Can ANCSA help?* I think so. Why go off and form some other organization? Why build a bridge again when you've got it started and you've got a good base? What's been done is a great thing, and I think we're continuing on and we will continue on. We don't need to start all over.

A lot of people in my age group are in that same situation. I believe my age group tends to be a little bit more educated. Our parents and the ANCSA generation really pushed their children to go to college. I think we were provided more opportunities than our parents. So maybe we'll be able to look at it from both sides of the fence. Maybe I'm off base, but I think my generation doesn't know enough about ANCSA. And what do you do? You don't have ANCSA 101 to bring us all up speed. I think our generation has really got to get more involved.

# *NANA Region*

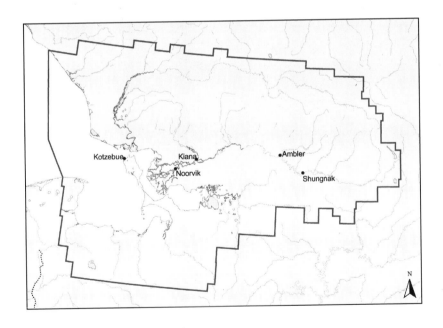

*MAUDE BLAIR was born on November 26, 1975. She grew up in Kiana in Northwest Alaska. She graduated from the University of Alaska Fairbanks in 1996 with Bachelor's Degrees in Broadcast Journalism and English and worked for NANA Regional Corporation in Anchorage as a Communications Specialist. Blair is attending law school and wants to become an attorney and return to work for NANA.*

*Although she was born after 1971, Blair is a shareholder in NANA Regional Corporation because a majority of the shareholders voted to issue stock to those born after the Alaska Native Claims Settlement Act. She was interviewed August 25, 1998, and at the time she was working for NANA.*

I feel that compared to the legislation and what happened in the Lower 48, it was a very good piece of legislation. The first way it affects me is that I work for NANA. It was a company created by ANCSA, which has been very beneficial to our people.

I grew up in Kiana, which is 40 miles northeast of Kotzebue. It's a village with about 350 people in it. I have an older half-sister from my dad's first marriage. She grew up in Arizona, so I was really the oldest of the next three kids. I have a younger brother and a younger sister. My mom is Inupiaq Eskimo, and my father is white. My father was a teacher, and my mother was a housewife. It was always neat having summers off. We'd fly down to Arizona or California or back to Ohio to see Dad's family. Everybody was always convinced we had it backwards – Arizona in the summer and Alaska in the winter (laughs). We liked it just fine, though.

My older sister is five years older than me, so she's 27. My brother is 20, and my sister is 18. I'm 22. We are all shareholders because we belong to NANA. And I think we were all shareholders from birth because my mom gave us all 10 shares back before the '91 amendments, when they decided to allow "afterborns" in.

My dad grew up in Ohio. He went to school at Arizona State University, got recruited by the BIA and they brought him up to Noorvik about 30 years ago now. He was a teacher for 20 years, mostly in Kiana, and married my mom in 1974. My mom grew up in Shungnak and then moved to Ambler when that town was founded (in the late 1950's). Her father was a pastor, Tommy Douglas. He's well known up there. Everybody knows who I am because of my family.

My mother had a very traditional lifestyle. They have a camp on the river, which is just great. It's just this little cabin out in the middle of nowhere. And we actually spent one summer there, and it was a very fun summer because we went out fishing, and we did the berry picking – we had to do all this stuff. It was fun.

*Your Native language?* She refused to speak it to us, growing up. Because she was in that age group that was beaten if they spoke their Native language in the schools. I mean she spoke some words to us, but every time we asked her to sit down and really talk to us and teach us, she said no. She did speak it with her friends. That's why we were always asking her. We wanted to know what she was saying.

They finally started having Inupiaq classes, and once we finally all got into school, Mom's excuse was, "Well, you should be learning it in school."

And we'd say, "No, Mom, we should be learning it at home."

And now she finally says, "I should have started you guys speaking Inupiaq."

We say, "Yeah, that's what we were trying to tell you."

I've always had a sense of being an Alaska Native. We grew up in the village. I was treated just like everybody else. Except for once in a great while, you'd get somebody teasing you about being a half-breed or the white kid or something like that. And that always just rolled off my shoulders because then I went home and ate dried fish and seal oil, and all that stuff. So it's like, "What are you talking about?"

*Discrimination?* No, because for the most part we were in the village where it's pretty much Native, about 90 percent, I'd say. And the rest of the time we were off traveling, and everybody else in the country thinks it's the greatest thing that they got to meet little Eskimo kids, which didn't really feel like discrimination. You know, we were special. It was kind of neat.

It's just really comforting to know that I belong. In one job I had, I was the "token Native." I hate calling it that, but that's why they hired me. That's why I was there. I was the only Native. Everybody else there was white. About six months to a year after I started working there, they hired a black person. We were the only two minorities in the entire building, and I hated it because every time a Native issue came up, "Oh, Maude will report on that because she knows about it." And, if it's something to do with Doyon, then, well, no, I don't know about it. I have to learn, just like everybody else. So I hated that because there was just always this assumption that if it had anything to do with being Alaska Native that I knew about it.

But that's why I love working at NANA now. Because it's

people from my region. They speak words that I understand. And it's like one big family.

*Education?* We moved away from Kiana when I was 13 because my dad had already done 20 years of teaching, and he wanted me to go to a better high school because I was already doing English classes with the seniors in Kiana. So we moved to Kotzebue which has about 4,000 people and a much bigger high school. I was in the tenth grade. And there was just so much more to do. I was a cheerleader. I was in the Honor Society, Student Council, Future Homemakers of America. I did everything. It was fun.

*Social ills in the community?* My parents sheltered me from all of that stuff. I find it strange now to go back to Kiana now and see people who are drunk walking in the streets because I never saw that as a child. I had to be in the house by eight. *They were strict?* Very. *Did you see more problems in Kotzebue?* Not really because I wasn't at all interested in anything like that. I did a lot of reading, worked at the hotel-restaurant and at the radio station, so between all of my school activities and work, plus the fact that I was there from the age of 13 to 16, I didn't have time to see much.

*Higher education?* I never had a choice. Because my dad was a teacher, it was just assumed from birth that we would all go to college. And we have. It's really nice to just have that assumption there. I just helped with a journalism camp a few weeks ago, and they wanted me to talk to one of the girls. She was a Native from a village about the same size as mine, and she had this assumption that she could never go to college. And I said, "No, no, no. I will talk to her because I went to school on scholarships. There's absolutely no reason she can't go." So I'm very happy that with my family it was just, no, you're going. And we never questioned it.

*Has church been a base for you?* I think so because even when I got off to college, I was 16 years old, in a strange town, surrounded by a lot of different people, I started going to church. I belonged there, and later people at school started accepting me as an intelligent human being, not as just this little kid. So it was nice. It always helps you to settle in to a different place. I kept challenging myself there at UAF, too. The first semester, I had 19 credits. I was a cheerleader, and I had my own radio talk show. So that kept me pretty busy, too.

I have a degree in English with an emphasis in writing and one in broadcast journalism. I was in the seventh grade in Kiana, and a cameraman from a TV station in Juneau came up and did an artist-in-residence program. And I loved being behind the camera. I loved doing the interviews. I loved all of that stuff. So when I got to Kotzebue, I started working at the radio station, KOTZ, and I liked that a lot, too. And between all the English classes I was taking at UAF, I just figured it would be easier to get another major in that, instead of using it as a minor. I just did both.

I worked in Fairbanks about a year and a half. And I did an internship there before I even started working there, which was about three months long. That's why they hired me because they saw what a hard worker I was.

My boss over at NANA is actually with the Alaska Broadcasters' Association, and she's pretty high up there in the ranks. So she was putting together this list of people to receive awards called "Goldies." Well, I won one, which was rather amazing to me. And she saw my name on the list and said, "I know this girl, and we have to get her in here if she's winning awards up in Fairbanks at a TV station." She called me up. We talked off and on for about three months, and then I finally moved here.

I plan to stay at NANA and then come back to NANA after school. I'm going off to law school next year. It's actually kind of a joke in my family. I've always wanted to be a lawyer. I've always found it fascinating. And when I was in high school, filling out applications, my dad said, "You can't be a lawyer. There are only honest people in my family." (Laughs.)

So I said, "OK, well, I'll do this other love of mine, which is journalism." And so I did, and now that I'm finally done, I look around and see that maybe I don't really want to be in journalism. I want to see if I can succeed as a lawyer, too. *The school?* Arizona State University, my dad's alma mater. Our lawyer at NANA is very excited about it, Jacquie Luke.

*Native culture?* My favorite time of year in Fairbanks was always the Festival of Native Arts because I got to see people from home, and I got to watch dancing from home. I got to listen to music from home and see arts and crafts. And it was always so much fun just to immerse myself in that much culture. Here? Well, I feel like I kind of immerse myself in it everyday at work because everybody there is from my region. Every once in awhile I hear an Inupiaq word, and I go, "I know what that means." So it's really nice. And I just keep bugging my mom for different things. The last time I was up at home, I got this song book that's both in Inupiaq and English so that I could just read up on the songs.

*Native hero?* You know I've always been fascinated by the Maniilaq stories. I've heard those since birth, and pretty much everybody in the region says they're descended from Maniilaq, but that's what my mom always told me, which I always found fascinating. I don't know. Sometimes I just feel this real connection to him. I can't explain it.

*Anyone else?* Now that I'm working at NANA I have this great admiration for our President Charlie Curtis because he does so much there. And he does it good-heartedly. He's one of the nicest guys that I know. And I've known him since childhood. He was the father of one of my close friends in Kiana, and so he was very happy to see me working for NANA now. And it's just nice. It's like having an uncle to work for. He's a great guy. And he does a lot, and he's really smart. And it's nice to see that.

*ANCSA?* I feel that compared to the legislation and what happened in the Lower 48, it was a very good piece of legislation. The first way it affects me is that I work for NANA. It was a company created by ANCSA, which has been very beneficial to our people. I've sat down and talked to Willie Hensley about that because he's from our region, and he's a friend of my family's. And I just think it's fascinating. I would have loved to have been there when it was going on. It was so long ago now.

*What about the idea of creating corporations?* I think it's a good idea now. If I had been there back then, that would have scared the living daylights out of me because how many Natives back then had any business experience or any corporate experience? Anything like that? I mean they had to start from scratch, and that's a daunting task no matter what you're doing. And when you're doing it for 3,000 people who are depending on you to do it right, it's pretty scary. I mean our corporation now just does so much for our people. We have the world's largest lead and zinc mine on our land, and we made a deal with Cominco saying that you have to hire as many Natives as you can. So that's what they're doing. And so many people in our region work at the Red Dog Mine. And it's wonderful to see people who can live in their village and go to work. Because there aren't that many job opportunities up there.

And then we have other programs through NANA Regional Corporation that keep the culture up – the elders programs and Camp Sivunniigvik, which is a kids' camp where you go and you make birch bark baskets and you do beading and you cut fish, and it's fun. I finally went up there for the first time this summer, and my mom was the birch bark basket woman, so she had me sit down and make a little basket. And that was a lot of fun. And it's just great that our corporation can do that.

*Is there a clash between profit and culture?* I think it's balancing the profit-making with the commitment our president made earlier this year, which was number one to become a one-billion-dollar revenue corporation and number two to provide jobs for every shareholder who wants one. And the clash there comes in with attitudes toward work. We are developing an orientation, not only for our people, but for non-Natives who work at Cominco, showing them how the different cultures work. We're working on getting our people to know that when the alarm clock rings and you're hired to do a job, you have to get up at five in the morning and go to work. We have a lot of people who just don't feel like getting up that early and lose their jobs because of that. I mean we're a very laid back people culturally. They're used to working on their own schedules and to all of a sudden have to do what somebody else says, that's a really big conflict. So the other part is telling all the non-Natives who work up there that this is what their culture is like. They do get up late, but they stay up late and they work hard.

It's hard because not every shareholder wants one and not every shareholder who wants one can keep one for very long. And if they're down here in Anchorage – this has become one of our biggest problems – they don't want to work at the Courtyard for four or five dollars an hour. And we just don't have all that many big-paying jobs, and they don't realize that everybody else starts at the bottom and works up. So it's kind of an education thing going on there.

NANA has been very successful, and a lot of other corporations haven't been. I'd love to stick a hand out and help them any way that I can because I want all of the Native corporations to succeed. And at NANA we have great policy where we don't just try to hire our shareholders. We try to hire shareholders of any Native corporation. And it's really interesting to see how different people feel about different corporations. We have this human resources trainer who does North Slope orientation every Monday. She said in one of the classes a NANA shareholder was just going on and on about NANA doesn't do enough for its shareholders. They don't provide enough jobs and they don't provide enough money to the villages to do different things. And NANA's just a terrible corporation. And another shareholder was in there, saying, "No, what are you talking about? Our corporation's a terrible corporation. NANA does everything for you guys." And then another shareholder jumps in there and says, "Uh-uh. No, no, no, ours is the worst corporation. And NANA's still the best because look at how my corporation works." And so these two shareholders are comparing how bad their corporations are, and the trainer says that the NANA shareholder just kind of got smaller and smaller into his chair.

But I think NANA's been very lucky. The people who have been in charge have hired great people to work there. And they've done a lot for the corporation. And that hasn't happened everywhere. And I want it to. I want all of our corporations to be successful.

*How do you feel about 7(i)?* I think it's a great idea. It helped NANA a lot at first. We looked around and we said, "We don't have any natural resources. There's oil on the North Slope. There's timber in Southeast. But what do we have?" So they started doing service industry stuff, down here in Anchorage and on the Slope and places like that, and then they developed the Red Dog Mine. So, all of a sudden, we have the service industry, which is going wonderfully and making a lot of money for us, and we also have this mine. It's on NANA land. It's hiring NANA shareholders. So it's good for us economically and socially because it provides jobs to all of our people. And it all goes back into itself because we needed help to begin with, and now we're giving help to others.

*How do you feel about the fact that NANA added children born after 1971 as shareholders?* The first inclination was, "They're our children. They're Natives, too. We have to include them." And I'm very proud of the fact that they did. And they didn't mind at all about taking the smaller dividends. It's just involving the younger generations, not only in the culture, but in the corporation that is based on that culture.

*If you weren't a shareholder would you feel differently?* I definitely would feel differently because I have friends who don't belong to Sealaska because they didn't vote to include afterborns. And they're bitter about that. I can understand that because if I were part of this culture and not part of the corporation, I would be a little upset. *What about the fact that the dividends will be a lot less?* I don't even care about the money. The big part is that I am a part of this corporation.

*Your feelings about changes to ANCSA?* Well, first off, there's the "afterborn" legislation. I guess it was part of the "1991" amendments. And I like that. Each corporation has to make their own decision. They decided what was best for their corporation, and that's great. If they don't think that they can handle having all those people as shareholders then, that's fine. But NANA could, and I'm very proud of that. Other than that, I'd have to see what the other changes were.

*Your feelings on the success and political clout of some corporations?* I feel that's great. Alaska Natives, historically, haven't had much of a say in government. Up until 1971, actually 1969-70, they were pretty much ignored until it was discovered that there was oil on the land that they lived on. And NANA, ASRC and CIRI all have pretty big voices when it comes to politics and anything happening on a statewide level. And that's great because we finally have a say in things.

*Personal goals?* I kind of want to be the president of my corporation. But that is such a huge job, and it's just so daunting that I don't know if I could actually do it. Charlie does so much for the corporation. He is on call 24 hours a day to do stuff for the corporation. And he does it. And that would just exhaust me. He's a great guy, and I hope he stays around. But, I was joking around with our chief operating officer and Helvi Sandvik, our vice president of operations. She grew up in Kiana, too, so I've known her for years. I said, "Well, I'll be the next president."

And they said, "Well, great. We'll start grooming you now."

And I said, "Wait, wait, wait, I was just kidding." And I still don't know if they were kidding or not. That's the other fun part about working at NANA. You're just so close to vice presidents and the people who run the company. It's not like there's a separation. You can go up to them any time of day and start talking to them.

*Your goals for your children?* That's where I don't know what I want to do because I would love it if I could raise my children in Kiana. But there aren't really any jobs I could do in Kiana. I mean unless I got a teaching certificate. And I don't know that I want to teach. It's kind of scary in its own right. But I want them to be surrounded by our culture. And I guess Kotzebue would be close enough to it that we could get out to a village or a camp every weekend or whatever. But I want them involved. I want them to grow up eating seal oil, just like I did. I think it's a great community to grow up in because you hear all the time about it takes a village to raise a child. Well, that was true for us. You didn't just punish your kids if they did something wrong. You punished other people's kids if they misbehaved in your house.

But everywhere up there, you just have such a close community. And you don't even have to be from the same village. I knew people in every single village in our region just because of all that traveling that goes on. There are so many more opportunities up there. If I had gone to school in Anchorage or even in Fairbanks, there's no way I would have been a cheerleader and been on student council and been in FHA and done all the stuff that I did.

I would like to see in the next generation a lot more people finishing college. It just disappoints me so much that I am one of two in my graduating class to finish college. I'm also pretty much the only one that doesn't have a child yet. I just want everything to be so much better for the next generation. I want everybody to have a job. I want everybody to have an education. I want them to be able to come back to Kotzebue or Ambler or Kiana and just do great things for those villages. They are fun places to grow up in and they are fun places to live.

*Can ANCSA help with that vision?* I think so, even through the Native corporations that it created. We have a scholarship committee that gives out 70,000 dollars per year to students. We provide jobs for shareholders. Right there, ANCSA's a success because we can give all this help to our shareholders. We can do so much for them. It's just getting them to believe that they have to take care of the rest of it, and they have to stay in their classes and pass them and then stay in school. And they're realizing that it's not just up to NANA to provide for them. They have to take an active part in their lives and say, "OK, you know what? I'm going to do this, and I'm going to succeed." And that's what I want for them. I want them to realize that they can succeed. There is nothing standing in their way.

I think about the drug abuse now, because I'm finally old enough to see it on my own. When I go back to the village, I get invited to parties. And I think, "Why are you wasting your life doing this? You could be spending this money." And up there in the dry villages a bottle of alcohol goes for about 75 to 100 dollars. And they're spending this money on alcohol instead of taking classes at Chukchi Community College or finishing high school or just doing something. And that just breaks my heart.

I occasionally take a drink, but NANA has this "no tolerance" policy that I just love. If you show up for work to go to Red Dog or to the Slope, and you're drunk, that's it, you're fired on the spot. That goes for everybody in Anchorage, too. If you show up for work drunk, that's it, you're fired. If you're found drinking on the job, that's it, you're fired. We used to have a dorm up in Fairbanks that was absolutely no alcohol, absolutely no drugs. And they were very strict about that. They kicked a lot of people out. And I think that's a great policy. Yes, some people can handle it. But this is what scares my dad about drinking: he's afraid that I will be one of those people who can't handle it. So I watch myself very carefully.

I feel it's very serious (with my age group). That's why I'm just so careful about watching myself because I want to do so much more than just sit around being a drunk. And I think part of why they're doing it is they don't realize that they can go to school and they can do all this stuff, too. It's not just those really smart people, everybody can do this as long as you sit down and study and get the work done. And they're just resigning themselves to what they've always seen in their lives. They're resigning themselves to what they think is the only option. And I just have this whole other vision.

It's hard. That's what I've been trying to do on a small scale, and that's what I'm going to keep trying to do. Every time I go back, I tell all my friends, "Well, start taking classes at Chukchi Community College. Look for a better job if you don't like the one you have. And if you do like it, do the best that you can and stick with it." One of my friends from high school – I still haven't given up on her. And I'm not giving her any relief. She's so close to getting a degree. And every time I talk to her I bug her about it. She's one of those who left college after two years because she was pregnant. That just disappointed me so much. Her kids are great. I love them to death, but I still want her to finish college. And she can do it, and I'm going to make sure she does.

*RODNEY "BUTCH" LINCOLN III is currently employed as an Accounting/ Financial Analyst for Arctic Slope Regional Corporation. He was born on January 7, 1974, in Kotzebue.*

*An Inupiaq Eskimo, he is a shareholder of NANA Regional Corporation. The corporation is one of three Native regional corporations that voted to issue stock to shareholders born after December 18, 1971.*

*Years ago the Inupiaq name of Lincoln's great-grandfather was taken away by church missionaries who settled in Kotzebue, and he was given the Western name, Abraham Lincoln. Lincoln feels that as a member of today's generation of young Inupiaq adults, he faces a challenge to preserve the Inupiaq culture, while learning how to succeed in Western society. Lincoln is well known throughout Alaska as a star basketball player and role model, and he was the first Eskimo to earn a scholarship in 1992 to play for the University of Alaska Anchorage men's basketball team. As point guard for the UAA Seawolves, Lincoln was named team captain by his teammates for the 1996-1997 year.*

*Lincoln graduated as Salutatorian of his Kotzebue High School class in 1992, and has a Bachelor's of Business Administration/ Accounting and Finance degree from UAA.*

*Lincoln and his wife Robyn live in Anchorage. Lincoln welcomes the opportunity to gain valuable work experience in Finance. His long-term goals are to be qualified to effectively address the future economic needs and challenges of the Inupiaq people. He was interviewed December 4, 1998.*

S ome would say I was too busy playing basketball, and I would agree with that. I was much more accurate with a jump shot than I was with a shotgun. (Laughs.) Now that I look back on that – I received a scholarship to play basketball, and it's given me an education. I can't say that I regret it, but now that I look back and my father's passed away, I don't have the opportunity to go out and do the hunting and do some of the other things that I did at one time.

My name is Butch Lincoln. My real name is Rodney Lincoln, III. I'm named after my father and grandfather. I was born and raised in Kotzebue, Alaska, an Inupiaq Eskimo. I graduated from Kotzebue High School in 1992. I went on to the University of Alaska Anchorage and received a Bachelor's Business Administration degree in accounting in '96 and then a BBA in Finance in '97.

I played basketball for the University team, and upon completion of college, I have since moved to Arctic Slope Regional Corporation as an accounting/financial analyst. I've been at Arctic Slope for about a year and a half now. Married, no children.

I have three brothers and one sister. I'm the oldest. I spent some of my childhood with my grandmother, while my brothers and sister were raised by our parents. I was closest to my grandparents. My grandfather used to work on the Slope and he would go off for his two weeks for work, and I'd stay with my grandmother because she was home alone. That went on for a year or so, maybe even a couple of years. And then my grandfather passed away, and I just moved in with my grandmother. So I spent a good part of my elementary school years and high school years with my grandmother.

My mother right now is an education specialist for kids from the Kotzebue area entering college who are seeking funding from organizations such as NANA Regional Corporation and the Kotzebue IRA. These are Native organizations that give money to college students. She helps students fill out the applications and receive the proper preparation with the essay question. I worked with my mom for awhile there when I was getting out of high school. And she's been doing that for some time now. As far as my father, he's been deceased since three years ago.

Both my mom and dad were born and raised in Kotzebue, as well. Both sides of my family are in Kotzebue.

I know that my grandfather on my dad's side was originally from Wainwright. He was half Inupiaq and half German. German whalers, I believe, came up north of Kotzebue. On my grandmother's side, my dad's mom is originally from Nome. And she has some, I believe, Swedish, in her as well. It might be one of her parents came up as a gold miner during the Gold Rush there in Nome. So there's a mixture of some Inupiaq and some other nationalities on my dad's side, and he was half Inupiaq. As far as my mother, both her parents were full Eskimo.

My grandmother spoke some Inupiaq off and on, but it wasn't something that I picked up from her because she rarely spoke it. There wasn't enough spoken in the house. I would say she more understood it when people talked than she actually spoke it. So speaking the language wasn't that prevalent in the house. Now on my mother's side, if I had been living with my grandparents there, they speak fluent Inupiaq. Anytime I was in their house, it was spoken.

I wouldn't say I learned it. I actually do not know a whole lot, except for maybe a few phrases. I can understand more what people are saying or trying to say because of words that stick out or words that you recognize. But as far as speaking, no, I do not speak it.

*Subsistence activities?* As a kid, I commercial fished with my father since I was old enough to get in the boat – maybe eight or nine. And then I commercial fished all the way up to when I was 17 or 18. So there was a lot of that in the summer. Added to that, there was traditional hunting in the fall. You know, you went out for caribou and ducks and geese. In my case, I did a lot less of it than maybe my brothers did. Some would say I was too busy playing basketball, and I would agree with that. I was much more accurate with a jump shot than I was with a shotgun. (Laughs.) Now that I look back on that – I received a scholarship to play basketball, and it's given me an education. I can't say that I regret it, but now that I look back and my father's passed away, I don't have the opportunity to go out and do the hunting and do some of the other things that I did at one time.

*Your start in basketball?* Out in the Bush, in the smaller communities of Alaska, basketball is like it is in rural Indiana or rural Kentucky. Out in these places, there's not a whole lot else for kids to do. Basketball is king out there. So, not only was I so involved in the sport, but so were my friends. I don't know if you've ever been out there, but there's a lot of basketball. People love to watch, and kids love to play it. It was something that I did as a kid because I loved it. As I got older, fortunately for me, I had people around me that said, "Hey, you're pretty good, you ought to take this a little seriously and see how far you can take it." And with that comes school and some of the other things that you need to succeed in school and in basketball. I was real fortunate because I had older people – coaches, and older friends and my family – that helped me get to where I was. And that was to UAA.

*You're not really tall.* No, I'm not. My wife would say I'm about 5'6", but I say I'm about 5'7". (Laughs.) Just like in anything, you've got to make up for some weaknesses with some strengths. For me, I think I tried as well as I could to hide my weaknesses and show my strengths. And then the other factor in basketball is school. That's more important in a lot of cases than the basketball because you've got to have the grades to play. And if you're a good student – coaches will take a great student and a good player over a great player and a bad student because the bad student's the waste of a scholarship. So I had school going for me. I always took it seriously, and coaches knew that I was a good student and that I worked hard.

*Why basketball?* I can't explain why I enjoyed playing it so much as a kid. But, again, as I got older, I started thinking that I'd like to receive an education, I'd like to do something to start a career, to do some of those things. And I realized that basketball was maybe my way out so to speak and that you can receive an education while doing something you enjoy. So I would say during the last three years of high school, it not only was something I loved to do, but it was also kind of an investment. It was something more than just recreation. It started to become maybe a little work. You're looking to go on after high school.

I would say overall I was a good student. Fortunately for me, I had my parents and my grandparents who took school very seriously. I wasn't allowed to go out until my homework was done. I had strict curfews. My parents and my grandmother were really good about keeping on me when I was younger, and it set a foundation for later. In high school they really didn't have to do a whole lot because I was used to succeeding in school and giving my best.

In school, I enjoyed math, and that was what I was best at. As far as the verbal, the English part – I struggled with it. That's probably why I didn't enjoy it as much as I did the math. Still to this day, my English – verbal skills, written skills – they're a little harder to get than the math. And I found out for a lot of people it's just the opposite. For me, I seem to do really well in math.

I'm the first in my family, the first one of my grandmother's grandkids to graduate from college with a Bachelor's. I had an aunt who received an associate's degree when she was going to school. My mother went to the University of Alaska Fairbanks. She went to a boarding school at Fairbanks in high school. This was back in the '60s when it was not normal to leave and go to high school and then go on to college. She went on to college for a year and then she had to come home. Her mother became sick and was wheelchair-bound. So I believe if that hadn't been the case that she would have graduated from college. She knows the importance of education. So while I say I'm the first in the family, I believe she would have done it if she had had the opportunity to.

*Social ills in the community?* It's real unfortunate, but there are problems like alcoholism, drug abuse, the list goes on and on. Suicide, domestic violence, all of those ills – unfortunately they trickle down and they affect, not only those who are directly involved, but they affect family, friends. They affect kids, the elderly. I had seen a lot of that. Friends of mine. Family members of mine. Each person reacts how they choose to adversity, to hardship. I've always asked myself what I could do to not have to go through those things. I think I used some of those problems – diseases – as an incentive for me to go the opposite way. Some people allow those things to drag them in. I think those things scared me, and I wanted to get away.

Most kids in a town like Kotzebue or somewhere – you know

someone who has problems with alcohol or drugs. Or, you know someone whose parents are divorced. Or you have a relative who has committed suicide. Everyone's so connected that it's real hard not to be faced with some of those problems. When you see those problems every day, I kind of looked around and said, "I don't want to deal with these when I get older. What can I do to better my situation?"

*Your education?* I can't really say a lot of bad things about the education because I did well here at the University. I was prepared to come to college. I did well in the classroom, so I believe that my education in Kotzebue was sufficient. It was above standards, so to speak. One of the problems I always had with the education – in Kotzebue, there's a high turnover in teachers. Maybe that's a problem everywhere. But I think it's more of a problem in rural Alaska than it is maybe here in the city. But then again, in the city you have a lot more kids, so you're not as close to the teachers as you are there. But there was a high turnover rate. Sometimes you think people working there are just waiting to get out of there. That kind of hurts and diminishes the effectiveness of the education. Again, that's just my opinion. I don't have any specific examples.

*Discrimination?* No, I don't know if I've been real fortunate, but I cannot recall any one case where my Native race or being a minority or being from rural Alaska has ever been brought up. I can name a thousand instances where it's been used as a positive, as kind of what's made me "different." I've been touted by the media as the first Alaska Native to receive a scholarship at UAA to play basketball, so there have been cases like that where they've used minority status or my Alaska Native status as a positive. But I can't name a time when I was ever discriminated against. I can remember my mom telling me it was a little different when she was in school in Fairbanks. So maybe things have changed. When I think of my friends, I don't think I've heard of a lot of problems with discrimination.

*You were the first Alaska Native to get a basketball scholarship?* To play basketball, I believe, yes. It's something I've read. No one's come up and said, "Hey, wait a second, you're not. I am." (Laughs.)

*Was there a time when you had a sense of being an Alaska Native?* Not really. I don't know if it's because I'm not full Inupiaq that I was never shocked when I came to Anchorage. Kotzebue was large enough to where everyone wasn't Eskimo. There were

Caucasians. There were even a few blacks and there were different types of Alaska Natives. So it's a big enough community where you get to see other people. And as a youngster, I always came to Anchorage every so often. So when I came to college, I'd been to Anchorage numerous times. There was nothing really that I didn't expect. I wouldn't say there was a specific time when I realized that I was Alaska Native.

*Do you have a tie to your culture?* I feel I do. I feel I have an obligation in the future to help the people of my area and to help the people of the state. As an Alaska Native I would like to educate myself to better the lives of Alaska Natives. That's one of my goals – in an economic sense – to gain professional knowledge to maybe someday make a difference for Alaska Natives.

*Native hero?* Well, I have my parents. And they're Native. I've always thought of them as role models. Growing up and going through college, people have identified me as a role model because of my success in the classroom, success on the basketball court. And while I've accepted that, I remember when I was a kid. I never thought of any basketball player as a hero. I always thought of my parents as being role models, and I always looked at them to gain knowledge, to see the values that they lived for. So when I watched basketball I never thought of players as being role models.

But basketball takes a lot of discipline. Yes, athletes or people who are dedicated to a sport or to a profession – to anything – it takes a lot of time, takes a lot of sacrifice. That was one thing I mentioned earlier. I felt I sacrificed a lot of my subsistence activity with basketball. One of my ways to justify that is to say for the next 10 years I will do more of that now that I have the time. I have the opportunity to do some of those things I missed out on when I was so busy playing basketball.

*You mentioned basketball as a way out?* I don't think you should judge how successful you are on whether you get out of town or you move away or you go to school. There are successful people who don't go to college. But, for me, I couldn't decide if I was successful if I didn't know what people were doing on the other side of the hill. For me, I wanted to go elsewhere just to see exactly what everyone else was doing. To go to school at a large university. And fortunately, playing basketball, I got to travel to a lot of places. We went to Germany. We've been to the Bahamas, Hawaii, California, Texas. So you go to all these places, and you get to see other parts of the world and see how other people live. Each time I've gone somewhere I've always said, "Gee, I'm happy to live in Alaska. I'm happy to be from Kotzebue." But I think I needed to go elsewhere to appreciate all these things. If I never had gone elsewhere, I would have never known.

You'd be surprised at UAA's schedule. They're only a Division II team, but in terms of where they travel, it's right up there with the best schools. They go to Hawaii every year. If you look at some of the national power schools, a lot of them cannot say that.

I saw a lot of things I hadn't seen before other than the obvious things – sunshine and white sand beaches. I remember when we went to the Bahamas. On the television, in the media, it's painted as a beautiful place for tourists with nice restaurants, nice beaches, all of those good things. While that is there, there's another part of that country that they don't portray, and it's a lot of the people are very poor. Once you get off the beaches, out of the touristy places, the common people, the citizens – a lot of them – appeared to be very poor. It makes you feel lucky as an Alaskan, as a Native who lives up here. You get quality education. You have opportunities for work. You have opportunities to go to school. You have land where you can fish and hunt. And down there, I remember driving from the hotel to the gym – you had to drive through the town – and you could smell sewer. A lot of them didn't have running water. So when I go places like that, it makes me feel lucky.

I think overall young Alaska Natives should feel lucky because any young kid who wants to go to school, in my opinion can go to school if he wants. Because there's enough money out there. There are enough scholarships. There are just so many opportunities for kids. And I think sometimes we don't appreciate some of those things.

*Do you still play basketball?* I still do occasionally. People ask me if I play, and I don't know if recreational basketball is actually called "playing," but I play with a lot of former players that I've played with at UAA. It's good to go to a gym and see all of the friends you've made and the people you've played against and keep up. All of them are friends now. But other than that, it's pretty much over. There's no NBA or there's not anything like that. And that's fine with me.

I'm realizing that it's different once you get out in the real world and get a full-time job. I tell my wife, "School was easy. I wish I could go back to school again." (Laughs.) She can go to work, and I'll go back and go to school because college years were fun. I'd encourage most young kids to go to school. While there's a lot of work, there's a lot of fun. There are a lot of good memories of going to college.

*Was ANCSA a good thing?* I believe it was a good thing. I think about each corporation that was formed under this act: some have been more successful than others. But if it were not for the corporations stimulating and pushing for economic development and growth and job opportunities – if it wasn't for that – what would a majority of the people be doing? I think setting up the corporations with shareholders being Alaska Natives has made sure that business is done with the best interests of the Native people.

*The people who worked on it?* One of the persons that I am most familiar with is Willie Hensley. He's from Kotzebue, and I know him. I've known him for some time. As far as what he did during those years of forming the act, I'm not sure. But I'm well aware of his career. I've kind of kept track of what he was doing, because he always seemed to be doing good things. Now he's with Alyeska Pipeline Service Company.

I think setting up the corporations was a good idea. *As opposed to reservations?* I couldn't say because I don't know a whole lot about reservations. I've never been on one. I don't believe I know anyone who's lived on one. So I can't speak about the quality of life or the opportunities they have. But I know as far as setting up the corporations, it has given young people like me a chance to receive an education and know that if you educate yourself in business you can go back and have a place to learn more and to apply your education. It encourages kids to learn about capitalism.

I received scholarships from NANA and a number of other agencies and organizations from up in Kotzebue and a few even down here in Anchorage when I was going down here to school.

*Are you familiar with any changes to ANCSA?* I think adding young people is a good idea. Young people's needs for the land and the opportunities are equal to the older people's. For one, it's never been a custom of the Native cultures to not share. That's one of the foundations of each culture – sharing. And including young people is not only sharing, but I think it's fair. They're just as much a part of Inupiaq culture as some of the older people.

Different people have different agendas and different goals.

Whether it's a mistake for other corporations not to include young people, I don't know. But for NANA, I feel it was the right decision. I am a shareholder because they added young people. My wife is Alaska Native, and she's Bering Straits from Nome. She is a shareholder because she was born in 1971. I'm not sure what her views are on that. I'm a shareholder of the village corporation in Kotzebue, Kikiktagruk Inupiaq Corporation, KIC.

I think it's real important to have young people a part of the corporation. As I said earlier, it gives children just one more opportunity, one more avenue. Someone who is interested in business or accounting – some of those things – has a place where they can get help to receive an education and they can apply their education and come back and work.

*Is there a clash between culture, business?* No. I would think between culture and business, you can take a lot of values from your culture and apply them to business to help you succeed. I think of some of the culture from the Kotzebue, Arctic Slope regions. ASRC has some posters made up on how the Inupiaq culture ties to the business culture. One of them is taking the long view. They show an Eskimo looking out on the ice. It's things like that. Another one is business can be a harsh world, and it shows a polar bear getting ready to eat a seal. Just different things like that. And then when you think of some of the other values – knowledge of your culture – that says to me that you've got to be knowledgeable about what you're doing, whether it be in business or when you go out hunting. Or, be prepared for storms or things that you don't expect. And in the business world, you need to have that attitude. You've got to know what you're doing. You've got to have some backup strategies. I think a lot of the things go along the same lines.

I do appreciate ASRC, first of all because they've given me an opportunity to work. Not only that, they've given me a real opportunity to learn more. They as a corporation are really strong about younger people being leaders of the corporation in the future. I can appreciate that as a young person. My hat's off to them for showing that commitment. They have a management trainee program where they encourage young people to apply. Maybe they want to go to school, and once they're done with school, you assign them a mentor. And they see that you are prepared for future roles as managers and executives. I'm real impressed with their commitment to preparing younger people.

One thing I think I'd like to see corporations do is to use their size and their clout to see that they're continually providing a stimulant to the economy, providing jobs to the people, encouraging the young kids to go to school and providing funding to go to school. All of our regions have a lot of different resources. Some have minerals. Some have oil, some have trees. There are a lot of resources on the land, and I'd like to see the corporation continue to not only develop that land and provide jobs, but also to protect it and see that the wildlife and the environment are not hurt from this development. And I think they've done a good job up until now, and I think they'll continue to do a good job.

*Your own goals?* I'm a real goal oriented person. I told you earlier by the time I was in the ninth grade, I started thinking that basketball was just as much an investment as anything. I wrote a letter to my aunt in ninth grade telling her this is what I wanted to do: I wanted to receive a scholarship to play basketball. And I did it. So now that I'm done playing, it doesn't mean I'm done setting goals. I still have goals: I'd like to get my MBA. I'm looking into schools right now. I'd like to have that by the time I'm 29. And then from there, as far as where I'd like to work, what I'd like to do, I'm not sure. But I do want to stay in Alaska. And I do want to work for a Native organization whether it's a regional corporation or a village corporation or some other type. That's where my interests lie and that's where I'd like to help. I'd like to help other Alaska Natives. But I feel that I need to go out to get an education, to gain the knowledge to do that.

Some people can help by providing services – my wife is in social work. She can help people with their problems. I'd like to help people by providing jobs, by seeing that maybe a company is financially sound and able to provide dividends which are a vital part of many Alaska Natives' income. I'd like to someday be a part of a company that protects the environment of the people, ensures that development does not mean lost land or lost habitat or wildlife.

I talked about the importance of education – younger people. I think that that's where it's at. Whether you want to be a truck driver or professor, you've got to educate yourself. You don't have to go to college. Maybe you want to go to the military or become a barber, but you've got to go to school. You've got to get the training somewhere. I think it's real important for younger kids, once they're done with school to take that step. Because if you're sitting around, it becomes harder to get out and make that move.

In a town like Kotzebue, most kids don't get further education. If you got a kid that's walking the fence asking should I go to school? They're going to have a lot of friends who don't. It's a given that most of the kids don't go to school. And the longer you're home, the more comfortable you feel and the more tied down you get.

*JACK ZAYON is a NANA shareholder who was born in Fairbanks on November 15, 1972. He grew up in Fairbanks, but spent time as a child and teenager in NANA Region villages in Northwest Alaska. His mother, also a NANA shareholder, was born in Kiana and raised in Noorvik.*

*Zayon graduated from Lathrop High School in Fairbanks and then went on to the University of Alaska Fairbanks. He received his Bachelor's Degree in Business Management from the University of Alaska Anchorage in 1997. Throughout his college education, he was employed by NANA in various capacities during summer and holiday breaks, which allowed him to pay for school.*

*Zayon's long-time dream and vision has always been to help empower and develop opportunities for his people. It was this vision that led him to the development of the Alaska Native Professional Association, a membership organization for young Alaska Native Professionals.*

*Zayon is also very interested in Alaska Native cultures and seeks to foster the resurgence of cultural pride. He hopes to set up a conversational Inupiaq language class for Alaska Native children and adults in Anchorage, as well as help with summer cultural camps to instill Inupiaq values.*

*Zayon participated in Leadership Anchorage, a program formed by the Alaska Humanities Forum with a grant from the Pew Charitable Trust to foster and develop leadership skills.*

*He is employed by NANA Development Corporation as a Business Specialist. He previously worked for Dynamic Capital Management, Inc., in Anchorage as a Marketing Specialist and Stock Analyst. He and his wife Kristen have one daughter, Emma Elizabeth, who was born June 17, 1998. He was interviewed July 13, 1998.*

I have this one vivid memory. I was a little kid and I was being dedicated to the Lord in a Friends Church in some small village somewhere. And I'll never forget being around those Native elders – the comfort that they were giving me and the praise. . . I remember being passed from elder to elder and being prayed for by all these elders. It was a nice feeling. I remember this flood of emotion coming over me.

I was born in Fairbanks and grew up there. I was the youngest. My next older brother is seven years older. The oldest child was 12 years older than I. My father was born and raised in Philadelphia. He joined the Army and was transferred to Fairbanks, and that's where he met my mother. She already had a couple kids at the time. I found it very admirable that he married into that. My parents are Jack and Nina Zayon. They are both in Anchorage. My mom is 63 and my dad is 58. My father has always worked in construction as a carpenter. Mom was a nurse, then a full-time mother, and now she's working for Maniilaq Association as a patient support worker. I am half Inupiaq Eskimo and half Caucasian. My mother was originally born in Kiana but was raised in Noorvik. We had a lot of Inupiaq culture in our family. We grew up eating our traditional foods, fishing and picking blueberries.

It was somewhat challenging growing up in Fairbanks, being half Inupiaq and half white. Some of the perception about Natives among non-Natives in Fairbanks is that they're drunks and they're down on Second Avenue. I experienced racism on a weekly basis, and it was tough. A lot of my friends would make fun of Natives – without even knowing that I was Native because I looked like I could have been Hispanic or Hawaiian. I took it personally but would hold it in. I couldn't really take the racial remarks until I got into junior high. It was about junior high when I started to feel more confident and proud about my Alaska Native heritage.

A pivotal point for me when I started getting more pride in my heritage was when I was in about eighth grade and I moved to Kotzebue. My dad got a construction job there and my mom also wanted to get back to work after being a full-time mother for so many years. I moved back up there with my mom and my dad and my older brother Michael, and we lived there for about a year and a half. And that's when I really saw something kind of interesting. Even though I was half Eskimo and half white, I saw some racism against me by some Natives because I was "white." It was very strange, and I never thought that would have happened, but some racism does also exist amongst our Alaska Natives.

When a new kid comes to town it's kind of like that in a smaller town, I guess. And I think that resentment might have come from experiences that these Natives had when they came to the city. They'd notice how they were treated by the majority of the people who are Caucasian. I started fitting in as time went by, really enjoying it and taking pride and learning about my culture by trying to learn as much as a I could about the language – taking an Inupiaq language class and also being immersed in potlucks, fishing and hunting.

In Kotzebue, almost everyone I hung out with was Inupiaq Eskimo. Once I started to meet them, I noticed they were different from Natives in Fairbanks. They had more pride in who they were, maybe because they hadn't experienced as much racism as I. I took an Inupiaq language class for a year when I was there, which I think is critical for preserving culture. I think it might be mandatory in some villages for them to take their language.

Everybody pretty much knows that it's very difficult to maintain cultural ties in today's society. It started with my mother's generation when she was pulled away from her family to go to Mt. Edgecumbe. The children weren't even allowed to speak their Native tongue. They would be punished for it.

*Sports?* All three brothers grew up playing hockey in Fairbanks. We were all pretty good. And then when I moved to

Kotzebue, I took a year off. But I really enjoyed learning about the different Native games. One thing I wished I had more of when I was growing up in Fairbanks was that they had more cultural activities for the community. Now they are getting better about it. I wish I had been more a part of the Native Olympics and stuff like that.

I couldn't really talk to my parents about feelings about racism and discrimination. I never was able to have real personal discussions with my dad until the past few years. On the other hand, I did have a pretty good relationship with my mom. She was a Christian lady and actually my grandpa was a pastor in Noorvik and was also a legislator for the region. I've been proud that James Wells was my grandpa and hear he was a great guy. I've always thought about the possibility of getting into politics. Who knows?

Since my mom was a Christian, we were pretty close in that regard. She was definitely concerned if anything was wrong, but I still felt that I really couldn't talk to her because I didn't think she could relate to my problems. It was mainly embarrassment – being half Native and being around white kids who would make fun of Natives. I really didn't think she would understand that, so I really didn't talk with her about those issues.

I could talk a little to my brothers and sisters because they kind of got the same thing I did. I guess they kind of just closed it all in. At times I remember them talking to my parents a little bit about it. But my dad never really said anything about it. All my mom could do was sympathize. Racism – it was the little things, kids calling me "Muktuk" or just kids imitating the way they thought Natives talked. They'd give them an accent and just make fun of them. They'd say, "whale blubber eater," little things kids do that have a negative effect on you.

I went to elementary school at Hunter Elementary. I excelled in art. One of my pieces went to Juneau. I used to win those Christmas art competitions for the pictures in the calendars just about every year for my grade. I excelled in sports. They'd have marathons in gym class and stuff. I'd win those just about every year. My sixth grade year, I won the Principal's Award. I guess it's kind of prestigious for elementary. It's an award that the principal gives out to a student who's been there from kindergarten through sixth grade and who they feel had been the most outstanding student. I got decent grades.

We did some camping growing up. My dad liked to take us

fishing and camping. We got a lot of food from the relatives, ate a lot of Native food in Fairbanks. Aside from the racism, I had a pretty good childhood. I moved back to Fairbanks when I was in ninth grade, and I played hockey for Lathrop High School my junior and senior year. One of the highlights I'm most proud of was my junior year of high school where I was selected for Boys State, and there were only two students selected out of the whole high school who were chosen to come down to Anchorage and learn about the legislative process. I ran for Commissioner of Natural Resources and won. We had mock political campaigns and issues. It was a two-week training program, kind of like boot camp. We'd wake up at 5 in the morning, go jogging, go to breakfast, come back for sessions. As commissioner of the Department of Natural Resources, I wanted to have a major say with the direction of natural resources in Alaska.

My father knew a lot of the Native issues. He loves to read, so he always knows about the issues but he never really took a stand on any of them. He always knew what was going on with NANA, but he never really participated in any of the issues. He loves Eskimo food.

My first memory of being Native? I have this one vivid memory. I was a little kid and I was being dedicated to the Lord in a Friends Church in some small village somewhere. And I'll never forget being around those Native elders – the comfort that they were giving me and the praise and just being dedicated. In the Friends Church, dedication is almost like baptism. It's a ceremony of giving a child to the Lord. I found it very comforting. I remember being passed from elder to elder and the prayers. I remember feeling this flood of emotion coming over me.

*Alcohol?* Yeah, I did have some exposure. My oldest brother was 24 when he died from choking on his vomit after he'd passed out and was put on his back. I remember his last few years of his life he struggled with alcohol and Christianity. I remember a few times he would come home with cuts on his face from getting in a fight. I'd known at that age it was from alcohol, and he never really could handle it. It eventually led to his death in Kotzebue. He was studying there at the vocational school in Kotzebue. And that was when I started realizing that alcohol really was a problem for Native people. I know it is an issue and challenge facing Alaska Native people today. Alaska Natives have been exposed to alcohol for less than a hundred years, whereas other cultures have been exposed to alcohol for thousands of years. So it's something very new to people. Alaska

Natives don't have a high tolerance for it and are very susceptible to alcoholism and the abuses that go with it.

I've experimented. The first time I got drunk was in seventh grade. We used to go get these buyers downtown. Most of the time Natives would buy for us for some money. It was terrible. But it's a reality and kids today are doing the same thing. We'd always find out whose parents would be out of town for the weekend. We'd bring the bottles to school in our backpacks and go to their place on Friday and get drunk. Then, when I moved to Kotzebue in the eighth grade, same thing. We always had people buy for us. I noticed a lot of partying went on in Kotzebue, as well. I've talked to other people, and they say it's pretty much that way in all small communities. It seems like their complaint is there's never really anything to do. So what do they do? They party.

As a kid growing up, I never thought about college. A girl I went out with in high school had a big impact on my future goals. She was a couple years older than I was and she was a very smart girl. She was salutatorian for Lathrop High School when she graduated and she started encouraging me to think about going to college. I never even really thought, me? Go to college? Me, the only one out of the whole family even graduating from high school? That was a big deal. So I got these dreams and aspirations. My family was very happy and very proud that I graduated from high school because my brothers and sisters all dropped out, for whatever reason. Being the youngest, I learned from many of their mistakes.

I don't know what made me more confident than them. Although my older brother Mike was very popular. He was the best hockey player in the state of Alaska for a few years for his age group. I know he was always kind of embarrassed because of the racism. He always hung out with the really popular kids, and they'd also make fun of Alaska Natives. And I felt that it hurt us, hurt knowing that it's part of who you are.

I called the University of Alaska Fairbanks and asked them about enrolling, and I asked if they had any programs for Native students. They pointed me in the direction of Rural Student Services, and told me what to do. My first major was biology. I wanted to be a doctor. I had big goals coming out of high school.

Discipline is different in the Native culture. From what I know, parents don't really spank the kids. We never really had that in my family. I wish they had been a little more strict in a lot of ways. I believe consistency with discipline is very important and will do things a little differently with my children.

I ended up majoring in business management. I got an internship down here one summer in Anchorage with a man named John Shively at NANA. At that point, I had been getting burned out, thinking that being a doctor was going to take way too long, so I changed my major to business, transferred my credits over. I really didn't know what I wanted to do my freshman year of college, so I chose pre-med. I had some experience with the medical field because I did some volunteering in some hospitals, and I was in the Della Keats summer enrichment program, which is a six-week program that gets high school students ready for college and lets them know in advance what you have to look forward to in your studies and the challenges.

I love business, but then again, I get a compassionate side from my mom being raised in a church. My mom's a very compassionate person. Right now, she works for Maniilaq Association as a patient support worker and translator here in Anchorage. She helps people who come in from the village, helps them to get adjusted to Anchorage, arranges things for sick and dying people. It's a tough job, but she really enjoys it.

When I graduated from college it felt really good. I believe if you have a goal and you take little steps to get there, then, it's no problem. Sure, there are going to be trying times, but you know if you have a clear vision and break your goals into little steps, it's not as big a deal.

At UAF I felt very comfortable being an Alaska Native. UAF has a really good support network, Rural Student Services. At that age, I'd grown to realize that I am who I am. I had learned to accept myself for who I am. If people make fun of Natives, you know, they are shallow.

I knew about NANA, growing up, because of the dividends that I didn't receive – and my brothers and sister did. I'd been to a few meetings growing up. I'd hear some complaining about what's going on with certain issues. I never really listened in depth. You've always got people out there complaining, talking about different things that Native corporations aren't doing for them.

I really enjoyed working for NANA. I wrote a tour guide manual for Tour Arctic up at Prudhoe Bay. That was a fun project. I went to the different oil companies here in town and found out what they did and how they did it. NANA also has a really good program that they use to put their students through college – summer hire program. They go up there to the North Slope and clean up the whole environment from well pads to the tundra. Mainly, they're just young college students. NANA employed me as a supervisor for the summer hire program. I made good money in the summer and that allowed me to not work during the school year. This kind of brings me back to working for a Native corporation, which I originally wanted to do straight out of college, but I also wanted to get some professional experience outside a Native corporation.

I've been married for almost four years now. We just had a little girl. She's four weeks old. We named her Emma Elizabeth, and she's completely changed my life for the better. Even though she's only a quarter Inupiaq, I still want to teach her about her culture, submerse her in it by taking her up North when she's still a young child. I want to take her on a river – letting her see it, experience the culture and not just read about it. Make sure she calls her Eskimo grandma *Ana*. Just little things like that. Teach her to be proud of being Alaska Native.

Because NANA added "afterborns," I am a shareholder. Our daughter will be, too. We're going to enroll her, and I think that's wonderful. There are so many different benefits. For one, shareholder hire. If I weren't a shareholder, I probably wouldn't have been hired for NANA's summer hire program. Their summer program allowed me to make enough money to live off during the school year, helping me to focus on my education. I have a lot of Alaska Native friends who aren't shareholders. They feel very unfortunate that they're not shareholders. I actually have a friend right now who's been working on getting something organized to present to his Native corporation to get them to enroll afterborns. I know it bothers a lot of afterborns.

I think being a shareholder gives you a little more pride in your region and in being an Alaska Native because, especially in Alaska, the Native corporations play in the same game as all the other big corporations in the state do. I believe enrolling afterborns would give them more pride and more incentive to learn more about their Native political issues so they can hopefully go to work for their Native corporation someday. It's definitely not just a check. It's the pride, job opportunities, feeling of belonging.

*Do you have a Native hero?* I have a few. I wouldn't call them "heroes," just people I look up to who are Alaska Native. One is Will Mayo from Tanana Chiefs Conference. I'm very impressed with the way he sees things and the way he's able to convey his message to the public. He's very passionate about his people, and to me that's very admirable.

Also, I have respect for Perry Eaton. I know him a little bit. I'm always impressed by his knowledge on Native issues. Some of the people that I really look up to are people who convey taking pride in your Native culture.

I'm impressed by what Willie Hensley (one of the architects of ANCSA) has done for Alaska Natives. All the accomplishments he's had, how successful he's been, breaking trail, you might say, for Alaska Natives. I admire him for just diving in to ANCSA and doing what he could for the Native people and making sure we were heard.

Charlie Curtis (current President of NANA) does a wonderful job. I'm not too knowledgeable about how all the other Native corporations work, but just seeing him moderate meetings and answer questions at shareholder meetings is impressive. A lot of the shareholders ask some very tough questions – and they're entitled to.

I'm very impressed by Julie Kitka (President of the Alaska Federation of Natives). She's a wonderful person. I had the opportunity to work with her a little bit on Anchorage Native Vote. I was the vice chair for one summer. I got a chance to see how compassionate she is, yet how tough she can be. She's a tough lady. She's smart. She makes sure she gets our voice heard. And I really admire her for that.

There are many other Native leaders I'd like to meet who have a wealth of information like Roy Huhndorf and Carl Marrs from CIRI and leaders from the Arctic Slope Regional Corporation.

*ANCSA?* Recently I've been getting more involved in reading on different Native issues, discussing Native issues. I think at the time ANCSA was a good idea. My understanding is that at the time of the passage, most Natives were unaware of the way things are set up in a corporate environment, the laws and regulations. I think they did a good job with the resources they had. I'm not sure, but probably some of the issues were determined in spite of the fact that the people who were working on it couldn't be truly representative of all the Alaska Native groups. They worked with what they had. I'm sure there were a lot of limitations and pressures that the government may have been putting on them that today they wouldn't have gone along with. Maybe they weren't allowed enough time to think strategically through the issues. I think ANCSA was good in a sense because it pushed the Alaska Natives to band together and start thinking more along the lines of capitalism. Kind of pushed them into a Western culture, you might say. Kind of forced them to become educated on issues that would affect their future. A lot of things didn't go well with ANCSA corporations as far as early management. There was a lot of inexperience, just because the Natives hadn't had that experience working in a capitalistic system. A lot of bad investments lost them money, I understand.

I've talked with some white influential people and was surprised. I got the impression they didn't like ANCSA because they feel that it's blocking Alaska Natives from being assimilated into the larger mainstream urban towns like Anchorage. They didn't come out and say it, but I got the impression that they think Natives have too much political power in the state of Alaska. They said Alaska Natives need to move to places like Anchorage because there's no industry in the smaller communities. One person in particular, a vice president of a bank, I was just kind of flabbergasted that he thought ANCSA was a horrible idea. I just couldn't believe what I was hearing. He rambled on about how because the rural villages didn't have roads, railways or any larger modes of transportation, there would never be any form of economy. So in essence the people need to move to more urban areas because it's too expensive to fund these villages' education and other services.

I think ANCSA accomplished what it could at the time. There are so many different views on ANCSA. It seems like there are so many different pros and cons of ANCSA. A lot of people talk about the perception of the regional corporations being greedy versus the village corporations and the village corporations not getting enough say. The Native corporations: I feel they are doing the best job that they can. You can't please everybody. It might be kind of a hard concept for shareholders in the villages to grasp, as far as the offices in Anchorage being greedy in the sense that they're not hiring enough shareholders. And I agree with that and I don't agree with that. Say, for example, when NANA opens up a new hotel. You have to put someone that's trained and educated into managerial positions because they know what it takes to run a hotel. I know Native corporations strive to train the people and give their shareholders the incentive to excel in their positions – so they can have the better paying jobs.

Right now we're trying to get an Alaska Native professional association started so we can bring together the Alaska Native professionals and learn about the issues in Alaska and what we can do to network. I actually brought our mission statement: "The mission of the Alaska Native Professional Association is to identify, develop and nurture professional relationships with our peers and to foster Alaska Native leadership through community involvement." Playing a role as mentors to the Native students in college. "Membership is by word of mouth and is open to those who meet the following conditions: those who are tribally enrolled members of an Alaskan tribe; or are a shareholder, or a descendant of a shareholder, of an ANCSA Native regional or village corporation; American Indian; and who have a four-year college degree or equivalent professional experience; and who are 39 years of age or younger."

I think ANCSA was also good in a sense in that it brought the Alaska Native community together – forced them together. Today, there are a lot of younger Alaska Natives out there and there really isn't anything bringing them together – to meet each other and become educated on the issues. So that's going to be a goal of this group.

*Does participating in profit-making ventures detract from culture?* That's a tough one. I guess I don't think so. In my experience, I've seen the values Alaska Native corporations push – traditional values that incorporate into business. They're fair. I see that if the Native corporations can incorporate those values into their business, it's good business. I'll try to make a point, and it's a little off from the direct question you've just asked. In smaller village communities, when young adults go off to college and they come back – after they have a degree, people treat them a little differently. They think they're a changed person, and I think that's a problem and a misperception. The person might have a degree and they might be a little more educated, but they're not a different person. I've witnessed it in my family situation. It's probably not that way with just Natives, but with anyone that goes away to school. Other people might be envious or they might think that the person thinks they're a hotshot, and I think that's an issue that needs to be addressed. I think if our people are going to be successful in the future, Native corporations need to push education really hard.

*What about the success of some of the corporations?* It makes me feel wonderful. I hope to see that the other Native corporations will follow in that success. I think there's a lot of potential for Native corporations. Look at CIRI, ASRC, NANA, Doyon and some of the others. They have the ambition of becoming global.

*Political Clout?* I think it's important that each Native corporation is involved in lobbying issues that face Alaska. They are such a big part in the Alaskan economy that they should have their say in the way issues are decided.

*Personal Goals?* My personal goals – they change. Ever since I've been a little kid I always wanted to be president of my Native corporation. Recently, I applied to this program in Anchorage called the Leadership Anchorage Program. The program focuses and emphasizes leadership in many regards as far as civic leadership, but also learning about different leadership models. One of the goals is for me to get accepted into that program so I can learn more on leadership, personal reflection, what works and what doesn't. Then, eventually, I'd love to see this Alaska Native Professional Association that's being formed get more Alaska Natives on more boards throughout Anchorage.

Right now is kind of a critical point for Alaska Natives, to get more involved and become more educated on the issues. It's vital to train more Alaska Native professionals to become aware of ANCSA issues. Because my generation right now, we're going to be the ones leading the Native corporations in the future, 10 years, 15 years down the road. And I hope to see that this Alaska Native Professional Association kind of pulls them all together and meets with different Native corporations.

My goal for my daughter would be to definitely raise her with discipline. Teach her to think for herself. Teach her to be a good-hearted person, like my mom taught me. Teach her to appreciate what she has. Respect your elders and immerse her in traditional Alaska Native values. I want her to be able to identify with her culture, know her past.

*Your vision?* A vision would be to have the subsistence issue worked out, see more of a resurgence in our cultures, see more Alaska Native leadership statewide and see our people working in harmony with the Legislature. I think subsistence is such a huge issue right now, and it's vital for the state. I think it's a very divisive issue right now. It's hard to say what's going to happen in the next 10 years, but I would love to be involved. To put it simply, I'd love to see more younger Alaska Natives uniting and working toward the betterment of all our people. I think the experienced Alaska Native professional working with younger Alaska Native professional is going to help the transition of leadership for people's futures. The Willie Hensleys aren't going to be around forever. And who's going to fill his shoes? You've got to think about the future. If the Native corporations got together and really focused on getting a strategic plan put in place, then I think that would have a very positive impact on the future of Alaska Native people.

They need to come together without their own political agenda. They need to leave that at home. They need to focus on what are we going to do now to start training and educating Alaska Natives. Not only for the Native corporations, but for positions in the Legislature. I would hope that this Alaska Native Professional Association could maybe someday get some help from the Native corporations in having professionals in their industry, in leadership, like what Leadership Anchorage does, having the best training you can get for the future of our people. The older I get, the more mature I get, the more I read on the issues, I feel like I see the challenges that are being put on Alaska Natives. The more trained and the more knowledgeable, the more confident I become on helping the Native community.

# *Sealaska Region*

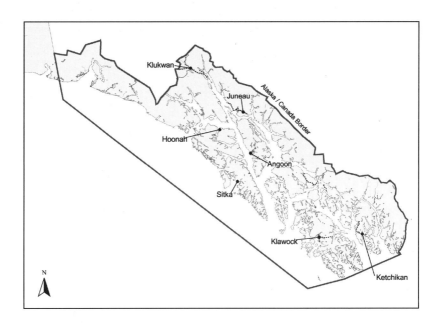

 **JAELEEN KOOKESH ARAUJO** *was born February 16, 1973, in Juneau and raised in Angoon in Southeast Alaska. The small village of Angoon has just over 600 people and is situated on Admiralty Island. Its economy is based on fishing.*

*Araujo is the daughter of Albert and Sally Kookesh and she is a member of the Dog Salmon Clan of Angoon.*

*Araujo has a Bachelor's Degree in Political Science from Stanford University and a law degree and certificate in Indian Law from the University of New Mexico. She is currently employed by Van Ness Feldman in the law firm's Washington, D.C., office, where she practices primarily in the fields of Alaska Native and Federal Indian law.*

*In 1997, Araujo was honored with the top award given to an Alaska Native youth by the Alaska Federation of Natives.*

*She was married on August 15, 1998, to Todd Joseph Araujo. Her husband is a member of the Wampanoag Tribe of Aquinnah in Massachusetts. He is currently a staff attorney for the National Indian Gaming Commission. She was interviewed February 12, 1999, from her office in Washington, D.C.*

W e have the land base, but we have more than that. We have the resources to do something with that land base. Unlike the reservations in the Lower 48, we don't have to go to the Secretary of the Interior and ask for authority to do whatever we want to on our lands.

I was born in Juneau. I grew up in Angoon, Alaska, in Southeast. It's a small community of just over 600 people. The population kind of fluctuates. It's just outside of Juneau, in between Juneau and Sitka on Admiralty Island. It's a Tlingit community.

I did all my schooling – from pre-school through graduation from high school – in Angoon. The only time I did not live there during my younger years was when my mom and dad, Albert and Sally Kookesh, were going to college. So I spent some time – a couple of my first years – in Seattle, Washington, when my dad was in law school at the University of Washington, and my mother was an undergraduate at the University of Washington. I vaguely remember that because by the time we moved back home when my dad and mom finished school, I was about four years old.

I have four siblings. I have an older sister named Elaine, a younger sister named Reanna and two younger brothers, Albert and Walter. I also have a niece and nephew named Chenara and Edward. Most of my family on my dad's side is from Angoon, and most of them live there. My mom's family is from up in the Doyon Region. Her maiden name is Woods, and her family lives all throughout Tanana, Rampart and Manley Hot Springs.

For me, growing up in Angoon – it was just all that I knew. Now that I've left there – and have been away at school and now here in Washington, D.C. – I realize what a unique experience it is compared to most people in this country. Growing up in a small

Native village and being raised not only by my family, but by my community, you realize the community structure was amazing there. If I wasn't learning lessons from my own parents or my own uncles and aunts, it was from other elders or members of our community. So I really feel like I've been blessed, growing up in a place like that with all the traditions and the community aspect of it.

In terms of my family, we're very close. My parents have always instilled in me the importance of education, which is why I went on to college and then on to law school. Even from my earliest years, my parents were going on to college themselves, so I always knew that education was an important area to develop.

*The community was very strong?* There was just something about growing up in Angoon. It's a very small community, and people who have no concept of a small village ask me all the time, "How did you grow up in a place like that. It's so small. Wasn't it boring? Did you have anything to do?" But it wasn't like that for me. I never felt bored. I never felt like there weren't things to do. It was almost like the world was my playground. We found things to do in the community. We didn't have TV until I was in the first grade, so we figured out things to involve ourselves in. We were involved in different things like beading and our Indian dancing and things like that. I'm not going to sit here and say that things haven't changed, especially every year with the loss of another elder.

I remember the way it was. I think a lot of people there know what I'm talking about, and they still feel that community aspect. I still feel it, but it was just a very different time, and there was just something about growing up in a small community at that time. I have good memories of my childhood.

*Were there problems with alcoholism in the community?* My parents – neither of them drink or smoke, so personally I didn't have to experience that. I didn't grow up in that kind of environment. Although I did have relatives, and I had other friends in my community who did have to deal with issues like that. So I did know that they were out there, but I think in a lot of ways I was very protected and isolated from those types of social ills. I knew it was there, but my parents just really protected me from that type of environment.

Angoon is a dry community, and I think it was a lot harder to get things like that into our community back in those days – not so much these days. I think a bigger problem today is the issue of drugs, not just alcohol.

When I was growing up in high school, it wasn't considered the "in" thing to do – go out and drink or do drugs or whatever. I went all through school, even high school, and I never touched a drop of alcohol. When I got to college, people were shocked that I'd never had alcohol in my life. That was also another unique experience I've had. I still to this day don't drink alcohol. I'm not going to sit here and say I've never tried it. That's what the college experience is about. But I tried it and didn't like it and have never done it again. It's just one of those things.

My husband and I – both of us – are very proud to say that our children will never see us drink alcohol. And there are always these negative views about Native people being alcoholics, and I, for one, am not going to be someone to perpetuate a stereotype. I've always been an athlete and tried to be very healthy, and when I was in college, it just didn't feel right. It has something to do with having my peace of mind. I really cherish that. I didn't want to do anything to mess that up.

*Why did you pursue higher education?* My parents were setting the example, and they talked more about education as I got into high school. I was always one of those students who the teachers and community members saw some potential in. I was "tracked" to go on to college. Unfortunately, I have real problems with students being tracked because I know that I had classmates who were just as bright as I was, but weren't tracked for college. I've just been lucky. My parents saw some potential, and they always stressed that it was important to go to college. They would talk about possible schools that I could go to, and they encouraged me to apply to some of the best schools.

In a small community like Angoon, a lot of the counselors that worked there would encourage you to go to a small school or a community college. My parents were saying, "Why don't you apply to bigger schools? Why don't you apply to Stanford?" So I went ahead and did that and actually got into Stanford, so it worked out great. I almost didn't believe that it was possible myself, coming from such a small school. I graduated with a class of 10, which was a big class in my community. We didn't have as many academic opportunities in a small high school like that.

It was just my parents' example. I mean very few people at that time had a college education. I saw how it helped them in their lives to do things in terms of developing their own businesses. They have a fishing lodge and a small store and a restaurant that they run. So I saw how it helped them with their own business endeavors, but also with my dad – to be able to provide services to the Native corporations, our village and Southeast Alaska and also to be involved with other Native organizations. It just seemed like with the education you could do a lot more, not only in pursuing your own dreams, but helping your own people.

*Did you participate in subsistence activities?* Yes, some. When I was little we used to go fishing with my dad. As we got older, it didn't happen as much. In the summer time also we smoked the fish. We'd go out and have big family affairs of beach seining so that we could get sockeyes for smoking. And then we'd help my mom tend to the smokehouse in the summer time and make sure that the smoke is constant and that the fire doesn't get too hot or too low. Also, we helped with things like clams and seaweed, picking berries or whatever.

It was always there. I guess I didn't think about it so much because they were just activities that we did. But I was involved in those things. *You must miss that.* Yes. Everybody goes off in the summer time to get sockeyes, and they're all canning fish and smoking fish all summer. I don't only miss having access to fresh fish or smoked fish, but it's that whole social activity. Helping my mom cut the fish or tend to the fire or move the fish so that it doesn't stick on the poles in the smokehouse.

*Did you learn any of your language?* Unfortunately, no. Both my parents went to Mt. Edgecumbe High School – boarding school – and neither of them knew their languages. So it's really hard if you don't have parents who speak their language to learn those things. We had classes in high school, even elementary school. So I know a few greetings and certain phrases, and I knew all the songs from our community dance group. But I just can't speak the language. It's really something that I struggle with. It's a goal that I really would like to pursue at some point. I know we have more resources available for things like that, especially through our corporations and their heritage foundations. Sealaska, for instance, has "Beginning Tlingit" tapes so you can start to learn some of the language. And they have other Tlingit language books.

*Did you experience discrimination?* Growing up in Angoon, there were predominantly Tlingit people, so I think people who got picked on the most were the non-Natives that lived there, the teachers' kids or whoever. I was always kind of uncomfortable leaving my "comfort zone," which was my small community. Going into places like Juneau or Anchorage or Fairbanks or wherever – although it wasn't explicit and nobody would actually say something to me or my family members or community members around me – you could always tell that there was kind of a negative view of Native people as poor, as uneducated. It's very different now. I'm a lot more confident in who I am. I don't feel in any way inferior to non-Native people. But you kind of felt that negative attitude if you left your home community.

*Was there a point when you knew you were an Alaska Native?* I always knew I was when I was growing up, but it's just kind of something that you take for granted. It just seems like it's there, and you don't realize how important it is until you actually leave your home community, which is predominantly Native. When I went away to college at Stanford, it was just me on my own. And standing there on my own, I had to really define who I was and who I am. Going away to college just made me realize what an amazing background I have. I'm Tlingit and Athabascan. I'm a Native person. I have a unique experience growing up in a Native village. I grew up practicing our traditions and learning our dances and our songs.

Even in just my short lifespan, I feel like we've lost certain traditions that we have. I don't want that to continue. I want to be one of those people who will try to save some of our culture and traditions. I guess leaving that home community, which was so rich with culture and tradition, helped me realize what a rich history and tradition we have.

*Did you participate in the dance group?* Yes. More so when I was younger. In high school, I was involved in four different sports – cross country, basketball, volleyball and track – through the school year, and I was traveling all the time. But in elementary through junior high, we had a great dance group. We would travel all over.

*Do you have a Native hero or heroine?* Two people that I think of right off the bat are my parents. Doing what they did – going off to college, getting that education while having young kids to take care of, focusing their energies to get that education so that they can take care of themselves and they can take care of us and work for their people. My dad has worked tirelessly since I can remember on Native issues and with Native organizations. He's just always been an inspiration. And my mom – for always just being there in the home, but also taking care of our family businesses and making sure that we knew traditions on both our Athabascan and Tlingit side. They're two inspirational people in my life.

Of course, another person I can think of is Elizabeth Peratrovich. Significantly, to me, Elizabeth Peratrovich Day is on my birthday. For her to be able to stand up before the Alaska Legislature as a Native woman – standing up and saying her piece on behalf of Native people – that's very significant to me that she had the strength to do something like that. I know that our Native women are very strong people, but at that time, I'm sure it was very out of the ordinary for someone like her to stand up against discrimination.

*You are married?* Yes, soon to be six months. We got married in Angoon on August 15th, 1998. My husband's name is Todd Araujo. He's an attorney as well. Actually he's a member of the Wampanoag Tribe of Aquinnah in Massachusetts. They're from the island of Martha's Vineyard. He works for the National Indian Gaming Commission. *You feel that you have a lot in common?* Yes. Even though I'm an Alaska Native, I think there are a lot of issues that touch us as Native people all across the country. I've always known that I wanted to marry a Native person, whether from Alaska or some other Native tribe. It's just always been an important thing to me. Especially since we have issues of blood quantum and enrollment and things like that. Most people don't realize that as young Native people, it's something we have to think about. Even with my parents marrying from two different tribes, I'm sure it was a big issue when they were getting married as well – getting married outside the tribe.

*Your feelings about ANCSA?* I think it was a very necessary thing at the time. I mean with the State coming in and taking all this land with the Alaska Statehood Act. When Alaska became a state, the Alaska Natives were in danger of losing title to all the land that they had. We needed something to protect our Native lands. I understand why it came about, just in terms of my studies of federal Indian law. I think the government had realized that its other Indian policies hadn't really worked – the Allotment Act, termination, the Indian Reorganization Act, and whatever other policies that they've used to deal with Indian tribes. I see how this new concept of corporations sort of came about – because they wanted to try something different.

But also it's amazing to me that this foreign type of organization was imposed on our Native people. I mean, we dealt with it, but it was just kind of a crash course in learning how to govern and organize corporations and deal with boards of directors. Our Native people had to learn really quickly how to be corporate executives and shareholders. On the one hand, I see how something new had to come about to deal with our Native people because other policies weren't working.

I can't even fathom the panic at the time. "OK, now we have land, and we're supposed to form a corporation with all this money. But we don't know anything about it. What do we do now?" I'm impressed with how our people were able to master this corporate structure and to deal with bottom-lines and all those types of things, acquisitions and economic development and whatever. I've always been impressed with that.

I feel like a lot of the corporations have been very successful and over the years have gained a lot of knowledge in running these corporations and in training their youth. I also feel like while it was a necessary act when it happened, I think there are a lot of flaws that unfortunately we have to deal with now – things like extinguishment of aboriginal title. The fine print that just got overlooked when the act was actually signed. I guess there's always a give and take when you want legislation passed to protect you. Sometimes you're going to lose things. But now that we have it we just have to keep moving forward and deal with it.

And then, you always have the "New Natives" issue of those born after the act passed. Did they meet the deadline of December 18, 1971, to become shareholders? As a New Native myself, that's an issue that weighs heavily on my mind all the time.

I am a shareholder, thanks to my parents gifting me shares, but there are a lot of young Native people out there who are never going to be shareholders. If you have one parent with several children, they can try to allocate shares to all of them, but some may be left out. Or, maybe you have a Native child who has been adopted who doesn't have parents with shares – whatever. There are going to be a lot of young Native people left out of this corporate structure, and it's really sad. Eventually, there may be a problem because you're going to have a lot of young, talented Alaska Native people going out to get educated. They're going to have a lot of expertise and education in ways that might benefit the corporation, and yet you have to wonder if they're really going to want to be involved in these Native corporations that they don't even belong to.

I do want to be involved in the Native corporations because this is my ancestors' land that they're managing and developing and protecting. Some young Natives might not feel the same way. They have nothing to gain from these corporations because they're not shareholders, and none of their siblings or family members are either, so why should they take part in providing any type of benefit to the Native corporation?

*What about those corporations that have added the New Natives?* I think it's great. I guess I just get so frustrated with the whole argument that people have about further slicing the pie and cutting the pie into smaller and smaller pieces, which means they get smaller and smaller dividends. In talking to other young Alaska Natives when I worked as an intern at Sealaska Corporation, we were saying, "Who says the pie was baked only for you?"

This Alaska Native Claims Settlement Act – I'm sure – was enacted for the purpose of protecting the Alaska Native lands for all Alaska Native people and all the generations that follow. Unfortunately, with the deadline, it appears to benefit only certain generations, and those that follow may never receive any type of benefit. So I think it's very important that other Native corporations follow the lead of those that have allowed New Natives in, even if it's through different types of stock structures, such as life estate stock or whatever.

*Was it a good idea to create corporations?* I think so. They were given money and land, although I don't like to say they were "given" land. They "retained" some of their land. And with the corporation, you have the resources to do economic development. If you go to any of the reservations in the Lower 48 – and I've been to several of them – yes, they have a land base. But they weren't given money to start a corporation or a development organization or whatever to further add to their resources to provide services to their people. The tribes with reservations are constantly struggling to create economic development, to be self-sustaining by doing such things as gaming. Unfortunately the land that was given to most of the tribes isn't the best land for economic development, so they have to do things like gaming or other things. Well, actually gaming is the best thing that's worked for them in the recent years.

With the corporations, we have the resources to further develop our land base to add to our resources, to add more economic stability to our corporations, to provide for the future. Just like the reservations, we have the land base, but we have more than that. We have the resources to do something with that land base. Unlike the reservations in the Lower 48, we don't have to go to the Secretary of the Interior and ask for authority to do whatever we want to on our lands. The reservations in the Lower 48 – their land is held in trust by the federal government, so it's basically the federal government's land, and the tribes are being allowed to use it. That's kind of a way to look at it. I think we have a lot more autonomy in the corporate structure.

*What are your husband's reactions?* Like most Native people from outside of Alaska, he didn't really know much about the Alaska Native structure until he met me. Now he probably knows more than he ever wanted to. (Laughs.) I think most people look at it very strangely. They say, "Corporations? Native people running corporations? That's very odd." And they think that's not a very traditional way to run government or to manage your resources for Native people. I'm not saying my husband says this, but I think generally most Native people from down here think that it's a very foreign structure to impose on Native people. But I can only point out that the Indian Reorganization Act itself required Native people – tribes in the Lower 48 – to form tribal councils and to have a chairperson or a president. That's not something that they used to have, either. They used to have traditional councils, or, they had chiefs. They had their own types of governments. And then the federal government imposed a different type of government on them as well. So it's not something that just happened to the Alaska Native people. I think more Native people in the Lower 48 states need to realize that they also have a form of governance imposed on them by the federal government.

More focus has come on to the Alaska Native Claims Settlement Act because of the Venetie decision, so more people are curious about the Alaska Native structure and what was lost and what was gained. Unfortunately, the Venetie case didn't come out very well, so I think there's more of a negative view of ANCSA. It looks like it did away with aboriginal title and maybe sovereignty aspects in terms of having your own tribal courts and tribal jurisdiction and things like that.

I think there's a negative view, but the more we educate people about it, the less negative view they have on it.

*What about the amendments to ANCSA?* Yes, you have the

1991 amendments. I remember when I was younger, there was this big worry about the shares being sold to non-Natives. We don't have to worry about that any more, thankfully, with those amendments. I think there have been some changes for the better. There were things in the original act that were very confusing and ambiguous, such as with Section 7(i) calling for the sharing of resource revenues. Maybe eventually we'll get it right, but I think there are always going to be issues surrounding it – subsurface estates, surface estates, all that kind of stuff.

*Goals for the future?* For now, I'm out here in Washington, D.C. I work for the firm Van Ness Feldman, which does work for some Alaska Native corporations. We're D.C. counsel for those corporations, meaning that we do work that needs to be done in Washington, such as legislation or legislative monitoring. I came out here hoping to get experience that I can take back to Alaska eventually. I know home is always going to be there. I do miss it now, but I do want to have some experience and something to take back when I go home. I do plan on going back to the state of Alaska, hopefully to work for one of the Native corporations as an executive, in a general counsel capacity or to work for a law firm that works for Native corporations in Alaska.

*What is your vision for the Native children of the future?* Education. It's always been instilled in me that it's important, and I still continue to believe it's important. Society has changed so much that it's very hard to have any type of job or employment without some type of training. Also, I think there needs to be more education about our cultures and traditions and language – if not in our schools, in our communities. As I said, even in my short life things have been lost.

More needs to be done to instill confidence in Native youth in who they are and in helping them realize – as I do at a later age – how significant it is that you are a Native person and how rich your culture is and how rich your traditions are. How unique our lives and perspectives are compared to most people. I really want to stress education, not only in the mainstream society sense, but in the cultural and traditional sense.

*ANCSA in the future?* I think we need to continue to train young Natives to gain expertise in the corporate structure or in fields that the corporations will be getting involved in, whether it's tourism, economic development, acquisitions, investments, natural resources issues. I think that's something that's going to be important for the corporations' future. In terms of ANCSA itself, I think it's going to continue to evolve.

The name of the act makes it sound like that's it, we're done, the slate should be clean between the government and the Alaska Native people, but I don't think that's the case. We have to continue to use the act – not really to gain more from the government, but to maintain what we have. Although we were given some things through the act to try to protect our land and our culture, if you just look at some of the recent Supreme Court decisions dealing with American Indians or Alaska Native groups, there's kind of a slow chipping away at what we have. And I think we really need to stand on ANCSA and use it to protect what we have now, so that we don't lose any more.

Being a young Native professional – most people perceive of me as having "left home" and having become too educated to be part of the community any more. I just want to stress that that's never been the case for me. I'm always going to be from Angoon. I'm always going to be from Alaska. I'm always going to be Tlingit and Athabascan. And my education has never been a way for me to "get out." It's something that I want to use for the benefit of Alaska Native people. Not just for me.

Even though I'm out here in Washington, D.C., it's not because I want to get away. It's because I want to have more to bring back when I eventually come home. A lot of times there's a negative view of those of us who have been educated and go away from home, and because of those perceptions, that we don't want to belong in that place any more. But that's not the case. That's something I think people should know about those of us who are young and educated and who are going out and doing things outside the state of Alaska.

I am where I am because of my parents, my community, because of all the support I've had not only from the people of Angoon, but from all the Native people in the state. Receiving the Roger Lang Youth Leadership Award at the Alaska Federation of Natives Conference just kind of evidences how I am supported not only by the people of my own community in Southeast, but by the people of this state who need some of us to go out and be educated and provide our expertise and education to the Native people when we get back home.

*RICARDO GUCHXWEINA WORL was born January 4, 1962, and grew up in Juneau, Alaska's capital, as part of a large extended Tlingit clan. He is a member of the Thunderbird – Shungookeidee – Clan who originate from the village of Klukwan. His ancestors come from the House that was lowered from the sun.*

*His parents divorced when he was a child, and he grew up living with his mother Rosita Worl, a well known Tlingit leader. The family moved to Anchorage in 1970 so that his mother could complete her undergraduate degree.*

*After graduating from high school in Anchorage, Worl went to Dartmouth. He graduated from Dartmouth in 1984 with a degree in Anthropology.*

*His first job out of college was as the marketing director of a statewide monthly magazine that had been founded by his sister and other family members called* Alaska Native Magazine. *His mother was the publisher/editor, and his brother the general manager. The magazine eventually ceased publication, but family members felt they added tremendously to their own experience as well as providing a valuable service to the Alaska Native community. Worl next took a position with Sealaska Corporation, then worked as a legislative staffer, and then as a loan officer for the National Bank of Alaska. Currently, he is employed by the Tlingit & Haida Regional Housing Authority.*

*Working with younger Alaska Natives has remained one of Worl's highest priorities since returning to Alaska from college. He volunteers a substantial amount of time organizing and participating in Native youth activities.*

*Worl is a shareholder in Klukwan Native Corporation and Sealaska Corporation. He and his wife Lisa, who is also a Tlingit from Juneau, have a daughter and a son. He was interviewed January 6, 1999.*

**M**y background is in anthropology and so I'm always looking at a different perspective on the corporations. Yes, we are a corporation, which is a Western institution, but at the same time the corporation and its corporate leaders and the board members have "tribalized," shaped, changed these corporations to meet some of their needs, some of their values.

I grew up in Juneau, Alaska. I come from a family with an older sister and an older brother. I am the youngest of three, but I also grew up with an extended family, several aunts and uncles, my grandparents. They were all a very big part of my life. They were raised in a traditional manner: There were three sisters, my grandmother and her two sisters. They all had children, and they were all raised under one roof as brothers and sisters, even though technically they were cousins. But they were brought up as brothers and sisters. And so I spent a lot of time with my aunts and uncles. My aunts would take me out with them whenever they went berry picking or on picnics to the beach. My uncles – I spent a lot of time in the summers fishing with them. We did some commercial fishing as I got older.

We did a lot of traveling because my mother, Rosita Worl, came up to Anchorage and went to Alaska Methodist University for her undergraduate work and then went back East to Harvard for about three years when she got her Master's. So we lived in Cambridge. But we always came back to Juneau in the summer time, and I spent time with my dad and my aunts and uncles.

Usually in the summers, if we weren't fishing or spending time outdoors, we were involved with the Gasaan Traditional Dancers dance group. We'd perform at ceremonies. But also it was at the very beginning stages of the tourism performances. We'd perform on ships. They weren't very frequent back in the early '70's. There might be three or four ships during the summer that we'd perform for.

Later on in junior high, we lived in Barrow. My mother, after leaving Cambridge, lived in Barrow for about four years. She was doing her field work for her dissertation, studying Eskimo whaling. That was a whole other cultural experience that gave me a different perspective on rural Alaska. Definitely Southeast rural Alaska is very different from other rural Alaska communities. In Barrow, they were a lot more dependent on subsistence, on whaling. And it was also before the North Slope Borough started receiving money from oil development. In fact, we were there from 1974 through 1976, so the money had just started to trickle in.

Being an Alaska Native, I felt when we first moved there I would have had some acceptance. It was primarily at that time almost all Inupiaq Eskimo population. The non-Native population was very small. But, to my surprise, the first year my brother and I were there we got in a lot of fights. Some of the kids gave us a hard time, called us "honkeys," even though we were Alaska Natives. I think it was just a general term for outsiders.

But after being there a couple years and being involved in the community, people began to understand the role that my mother had in the community, working with the whaling captains who generally tended to be the community leaders. We sort of earned a little more respect in the community.

My father is Filipino. He was in the Coast Guard, and he's retired. Actually, in Juneau and Ketchikan it was pretty common for the Indians to intermarry with the Filipinos. And it was an historical-social factor in that there was a big population of Filipinos who came over to work in the mines and in the canneries during the world wars. At that time, there was also a distinct division between the whites and the Indians, and along came another minority faction. The whites and Indians didn't intermix at all, so it was a natural mixture. Filipinos and Indians got along, so you see a lot of what we call "mestizos," mixed-blood Indians.

*Do you feel a tie to the Filipino culture?* Not so much in that I didn't spend a lot of time with my father or his family. He was always working, and my parents were divorced when I was about five.

Definitely, I grew up identifying with the Tlingits. I spent most of my time with Tlingits in my family.

*Did you experience discrimination in school?* In Juneau there definitely was discrimination. At that time I suspect the Indian people were not as well off back then. The corporations and some of the federal funding have turned things around, and now Native people seem to be more in control of their destiny and of their livelihood. Whereas, back then I think there was a lot of animosity and uncertainty and definitely not the type of economic influence that Native people have now today.

One of the most memorable instances of racism was when I was in third grade. Racism is racism, but I think it's just a lot of ignorance and misunderstanding about Native cultures. We were having music lessons, and my third grade teacher played the piano. She flipped a page on one of her piano music books, and the name of the song was "Ten Little Indians." She recalled that I was active with an Indian – Tlingit – dance group. And so she tried to coax me to get up in front of the class and perform this Tlingit dance while she played "Ten Little Indians" on the piano. You know, I told her, "I can't. I don't have my regalia. I usually dance with a blanket."

I was just a third grader, and you have this authority figure really pushing you. She said, "Well, you don't need a blanket." She gave me somebody's coat and wrapped it around me and said, "Here's your blanket." And she led me up to the front of the class. And I stood there while she played her piano music, "bomp-pomp-pomp-pomp, bomp-pomp-pomp." I couldn't dance. I couldn't move. I was just so embarrassed.

*Did the teacher understand what she had done?* I doubt it. I didn't mention it to my mother until years later. I was just so embarrassed that I couldn't dance. Not only was it not the right kind of music, and I didn't have the regalia, but in Tlingit tradition, when you dance, you have to dance in respect and also to show your pride for your family, your father's clan, your own clan. And to be forced to do that with no real ceremonial background, being that young, too – it was too much. *What about the reaction of the kids?* I don't remember. I just remember being in total shock, I guess. Your adrenaline is going. I was frozen basically. I just remember her playing the piano and staring at me, and the kids were staring at me.

When I told my mother that story years later, she couldn't believe it. She was angry.

That was in grade school. In junior high, we were traveling quite a bit, but there was a semester where I spent junior high in Juneau. It was pretty apparent that the non-Native kids gave us a hard time, called us "salmon crunchers." But I do recall in one of our art classes at that time some of the Indian Ed programs were starting to penetrate the curriculum. And there was a period for Native art appreciation. We did some Native design.

And then I went to high school here in Anchorage. I graduated from West High in 1980. It was a little better. There was a pretty big Native population at that time with kids from all over the state, Eskimos, Aleuts, Athabascans. And at that time I became a lot more involved in school activities, sports, student government, orchestra – a lot of the activities that some of the other Native kids weren't involved in, especially student government, Honor Society. I don't know if that's still the same. For some reason I always felt comfortable in trying something new, regardless of racial makeup of the group.

But I was never ashamed to identify myself as Alaska Native. It was the same way in college. When I went to college at Dartmouth, the Native Americans were a fairly small group – probably only 20 of us out of a class of maybe a thousand people. And they pretty much stuck together, the Native Americans. And I did a lot of other activities, sports, fraternity, Senior Society.

For some reason, I guess I have enough confidence to venture out and do other things. But the tradeoff for that was that the Native students felt that maybe I wasn't "really" Native because I'm doing all these other things. But I was still involved with Native programs. At the time I was in high school it was Cook Inlet Native Association. They had a lot of functions. The ski program was probably one of the best things they could do for high school kids. It got them into a sport up at Alyeska, which was traditionally for the affluent families. Lift tickets back then were 15, 20 bucks, which was a lot. And then all the ski equipment – they provided it. They provided the transportation. It was a really neat program. In the summer time, they had summer camp for Native kids. As a high school student, I worked as a counselor to younger grade school Native kids.

I guess you always feel like you have to prove yourself as being committed to the Native culture, Native community when you venture beyond into the non-Native activities. I've always felt that I had that balance.

*Your education?* I always liked school. My mother, being a very strong, academic-oriented person definitely had a big role in that. My three years up in Barrow slowed me up some. Again, it was at a time before the oil money had come in, so they had just moved out of being a BIA school. In fact, I remember seeing some of the furniture around had "BIA" written on it. So academically, the schools in Barrow were not up to par. So when I moved here to Anchorage to West, I was a little bit behind in terms of mathematics, writing, some of the real basic stuff. I spent a lot of my high school kind of catching up.

But even though I lacked in some of those areas, my mother forced me to sign up for the honors courses, which tend to be challenging. I probably got C's in those courses. But it did force you to learn a lot more. I guess I was fortunate she made me do that, although at the time, (laughs) here are all these kids, they're straight-A, 4.0 students, and I was pretty average. But the courses I was taking were more challenging.

*Did you always know you wanted to go to college?* Yes, I guess so. I think having a chance to be with Rosita while she was in her master's program and being exposed to the type of people at Harvard had an effect. Even though we were kids, she made a big effort at involving us in everything that she went to. So we were around a lot of other people at Harvard. I think that helped. And just her expectation that, "You're going to college." It was just not anything that we ever questioned or was optional. Plus the fact that my sister was going to college, and my brother went off to college. I was a sophomore in high school when he was a freshman in college.

*Do you remember when you had a sense of being an Alaska Native?* It was something that I've always grown up with. I don't recall when I realized what it meant to be an Alaska Native. Maybe I started realizing differences between Native people and non-Native people kind of early on, even in Juneau. My first perception of the universe was that everybody's like my family, like Indian people. As I got older in Juneau, I started realizing differences between people – body language, how they treated you, how they looked at you, the kind of language they used with you, the tone they used with you. Definitely in high school here in Anchorage, I was aware of differences.

*Do you have a Native hero or heroine?* I guess I have several. It's interesting. I view them as heroes. I had a very romantic notion about Native people and how you're trained. You feel the community's behind you. You go off to college, you come back and you bring skills back and put them back to work for the community. That's just ingrained. That's the expectation. Everybody's really proud of you, glad that you went off and got your education and you're coming back.

I remember in college people would ask me, "Well, what are you going to do after college?"

"I'm going back to Alaska."

And they couldn't understand that. "What's in Alaska?" There didn't seem to be a lot of job opportunities. I didn't have a real answer. At the time, we did have our family business, *Alaska Native Magazine*. I knew I was going to do that. But I guess they couldn't understand why I would want to come back to Alaska when they're going to work in Chicago, San Francisco, New York City or Boston for some investment bank or advertising agency. And I was going back to Alaska.

I told them, "I'm committed. I'm going to go help my people."

And I had this notion when I came back I was going to be greeted with open arms by our leaders, and they were going to take me under their wings and show me the ropes. I found when I got back here it wasn't that way. It was actually – I wouldn't say there was resistance – but it wasn't as open as I thought it was going to be. I guess at that time I came to realize that's part of Native politics. I'm still learning about it. We can be hardest on ourselves.

I do have heroes and definitely people I aspire to be like, people I look up to. I would say Perry Eaton (who headed the Community Enterprise Development Corporation) had a big influence. Byron Mallott (former CEO of Sealaska Corporation). Morrie Thompson (former CEO of Doyon, Ltd., who was killed in a plane crash January 31, 2000). Definitely my mother has been a really big influence. And definitely Tlingit leader Daanawaak, Austin Hammond, who passed away several years ago. He was clan chief out of Haines. In fact, I remember I learned how to dance the old Tlingit style watching him dance before he got older and couldn't dance any more. Traditionally a lot of men would go into a trance, be in a spirit state when they were dancing. I remember watching him. His motions were not only stately, but he definitely had the spirit, and it came out during his performing these dances. Also, I admired his ability to communicate with kids. Until he died, his life was dedicated to his grandchildren.

I feel I have that same commitment through my personal involvement with Native youth. I still coach and teach Native Youth Olympics. I'm involved with Junior Achievement. And that's one of the chances I have to get into the schools. I've coordinated several youth conferences and make sure that I attend the AFN Native Youth Conference. Just to listen, mostly. Even though I'm feeling older and a little more distant, I still have a big interest in the kids and a big commitment to them. And I make certain I'm available. And I keep an eye out to see who has a lot of potential and make sure that they get help if they need it.

*Do you have a tie to your culture?* Yes. For awhile I guess I felt other people had a lot of uncertainty about me because I had adopted certain aspects of Western culture. I like certain types of dress. I guess there were a lot of differences visually, there's my language, and I'm educated. My style of communication might be more Western. But inside, definitely my values, my connection to the Native people have always been there. My entire career has been committed to the Native community. I worked for a Native corporation, a Native-owned business, *Alaska Native Magazine* which was committed to the people. I worked for two Native legislators. I worked for Cook Inlet Tribal Council, working with Native educators. So there hasn't ever been any reason to question my "Nativeness." It comes back to, as people get to know me and my career and my commitment to the community, I've become more comfortable in venturing into non-Native activities, non-Native organizations.

I guess what it comes down to is balancing the Western world with the Native world. I feel I definitely have a sense of acceptance in the non-Native community and also the Native community. And it's not always an easy thing to balance, especially when I travel out to the village. With some of the tribal village people there's definitely some tension – rural versus the urban corporate Native groups. I've seen it at AFN. There's still that division. I guess I've always been aware of that dichotomy.

*Your feelings about ANCSA?* It's something that I've studied almost my entire life. It is a big part of me. It's a big part of our community. I think it's a good thing. I know there are a lot of people – even our own people, a lot of Native Americans – who feel that ANCSA is not a good thing and that it's too Western and that it jeopardizes our relationship with the land. The Western values of ownership and business are too conflicting with the Native values. Personally, I know it's been a good thing, economically and politically. Native people would not be where they are today without it. In just Southeast alone, Native corporations are the largest employers, the largest private landowners. The combined economic impact that they have on the region rivals that of our natural resource economy. It has provided economic growth and opportunity for our people. There's just no way we would have been able to accomplish that if we had had to rely on federal funding and government projects.

*(Gestures toward a window.)* An eagle just flew by the window. That must be a good sign.

So there were the unquestionable economic benefits that ANCSA has provided Native people. Related to that, the economic force translates into political power. We definitely have an influence with AFN, and also each regional corporation individually in the respective regions carries a lot of economic clout. I think the corporations are now maturing, and at some point they're going to be able to – in a meaningful way – flex their political muscles. Even at the federal level, with the "1991" amendments, the fact that AFN was able to get a bill passed through Congress in a very short period speaks to some of the political influence that the corporations and AFN have. And it has to do with the fact that we've spent so much of our energy and time interpreting the legislation, working with Congress. That's benefited us, in that sense.

There is the issue of corporations being "too Western" in that ANCSA did change the relationship between Native people and the land. Prior to land claims, every tribal member was entitled to use and occupy traditional tribal lands. Whereas now, after ANCSA, in order to benefit from tribal lands you have to be a shareholder. And as for shareholders, that's the only part that I feel is a weakness. We're leaving our kids out because those born after 1971 are not shareholders. I'm glad to see a number of the corporations have opted to issue shares for them. I believe all Native kids are entitled to participate in the land claims. That's their given birthright. But that has been one of the tradeoffs for these corporations.

We've definitely seen it in Southeast where our traditional values tell us that we're all supposed to share equally. We've got to take care of our kids. They're entitled to that. But on the corporate side, when it comes to issuing stock to "New Natives," Sealaska Region has been split right down the middle. Half of our people say,

"Well, no, because if we issue shares to our kids, to the New Natives, it's going to decrease the value of my shares and decrease how much money, benefits I will get from the corporation."

That is a Western value. And it's just one of the conflicting values where the Western value is starting to win. It's something that since high school I have taken on as a personal challenge: To see that our kids get shares. I've tried to help other people understand that the intent of land claims was not to give dividends, to put money into the pockets of shareholders. The original intent was to secure ownership and control of Native lands. That's what our elders, our ancestors wanted, to make sure that we have this. The dividends, the economic benefits, the scholarships, the economic influence – that has all been a bonus. That's all gravy for Native people from my perspective.

I'm in the process of gifting shares both in the village corporation and also the regional corporation stock to my daughter. My wife is also a shareholder. She's the eldest. She's got three younger sisters, and she's the only one who was born before the cutoff date in 1971. So she's a shareholder, but her sisters are not.

*You're working to have Sealaska issue stock to young people?* Yes. And I know the corporation wants to, but because the shareholders are so divided on it, my feeling is that the corporation needs to take a little bit more of a leadership role in influencing our shareholders and saying, "Yes, if we do give the stock to New Natives it will decrease the benefits you're going to receive. But our traditional values, our original intent with the land claims – there are so many reasons why our kids should have stock."

And it's scary to think about. There are almost as many Native non-shareholders now as there are Native shareholders. It's getting close. What's going to happen when these kids become shareholders when they inherit their stock? Are they going to want to sell their stock? It is a possibility, although surveys of shareholders now show that they want to maintain their stock. But will that carry over to this next generation of shareholders who inherited their stock? They feel like they're left out because they're not able to vote. They're not able to participate. They're not entitled to any benefits from the corporations. Yet, we know they want to be. Everything they talk about at these youth conferences is they aspire to be a corporate leader. Yet, they are not shareholders, they're not entitled in any way to the benefits of these corporations.

That's one fear I do have. A term I've heard used before is this is the "sleeping giant." When the stock goes over to the New Natives, what's going to happen? What values are they going to have with regard to corporations?

By law, we had to be a profitable corporation. So we have benefited from that, but the tradeoff has influenced some of our traditional values.

At the same time, our economic advantages have helped us carry on and maintain our traditional culture. You look at how much money corporations have put into lobbying, into protecting subsistence, into protecting the Native culture – there's a lot of political legislation, both on the federal and state level. And I think a lot of it goes unnoticed by our people. Our corporations are funding lobbyists who are keeping an eye on certain legislation. It benefits our people directly and indirectly, but they may not be as aware of it.

Our corporations have taken on their social obligations. And that's another issue. Other corporations don't have the same type of commitment as Native corporations do. Their commitment to the tribe, the culture, the social well-being of shareholders goes well beyond what other Western corporations would have.

My background is in anthropology and so I'm always looking at a different perspective on the corporations. Yes, we are a corporation, which is a Western institution, but at the same time the corporation and its corporate leaders and the board members have "tribalized," shaped, changed these corporations to meet some of their needs, some of their values. Again, there's that idea of benefiting the elders, the non-pro rata distribution. The amount of capital they contribute to the social well-being of the shareholders is another tribally influenced aspect. You look at other corporations – they benefit their shareholders strictly bottom-line, money, the value of dividends. Whereas, Native corporations – I know one corporation spent as much as 20 percent of its revenues on non-business, social-type benefits for its shareholders. So, I guess I feel that we have taken on this Western institution, but I think in the future, we're going to see the Native corporations evolve into corporations that are a little more tribally influenced to help carry on these values.

The 7(i) revenue sharing provision – there are no other corporations that have that type of covenants. That was originally intended to help the corporations who didn't have as many natural resources. It's very controversial, especially for those corporations who are paying out. They feel it's unfair. And that is a big factor. It's only Native regional corporations that have that obligation, but again, it's the sharing.

The stock restrictions, allowing them to issue shares to New Natives, having the option to give their land back to the tribes – there are other issues – Native corporations definitely are different because of values that their owners and leaders have. We've been able to re-shape the corporations, make them different from other corporations.

*Personal goals?* I guess for as long as I can remember I've always wanted to be in a position where I'm doing the most I can to benefit the welfare of Native people. It's been ongoing. I haven't had this vision where I'm going to be a leader of a corporation one day. But it has always consistently been, no matter where I am, I try to figure out, "OK, how does this affect Native people? Is this job, is this organization, is this program that I'm working with – is it doing as much as it can for Native people?"

I have a 17-month-old daughter, Miranda Rose. She just had her Tlingit naming ceremony in Hoonah in October. We're due for our second child at the end of March, early April. It's exciting. I feel like this is what I'm supposed to be doing – being a father. And my commitment to children, the younger people, is even stronger now. I'm a lot more aware of the institutions, the organizations that influence our kids. I think that's another area where our corporations can help. We really need to look at grooming our kids. We've learned to rely so much on schools to provide a lot of training and things that our kids need which traditionally were done by the village, by your clan members or your tribal members. But we have this dependence on government, schools. And that's another thing we're going to evolve in and that's parent involvement with their kids, with the schools.

Native people of my parents' generation have had negative experiences with schools – the BIA schools, schools where kids were taken from their parents. My mom was a little child when they took her off to a boarding school where she was beaten for speaking Tlingit. And that isn't that long ago. That has had an influence on how they raised their kids and their expectations of schools and being a part of the school

*Your vision for Native people?* It's definitely exciting. There's a lot of fear that we are losing our traditional culture, the language. And that is definitely a fear that's founded. I agree. I do fear that. And I certainly do all I can to minimize that. I try to learn as many

Tlingit words as I can. I attend potlatches. I observe as much as I can.

It's hard because in the Western world you have to have a job to sustain your family. It's changed. Our commitments of our time have changed. It requires a certain amount of dedication to the Western world. You have to have a job, a house, responsibilities. And that takes away from the time that we can commit to the culture, to being every day with your grandparents, with your elders, to doing subsistence activities. Especially in the urban areas, it's harder. And that's where a lot of our population is migrating to, some of the bigger urban regional hubs. So there's that conflict there. But at the same time while we have this fear, I also feel good in that our culture is changing. It's evolving. It's growing. I mentioned that the corporations are a big part of that, but also our kids are a big part of that. At the youth conferences, these kids get up, and they are confident in not just their education, their personal skills, but also the fact that they identify themselves as Alaska Natives. When I see that they understand the Native issues – I see they have this commitment to Native people – I'm comforted that we're going to continue to evolve. We're going to continue to grow. I wish I could help our elders understand and have faith in the young Native people.

We're kind of in a transition phase now. In the '80's, a lot of the leadership of the corporations – of the nonprofit organizations – came from a pool of political leaders. Prior to land claims, in order to achieve the land claims act, we had to develop a lot of political leaders because we didn't have economic leaders. The opportunity wasn't there for business. So there were no business leaders, so to speak. After ANCSA, these political leaders stepped into the corporate boardroom, went onto the board of directors, became the CEO's. And they brought with them that political leadership and experience. So we had this period where it was rough, a shaky start. Corporations were losing money.

But now, we're seeing a lot more people coming up through the ranks who have more education, more business experience, more exposure to Western finance. And that's also at the same time while the Alaskan economy has really grown, changed and matured. Definitely in the future we're going to see a lot more savvy Native business leaders. Not that we haven't had great leaders, I just think we're going to become more focused.

I hope that one day we're able to see the corporations combine their economic force. I think we're working toward that. There are still a lot of political factions, political differences within the regions and on a statewide level. But if that were ever to happen – it's exciting to think from a financial perspective about what they would be able to do – the projects, the accomplishments, the combined economic force of Native corporations.

# Thirteenth Region

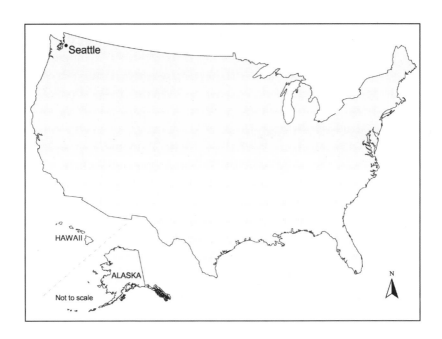

 **BRENDA (MAMALOFF) TAKES HORSE** *was born January 23, 1957, in Canada where her parents were living while her father attended school there. When she was about six months old the family moved to Kodiak where she lived until she was in first grade. Takes Horse's father, Fred Mamaloff, is a minister. Through his assignments to various parishes within Alaska, the family also lived in Juneau and Fairbanks. Mamaloff is originally from Kenai, and today he is believed to be the last living speaker of the region's three dialects of Dena'ina Athabascan.*

*Takes Horse is a member of the Kenaitze Indian Tribe and is enrolled to the Thirteenth Regional Corporation. She attended high school in Montana. Her family lived at Crow Agency, the capital of the Crow Indian Reservation. It was there that she met her husband of more than 20 years, Dennis, a member of the Absaroka (Crow) Tribe.*

*She attended college in Montana and Wyoming. She has worked for the U.S. Bureau of Land Management for more than 20 years and today is the Native Liaison for the BLM Alaska State Office in Anchorage. Among her professional goals is increasing Native representation in the workforce. Takes Horse was instrumental in the creation of an organization of other Native Liaisons within federal agencies and currently serves as the chair.*

*Takes Horse said that the opinions she expressed in her interview were her own and were not related to her professional position.*

*She and her husband have two children, Travis, 12, and Caleb, nine. The family lives in Eagle River. She was interviewed June 29, 1999.*

**B**ut we chose the Thirteenth. I am not sorry. . . The power is in the tribal government, not in a corporate structure. But I optimistically think that the two can become collaborative. I don't think that it has to be that the tribe wins or the corporation wins.

My parents met in the fish cannery in Kenai, and I was raised the first six years of my life in Kodiak. We moved Outside for a year to Portland, Oregon, then back to Juneau for a year, then to Fairbanks for the third through the sixth grade. After that, my dad was transferred to northern Montana for two years and then to the Crow Reservation for the remainder of the time they were in Montana. I was married in '78. My parents left to come back here in '79.

I was born in Canada before the law that says children born of American parents on foreign soil are automatically citizens. That was not until 1962. So when I was going to school in Fairbanks, I had to become an American citizen. I have the paperwork. (Laughs.)

*Your parents' names?* Fred Mamaloff and Evelyn – her maiden name is Heinrich, and she came from Minnesota in 1947. *She's non-Native?* Yes, she claims to be from the "Germanic tribe." *Your father is from where?* Kenai, so he's Athabascan Dena'ina. Also, I had a grandmother who was from Atka, so I guess we're Athabascan and Aleut.

I was born in Camrose, Alberta. My dad was going to college. I think I was six months old when we moved to Kodiak so I don't remember Canada at all.

My parents met in the fish cannery in Kenai. My mother was a school teacher. She taught in Palmer, Aleknagik and Ninilchik. As she was trying to work during the summer, she would work in the cannery. That's how she met my father. He was the foreman. Back then in 1952, it was considered a mixed marriage.

My father was going to college to become a minister. He became a minister and that's why we moved to Kodiak, and that's what moved him around. He is supposed to be retired, but he is not. He's 73 now. It's the Church of God, a Bible-based church, and he was one of the first and is still the only Native minister of that denomination. I have no brothers and sisters. They tried many times to adopt, and they had many, many foster children.

*Were the foster children Native or non-Native?* I don't remember them being any designation. I do remember the ones that they almost adopted were Native. But I don't remember specifically, Native, non-Native. It was just people. At that time the only hospital was here in Anchorage. When people came from the Aleutian Chain, they would get stuck there in Kodiak. Who else to take care of them, but the local ministers, especially a Native one? Most of the Native people that we came in contact with were Russian Orthodox. My father was supposed to become a Russian Orthodox priest and ran away and joined the Army. He understood the Russian Orthodox belief system and was sympathetic. Anyway, as a Native person, he couldn't stand to see some kid stranded. Sometimes they stayed with us four, five or six weeks, until the weather lifted and they could get back into some of those really remote locations.

I remember there was always somebody there. My dad would be bringing someone home to feed. They didn't have welfare back then. We didn't eat real fancy food, but that was his way of helping and sharing – cook up a fish and invite the "hobos" or the "bums." On an island, everybody knows everybody. There were only 50 miles of roads or so.

I went to kindergarten in Kodiak. Then I went to first grade in Portland, Oregon, where my dad was finishing up his school, and then to Juneau, where he filled in for a guy that was in Juneau.

My parents truly believed in touring wherever we went. Because there was only one of me, they could afford it. Plus, they could always mix business with pleasure – go and do a service somewhere. When we lived in Juneau, we took the ferry everywhere, and they wanted to show me all the different things you could see. Their belief was that where you were – that's where you needed to become familiar with the foods – go berry picking with the local people, go fishing with them. When we lived in Fairbanks, they took a big tour of the North Slope. So they took me to Kotzebue, Barrow,

Nome. This was during solstice one year. Back then it wasn't that terribly expensive. They really believed that you needed to be aware of surroundings, what people eat, how to harvest the herbs from that part of the country. My mother has always been an avid organic gardener.

*After Fairbanks?* We moved to Eureka, Montona. Dad was just filling in for someone. That was for two years, so seventh and eighth grade, I went to school down there in Eureka, which is a very, very small place. *High School?* I went to high school in Hardin, Montana, but I lived in Crow Agency. We moved to Crow in 1971. And I went to high school there. When I went to high school it was 50 percent Native and 50 percent white. But I lived on the reservation, and my dad pastored the church there in Crow.

I got a very unique perspective to things. There are not many people, I've learned, who have my perspective.

*When did you have a sense of what it meant to be an Alaska Native?* From Day One. I didn't have much choice. We were very poor. Ministers don't make any money, and Dad was very adamant about – so many things to eat and so many things to do, and all of it related to the way he was raised. Clamming, fishing. He fancied himself as an amateur marine biologist. By the time I was in kindergarten, I knew the genus species names of all the little animals that stuck to the piling underneath the docks – what they did, what they ate. I don't remember it now, but I do remember being able to pick out different things and if they were edible. We didn't live in Kenai, but every year all through this time my mom and dad would make an effort to go back for commercial fishing. All my relatives are in commercial fishing. We have setnet sites in North Kenai, and if it wasn't every year, it was every other year that we would go and spend at least the run, which is almost the whole month of July, in Kenai. Quite possibly we'd stay up into September for moose hunting. The whole family would move out into the woods for about a month and still does.

I struggle with this a lot because of being called names when I got down to the Lower 48. I didn't recognize that there was a difference between my parents when I grew up here. It wasn't pointed out to me. I didn't know what the names meant, and I think that's when I really figured out that there was a big difference and that my mom ceased to be of the "Germanic tribe," and "became" an Indian. She learned very quickly and liked to do things like berry picking, gardening, hunting, being outside, fishing. My mother is very small in stature, so she couldn't do some of the things that Indian women traditionally did because most of the chores were divided between the men and the women. This has carried through in that now my husband and I do things together. That's very nontraditional.

*Discrimination?* When I went to the Lower 48 – that's the big distinction I made about growing up up here and then moving down there when I was in the seventh grade – I realized that there were people out there that had some really strong views. We lived near some of the Freemen – and they were pretty negative. But I was always taught that it wasn't my problem. It's theirs. And it all goes back to whether you're going to let it bother you. If you can't change their mind, you can change your reaction.

Here I was surrounded by other Native people. My dad was a Native minister, and he pastored congregations that were not predominantly Native, but most of the people that did things with us were Native. It revolved around subsistence activities, berry picking, hunting, fishing. It wasn't until I moved to the Lower 48 that I figured out that some people take vacations in the summer. I couldn't understand why anybody would want to do that. There was too much to do up here. If you take a vacation, it should be in the winter. Why would you take a vacation in the summer?

*Your Native language?* My dad was very adamant about me succeeding in the white world. He was forced to learn Russian and English and spoke Indian at home. He did not want that to happen, so they chose English and that's what they did. Besides my mother is not a speaker. And so the language part – we still use little pet words to refer to things – hot and cold. But they are more "family" words. Like I said earlier, I'm still trying to update the Athabascan dictionary with James Kari of the Alaska Native Language Center to at least have a record of how it should be. He worked previously with Grandma Bertha Monfor and Uncle Pete Kalifornsky to put this thing together. As far as I know and as far as Mr. Kari knows, my father is the last one that knows all three different Athabascan dialects of the Kenai area.

*After high school?* I went to college at Eastern Montana College (now Montana State University Billings). I went about two years there and then I got a music scholarship for Sheridan Junior College in Sheridan, Wyoming. I went to school there for about a year, and then my husband got laid off and I moved to Billings and worked full-time for the Bureau of Land Management.

My husband is a Crow. Takes the Horse From the Enemy is the name that his great-grandfather earned.

I married the boy next door, then my parents moved back up here. My husband and I stayed down there for quite awhile. My husband's parents were elderly. He's the youngest, and we stuck around to help them out. Then he got laid off from another job, and we moved up to Kenai in '84. At that time we'd been married awhile and I said it was his turn to become acquainted with my family. I'd never lived in Kenai before, so this was a first for me, too. So we lived in Kenai from '84 to '87. My dream – don't laugh – was to work at the fish cannery where my parents met. I worked there only about two to three weeks in the egg line. But at least I got to do it. It's very hard work. It's supposed to be for younger people (laughs). But it was something I realized I wanted to do. And then I worked for my tribe, Kenaitze Indian Tribe, for awhile, and then I worked for the State of Alaska Division of Public Assistance.

*A Native hero?* I thought about this quite awhile. I really think this needs to be elaborated with my children. I have two boys, nine and 12. Travis is the 12-year-old. Caleb is the nine-year-old. I try to educate them that there were great Native heroes in the Lower 48 and here, in their father's tribe and my Athabascan neighborhood. But I guess there are not many people that I know who are my heroes that other people know. So, from down South, I did a little a bit of research on Sacajawea. What a forerunner for Native women working. She had her own day-care system. There are probably more that I should say. I think the people that went before me in the federal government are noteworthy. I would not be able to do what I'm doing today had it not been for people going before me, forging the way.

*Your feelings about ANCSA? Do you remember when it was passed?* Yes, I remember getting legal notification from here. The way it was posed to me at that time – and I was a freshman in high school – was that Number One we had to prove we were Indian. The government was disputing the fact that we were Indian. Number Two we had to trace our ancestry to prove we were Indian. The next point was that there were these 12 corporations that we could not join because we weren't living here. I'm just saying the way it was phrased to me, and I have learned since that was not accurate. We could have made a choice. But we chose the Thirteenth. I am not sorry. I am not embroiled in the politics, nor do I have the big dividend payments that have caused a lot of substance abuse in my family. I guess when you're poor you can't afford it. (Laughs.) Those are just my personal views.

*Alcohol problems?* I don't want to say that my family had more than anybody else or less than anybody else. I do want to identify that it's a problem. I'm glad that it didn't snap me up, although it could have. My parents were very pivotal in instilling some values and ways of thinking that addressed that kind of thing.

But I think ANCSA did put a wedge between families and between tribal members because it added a couple more layers of government to some people that didn't even understand the government system that was already in effect. It tried to make corporate people out of tribal people with no training or insight into why. And there wasn't much time for coordination so there wasn't much communication that happened either about it.

And I view it as a termination measure. I get upset when people introduce themselves and identify with their regional corporation before the tribal identity. We are born to a tribe. ANCSA was created in '71. And if ANCSA goes away or gets cancelled or whatever happens, the tribe will still be there. I guess I'm equating a tribe – my view of the tribe is a family environment. That's a good thing to be in that kind of environment. For awhile I didn't want to be. And when you're growing up you don't want to do everything that everyone tells you to do, so for awhile I resented being a tribal person.

You have to understand where I was at the time, too, when I was a teenager in Crow Agency. The Crow Tribe is not an IRA tribe. They've had a long history of trying to help the federal government – and getting screwed in the process. They are very arrogant people, and I'm not saying that with a bad connotation. It's their strength. But nevertheless, you are born to a tribe, and you have no choice. You have to get to where you embrace this. It's like being born to a Jewish family or a very strong Slavic family – you've just got no choice. You're one of them.

*Your feelings about the corporate structure?* The very concept of stock is hard to imagine from someone just off the street – all of a sudden you give them a hundred shares of a corporation. It doesn't really mean too much. And that's where a lot of Natives were coming from. I wasn't here at the time, but I do have connections and relatives, most of whom are members of CIRI. And there was a lot of politics going on. I had a lot of relatives in and out of the politics and getting very upset about things, which I could never understand.

The power is in the tribal government, not in a corporate structure. But I optimistically think that the two can become collaborative. I don't think that it has to be that the tribe wins or the corporation wins. The intent was that the tribes and corporations work together. I don't think this has happened the way that it was envisioned. But I think initially it was designed to work, but I don't know about the effects.

*How about the idea of adding young people?* I think they're trying. They're going down the right road. Part of this is not a corporate type of thing. A piece of paper can be split up. It's a tangible thing. I don't know about creating stocks. I'm not real educated on how that's done. I don't think it's a big issue. You have a certain amount of stock and however you split them up should work. They've passed measures now so that stock isn't sold on the market. I'm glad to see that that's happened. I'm real hesitant about getting too opinionated about that kind of stuff. You can have a person that has stock from all 12 different regions, and then what?

Also, this is not a corporate gripe, but a lot of constitutions of tribes have rules that say people can only be members of one tribe. So if I married a white guy, I wouldn't have a problem registering my kids to my tribe. But since I married another Indian, we have to pick which one to register them to. I don't agree with that. This is more like a tribal gripe.

In my marriage to my husband, we have nieces and nephews that are more "Indian" than us and cannot receive any services because they're not one quarter of a certain kind. So, I look at the big picture and think that ANCSA is headed into fractionalization in the same way. Fractionalization of allotments is happening in the Lower 48, and it's happening here. If we're really into keeping track of what kind of blood you have – what other group of people has to keep total records on how much blood and whose it is? Now, I do believe that's what ANCSA was trying to eliminate.

Some people are angry about the fact that the Thirteenth Region has had difficulty becoming financially successful. People feel they have no choice, and that's what they're angry about. I felt the same way, that we didn't have a choice. But I've looked around, and I kind of like not having that kind of identity. It does pose a problem, though, because what are they going to do with those Thirteenth members who are starting to come back home? In 1971, how were we supposed to know and how were our parents supposed to know? It was in our hearts that eventually we would all come back. There are people that live in the Lower 48 that are from here that stay there, but this is our home. This is where we will be. If the rules say such, we cannot fight the rules. Plus, we didn't have a lot of money to hire an attorney, which we felt we would have had to do. The Crow Reservation down there had not a clue on how to help us and neither did the BIA. ANCSA to someone from the Lower 48 is a very confusing document. And it rules so much of what we do up here, in the federal government anyway.

*Your husband's reaction to ANCSA?* He's got mixed views. At the Crow Reservation, they have their own judicial system, their own jails. They have their own cops. They have their own welfare department, and the tribe runs all of this. There's a certain beauty to that, and there's a certain problem with that. If you're not related to the right people, it could be a problem. And my husband was never related to the right people. His family group is more into the spiritual realm than the political realm. He thinks ANCSA's stranger than heck – why they would all of a sudden make tribal people corporate people? It's very confusing to him.

*Do you keep up with Thirteenth?* I get their newsletter. I guess that's about the only way you can keep up with their activities. *Would you run for the board?* Oh, no. I'm not a political person. That's not something that would appeal to me at all.

Some corporations have been very successful financially. I think that's great. I think that's how it was supposed to work. I just wish that they would dribble that on to the tribes. They're the moneymaking people. They have the power to fund things as they see fit, and you would think that shareholders of these corporations would be pressuring regions to support village programs. I understand that regions are supposed to make money. I think it's possible to make money and still do some things. Although I don't think regions should be in the social services business. I think that is better handled by village corporations or tribes who have a close contact with people right there.

*Why do we still have sanitation problems in Bush communities?* It isn't totally the State's responsibility. Yes, the state could do something about it, but so could the regions. They're supposed to be making money. Maybe they need to do a better job of telling shareholders what they're making money for and what they do. It appears to common folk as a great big business that we're not even involved in. I'm just speaking as one of the common folk.

*Your job?* My job is as the Native Liaison for the Bureau of Land Management. I am located – organizationally – under the state director. I work on the coordination of resource management with Alaska Native groups. And I use the term "groups" to mean individuals, communities, tribes, tribal governments, regions, consortiums.

In doing my job I met several other Native people who are working for federal agencies. We formed a group of Native liaisons. We are all facing the same issues. We all feel that we're one little person in a big organization. We try to help each other decipher things, interpret things, bounce ideas off each other. I have Native people who work with me in this group in the Air Force, the Corps of Engineers, in U.S. Fish & Wildlife, in the National Park Service, Minerals Management Service, Environmental Protection Agency, the Forest Service and others. We have agreed to meet twice yearly. We started out by trying to define ourselves. A lot of the questions we get asked by tribal people are very hard to answer: What's trust responsibility? What are fiduciary responsibilities? Each agency has a different mission and with that, different authorities, and with that, a difference in how we deal with Native people. Most of the time, it falls on the Native liaison to talk about these differences.

Our agencies are trying to do what's right, but we've got a lot of things to get through, such as our authorities that say we're a public organization as opposed to a Native organization. We serve the public, so it's difficult to put into words how we can define our trust responsibility in that respect. We bounce ideas off each other. We're all asked to brief people in high levels, and a lot of times we are briefing people that we know don't have a clue about Native culture. Where do you start? You don't want to offend your headquarters people from Washington. You somehow need to present this information respectfully and maintain your dignity in the process. What we mean by that is that too long have Native people been portrayed as: Let's dress them up and have them come dance. That way we'll educate people. That does to some extent, but working side by side with people is better. I have refused to participate in a lot of "costuming," which is what I call it. I don't have a costume. I have regalia. I have an outfit, but I don't have a costume. Sometimes, the federal government in its wish to be inclusive tries to categorize Native people as "costumes."

There is a difference in a definition of a word. They see one of our words in the federal government and say, "What does that mean?" Because it doesn't mean the same thing to the federal government as it does to Native people. Nor does it mean the same thing within the federal government or within all of Alaska. So those are some of the issues we deal with. They are pretty heavy issues. We try to coordinate with the Alaska Federation of Natives and the Alaska Inter-Tribal Council. AITC represents the tribes. AFN is tribal, but they're also heavily corporate. And they both have valuable places in making decisions.

Our group is a good conduit for sharing information, for helping each other. We try not to be exclusive, but we're for Native people working for the federal government that are in these positions.

I am the chairman. We've said we were going to have a rotational chair, but since I've formed this thing, I've been the chair. I've been trying to get rid of it. (Laughs.)

*Your goals?* I've thought about that. What I have learned in my life is that it's good to set goals, but what I want my children to understand is that when you set goals you'll have to switch gears many times. The ability to roll with the flow is a whole lot better than the skill of building goals. I've had many goals – one of them was working in the cannery. But for very many reasons, a lot of them haven't happened. But I believe there are no such things as accidents, that the Higher Power has put us here for a reason and we just have to struggle around with what it is. It's good to make goals, but my immediate goal is to get through the teen-age years with my children. I have had to take my life a day at a time, and in the job that I'm in it's very intimidating to deal with 227 tribes. The only way I can get through my job is one day at a time, one tribe at a time. If you think bigger than that, you're working on an ulcer.